COUNSELING RESEARCH

QUANTITATIVE, QUALITATIVE, AND MIXED METHODS

Carl J. Sheperis
Walden University

J. Scott Young
University of North Carolina at Greensboro

M. Harry Daniels
University of Florida

Boston Columbus Indianapolis New York San Francisco Upper Saddle River
Amsterdam Cape Town Dubai London Madrid Milan Munich Paris Montreal Toronto
Delhi Mexico City Sao Paulo Sydney Hong Kong Seoul Singapore Taipei Tokyo

Vice President and Editor in Chief: Jeffery W. Johnston
Acquisitions Editor: Meredith D. Fossel
Editorial Assistant: Nancy Holstein
Vice President, Director of Marketing and Sales Strategies: Emily Williams Knight
Vice President, Director of Marketing: Quinn Perkson
Marketing Manager: Amanda L. Stedke
Senior Managing Editor: Pamela D. Bennett
Senior Project Manager: Mary M. Irvin
Senior Operations Supervisor: Matt Ottenweller
Senior Art Director: Diane Lorenzo
Cover Designer: Diane Ernsberger
Cover Art: SuperStock
Full-Service Project Management: S4Carlisle Publishing Services, Ashley Schneider
Composition: S4Carlisle Publishing Services
Printer/Binder: Hamilton Printing Co.
Cover Printer: Phoenix Color Corp.
Text Font: Times New Roman

Credits and acknowledgments borrowed from other sources and reproduced, with permission, in this textbook appear on appropriate page within text.

Every effort has been made to provide accurate and current Internet information in this book. However, the Internet and information posted on it are constantly changing, so it is inevitable that some of the Internet addresses listed in this textbook will change.

Library of Congress Cataloging-in-Publication Data

Sheperis, Carl.
  Counseling research: quantitative, qualitative, and mixed methods/
Carl J. Sheperis, J. Scott Young, M. Harry Daniels.—1st ed.
      p. cm.
  Includes bibliographical references and index.
  ISBN 978-0-13-175728-8
1. Counseling—Research.
I. Young, J. Scott. II. Daniels, M. Harry. III. Title.
BF636.6.S54 2010
158'.3072—dc22

                                2009017024

10 09 08 07 06 05 04

www.pearsonhighered.com

ISBN 10:   0-13-175728-8
ISBN 13: 978-0-13-175728-8

To Donna for your undying support in every phase of this project and every phase of our lives.

Carl J. Sheperis

Dedicated to the memory of Dr. Nicholas A. Vacc, who inspired both excellence and innovation in the practice of research.

J. Scott Young

For my wife and daughters - Diane, Gretchen, and Erin

Harry Daniels

PREFACE

As a counselor-in-training, you might regard the research aspect of your program of study as a strange bedfellow for your clinical training. Of course, your preliminary interests (depending upon your emphasis area) are to learn how to develop peer-mediation programs for a school district, learn how to address the symptoms of mental illness, understand the various implications for a disability on an individual's vocational future, or learn how to address roommate relational issues through residence-hall programming. Because you want to learn the essential skill sets to become an effective counselor, it is probably difficult to see how research fits into your academic plan. As you read through the chapters of this book, we hope it becomes clear that research and counseling are integrally intertwined, and that you need research to help you maintain best practices in the world of counseling.

Our goal, through this text, is to help you integrate research into the process of building your counseling skills. Through this text, you will be exposed to the foundational principles of research and how they apply to the counseling profession. We will guide you through the various aspects of counseling research and expose you to quantitative, qualitative, and mixed-methods approaches.

APPROACH AND ORGANIZATION OF THE BOOK

This book was designed as an introductory research text for counselors-in-training and assumes no prior knowledge. We undertook this project due to our concern that there are few text options for counselor educators who teach research to master's-level counseling students. It was our desire to create a book that is geared toward the issues counselors face when conducting research and that it be presented in a direct, easy-to-read manner using counseling literature and examples to communicate the information the typical master's-level counselor needs to know. In short, we wanted to write a student-friendly book that we wish we had had when we were taking our research courses.

This book is arranged into 18 chapters and 2 appendices. In Part 1, we lead the reader through the steps a researcher takes to begin a study—including reviewing the literature, developing research ideas and appropriate research questions, and deciding on a methodology that best suits an investigation of the topic. In Part 2, we explore quantitative approaches to research methodology, followed in Part 3 by a discussion of qualitative approaches to research. Part 4 covers mixed-method designs, data analysis, and writing up one's findings into a research manuscript. The book closes with a discussion of multicultural counseling issues in research.

We begin each chapter with Learning Objectives for the content, with the hope that these objectives will assist readers in focusing their study to critical areas. Similarly, each chapter ends with a set of review and discussion questions designed to provide a summation of important content and its application. In the main body of the chapters, we provide many examples drawn from the counseling literature to give the reader a real-world context for the material discussed. All chapters are written with the overall intention that a reader will finish the book knowing how to execute a research project from beginning to end. Furthermore, and perhaps most important, demystifying the research process is a central purpose of this book. It is our desire that master's-level counselors become both consumers and producers of counseling research with the belief that, yes, I can do this!

ANCILLARIES

Ancillaries for this textbook:

> *Instructor's Manual:* This manual is constructed to provide the research professor with instructional aids for each chapter, including: chapter overview; outlines (talking points); keywords and definitions; suggested learning activities; and a test bank.
>
> *PowerPoint Lecture Slides:* Instructors are provided with a bank of lecture slides that detail the essential elements of each chapter in the textbook.

ACKNOWLEDGMENTS

Editing a textbook on research is an arduous task and could not be completed without the support and dedication of a large number of individuals. First and foremost, we would like to thank our editor, Meredith Fossel, for believing in our project and helping it come to fruition. We would also like to thank the rest of the support team at Pearson for their work on editing and production.

An edited textbook does not come to fruition without the scholars who contribute their work to the venture. We would like to thank the individual chapter authors for sharing their expertise, time, and dedication to advancing research in the counseling profession.

We could not complete the project without individuals who volunteered to review our first draft of this manuscript; their suggestions were invaluable. We would like to thank Joseph C. Ciehalski, East Carolina University; Charles D. Palmer, Mississippi State University; and Elizabeth Thrower, University of Montevallo. We specifically thank Rosanne Nunnery and Jan Lemon (doctoral students at Mississippi State), who served as our editorial assistants for the project.

We want to acknowledge our mentors who ignited our lasting interest in research and our colleagues and students, whose enthusiasm for and curiosity about the human condition sustain us. Our contributions to this text would not have been possible without them.

Carl J. Sheperis

J. Scott Young

M. Harry Daniels

ABOUT THE AUTHORS

Dr. Rick Balkin is an associate professor at Texas A&M University-Corpus Christi. He has practiced in psychiatric hospitals, outpatient clinics, and community mental health centers since 1993. Dr. Balkin holds professional licenses in Texas and Arkansas and has a specialization in supervision. He is also a Nationally Certified Counselor. Dr. Balkin served as president of the Association of Assessment in Counseling (2008–2009), and has served as the executive editor of the *Journal of Professional Counseling: Practice, Theory, and Research*, Statistical Consultant for Counseling and Values, and the associate editor of *Quantitative Research for the Journal of Counseling and Development*. His primary research interests include counseling outcomes, program evaluation, counseling adolescents, and gender and ethnic differences in counseling. Dr. Balkin most often teaches the clinical coursework and research components.

April Whatley Bedford is an associate professor and chair of the Department of Curriculum and Instruction at the University of New Orleans. She teaches courses in literacy, children's literature, multicultural education, curriculum, teacher development, and qualitative research methods. April is on the Publications Committee of the Association of Childhood Education International (ACEI); a past president of the Children's Literature and Reading Special Interest Group of the International Reading Association (IRA); and an active member of the Children's Literature Assembly of the National Council of Teachers of English (NCTE). She chaired the 2008 Notable Books for a Global Society Book Award Committee and is a co-editor of the *Journal of Children's Literature* and the ACEI quarterly publication, *Focus on Elementary*.

Kristy A. Brumfield, Ph.D. is a clinical counselor with a special emphasis in early childhood play therapy and an associate professor at Xavier University in New Orleans.

Dr. Matthew R. Buckley has been a mental health counselor for the past 15 years and a counselor educator for more than a decade. His research interests include counselor development, group work, supervision practices, how theory is integrated into practice, and the regulation of professional counseling. Dr. Buckley currently serves as the Program Director for the Master's Degree in Mental Health Counseling and a faculty member at Walden University.

Craig S. Cashwell is a professor in the Department of Counseling and Educational Development at the University of North Carolina at Greensboro. He has published more than 70 journal articles. His research interests primarily focus on the competent and ethical integration of spirituality into the counseling process.

Tiffany Chandler is a doctoral student in the school psychology program at Mississippi State University. Ms. Chandler recently completed an externship in Forensic Assessment and is preparing to complete an APA internship. Ms. Chandler is interested in issues related to juvenile offenders and anger management. She has presented at state, regional, national, and international levels.

Dr. Catherine Chang is an associate professor in the Department of Counseling and Psychological Services at Georgia State University. Dr. Chang's major areas of interest include multicultural counseling and supervision; racial identity issues; privilege and oppression issues; and Asian and Korean American issues. Dr. Chang is a past recipient of the American Counseling Association's Research Award.

Dr. Teresa M. Christensen graduated with a Ph.D. in Counselor Education and Counseling from Idaho State University in 1999. She is a Licensed Professional Counselor-Board Approved Supervisor in Louisiana, a Nationally Certified Counselor, and a Registered Play Therapist–Supervisor who has counseled children, adolescents, and families for more than 10 years. She is currently an associate professor of counseling and chair of the Post-Graduate Counseling

Children & Adolescents Certificate Program at Regis University. Dr. Christensen teaches courses and conducts research related to child, adolescent, and family counseling; play therapy, child abuse and trauma; and group work, clinical supervision, and qualitative research.

M. Harry Daniels is a professor and former chair of the Department of Counselor Education at the University of Florida. Dr. Daniels uses the scientist-practitioner model as a guide, believing that counselor educators need to be skilled in both domains. Within this framework, he is interested in knowing how people construct their reality, particularly through the use of imaginative language, and the strategies that they use to regulate their emotional responses to life events. Dr. Daniels is specifically interested in the strategies parents and teachers use to influence children's emotion regulation abilities.

Susan H. Eaves, PhD, LPC, NCC, ACS, is a clinician with Weems Children and Youth Services. She received her graduate degrees from Mississippi State University in Counselor Education. She is the recipient of several state, regional, and national awards for her service and research. She is actively involved in her field as a clinician, researcher, grant writer, and presenter. Her professional interests include Borderline Personality Disorder, parenting, sexually risky behaviors, and self-injury.

Dr. Anastasia Elder is an assistant professor in the Department of Counseling & Educational Psychology at Mississippi State University. She obtained her doctorate from the University of Michigan and currently teaches research methods and statistics courses, while conducting studies and helping students on their research projects.

Vanessa Esparza is a Prevention Services Coordinator for a public non-profit community based agency in the Southeast. She completed her master's degree in Educational Psychology from Mississippi State University. She now works in collaboration with youth, families, schools, and organizations in the community to promote and advocate for drug free and safe schools and neighborhoods.

Dr. Geneva Gray is a faculty member in community counseling at Argosy University Atlanta. She earned her Ph.D. from Georgia State University and is interested in issues related to addiction, LGBT, multiculturalism, and counselor education.

Dr. Kim Hall is an assistant professor in the Department of Counseling and Educational Psychology at Mississippi State University. Dr. Hall graduated from Mississippi State University with a doctorate in School Counseling. Her research interests include problem-based learning and school counselor accountability.

Danica G. Hays, PhD, LPC, NCC, is an assistant professor in the Department of Educational Leadership and Counseling. Her research and clinical interests include intimate partner violence intervention; diagnosis and assessment; research methodology; and multicultural issues in counselor preparation and community mental health. Dr. Hays is the editor of the *Journal of Counseling Outcomes, Evaluation, and Research.*

Dr. April K. Heiselt is an assistant professor in the Counseling and Educational Psychology Department at Mississippi State University. Her teaching emphasis is in Student Affairs in Higher Education. Her primary research interest centers on the impact of civic engagement on student and faculty learning. She is currently employing the use of mixed methodology to explore the intersection of service-learning and leadership on first-year college students. She is the author of a variety of academic journal articles and conference presentations.

Dr. Kristin N. Johnson-Gros graduated from the University of Southern Mississippi with her doctoral degree in School Psychology. She completed her pre-doctoral internship at Munroe-Meyer Institute in Omaha, Nebraska. She was an assistant professor at Mississippi State University before joining the school psychology faculty at Eastern Illinois University in August 2008. She was a practicing school psychologist in Mississippi and Louisiana for several years. She has national certifications in Crisis, AIMSweb, and as a School Psychologist. She was the lead writer for the Mississippi Department of Education on *Response to Intervention: Procedures and Technical Manual.* She has presented at the national, regional, and state levels on Response to Intervention, Academic Interventions, Curriculum-Based Measurement (CBM), and Teacher Support Teams. In addition, she has peer-refereed publications in areas of academic and behavioral interventions as well as other publications.

Kerrie Kardatzke is a doctoral student in the Department of Counseling and Educational Development at the University of North Carolina at Greensboro. Her research interests include intimate relationships of adult children of divorce and dating violence. She has co-authored a number of journal articles, and is passionate about bridging the gap between research and practice in the counseling field.

Sandra Trupiano Landry is a doctoral student at the University of New Orleans in the Department of Curriculum and Instruction. She is interested in qualitative research approaches and understanding the lived experiences of research participants.

Dr. Sang Min Lee is an assistant professor in the School Counseling program at Korea University. He has developed a keen interest in advanced mathematics and statistics, and has been involved in research projects that require the use of large databases with sharp analytical skills. Areas of research interest include counselor training, school counseling, and counselor burnout. He is currently involved in several funded research projects. Given his solid research knowledge, he published 37 articles in the past four years, with several more under revision and review or in preparation. In addition, he frequently makes presentations at academic conferences to disseminate research results to our community of scholar practitioners.

Edina L. Renfro-Michel is an assistant professor of counseling at Montclair State University. Her research interests include adult attachment, counseling supervision, and integrating technology into pedagogy. Dr. Renfro-Michel has published a number of journal articles and book chapters. She has conducted professional presentations at state, regional, and national levels.

Nicole Roberto is a mental health counselor at NewBridge Services where she serves the mentally ill adult population. She earned her B.A. at Rowan University as a Communications major and a Psychology minor. After graduating from Rowan, Nicole went on to pursue her M.A. in Counseling at Montclair State University where she served as a Graduate Assistant. Nicole completed the counseling program in August 2008 and is currently working toward professional licensure.

Carl J. Sheperis, PhD, NCC, LPC, ACS, is the Academic Program Director for counselor education and human services doctoral programs at Walden University. He has over 19 years of clinical experience in the assessment and treatment of behavioral disorders and psychopathology in infancy and childhood. Dr. Sheperis teaches master's and doctoral courses in assessment, research, and statistics. In 2005, Dr. Sheperis was selected as the Outstanding Counselor Educator—Pre-Tenure by the Southern Association for Counselor Education and Supervision. He is a past recipient of the Donald Hood Research Award for AACE.

Dr. Donna S. Sheperis is the Counselor Education Program Coordinator and an assistant professor in Community Counseling at Delta State University. She has more than 20 years of clinical experience in the provision of mental health services to diverse populations. A counselor educator since 1999, Dr. Sheperis teaches master's and doctoral courses in ethics, supervision, skills, sexuality, and diagnostics. Active in professional organizations at the state and national levels, she currently serves as president of the state licensed professional counselors' association.

Laura R. Simpson, PhD, LPC, NCC, ACS, is an assistant professor and coordinates the community counseling and internship program at Delta State University. She has 19 years' experience as a clinician. Dr. Simpson's interests include counselor wellness, secondary trauma, spirituality, and clinical supervision. Dr. Simpson has been the recipient of the Outstanding Research Award from both the Mississippi Counseling Association and the Mississippi Licensed Professional Counselor Association. She also received the College of Education Outstanding Faculty Award at Delta State University for 2007–2008.

Dr. Joshua C. Watson is an assistant professor of Counselor Education at Mississippi State University-Meridian. A Licensed Professional Counselor and Nationally Certified Counselor, Dr. Watson received his doctorate in Counseling and Counselor Education from the University of North Carolina at Greensboro in 2003. He has authored more than 30 journal articles, monographs, and book chapters and has presented at several national, regional, and state professional conferences. In addition to his academic appointment, he also serves as an elected member of the Association for Assessment in Counseling and Education Executive Council.

Kelly L. Wester, PhD, is an assistant professor in the Department of Counseling and Educational Development at the University of North Carolina at Greensboro. Her main research interests include research integrity, self-injurious behaviors, and professional identity in counseling. She has published an interactive DVD and handbook titled *Conducting Research Responsibly: Cases for Counseling Professionals,* which can be used by students, educators, or clinicians to better understand research ethics in counseling situations.

J. Scott Young, **PhD, NCC, LPC,** is Professor and Chair in the Department of Counseling and Educational Development at the University of North Carolina at Greensboro. He was a professor for 12 years at Mississippi State University and, in addition, has been a practicing counselor in private practice, agency, and hospital settings for more than 15 years. His leadership in the field of counseling includes service as president of the Association for Spiritual, Ethical and Religious Values in Counseling and member of the Governing Council and Executive Committee for the American Counseling Association.

Scott is co-editor of the book *Integrating Spirituality into Counseling: A Guide to Competent Practice* and the forthcoming text *Counseling Research: Quantitative, Qualitative, and Single Subject Design.* He has published numerous articles on the interface of clinical practice with spirituality and religion, and has received awards for his work. Scott received his degrees from University of North Carolina at Charlotte (B.S.) and University of North Carolina at Greensboro (M.Ed., Ph.D.) Scott is a National Certified Counselor (NCC) and a Licensed Professional Counselor (LPC). He is married to Sara DeHart-Young who is also a licensed counselor and registered art therapist. He and Sara are the parents of two daughters—Savannah and Sophie.

BRIEF CONTENTS

CONTENTS

Part 3   Qualitative Research Designs and Program Evaluation

Chapter 9   Grounded Theory Methodology (Matthew R. Buckley)   115

Chapter 10   Phenomenological Designs (Teresa M. Christensen and Kristy A. Brumfield)   135

Part 5   Ethics and Multicultural Issues in Research

Chapter 17   Ethical Consideration in the Practice of Research (Kelly L. Wester)   249

Chapter 18   Multicultural Issues in Research (Catherine Y. Chang, Danica G. Hays, and Geneva Gray)   262

CHAPTER 1

Contemporary Issues in Counseling Research

Carl J. Sheperis, *Walden University*

OBJECTIVES
After reading this chapter, you will:

- Be able to understand the purpose of learning about research in counseling.
- Be able to understand the principles of the scientist-practitioner model.
- Be able to understand the basics of data-based problem solving.
- Be able to comprehend the implications for counseling research in the world of practice.
- Be able to recognize the various journals dedicated to the counseling profession.

OVERVIEW

Research is essential to the success of counseling as a profession. In this chapter, you will learn about the marriage of science and practice in the counseling profession and be exposed to some models (e.g., the data-based problem-solver model) that will help guide your understanding of research throughout the remainder of the textbook. You will also learn about some counseling journals that contain research elemental to your practice as a professional counselor.

RESEARCH IN COUNSELING

Welcome to the world of research. Some of you may be wondering why you even have to enter into this world when your goal is to work as a counselor. It is important to recognize that as a profession, counselors are paying increasing attention to the efficacy of their practice. Changes in funding sources and managed care issues have forced counselors to examine interventions and outcomes within the various types of therapy settings. Thus, although you may never actually conduct large-group research projects, you need research skills to be an effective counselor. Throughout this book, the authors use real-world counseling examples to highlight the application of research to practice. It is our hope that you will learn to become scientist-practitioners and use the models throughout this book to increase your effectiveness as counselors.

The Scientist-Practitioner

Since the 1970s the healthcare industry, under the rubric of managed care, has been cutting costs. Managed-care organizations have eliminated all but what they deem to be medically necessary treatment by establishing a predetermined number of treatment sessions based on the diagnosis (R. L. Hayes & Dagley, 1996; Kent & Hersen, 2000; Sanchez & Turner, 2003). In order to practice and be competitive in this environment, counselors must be able to provide proof that interventions used are research based and empirically sound (Crane & McArthur, 2002; Kent & Hersen, 2000), and that they result in desired outcomes (S. C. Hayes, Barlow, & Nelson-Gray, 1999; Kent & Hersen, 2000). With evidence-based treatment becoming a focus of practice and training, attention has been directed to the scientist-practitioner (SP) model as a way to bring the subjective experiences of therapy and the objective evidence of science closer, leading to more effective treatment and thereby saving money (Corrie & Callanan, 2001).

S. C. Hayes et al. (1999) reported that a critical component of training counselors to work within the managed care era involves teaching them to function as scientist-practitioners. Although the scientist-practitioner model was developed for use in clinical psychology (Stoner & Green, 1992), it is a useful model for preparing individuals to function as counselors. The impetus for developing the SP model was to combine both clinical and research training, leading to an integration of research and therapy, thus ensuring *best-practice* efforts (Crane & McArthur, 2002). According to Sexton (1999), the integration of research and practice through an approach like the scientist-practitioner model affords counselors the best aspects of the art and science of counseling (e.g., clinical experience and empirically validated treatment approaches) in their effort to help clients with complex problems.

Counselor educators who are proponents of the scientist-practitioner model encourage counselors-in-training to approach all cases as formal research projects and to use empirical evidence in everyday practice (Cherry, Messenger, & Jacoby, 2000; S. C. Hayes et al., 1999; Lampropoulos & Spengler, 2002; Wakefield & Kirk, 1996). In other words, to develop a best-practice approach, you will be using the methods you learn in a research course throughout your work as a practicing counselor.

As part of the SP model, three roles have been delegated to the practicing counselor: (a) producers of new data, (b) consumers of research, and (c) evaluators of effective therapy. In this way, the scientist-practitioner model focuses on joining two separate roles: the scientist and the practitioner. In accordance with SP philosophy, the practitioner should be well versed in both research and clinical skills, which will result in counselors who are involved in research and scientists who are involved in practice (Crane & McArthur, 2002). Neither science nor practice is emphasized more than the other. Although, as a student, you may find that you do not have a specialized expertise in both science and clinical skill, you should have the ability to incorporate both into practice (Stricker, 2002). Foundational in the SP model is the premise that research and effective clinical skills can be integrated (Wakefield & Kirk, 1996).

Scientist-practitioners use data-based interventions that have been proven to be effective through research (Dougherty, 2000; Kratochwill, Sladeczek, & Plunge, 1995). Because the practice of counseling has become increasingly time-limited, it is important for counselors to establish goals, implement interventions, and obtain proof of outcomes in a timely manner (Noell & Witt, 1998; Wakefield & Kirk, 1996). Thus, counselors using the SP model acknowledge the importance of utilizing data to (a) determine the focus of treatment, (b) design appropriate interventions, and (c) evaluate outcomes.

As a student taking your first research methods course, you may have some difficulty making the transition from the practice of counseling skills in other courses to the analysis of data. While the SP method of conducting the practice of counseling may seem alien at this point in your training—relative to what you have learned about basic counseling skills (e.g., reflective listening, empathic understanding, and support)—it is important to recognize that it has already been a part of your training. As you have learned basic counseling skills, you have discovered that each counseling intervention has an appropriate time and place. We are suggesting that you make more formal decisions about the use of those interventions. In other words, it is important to use data as you work toward solving client problems. Over time, researchers have been able to evaluate the utility of various counseling practices, empirically analyze components of counseling practices, and determine the impact of matching presenting problems with specific counseling models (Sexton,

Whiston, Bleuer, & Walz, 1997). Thus, even the most inexperienced counselor should be using a data-based approach to counseling.

The Data-Based Problem-Solver Model

You may find that the data-based problem-solver (DBPS) model, a component of behavioral consultation, is particularly useful to a counselor-in-training. The DBPS is beneficial in that it provides trainees with the ability to rapidly assess needs, monitor symptoms, and evaluate outcomes (Edwards, 1987). The ability to function as a data-based problem solver will allow you to identify and analyze a problem, develop and implement a course of treatment, and evaluate outcomes within a short period of time. Empirically based literature is used to define problems, formulate treatment goals, develop interventions, and collect data. Thus, learning basic research methodology and being able to analyze the quality of a research article will be critical to your development as an effective counselor.

In essence, the DBPS model is an extension of the scientist-practitioner model and is based on the belief that counselors are obligated to use effective problem-solving strategies, which is the most effective avenue when approached from a data-based framework. The identification of problems is essential to this model. Problem identification is one of the critical links between research and practice because it facilitates intervention planning and implementation. Lack of specificity in this area has often deterred practitioners from moving forward in psychotherapy (Edwards, 1987). Ultimately, regardless of how effective a counselor may be, if the problems are not properly measured and assessed, intervention is disadvantaged and treatment is compromised. If practitioners are not clear about where they are going in psychotherapy, how will they know when they've gotten there, or even when they've gone elsewhere?

The World of Counseling Research

Now, it is hoped, you are beginning to see that because the world of counseling is moving toward evidence-based practice and data-based problem solving, an understanding of research is important in your training. Once you accept the importance of understanding research, we can move toward examining the various types of research applicable to the profession of counseling. Counseling researchers typically focus on two different aspects of the profession: (a) effective counseling models and (b) aspects of the individual counselor that affect outcomes. Each of these focal points has significant implications for the practice of counseling.

EFFECTIVE MODELS   It is likely that each of you has already been exposed to a large number of counseling theories as you enter graduate studies. Exposure to such a vast number of approaches poses a question: "Which theory is best?" You may find it comforting to know that while counseling is generally effective, there is no supermodel. Instead of one model outperforming another in research studies, researchers have found that certain factors in the counseling process play more of a role than the theory being used. For example, Lambert (1991) found that approximately 30% of outcome is attributable to common factors (the supportive nature of counseling, the value of learning, and action-oriented processes such as behavior change).

In addition to the common factors that affect counseling outcomes, empirically supported treatments (ESTs) have been found to have important effects on specific problems. ESTs are manualized (i.e., have specific steps to problem solving) treatment protocols that have empirical evidence to support their use in specific situations (Sexton, 1997). Sexton (1999) believed that ESTs should become a central part of training for beginning counselors.

THE COUNSELOR AS RESEARCH SUBJECT   The second focal point of counseling research is on the counselor. Like the research on counseling theories, we have discovered that a signature profile for a counselor does not exist. According to Sexton (1999), neither demographic variables (e.g., race, gender, age, and cultural background) nor professional identity (counseling versus psychology versus social work) have significant impact on the outcome of counseling as a process. What may be even more surprising to you is that researchers have found that years of professional experience are also unrelated to counseling outcome. So, if years of practice are unimportant, then why go through such a rigorous training program? The answer is simple: the number of years of experience does not always transfer to increased skill. In our profession, we have found that counselors' level of skill, their cognitive complexity, and their ability to relate to their clients are the key elements that affect counseling outcomes (Sexton, 1999). From this information, it should be clear to you that to become an effective counselor, you must have a blend of relational skills, analytical skills, and intervention skills. Your graduate coursework can help to increase your efficacy in each of these areas.

We believe that a course in research will help increase your cognitive complexity and help develop your analytical skills through designing and critiquing counseling research. Through your learning experiences, we hope to help you increase your understanding of and your ability to apply counseling research to the world of practice.

Journals Related to Counseling

As you read through the chapters of this book, you will be exposed to all of the building blocks of counseling research. Because counseling is such a diverse profession, we include quantitative and qualitative approaches to research. In addition, we review research procedures that combine quantitative as well as qualitative methodologies (i.e., mixed methods). In conjunction with the methods of research, we also review critical issues central to the research process (e.g., ethics, multiculturalism, writing, and reviewing the literature). While this text will serve as a thorough survey of information relative to the world of counseling research, it is important for you to review primary sources as well. We strongly suggest that you seek out research articles from professional counseling journals to help supplement your reading. There is no better way to understand the methodologies and issues discussed in this text than to see them in actual research studies (Table 1.1 contains a list of journals from the American Counseling Association and its associated divisions). We wish you luck in your continued studies and in your preparation as a scientist-practitioner.

TABLE 1.1 Counseling-Specific Journals

Journal Name	Organization	Publication Schedule
Journal of Counseling and Development (JCD)	American Counseling Association (ACA)	Quarterly (available online as well)
Journal of College Counseling (JCC)	American College Counseling Association (ACCA)	Twice yearly
Adultspan	Association for Adult Development and Aging (AADA)	Twice yearly
Measurement and Evaluation in Counseling and Development (MECD)	Association for Assessment in Counseling and Education (AACE)	Quarterly
Counselor Education and Supervision (CES)	Association for Counselor Education and Supervision (ACES)	Quarterly (also available online)
Journal of Humanistic Counseling Education and Development (HEJ)	Association of Humanistic Education and Development (C-AHEAD)	Twice yearly
Counseling and Values (CVJ)	Association for Spiritual, Ethical, and Religious Values in Counseling (ASERVIC)	Three times per year
Career Development Quarterly (CDQ)	National Career Development Association (NCDA)	Quarterly
The Journal of Addiction & Offender Counseling (JAOC)	International Association for Addictions and Offenders Counselors (IAAOC)	Twice yearly

TABLE 1.1   Counseling-Specific Journals (*continued*)

Journal Name	Organization	Publication Schedule
Journal of Employment Counseling (JEC)	National Employment Counseling Association (NECA)	Quarterly
Journal of Multicultural Counseling and Development (JMCD)	Association for Multicultural Counseling and Development (AMCD)	Quarterly
The Journal of LGBT Issues in Counseling	The Association of Lesbian, Gay, Bisexual & Transgender Issues in Counseling (ALGBTIC)	Quarterly
Journal of Mental Health Counseling (JMHC)	American Mental Health Counselors Association (AMHCA)	Quarterly
Rehabilitation Counseling Bulletin	American Rehabilitation Counseling Association (ARCA)	Quarterly
Professional School Counseling	American School Counselor Association (ASCA)	Six times per year
Journal for Specialists in Group Work (JSGW)	Association for Specialists in Group Work (ASGW)	Twice yearly
The Family Journal	The International Association of Marriage and Family Counselors (IAMFC)	Quarterly
The Journal of Creativity in Mental Health	The Association for Creativity in Counseling (ACC)	Twice yearly

Summary

In this chapter you were introduced to the role of science in your work as a professional counselor. Hopefully it has become clear to you that research and practice make good bedfellows. As you make your journey through the remainder of this textbook remember that evidence-based practice is an ethical necessity in your work as a counselor. Thus, it is important for you to consider carefully all of the various methods of research presented and to develop a sense of competence in understanding their applications to your professional work. While some of you will move on to become producers of research that will guide evidence-based practice, the majority of you will become competent consumers of research. Good luck in your journey toward becoming scientist-practitioners!

Review and Discussion Questions

1. Take a moment to compare the scientist-practitioner model to what you have learned thus far about counseling skills. What are some potential ways you can combine these two approaches? What benefits and drawbacks are there related to working from an SP model?
2. Think about a client and the presenting issues related to his or her case. Go through the elements of the SP and data-based problem-solver model and determine a plan of action. What empirical studies would be important to evaluate in your work with this client?
3. Take some time to review articles in some of the journals listed in this chapter. Do any of the particular journals seem to fit your professional interests? Consider joining the professional division that publishes that particular journal.
4. Pick out a counseling research article on a topic that interests you, and use it as a point of reference as you read through the text. Remember that it will be important to find additional articles that match the various models of research along the way.

CHAPTER 2

Getting Started

Donna S. Sheperis, *Delta State University*
Carl J. Sheperis, *Walden University*

OBJECTIVES
After reading this chapter, you will:

- Be able to present the benefits and challenges of conducting research in counseling.
- Be able to delineate the basic components of research.
- Be able to understand the characteristics of an effective researcher.
- Be able to understand the methods of developing a research hypothesis or question.
- Be able to outline elements of sampling.

OVERVIEW

Before you can apply the results of research to your work as a counselor, it will be important for you to learn about the research process. In this chapter, we provide you with a basic framework with which to understand and conceptualize a research study. We start with the most basic task of generating a research question and provide you with an introduction to a variety of components in the basic research study (e.g., generating hypotheses, determining a method, and selecting a sample). After introducing you to the basic elements of research, we provide you with some of the reasons for conducting research in the counseling profession and discuss the challenges of working with human research participants. The information provided in this chapter will be essential for your understanding of the more specific research procedures discussed later in the textbook.

GETTING STARTED IN RESEARCH

Being able to read, understand, and effectively apply research in practice is an important part of the counselor's job. To make critical judgments about any specific research study, one must have a functional knowledge of basic research concepts. In this chapter we introduce those concepts that are the foundation of the research process.

What Is Research and Why Do It?

Research is a systematic investigation that involves collecting, analyzing, and interpreting information in a sequential manner in order to increase our understanding of the phenomenon of interest.

Counselors who conduct research become interested in a topic and a specific question; they set about gathering the data needed to answer the question, analyze the data, and report results to others in the profession. To be confident that what we find is real, each step of the process, each characteristic of interest, and all aspects of the environment in which the information resides must be clearly defined. This process of collection and organization should be conducted and reported with as much precision as possible, to allow other researchers to reproduce and verify the validity of the findings. In the long run, research informs the profession and enhances your ability to use best-practice methods.

Basic Components of Research

Research is a search for truth that begins with a question. Counselors conduct research as scientist-practitioners, that is, as those who are accountable to the profession (Haring-Hidore & Vacc, 1988). Scientist-practitioners seek to better understand the challenges and events encountered in the discipline of counseling, which leads to better and more inclusive ways of working with clients and producing positive counseling outcomes. Research is not conducted purely for research's sake; it is conducted with the intent to benefit those we serve in the profession of counseling.

When there are gaps between what our clients need and what we are able to provide, an idea for research is born. In other words, the limitations of practice or the new and different concerns present in the client population drive the research questions that generate new knowledge. Put simply, there is a feedback loop in the scientist-practitioner model: practice drives client outcomes, client outcomes drive research, and research drives practice.

To begin, let us take a look at some of the basic components of research. We elaborate on these concepts in this chapter and throughout the text. In order to begin the process, a research question is generated. A *research question* is the general question that guides the direction of the research. It defines the relationship between what you want to know and how you intend to obtain this knowledge through research. Once a research question is identified, hypotheses are developed. A *hypothesis* is an inference or speculation that is indicative of the researcher's best estimation of the projected results of the research (Rosnow & Rosenthal, 2005). The hypothesis is based on an understanding of the subject under consideration and requires the researcher to apply reasoning skills in order to make a best guess about the topic to be studied. It is not necessary for hypotheses to always be correct; the results of research are intended to support or refute the hypothesis generated by the researcher. The whole point of the research is to test against the hypothesis in order to generate new knowledge.

Counselors, regardless of professional settings, are concerned with the characteristics of the people with whom they work (i.e., intelligence, interests, aptitude, achievement, and personality). It is not difficult to recognize that the people with whom we work vary considerably in almost every characteristic. Some people are more intelligent than others, some are more mechanically inclined, and some work with people better than others. In research we call such characteristics *variables,* which means they have more than one attribute or value (thereby making them capable of varying). The variable in a research study is observed or manipulated, and constitutes the means by which we structure our observations about the data. When we examine variables, we often want to know what effect one variable has had on another or what change was evident in a particular variable. Thus, identification of the variables under consideration is key to the research process.

Let us assume that as a counselor you have identified a broad research question, have made some preliminary hypotheses about this question, and have considered the variables that need to be studied. Your next step is to determine the type of *research design* that will be most appropriate for your study. Many research designs are presented in detail for you throughout this book, but it is important to take a broader look at research types as we discuss getting started.

Research techniques are infinite in scope, but they fall into clear categories in terms of types of data collected and lines of inquiry. Research designs that collect numerical or categorical data are considered *quantitative designs.* These data can be expressed in terms of real numbers, and include examples such as scores on the graduate record examination (GRE), the gender of participants coded as a 1 or 2, or ratings on a Likert scale ranging from 1 to 10. *Qualitative designs* collect data in the form of narrative answers and are often focused on a central phenomenon. According to Creswell (2005), qualitative inquiry focuses on the view of the participant, emphasizes the setting specific to the participant, and highlights personal meaning of experience for the participant. Qualitative inquiry is often employed when little is known about a particular subject. There are numerous methods of qualitative inquiry available to counseling researchers. In this text, we cover grounded theory, phenomenology, and narrative approaches to qualitative research. Each of these designs includes focused interviews and case studies as examples of qualitative data.

Experimental, descriptive, and relational research designs encompass virtually all methods of empirical inquiry. *Experimental research* attempts to define causality. It allows the research to control or alter one variable's effect on another. The variable being manipulated in this way is called the *independent variable*. The variable being studied is called the *dependent variable*, and the researcher measures the effect the independent variable has on the dependent variable. In experimental research, the researcher is interested in how the dependent variable responds as a result of the independent variable (Shavelson, 1996).

In general, counselors want to be able to study variables in a way that enables them to describe the variables' variation within and among the population under consideration. Additionally, the ability to control for, predict, or explain this variation helps counselors understand the variables.

Descriptive research is not concerned with cause and effect. Instead, *descriptive research* sets out to fully define the presence of a particular phenomenon. It tells us how things are, and it is often the first step in any research process because it empirically establishes the foundation for further lines of inquiry (Rosnow & Rosenthal, 2005). *Relational or correlation research,* however, looks at the relationship between existing variables and is concerned with linking or making an association between two or more phenomena. This type of research results in the ability to determine whether X and Y are related and, if so, the pattern and strength of the relationship (Rosnow & Rosenthal, 2005).

In summary, experimental research defines the variables and tells us how they got to be that way; descriptive research provides an overview of the actual presence of the variables; relational research describes for us how certain variables are in relation to other variables; and qualitative research focuses on the view and experience of the participant.

Importance of Sampling and Generalizability

In addition to determining your research questions and design, you will need to establish how the population for your study will be defined and sampled in order to gather the data. Of primary importance are the issues of sampling and generalizability. A target population includes all the potential participants from which the research sample could be drawn based on the research questions being investigated. For example, if you are interested in studying drug-prevention programs in schools across the nation, every participant in such a program would be part of your target population. You can imagine how difficult it might be to study all members of a target population. Try to conceptualize the time and expense involved in surveying every type of program and every participant across the nation. Another approach to conducting this line of inquiry would be to consider an accessible population or a group from which you can make reasonable inferences to the larger population.

As indicated, it is nearly impossible for entire groups to participate in a research project, so a more efficient yet effective way of conducting research is to study a subset of the population, or a sample. A sample is simply a portion of a total population. Representative samples provide researchers access to the data needed and can provide the same results as studying an entire population. Counselors determine the type of sampling method to be used prior to beginning their research. Generally, participants are randomly selected from the larger population to create a sample that is representative of the whole and free from bias.

Validity and Reliability

Counselors who are researchers are charged with designing studies that provide valid and reliable results. *Validity* is the extent to which the results of a measurement or procedure actually serve the purpose for which it is intended (Shavelson, 1996). For example, if the research is intended to measure students' satisfaction with their counselor education program, questions on a valid survey would address this topic rather than ask students about their family of origin and birth order. *Reliability* is the extent to which the results of a measurement or procedure are consistent from one measurement to another (Shavelson, 1996). You may have a scale in your bathroom that measures you in pounds and thus is valid because it measures what it is supposed to measure. If you weighed yourself three times in a row and got the same weight each time, you would view the scale as reliable. If each weighing gave you a different result, the scale might be valid, but it certainly would not be reliable! A reliable research design could be replicated, and the results would not be statistically different from the original study.

Problem Formulation and Hypotheses

A primary challenge in research is the formulation of the research problem and hypotheses. When a counselor is asked to conduct research, the area of research is often assigned. However, when conducting independent research, counselors act as scientist-practitioners and investigate areas of interest that will inform their practice. Once an area of interest is identified, the specific research problem is up for consideration.

RESEARCH PROBLEMS   Researchers focus on small slices of large problems. Quality research is, by design, very specific in focus and limited in scope. Beginning researchers often make the mistake of looking at broad research questions that cannot be practically studied. In their enthusiasm, their desire to investigate using broad strokes emerges. "What makes people happy?" is an example of a research question that is too broad. More often, it is the finer points that make up the most effective research efforts. While there is always the potential for the converse to be true (that the area of inquiry is so narrow it provides no real suitable information to affect best practice), counselors more typically find themselves having to pare down the area of interest to a manageable research endeavor. Scientist-practitioners want to make a difference, which is why they engage in research. Harnessing that enthusiasm into best-practice research methods is one hallmark of quality research.

The researcher approaching a new project is often overwhelmed by the prospect of making a choice of a *research problem.* The responsibility and future commitment attached to this stage of the research process loom large. Engaging in Socratic dialogue discussions with colleagues and reviewing research in similar areas can aid the counselor during this time. Defining the research problem may feel like circling around a target slowly. The counselor begins with a general idea, and then, through consultation and investigation, begins to move closer to what will ultimately become the final target: the actual research question.

RESEARCH QUESTIONS   A *research question* is a statement of the problem and its significance (Best & Kahn, 2006). A research question may be in the form of an actual question or may be a declarative statement. Regardless of the form it takes, a research question must be specific in its focus and intention. The significance of the question must be specified by the researcher to avoid simply collecting data to analyze for the sake of analysis. Ultimately, researchers must attend to the "So what?" factor about their lines of inquiry.

Here are some samples of research questions:

- Do drug-prevention programs at the elementary school level reduce actual drug use by participants?
- What is the effect of a peer-mentoring program on the recipients' attitudes about school climate?
- Do cognitive coping strategies affect the prevalence of depression in postpartum women?
- How does faculty mentoring affect graduate student research projects?

These types of research questions allow us to consider the next step in the research process: identifying the hypotheses.

HYPOTHESES   A *hypothesis* is a tentative or potential answer to the proposed research question that is informed by existing literature and understanding of the problem. In other words, it is not merely a guess about the answer but a best guess that has the backing of the researcher's understanding of the problem. A hypothesis must arise out of the refinement of the research questions and must be formulated prior to data collection; otherwise, it is not a hypothesis but a data-driven response to the question. Hypotheses are posed to be either supported or refuted.

Most research problems will result in major and minor hypotheses, which are then tested against the collected data. Hypotheses are stated in absolute terms and are never questions. Consider the following research questions and their corresponding sample hypotheses:

Research Question: Does involvement in social organizations affect the grade point averages (GPAs) of freshman males?

Hypothesis: Freshman males in social organizations have higher GPAs than those who are not in social organizations.

Research Question: Does a counselor's sense of spirituality affect his or her likelihood for suffering symptoms of compassion fatigue?

Hypothesis 1: Counselors who are involved in regular religious activities report fewer symptoms of compassion fatigue.

Hypothesis 2: Counselors who score at or above average on the Spirituality Inventory Scale score lower on the Counselor Compassion Fatigue Inventory.

While hypotheses are intended to be proved or disproved, the idea that a hypothesis may not turn out to be supported by the research can be difficult for researchers. They routinely hope that their best guess is supported by the data collected. Publication of research efforts may come to a standstill when the researcher does not personally like the results. Graduate faculty members often see this dilemma in the master's thesis or doctoral dissertation. A quality research project will be conducted only to have the author's original thought, or hunch, refuted. The researcher may have personalized the outcome and regret that the study did not confirm suspicions. The point is that having your hypothesis refuted does not mean there was a bad study. If the design is solid, the outcome is solid, and that is what counts in the world of research.

SAMPLING

Once a research question has been posed and hypotheses formulated, you will be faced with determining the most appropriate method for selecting the research participants. *Sampling* is a means of identifying and selecting a portion of the total population. Additionally, a good sample is a representative segment of that population in that it mirrors proportionately the characteristics that are present in the larger population.

To generate a representative sample, the researcher first defines the population of interest. Next, the researcher must design a plan for sampling that population. Most plans involve the use of random selection so that the sample is dependent on mathematical probability. In *random sampling,* every person in the population has an equal and independent opportunity to participate in the research. Essentially, all possible participants are part of the total population pool, and actual participants are determined by using random selection methods. Random sampling can be as simple as a systemic sampling method, which involves choosing every fifth person on a list of potential participants (Best & Kahn, 2006). Another random method might be to assign a number to every potential participant and then use a random number generator to select participants. This method is similar to drawing names out of a hat, and it allows every potential participant an equivalent selection opportunity.

It makes sense that sample sizes that are larger and make up a greater percentage of the actual population are more likely to truly represent the population being studied. This reflects the concept of *generalizability* and is a measure of external validity. As an example, assume there are 300 youths participating in an after-school tutoring program. A counselor asked to evaluate the participants' satisfaction with the program may decide to conduct a survey. The counselor who randomly selects one third of the population to receive the survey, or 100 subjects, will generally have a sample that is more likely to represent the whole group than the counselor who decides to survey 1 out of 10 youths, or 30 total research participants. This concept reflects the role of sample size, to be discussed later in this chapter.

Another sampling consideration is the use of stratified random sampling measures. Continuing with the example of the after-school tutoring program, let us assume that the youths who participate come equally from middle and high schools. The counselor charged with evaluating student satisfaction decides to conduct a random sample using an alphabetized list of participants. If, by chance, the researcher selecting every 10th participant from this list managed to survey 30 students who were all from middle schools, the results would not fully represent the overall population under consideration. The opinions of high school participants would be missing in the evaluation.

How can the evaluator ensure the integrity of sampling such a population? One method would be to use stratified random sampling methods, which ensure that identified subgroups are represented in the sample (Best & Kahn, 2006). In this case, the evaluator would divide the overall population into the two identified subgroups, middle and high school, and then randomly sample within these groups. In addition to grade level, gender or ethnic differences may be of interest to the researcher. Essentially, all of the characteristics of the population as well as the purpose of the study must be carefully considered while determining the sampling process for the study.

The random sample methods discussed thus far are considered simple random sampling methods. Such methods are not always possible for larger or less-well-defined populations than the one used in our example. For instance, think about the researcher charged with studying elementary school–based alcohol- and drug-prevention efforts in the United States. Generating a list of the actual participants in a national program would be impractical and absolutely untenable! Instead, it would be advisable to randomly select a number of states; from that list to randomly select a number of counties, from that list to randomly select a number of school districts, from that list to randomly select a number of elementary schools, and so on. This successive series of random samples results in a cluster sample, and it is a reasonable method to use when the overall population under consideration is too large for simple random sampling methods.

Random methods are not the only way to generate a sample. Many counselors who are conducting research engage in what are called convenience sampling methods. Convenience or opportunity samples are made up of the members of the larger population that are most accessible to the researcher. Such a sample is simply one that is gathered based on nonrandom methods. Asking for research participant volunteers is one way to acquire a convenience sample. Studying available classrooms or sending surveys to participants we have home addresses for are other ways that researchers utilize convenience sampling.

An additional sampling consideration is the concept of sample size. Realistically, there will likely be some trade-off between the most desirable size and the most practical size that can still provide valid results. While larger is usually better, there is no single percentage or absolute number that researchers must adhere to in order to ensure that an appropriate sample size has been met. Probability tables exist that can provide researchers with general guidelines for sample size however the process is more complex than simply consulting a table (see chapter 4 for a thorough discussion of methodological issues related to sample size). Sample size depends on the type of study being conducted; the nature of the population under consideration; and the practical considerations of available time, money, and other resources allotted to the project. Best and Kahn (2006, p. 20) provided the following considerations for sampling:

1. The larger the sample, the smaller the magnitude of sampling error and the greater the likelihood that the sample is representative of the population.
2. Survey studies should typically have larger samples than are needed in experimental studies because the returns from surveys are from those who, in a sense, are volunteers.

3. When samples are to be subdivided into smaller groups to be compared, researchers should initially select large enough samples so that subgroups are of adequate size for their purpose.
4. In mailed questionnaire studies, because the percentage of responses may be as low as 20 to 30%, a large initial sample should be selected to receive the mailing so that the final number of questionnaires returned is large enough to enable researchers to have a small sampling error.
5. Subject availability and cost factors are legitimate considerations in determining appropriate sample size.

Researchers can never be absolutely certain that they have captured a pure representative sample, but thoughtful sampling procedures create the best possible sampling outcome for the study.

Writing the Research

Now that we have thoughtfully considered the components of the research project, it is time to write a plan for the research (for a more extensive discussion, see chapter 5). In graduate theses or dissertations, this is called the methods section. To present our plan effectively, we identify the research question(s) and corresponding hypotheses. Then the subjects under consideration are identified, including the total population, the type of sample to be studied, and the sampling method selected.

Once the purpose and the population are clearly defined, the researcher must specify the instruments to be used. Any test, surveys, or experimental measures must be described, including their validity and reliability as well as the rationale for using these instruments. From this foundation of information, the researcher can discuss the specific procedures for the project, which is essentially the how, where, and when of the study. It is necessary to define each proposed step in the process so that any deviation from the plan can be discussed in the results section. The final piece of the methodology proposal is to discuss how the data will be analyzed, how they will be tested against the hypotheses, what statistical method(s) will be used, and why those particular measures are most appropriate. Following these steps helps the scientist-practitioner to ensure the foundation of a quality research project.

RESEARCH IN COUNSELING

Realities of Conducting Research in Counseling

We conduct research in order to develop new knowledge about a particular phenomenon. We apply the scientific method as a strategy to develop this knowledge. The ultimate goal is for the results of our research to affect and improve our ability to describe, predict, or explain characteristics, actions, and/or interactions within or between the subjects of observation (Gall, Gall, & Borg, 2006). In essence, counselors conduct research in order to facilitate effective clinical practice with the populations they serve (Sexton, 1996).

In counseling, *improving/controlling behavior* is one of the primary applications of research. While our thoughts are important, what a person thinks is not considered socially relevant until those thoughts manifest themselves in behaviors. For example, a person experiencing hallucinations does not necessarily attract attention until he or she "acts out" in public. Once the delusions are manifested, interventions are sought to explain and improve or control the behavior.

Research has become more and more prevalent as many counselors conduct research to be accountable to the profession. That accountability might be to satisfy requirements of third-party reimbursement entities or to justify the existence of programs (Sexton, 1996). Additionally, grant-funded endeavors require evidence of success in order for them to continue to receive funding. Counselors are often in a position of working with institutions that value their services but must continue to justify the need for the service. For example, school counselors are engaging in increased research efforts as they seek to provide statistical evidence of the effectiveness of their services (Whiston & Sexton, 1998).

Counselors have historically been at odds with research in the scientific community because they have often viewed studies as irrelevant to actual clinical populations (Sexton, 1996). In fact, the publication of research primarily in academic journals may have further alienated the practicing counselor from the new knowledge generated through empirical study (Sexton, 1996). Practitioners do not always see the connection between engaging in research and advancing their clinical abilities and improving client outcomes (Whiston, 1996). Increasing accountability, changes in research methods and designs, and a better understanding of the role research plays in the provision of counseling services has created a paradigm shift for the counselor as scientist-practitioner. The scientist-practitioner uses research as the basis for reflective practice and to generate ongoing rigor in clinical skills (Rowell, 2006). It is crucial that counselors do not fear research. At minimum, we must be critical consumers of the research we read. The tools for conducting quality research are provided to counselors in their training programs. All too often, we engage in regular research activities in our graduate programs but fail to carry that skill into our professional practice. As scientist-practitioners, we acknowledge the link between research and best-practice methods and strive to contribute to and improve the profession of counseling.

Ethical and Legal Considerations in Counseling Research

Research in counseling occurs within a set of ethical parameters designed to protect both the participants in and consumers of research (see chapter 17). These parameters were developed to cultivate *best practice.* Best-practice research is a worthy investment of a participant's time and resources. Additionally, such research is designed to result in a meaningful contribution to the profession of counseling (Bond, 2004).

In order to meet the standards for best practice, counselors must ensure that they are competent to design, plan, and conduct research. As scientist-practitioners, counseling researchers protect participants and end-users of research by adhering to established practices and consulting with colleagues or review boards to oversee their research efforts. Sufficient training, usually at the master's level or beyond, prepares counselors to understand research methodology and design as well as data analysis methods. Counselors practice under codes of ethics provided by their professional organizations, such as the American Counseling Association (ACA), National Board for Certified Counselors (NBCC), and others that govern this research into the client populations they serve.

Because counselors are often researching areas of vulnerability in people's lives, ongoing consultation and supervision are essential. The counseling relationship is one predicated on trust, and the counselor as researcher has no less responsibility to this foundation of the profession. Because counseling researchers are also clinicians, there may be dual relationship issues to address with participants. In program evaluation, for example, counselors may need to survey participants regarding the effectiveness of the services offered. Ethical research practice requires that the research relationship be independent of any clinical relationship. From a research perspective, this prevents the results of the evaluation from being influenced. From a clinical perspective, such a division protects the integrity of the ongoing client–counselor relationship.

In the chapter on ethics in research, the risks and benefits of taking part in a study must always be specifically outlined to participants. The counselor is responsible for providing this information in an informed consent [form] that can be clearly understood by those agreeing to join the study. The researcher has a responsibility to share with the participants the manner in which data will be collected, coded, stored, analyzed, and disseminated to protect the privacy of the individuals agreeing to take part in the research.

The Code of Ethics of the American Counseling Association (2005) provides counselors with this clear directive: "The primary responsibility of counseling is to respect the dignity and to promote the welfare of clients" (p. 4). The practice of research in counseling is likewise governed by this philosophy of ethical conduct. Ultimately, as scientist-practitioners, we strive to develop ethically sound research designs that address areas of inquiry that will make meaningful contributions to the field of counseling while protecting the participants and end-users of the research.

Summary

As a student of counseling, you should now be aware that counselors who are accountable to this profession conduct research to enhance the provision of effective services to the populations they serve. Part of being an effective counselor is knowing how to develop sound research designs in an effort to make meaningful contributions to the profession. Being an effective counselor also requires you to be a competent consumer of research that affects the professional landscape. Through this chapter, you have learned the basic building blocks of counseling research (i.e., types of research, development of hypotheses, and sampling). As you read through the remainder of the book, you will continue to add to your base and further your development as a scientist-practitioner.

Review and Discussion Questions

1. Take some time to compare some quantitative and qualitative research articles from professional journals. What are the basic goals of each of the research examples you have chosen? How does each example further our knowledge base?

2. Take a moment to consider the concept of target population. Consider a research topic that you might explore if you were a counseling researcher. What would be the target population for your study? How would you select a sample of that population?

3. Try to develop some specific research questions for the study you generated in question 2. Will you approach your study from a quantitative or qualitative perspective? What will help you make a decision?

CHAPTER 3

Reviewing the Literature

Donna S. Sheperis, *Delta State University*
Tiffany D. Chandler, *Mississippi State University*
Carl J. Sheperis, *Walden University*

OBJECTIVES
After reading this chapter, you will:

- Be able to understand the components of a literature review.
- Be able to present methods for organizing your review.
- Be able to search counseling-related databases.
- Be able to identify methods of analyzing the current literature.
- Be able to identify potential goals for conducting a review.
- Be able to delineate the basic components of APA style.

OVERVIEW

As a counseling student, you have probably read a number of journal articles or perhaps a doctoral dissertation. One of the key components of those research studies is the *literature review,* which offers an overview of the pertinent literature on a published topic. Consult any doctoral student or counseling researcher and you will quickly discover that writing about the relevant research surrounding a particular topic is an important but time-consuming task. Before actually writing the literature review, one must spend a great deal of time preparing for this task by researching the topic in question.

Some of you may take on this task as an assignment or as part of an independent research project. However, many of you will use the literature reviews of counseling researchers to help you complete assignments or make decisions about your practice as counselors. Thus, it is important for you to understand the principles of literature reviews in order to critically evaluate their quality.

In this chapter, we outline helpful tips for conducting a literature search as well as provide you with guidelines for writing, reporting, and understanding that information. Also in this chapter, we detail writing in the American Psychological Association (APA, 2001) format used by counselors, psychologists, and other professionals; discuss the program Endnote; offer a sample paper that will serve as a reference for you; and helpful websites to expand on this information.

REVIEWING THE LITERATURE

The reason for writing a literature review can vary, depending on the task at hand. Writing a literature review for a dissertation is much different than writing a literature review for a study that will be published in a peer-reviewed journal. The writing of the literature review is an extensive process that entails searching for, organizing, and summarizing the related research and literature on a particular topic. The manner in which a counseling researcher begins the search for existing materials depends on the scope of the area that is to be investigated.

According to LaFountain and Bartos (2002), there are five important aspects of the related literature in a research project, including (a) defining the perimeters of the investigator's field, (b) placing the research question in perspective, (c) learning which methods and instruments have been useful and which have less potential, (d) avoiding unintentional replication of previous studies, and (e) placing researchers in a better position to interpret the significance of their own results. Defining each of these roles before beginning a project will help ensure an organized, time-efficient, and thorough investigation of the literature.

Similarly, Eaves, Sheperis, Craft, Frasier, and Wells (2008) identified five steps that provide a framework for writing your literature review:

1. *Identify a topic for investigation.*   Any research project you begin will start with a question that sparks your interest. Once your interest is piqued, you will start to brainstorm general areas of interest to study.

2. *Locate the relevant literature on this topic.*   Having narrowed down the area of interest, you should begin the second step of the process by locating the existing literature surrounding the topic. This endeavor helps you verify that the work will be a valuable contribution to and an expansion of the literature.

3. *Critically evaluate the existing literature.*   It is the sole responsibility of the person conducting the research to be a critical consumer and evaluator of the research. It is imperative that, as a counseling researcher, you thoroughly read and analyze the existing information because not all of it will be useful for the purpose of the study. Narrowing down an area of interest and familiarizing yourself with the literature allows you to identify internal and external flaws in studies as well as consider areas for future research.

4. *Organize the quality and relevancy of information that outlines the actual writing process.*   Writing a literature review can be a time-consuming task. Organizing the literature will lessen your burden and allow for efficient writing.

5. *Present the wealth of information to the reader.*   Your audience must be able to understand the research that has already been done and determine the purpose of the research being conducted. The last step summarizes the first steps and leaves your audience well aware of the purpose, and more importantly, the benefit of the study.

RESEARCHING A TOPIC

Area of Interest

A literature review begins with your idea, question, or topic (LaFountain & Bartos, 2002). Of course, every research study should begin with a topic that the researcher would like to explore. VanderMey, Meyers, Van Rys, Kemper, and Sebrank (2004) suggested studying personal interests, topics mentioned in academic courses, and current issues. As budding researchers and scientist-practitioners, you should use caution in investigating topics that are either too general or too specific, overused, outdated, or of such lesser importance that they would not warrant further investigation. Considering these cautions, you should take some time to reflect on your ideas and areas of interest before engaging in the research process.

Once you have a general idea of what to study, a more systematic review of the literature needs to take place (Slavin, 2007). As the principal investigator, you must search and sift through all of the information encasing the topic of interest. This provides the foundation of knowledge regarding what has already been investigated and identifies any loopholes that can be expanded upon in future research. Before the literature review can ever be written you must locate, read, and analyze the information already published on the area of interest (Eaves et al., 2008). The next step is to review studies already conducted on this topic, giving careful consideration and attention to the benefits and limitations of each study, as well as the suggestions you may have for future research on your topic.

It is important to have thorough knowledge of the literature before defining specific questions and hypotheses. After acknowledging the past and present literature on the topic, you can then introduce your research question and begin demonstrating the necessity for and the importance of conducting the research.

Contribution to the Existing Literature

Taking on the task of conducting a literature review will require you to be knowledgeable about the existing literature, because you will have to report current findings and research on related topics (LaFountain & Bartos, 2002). It will be important for you to demonstrate how your topic or question of interest will make a contribution to the existing literature base (Eaves et al., 2008). By exploring the current literature and the uniqueness of your own research, you demonstrate that your work is not an unnecessary replication of a study (Slavin, 2007). In the steps toward accomplishing this task, you will have to somehow expand or clarify the preexisting literature. This endeavor should contribute meaningful knowledge and generally, "those studies that determine whether the hypotheses generated by a theory can be confirmed are more useful than studies that proceed completely independently of a theory" (LaFountain & Bartos, 2002, p. 31). Although we focus on writing the literature review, we should keep in mind the importance of conducting a study using sound methodology and its role in contributing to the ultimate usefulness of the study.

Narrowing a Broad Topic

Picking a topic to study and noting the importance of its original contribution to the existing bank of knowledge is a vastly intense process that ultimately acts as a filter for you to narrow your topic of study. Once you have identified an interesting topic, it is important to focus on a specific feature of that topic. VanderMey et al. (2004) suggested utilizing the following questions to help determine if the topic is manageable: "(1) Am I truly interested in this topic? (2) Does it meet all the assignment/ personal requirements? (3) Do I have access to enough information? (4) Is a paper on this topic feasible, given the time and page constraints?" (p. 449). Having a topic that is too broad prevents you from selectively identifying the scope of interest and may lead to ambiguity in the writing process. By limiting the research project to one or two research questions, you can better attend to those details and intensively study the purpose. Essentially, while you may be interested in many aspects of the topic, if you try to answer too many questions in one study it may become overwhelming. It is necessary to trim down your topic and research question(s) to a task that will be manageable. Keep in mind that follow-up studies and future research may address those questions you chose to leave out.

LOCATING, EXPLORING, AND ANALYZING THE LITERATURE

There are multiple types of sources and information available to researchers. Relevant literature may take several forms, including books, book chapters, published journal articles, and conference papers or presentations, as well as unpublished theses and doctoral dissertations (Cone & Foster, 1993). Consider the quality of ideas in the literature you are choosing to reference. Is it scholarly work? Does it have application to the topic? Is it based on a theory? The next section discusses and explains the many sources of existing literature available to researchers (primary and secondary sources) as well as tips for locating both print and electronic information that may assist researchers in the literature review process. It will be helpful to familiarize yourself with your library and the many information avenues that are readily available to you.

Scholarly Sources

The most commonly respected source of literature for you to consider is a published journal article (see chapter 1 for a list of counseling-related journals). Scholarly journals use an extensive process to review articles that are submitted, before publishing the final volume. Published journal articles require an editorial board to review the submitted work, make corrections, and vote to decide whether or not that article will be accepted for publication. Generally, these reviews are what are known as blind reviews, meaning that many of the reviewers are unaware of the article's authorship and make acceptance decisions based on the quality of the study and the article rather than the reputation of the writer. Prior to publication, each article has been subjected to multiple drafts before its final acceptance. The information has usually been peer reviewed, indicating that other professionals have read over the work, critiqued the content, and corrected errors. Thus, the information found in scholarly sources is more reliable due to the nature of the editorial process. Conversely, information found on unsecured websites should not be given the same credibility as an edited book or a published journal article.

To assist you in discerning scholarly versus nonscholarly sources, VanderMey et al. (2004) offered a few questions that may indicate if a source is trustworthy:

1. Is the author an expert?
2. Is the source current?
3. Is the source complete?
4. Is the source biased or unbiased?
5. Is the source accurate and logical?

By following these suggestions, you will obtain more reputable sources and strengthen the credibility of your work.

In searching for resources, be cautious of material on the Web. With the growing access and expansion of technology, it is possible for virtually anyone to post information via the Internet. It should not be assumed that the information is accurate, and should be considered more as a stepping stone. You may find interesting information available on the Web, but it is your job as the researcher to corroborate that information with scholarly sources.

Primary Sources

A piece of work that is considered the original report of research providing firsthand information on the topic or that is the first published account is known as a *primary source* (Cone & Foster, 1993; Galvan, 1999; VanderMey et al., 2004). A primary source is the direct account of an event, rather than someone's interpretation or explanation of what happened. For example, common forms of primary research are interviews, observations, surveys, experiments, and analyses of original data (VanderMey et al.). Depending on the nature of your investigation, these may or may not be suitable for your study. Galvan listed some additional examples of primary sources, including books and empirical research published in academic journals (e.g., theoretical articles, review articles, anecdotal reports, and reports on professional practices and standards).

Primary sources of information often provide meticulous descriptions of the methodology used in a study as well as detailed discussions of the findings. These sources should be differentiated from secondary sources, which provide a global summary of the results without the same in-depth detail (Galvan, 1999). It is important that you cite the information properly. If you cannot find the original article or material, do not cite it as though you obtained and read the article; be careful to follow APA guidelines for citing a secondary source (Cone & Foster, 1993).

Secondary Sources

According to VanderMey et al. (2004), *secondary sources* present a secondhand account of the information. Oftentimes, secondary information has been assembled, organized, and evaluated by someone who reviewed the primary source(s). Examples of secondary sources include textbooks, magazines, newspapers, television, and radio (Galvan, 1999). If this type of information is not appropriate for the task at hand, many journal articles, documentaries, encyclopedia entries, and nonfiction books are also common secondary sources (VanderMey et al., 2004). Remember, it is your job to sift through the information, critique it, and analyze what is most useful for the type of research project you are conducting. Both primary and secondary sources may potentially help the researcher establish a foundation of knowledge about the topic of interest, ultimately narrowing down the research question. There is a plethora of information in reference sources that can help you refine your topic. The exhaustive task of the researcher is to extract the relevant information.

Libraries

One of the most useful places to find information is the library. Whether you are a graduate student learning to navigate the inner workings of your campus library or a professional utilizing a public library, the depth of information at your fingertips is invaluable. Although electronic databases provide convenience in accessing information (and are described next in more detail), libraries often hold archival pieces of information and other types of primary sources that cannot be retrieved online. To develop some competence in conducting a literature review, it will be necessary for you to spend time in the library you plan on using to familiarize yourself with the library catalog, the reference desk, and any other system or program offered by the library that will help locate the information.

Electronic Databases

A popular method for locating literature involves choosing and searching a database specific to your topic of interest. There is a difference between an Internet source and an electronic source. Internet sources are free and anyone can have a Web page. Internet sites rarely make the best resources because you do not know if you are getting reliable information on "Joe Smith's Thoughts on Counseling." Instead, look for electronic sources that the library has paid a fee for use, such as ERIC and EBSCOHOST. In general, only published articles are found through such electronic databases. Using an online database is convenient and can be done at the library or from home with Internet access. Online databases search thousands of journals, books, chapters in edited books, government documents, newspapers, and theses/dissertations. Most databases allow you to limit your search with descriptors (detailed later in a section on search criteria) that report information related to the keywords you provide. Accurate descriptors and keywords save time as you avoid searching through unrelated information.

There are a number of databases for you to use when searching the related literature in counseling and similar fields of study. Some common databases searched in the social and behavioral sciences are discussed below, with a brief description of each.

ACADEMIC SEARCH PREMIER   This database is the world's largest scholarly, multidisciplinary, full-text database designed specifically for academic institutions. It provides full text for more than 4,600 periodicals, including full text for more than 3,600 peer-reviewed publications. This database supplies users with full-text journal articles in a variety of academic areas of study, including social sciences, education, humanities, engineering, language and linguistics, computer sciences, arts and literature, medical sciences, and ethnic studies. This database is updated daily.

DISSERTATION ABSTRACTS ONLINE   This database contains dissertations accepted from U.S. accredited institutions since 1861. Also included are selected international dissertations and master's theses beginning from the 1980s from all disciplines.

EDUCATION ABSTRACTS   *Education Abstracts* is database indexing abstracts of articles from more than 400 English-language periodicals. Full-text articles covering a wide array of subjects from preschool to higher education are available beginning from January 1996.

EDUCATIONAL RESOURCES INFORMATION CENTER (ERIC)   ERIC serves as a clearinghouse for all areas of education and educational research. It was established in the 1960s and contains more than 2,200 publications along with references for additional information and citations and abstracts from more than 1,000 professional journals.

MENTAL MEASUREMENTS YEARBOOK DATABASE   This database provides the text for the most recent versions of the *Mental Measurements Yearbook*. It contains information for more than 1,000 commercially available instruments used to measure personality, educational and academic skills, vocational skills, psychology, and other related areas. Each instrument is reviewed by selected individuals, and the database provides the name of the test author, publication information, the purpose of the test, scoring information, psychometric properties of the instrument, and a number of other valuable pieces of information.

PSYCH INFO   This database is produced by the American Psychological Association (APA). It is a collection of nearly 2.3 million citations and summaries of scholarly journal articles, book chapters, books, and dissertations, in psychology and related disciplines, dating as far back as the 1800s. This database also includes international material selected from more than 2,100 periodicals in more than 25 languages. Ninety-seven percent of the articles in this database are peer reviewed.

Search Criteria

Clearly, a variety of avenues exist for you to access the literature needed for a solid foundation and understanding of your research topic. When beginning your search in any electronic database, the use of relevant search criteria is critical. Most researchers begin with the general terms familiar to the subject. As you begin this process, be aware that what may seem like the most appropriate search term may not be the keyword to use in that particular database. For example, in your research on drug addiction, you may find that searching using the keyword *drug* reveals literature related to legitimate pharmaceuticals when you were primarily interested in illicit substances of drugs of abuse. In this case, just imagine the amount of time it would take you to wade through all of your search results to find the types of articles you were actually looking for! You may want to pair search terms, as most databases allow a few different slots for keywords. For example, pair the keyword *drug* with *illegal* or go one step further and specify a type of drug you are interested in studying. Trial and error, along with attention to the keywords highlighted and recognized by the particular database, will provide the best combination of terms to allow you to access the results you need.

When you begin to access the literature using your initial search terms, read some of the results for keywords that may be more germane to your subject. This will help you narrow down your results significantly. Additionally, the use of Boolean operators such as *and, or,* and *not* between your search terms will further focus your efforts. As you become more proficient with search options within a particular database and on your specific subject, you will be able to more quickly find results that address the core of your topic.

Here are some suggestions for searching electronic databases:

- As an example, from the electronic databases available to you through your library, select EBSCOHOST Web. Generally, there is also a text-only version if your browser is slow. EBSCOHOST is a global search that allows you to select specific databases.
- On this page, you will be asked to select your databases. Typically, Academic Search Premier, ERIC, and PsychINFO provide a variety of results in the field of counseling. You may select them all or choose only one to search. Play around with the combination that works best for you.

- Before starting your search, scroll down into the *Refine Search* area of your page. In it, you can select *full text* to ensure access to the article immediately. If your library does not have access to that article, there is probably a box where you can check Interlibrary Loan (ILL). Most libraries provide this service free, unless the article you have requested is particularly difficult to locate. If that is the case, your library may request a small fee to cover the expenses for retrieving the article. It is your decision to pay for the article. Remember that ILL can take up to several weeks. You may want to consider this service only if you have some time before your writing deadline; but understand that a responsible, exhaustive, literature review involves searching beyond the easily accessible, full-text electronic articles.
- Perhaps the most important option in the *Refine Search* area is the checkbox next to Peer Reviewed (Scholarly Articles, as described previously). Check this box every time. While it seems absurd to consider now, you do not want to have to justify a *Redbook* or *Newsweek* article as a scholarly resource.
- Numerous other options are available to you in *Refine Search* that can help you narrow your efforts. Investigate them to see how they can benefit you.
- *Search History* will keep up with your current search terms and results. You can use this page to combine two searches and find the articles common to both. It disappears when you log off, unless you have created a *My EBSCOHOST* account. This affords you the service of remembering the search terms you have used over time. Remember that you may not be successful searching for information on your first try. Playing around with the key terms, checking different boxes for peer-reviewed articles and full text, and searching all databases are important steps to finding the information you are looking for.
- Consider creating a *My EBSCOHOST* account that will keep records of all of your searches. Nothing is worse than having to ask yourself "Have I already tried searching *career assessment* AND *life span theory* before?" Conducting a thorough literature review takes a great deal of time and efficiency is essential!

Assessing Relevance

Once the information is found, it is your job to be a critical consumer of the research. In other words, while keeping in mind your topic, research question, and hypotheses, you decide whether or not the information you found is beneficial to the research project at hand. After you have checked the source to make sure it is reliable, you must question the content of the information. How will it be useful to your project? Was the methodology the same? Were the demographics of the participants similar? Are you expanding on a particular research study? It is imperative to first determine how the literature you are gathering is relevant to your project and then organize it accordingly. This will help in the writing process. Putting all of the information together and interpreting it is another large component of the literature review.

Storage of Sources

The information found in books, journals, and newspapers is referred to as *print information* (LaFountain & Bartos, 2002). This information is available at the library and organized by the library catalog. If you are unfamiliar with your library, oftentimes there are orientations and tutorials set up for individuals who need to learn how to search for research articles and other information. Most libraries have a reference desk or librarian available to walk researchers through the different processes involved in searching for the desired information.

It will be necessary to keep your print information all together and organized. Organization is a key aspect of compiling your data. You do not want to waste time searching and printing an article you already have. The only way to make sure this does not happen is to keep your project materials organized together, perhaps in a binder or in hanging file folders, so that you can reference the material you have already obtained.

Electronic information is more easily stored on servers, jump drives, and hard drives, but electronic information can be more difficult to keep track of. As previously discussed, EBSCOHOST, one of the most popular electronic databases, offers users an account option to store search results. Additionally, there are programs available that allow you to input information as you go, so you can keep records of all your information. One of the most useful is EndNote. This program allows researchers to create their own database of materials by electronic download of references. Students and other researchers may have access to this program at a cheaper price through their local or university library. EndNote is discussed in more detail later in this chapter.

As you begin your research, keep in mind that you will want to have sources that are as current as possible. Unless you are using seminal work (writings that served as the foundation, i.e., writings by Freud on psychoanalytic theory), anything more than 10 years old looks suspicious to the reader. In a similar vein, watch the use of textbooks as references because they are not generally primary sources.

Guidelines for Conducting a Literature Review

One of the main suggestions by authors proficient at writing literature reviews is to create an outline and process goals that will guide the necessary work for the project. *Process goals* are objectives you set for yourself to accomplish the task of reviewing the literature for a research proposal (LaFountain & Bartos, 2002). Define a process goal for conducting a literature review. Writing your own process goals helps you search the literature in the most effective manner. Following are some suggestions from LaFountain and Bartos (2002):

- This week I will schedule an orientation session at the university library.
- I will make an appointment this week to meet with a reference librarian to learn about the library databases.
- I will spend one hour per day for the next week reviewing the literature of a topic that I am considering for my proposal.
- I will search one electronic database per day for the next week, looking for literature related to a topic I am considering for my proposal.

Outlining short process goals helps you break down the assignment into more manageable pieces. This advice should not be foreign, because most of us have been taught from a very young age to break up larger assignments into smaller parts to make the assignment less overwhelming. It is the same concept with research. Writing a literature review and all of its components is a very large demand. By setting up steps along the way according to the project deadline, you can work on one task at a time while avoiding procrastination. If the project goes untouched and the deadline rapidly approaches, you may feel pressured and could inadvertently miss important pieces of information relevant to your project.

ORGANIZING AND PRESENTING THE INFORMATION

Much attention is paid to the experimental rigor and reported accuracy of a study (Henige, 2006). The literature review, however, sets the stage for the purpose of the research. A well-written literature review shares with the reader the rationale for the research as well as the place in which this particular piece of research fits within existing literature. In other words, the literature review helps you provide an answer to the question "Why?" about conducting the research.

Literature reviews apprise the reader of the current status of the area of inquiry and are comprised of multiple components. A literature review begins with an introduction to the topic. Within this introduction, an overview of the subject is presented in such a way as to illuminate the relevance of the subject through a description of the evolution of the topic and its current status in literature (Ritchie, 1995). This information may be organized as a historical timeline, or you may divide the existing research into categories that relate to your study.

The use of section headers within the literature review is key to creating a clear and logical flow of points to establish the foundation for the proposed study. Presenting ideas logically by grouping them into paragraphs and sections creates a well-constructed narrative reflective of organized and clear thought (Walker, 2003). The literature review is not a place to simply report study after study; rather, a well-written literature review creates an argument for the study being presented. Although it is often obvious to you, the author, the relationship between existing research and your proposed study is not always as clear to others (Heyman & Cronin, 2005). Thus, it is critical to organize the existing research by points of relevance and elaborate on the conclusions drawn by the existing body of research.

Organizing the Literature

In this chapter, we have already discussed the challenges in locating the existing research when we are beginning an exhaustive review process. Once this information is gathered, it then depends on you to make sense of the body of work for the reader. To accomplish this, you will need to report on the existing literature in context and elaborate on its role in understanding the identified subject.

It is helpful to organize the literature by its theoretical foundation and draw relationships between the current project and previous studies. Your responsibility is to analyze and synthesize existing literature to extract what is relevant to the research being presented (Ritchie, 1995).

Consider the following criteria, as suggested by Slavin (2007):

1. Is the study germane or relevant to your writing? The fact that an existing study is about the same topic area does not mean it will necessarily fit with your work.
2. Look at the methodology to determine if it fits your criteria; for example, you may wish to look only at qualitative studies or those with both pre- and posttest outcomes reported.
3. Is the study recent? If not, is there a rationale for including it in your work (i.e., is it seminal research)?

When you compile the data you should clarify and attempt to resolve previous discrepancies in the existing research. As a researcher, you must shed light on gaps in the previous research and discover new ways to interpret the information. Analysis of the existing information in the context of the study being conducted may answer questions from previous studies or corroborate the findings of other studies. At this point, you will suggest paths for future research, making sure to prevent any duplication of effort.

APA Style

Did you know that most research writing in the social sciences is APA style? As a student of counseling, you have probably been introduced to this style of writing for your academic papers. However, we have found that most students remain unaware of the nuances involved in effectively using this style of writing. *The Publication Manual of the American Psychological Association,* 5th edition (2001), provides a standardized formatting style for writing, organizing, and referencing research. According to APA, "(t)his standardization has greatly facilitated the communication of new ideas and research and simplifies the tasks of publishers, editors, authors, and readers" (APA, 2001, p. xxi). As you will see from the following discussion, the correct use of APA style involves far more than formatting citations.

FORMATTING   One of the questions you may have is, "Why do I have to use this style guide?" In APA style, writers and consumers of research share a common format, which allows them to concentrate on the content of the writing, because style issues are standardized. While beneficial to writers, the real use of APA style is to ease the path to reading scholarly work. Writers who carefully attend to the format will produce papers and manuscripts that are familiar to a larger market of readers.

As you may have already discovered, APA style may be easy to read, but the format is not easy to master. In fact, as you read our chapter, you may even find a few errors. Of course, we could assert that the errors were placed in the text as a learning check for you. However, the truth is that we are human, and it is difficult to address every nuance. In other words, you will likely receive a number of corrections as you attempt to write in APA style. Remember that practice makes perfect (almost).

APA style covers, among other topics, organization of ideas; grammar and syntax issues; language bias; and references. While research writers are generally well educated, and decent writers, sticking to form and using a consistent reference system can be challenging. In fact, the manual itself indicates that a number of exceptions can be found to every rule. We see the importance of mastering style but recognize that most of us maintain a heavy reliance on the APA manual as a reference item (we wrote this chapter with the manual open on our desks). As such, we cover some of the major components of the style here but refer you to the manual for more detailed information.

In preparation for writing your first draft, it is advisable to set the format to meet APA guidelines as soon as you begin to write. APA style, for example, uses 12-point Times Roman or Courier typeface. Margins are to be at least one inch at top, bottom, and both sides. While most word-processing programs are set to a Times Roman or Courier typeface, the default left and right margins of Microsoft Word®, for example, are 1.25 inches. Taking the time initially to change those settings will be helpful as you write your finished product. Newer versions of Microsoft Word® come equipped with an APA-style formatting function, as do other software programs that you can purchase independently. Using a formatting software program eliminates some of the potential for errors in basic APA style.

TITLE PAGE   After setting up your word-processing preferences, the next step is to create a title page. The title page in APA style includes a running head for publication, the title of your paper, author's name, and institution. Please be aware that the title page is numbered page 1 and is followed by page 2, the abstract. The abstract page contains a "brief, comprehensive summary of the contents of the article" (APA, 2001, p. 12). It is intended to provide the reader with a succinct and accurate snapshot version of the writing to follow. Even though it appears on page 2, it is typically one of the last sections you write—because you need the full paper to be able to create an abstract. When you do take on the task of writing the abstract, it should be an independent paragraph that does not contain any sentences from the body of your work. Finally, you are ready to begin the body of your paper on page 3, with the title repeated before the text begins.

HEADINGS   Now that you are prepared to write your introduction and review of the literature, you will need to decide on an APA heading style. "Levels of heading establish via format or appearance the hierarchy of sections to orient the reader" (APA, 2001, p. 111). The use of headers helps you create a structure and flow to the points you are making. You should note that the APA styles are guidelines for producing a typed manuscript. Printed textbooks such as this one vary in their treatment of headings, text, and illustrations. The style for a book is set by publishers to make the text more pleasing and easy to use. For your papers and journal manuscripts, APA recognizes five levels of headers, depending on the number of subheadings needed. These headings are:

CENTERED UPPERCASE HEADING (level 5)

Centered Uppercase and Lowercase Heading (level 1)

Centered, Italicized, Uppercase and Lowercase Heading (level 2)

Flush Left, Italicized, Uppercase and Lowercase Side Heading (level 3)

   Indented, italicized, first word and words after colon uppercase, rest lowercase paragraph heading ending with a period. (level 4)

When only three levels of headings are required, use levels 1, 3, and 4. For example:

Locating, Exploring, and Analyzing the Literature

Scholarly Sources

   Primary sources.

If your work requires a more extensive organizational hierarchy, the manual will further direct your use of headings.

Guidelines for Writing

Finally, you are ready to write! APA suggests addressing the content and organization of your literature review in a fashion similar to what has been presented thus far in this chapter. Scholarly writing requires the uses of *unbiased language;* that is, language that is free from stereotype or favoritism. Because the majority of research in counseling involves the use of human subjects, APA style provides guidelines for addressing research participants fairly and without prejudice or partiality. For example, APA style addresses gender-neutral language, sensitivity to labels, terms that reflect sexual orientation, racial and ethnic identity, disabilities, and age. The way in which the research is reported in your literature review can be as crucial as the results of the original study.

Within the body of your manuscript, you may need to use appendices, footnotes, endnotes, tables, and figures. APA style clearly affords the writer a common format for these items, recognizing that the writer must ensure that the item is necessary and integral to the writing. With the exception of endnotes and footnotes, these items are not typically found in the literature review but are often present in methods and results sections of research writing. As such, we refer you to the manual for more details on the structure of these additions. If you intend to include various types of tables and figures in your work, APA has developed an individual style guide that is independent of the APA style manual.

REFERENCES   The provision of accurate sources for the research you are reporting is critical to the well-written literature review. Not surprisingly, references receive a tremendous amount of attention in the APA style guide. APA style offers formatting guides for all types of references, including journal articles, books or portions of books, electronic media, and personal interviews. Following are examples of some of the more common reference types.

Journal article, single author:
Bryan, J. (2005). Fostering educational resilience and achievement in urban schools through school-family-community partnerships. *Professional School Counseling, 8*(3), 219–227.

Book, two authors:
Feerick, M. M., & Silverman, G. B. (2006). *Children exposed to violence.* Baltimore, MD: Brookes Publishing.

Electronic version of journal article available in print (APA has also developed a style guide for electronic resources that can be purchased for electronic download):
Faulconer, L. A., Hodge, D. M., & Culver, S. M. (1999). Women's disclosure of sexual abuse [Electronic version]. *Journal of Personal & Interpersonal Loss, 4*(2), 163–179.

Book with the group author as publisher:
Council for Accreditation of Counseling and Related Educational Programs. (2001). *CACREP accreditation manual of the council for accreditation of counseling and related educational programs.* Alexandria, VA: Author.

Third edition of a book:
Fenell, D. L., & Weinhold, B. K. (2003). *Counseling families: An introduction to marriage and family therapy* (3rd ed.). Denver, CO: Love.

Chapter in an edited book:
Starkey, D. S., & Rasmus, S. D. (2006). Individual and group assessment and appraisal. In D. Capuzzi & M. Shaffer (Eds.). *Career and life style planning: Theory and application.* Columbus, OH: Allyn & Bacon.

In-press chapter in an edited book:
Starkey, D. S., & Simpson, L. R. (in press). Turning group theory into group practice: The role of the experiential component in group facilitator training. In D. Viers (Ed.), *The group therapists' notebook*. Binghamton, NY: Haworth Press.

Works by the same single author during the same publication year:
Jourard, S. M. (1971a). *Self-disclosure: An experimental analysis of the transparent self*. New York: John Wiley & Sons.
Jourard, S. M. (1971b). *The transparent self*. New York: Van Nostrand Reinhold Co.

Plagiarism

It is impossible to discuss the art of writing well without mentioning the subject of plagiarism. An unfortunate reality, plagiarism is the presentation of another's ideas as if they were your own. In research writing, using another author's words, ideas, or even ways of organizing a topic without properly crediting the original work constitutes plagiarism (Cone & Foster, 1993). It is critical, as a developing scholarly writer, for you to find your own way of synthesizing and preserving material found in existing literature.

Plagiarism can be intentional, such as submitting another author's entire work as your own or including portions of such work in your own writing without a proper citation (Troyka, 1999). More commonly, plagiarism is unintentional. Beginning writers are often simply unaware of what needs to be cited and how to properly cite. Source citations simply provide the reader with a way to access the full body of the work being used to make the author's point (Henige, 2006). Understanding how to appropriately synthesize material from various sources, cite the work in the body of the text, and avoid the misuse or overuse of quotations facilitates writing that is free from intentional or unintentional plagiarism (Troyka, 1999).

Synthesizing and citing literature involves considering the source of the material. As the author, your own thoughts and ideas do not need to be cited or externally sourced. Similarly, information that is considered common knowledge does not require a citation. Common knowledge consists of "information that most educated people know, although they may need to remind themselves of certain facts" (Troyka, 1999, p. 487). Conversely, all material that is not considered common knowledge must be sourced.

Sourcing material involves providing the reader with the information necessary to retrieve the full body of the work being referenced. Every direct quote or indirect paraphrase will require a citation either in the body of the text, for example, "as Starkey and Chandler (2007) indicated, a well written literature review sets the stage for the rationale of the study. . .", or immediately following the idea presented, which will look something like this example: "a well written literature review sets the stage for the rationale of the study (Starkey & Chandler, 2007)." For maximum readability, it is suggested that you vary the manner in which you source your information to avoid patterns that might be repetitive or distracting to the audience. In other words, include the authors' names within the text if their presence adds to the understanding of the sentence, or decide to leave that information for the end of the thought if the authors' identities are not elemental to the writing.

Quotations

The use of text citations in APA format allows the author to properly credit the original source. As a student, you may feel the necessity to present a portion of an author's original work through the use of quotations. Quotations may add credibility to your writing. However, before quoting, it is imperative to ask yourself if there is any reason the author's direct words must be used. You may want to consider the following questions before using direct quotes: (a) Can the information be summarized or paraphrased? (b) Is it critical that you present the work in the original author's tone and intent? (c) Are the phrases used idiosyncratic to that author and worthy of quoting to preserve the integrity of the literature? If you answer yes to any of these questions, then quotations may be justified. If you decide that a direct quote is applicable, you will have to work toward smoothly incorporating quotations into the body of writing. As a writer, you should be conservative about the use of direct quotes and should make every effort to paraphrase first (Troyka, 1999).

Bibliography Management

A simple rule of bibliography management is that there should be a source for every citation and a citation for every source. If a source is in your reference list, it should be used somewhere in the body of your paper. If you use it in the body of your paper, by all means source it on your reference page. One of the most difficult components of scholarly writing is maintaining accurate sources and bibliography management.

You may have learned or developed a method for keeping up with all of your sources as you write. For some, this process is the most tedious, cumbersome, and error-producing portion of scholarly writing. Several companies offer software to assist with bibliography management. StyleEase (**http://www.styleease.com**) is a downloadable program that eases the formatting of the components of scholarly writing such as headings, tables of contents, appendices, and references.

Similarly, EndNote (**http://www.endnote.com**) can assist you in constructing a manuscript, organizing references, and creating an ongoing database of sources. EndNote provides a series of manuscript templates (e.g., APA style) for the user that allows you to insert references and text with minimal thought to formatting because the program formats your work for you. EndNote prompts you to complete text boxes that set up your title page in APA style, your abstract, and the body of your paper. As you type a source in the body of your writing, the reference information is automatically entered onto your reference page.

EndNote and other such programs ease your ability to acquire references and use them in your writing. When searching one of the many online databases previously discussed, results will often be made available to you in formats that can be directly downloaded to the software. You will be given the option of saving citations to a file formatted for the bibliographic management system and then exporting them into your personal reference library. There is one caution, however: you still need to review the reference to make sure it was correctly formatted on the database. Another major advantage of this type of electronic bibliography management is that it makes the references available to you for any number of writing projects. How many times have you remembered reading an article that would be valuable to you but you just cannot put your hands on it? By design, these programs create a paperless library for the researcher that allows for both ease of use and storage. Ultimately, electronic tools for bibliography management help the writer focus on the writing, not the burden of formatting or the fear of losing a reference along the way.

The Art of Writing

As previously discussed, the APA style guide is designed to assist you in preparing an organized, concise, and readable literature review. Heyman & Cronin (2005) have gone so far as to say that "writing style may be the single most important ingredient for success in publishing" (p. 402). In general, it is important to write from the broadest point, a general overview of the topic at hand, and end with the narrowest points, such as those points that speak to the gap in current research that you intend to investigate. The key to a well-written literature review is the art of synthesizing the material (Slavin, 2007). Too often, beginning writers assume that a review of the literature is simply a review of each individual study found to be important to the study at hand. Such an approach ends up looking like a listing of studies, with each paragraph beginning a synopsis of each author's work. A more appropriate approach is to present points that the literature makes in an organized and logical fashion using multiple studies to illustrate those points. For example, in a discussion of research related to student self-efficacy, the literature review may include:

> Smithers, Rogers, and Molpus (2000) offered graduate students in their programs APA workshops each year and found that students who attended these workshops felt more secure in their writing and tended to write more proficiently. Additionally, a 2006 study

showed similar results in graduate nursing students who attended an APA style training at their state conference (Knowles & Drury, 2006).

A more synthesized style of writing would report these two studies in the following fashion:

> Students who attended training in the use of APA style reported higher levels of security and self-efficacy related to their graduate writing style (Knowles & Drury, 2006; Smithers, Rogers, & Molpus, 2000).

Both ways of writing the information are accurate, but the synthesized version isolates the crucial point for the reader and presents it in a succinct fashion.

As you attempt to improve your writing skills, remember that effective research writers use a direct, clear, and concise approach to writing (Walker, 2003). By the time you reach the point of engaging in research writing, you have likely mastered the basics of writing form. However, even those writers who have the best understanding of basic sentence structure, grammar, and syntax need to follow clear editing procedures. In fact, it is estimated that editing, which occurs after the first version has been written, is comprised of about 70% of the total time dedicated to the writing project (Heyman & Cronin, 2005). As writers, we have a tendency to read our own writing using our own voice, missing inconsistencies along the way. Following your first draft, enlist the assistance of peer editors, who can review your writing from a more objective standpoint. Editing helps make you a better writer, so read your paper, read your friends' and colleagues' writing, and have them read yours. While writing, we all lose sight of our errors but can clearly see those made by others. It may be helpful to take breaks while editing; a fresh eye can help catch errors that could have been overlooked. Develop your own committee of editors, and share the task. Becoming a good editor helps you become a good writer.

Walker (2003) offered some practical tips for writers. He suggested that sentences be simple in terms of structure but that the structure be varied enough to engage the reader's interest. Ideas presented in well-formed paragraphs stand up to the scrutiny of scholarly writing. Finally, Walker suggested that if the reader has difficulty understanding your points, your writing loses credibility. Essentially, as a scholarly writer you will want your work to be clear, well organized, and readable. It is advisable to avoid jargon and hyperintellectualizing, which often sound good to the writer but are simply confusing to the reader.

As we have outlined in this chapter, it is important to keep a few things in mind when beginning the literature review process. It is critical to remember that writing is a skill. Intelligent, competent researchers often struggle with writing. While the results of your study may be your primary focus, a comprehensive but concise literature review is essential to set the stage for the research to follow. An exhaustive literature search is a component of writing up the research. As you write, keep the reader in mind, and write in such a way as to communicate clearly and effectively. It is important to be concise when writing. Providing examples is a useful tool to clarify a complicated subject without being redundant. The target audience should have a clear understanding of the purpose of the study, the voice of the researcher, and the findings and contribution by the author. A well-written literature review reflects the knowledge of the researcher on the particular topic. The use of timelines, editors, and ongoing revision will assist in creating a quality review of the literature, which will establish a foundation to showcase the research you have worked so hard to conduct.

In considering all the information you have accumulated in this chapter about conducting a literature review, obtaining relevant resources, following APA style, and writing effectively, take some time to review the following sample manuscript. As you read through it, look for elements of writing that may appear unfamiliar to you. For example, if you have not used an APA-style title page for any of your papers yet, pay careful attention to the running head and header on the sample. Also, look for any changes that you would make based on the information we have presented thus far.

Sample Paper
Running head: THE EFFECTS OF ATTACHMENT ORIENTATION

The Effects of Attachment Orientation
on the Supervisory Working Alliance
Keely J. Hope
Edina Renfro-Michel
Carl J. Sheperis
Walden University

Abstract

In this study, the effects of counselor and supervisor attachment orientations on the supervisory working alliance were explored. Matched pairs of counselors and supervisors ($N = 15$) completed the Experiences in Close Relationships Questionnaire—Revised (ECR-R) and the Working Alliance Inventory (WAI). Paired t-tests resulted in a significant difference in anxiety orientation between supervisors and supervisees. The results support the notion that an effective working alliance can be established regardless of contrasting attachment orientations. Implications for the supervisory relationship are discussed.

The Effects of Attachment Orientation on the Supervisory Working Alliance

Note that the title is placed again on the first page of text.

Note the use of first person plural. This is the correct format for writing in APA style. Writers often make the mistake of using the third person.

Attachment is a four-stage process beginning at birth and continuing through early childhood (Bowlby, 1969). During the attachment process, a child develops a framework for understanding and managing human relationships across the lifespan. Although individuals usually develop a dominant orientation related to a primary caregiver, different attachment domains (i.e., psychological states) can be activated across relationships (Sheperis, Hope, & Ferraez, in press). Thus, attachment theory provides counselors with a useful framework for understanding client interactions in relationships (i.e., romantic, friendship, and therapeutic) (Pistole, 1993). Because supervision is a type of relationship, it may also be affected by attachment orientation. Researchers discovered a correlation between attachment orientation and supervision satisfaction among counselors-in-training (Kim & Birk, 1998). However, the impact of attachment orientation on the supervisory relationship remains unclear. In an attempt to better understand relational aspects of the supervision process, we explored the effect of attachment orientation on the supervisory working alliance.

Review of Literature

Attachment is the first significant emotional bond experienced by an infant with someone perceived to be a source of protection and who provides a secure base to encourage a child's exploratory behavior (Bowlby, 1988). According to Bowlby (1969; 1980; 1988), attachment occurs in four stages. Stage one of the attachment process begins at birth, with an infant's communication of the need for proximity and physical contact through vocal and behavioral cues such as crying and grasping. During stage two, which occurs between 8 and 12 weeks of age, infants begin establishing indicators of caregiver preference through reaching and scooting. Stage three occurs from 12 weeks of age through the second birthday. During this stage, infants and toddlers begin to anticipate caregiver actions and adjust their own behavior in accordance with these anticipated events.

A consistent primary caregiver displaying affection and attention, as well as meeting the basic needs of the infant, has been hypothesized to promote a healthy attachment on the part of the child. Bowlby's fourth stage of attachment is characterized as an understanding of caregiver independence and the development of reciprocity in the infant–caregiver relationship. During these stages, consistency regarding the provision of behavioral reinforcement to basic emotional and physical needs is key to conditioning the child to utilize human relationships to gain a sense of security and comfort (Wilson, 2001). Children learn how to relate to others through the attachment process, and continue these patterns throughout the lifetime.

Adult Attachment

Historically, attachment researchers have focused on childhood interactions. However, an attachment orientation acquired during childhood often affects adult romantic relationships (Hazan & Shaver, 1994; Pistole, 1989). All attachment patterns exist on a continuum, with neither good nor bad attachments. In other words, individuals possess qualities of different attachment orientations but, in most cases, operate from a dominant orientation. Securely attached adults have feelings of self-worth and the belief that others will be responsive and loving. Thus, adults with a secure attachment orientation tend to have more successful and satisfying relationships than adults with insecure attachment orientations (Pistole & Watkins, 1995).

The Effects of Attachment Orientation on the Supervisory Working Alliance

Attachment orientations other than secure are often characterized by a negative sense of self or others. Adults with preoccupied and fearful orientations tend to be anxious or ambivalent about relationships and fearful of perceived rejection and loss. These adults gauge self-acceptance on the success or failure of their relationships and often cling to unhealthy relationships (Pistole, 1989). Adults with dismissing orientations often struggle with emotional intimacy, because relationships are seen as unsafe and threatening.

A central component among all attachment orientations is the degree to which a person struggles with intimacy. While intimacy is a crucial aspect of romantic relationships, it is essential for the success of other types of relationships as well (e.g., friendships or therapeutic relationships). Thus, a natural extension of attachment research has been toward understanding intimacy inherent in a therapeutic relationship. Although a power differentiation exists in therapeutic relationships, the therapeutic alliance is often emotionally intimate. Thus, clients often display similar attachment behaviors with counselors as with intimate partners (Pistole, 1989). Counselors modeling secure attachments can be a *safe base* for clients to explore their attachment orientations and relationship issues (Pistole, 1989). Additionally, counselors who display an insecure attachment orientation may disrupt the therapeutic relationship.

Attachment and Supervision

Intimacy in the therapeutic relationship is essential for success. However, it is only recently that the intimacy of the supervision relationship has been discussed (Hill, 1992; Kim & Birk, 1998; Pistole, 1989). Supervisors with an understanding of the attachment process can utilize the information as a teaching tool, a counseling tool, and a conceptual framework for the trainee–supervisor relationship. Because counselor supervisors often employ counseling skills with trainees, the supervisory relationship can mirror the therapeutic relationship (Bernard, 1997). For example, supervisees with anxious attachment orientations may feel less supported if their supervisors have avoidant attachment orientations. These supervisees may be seeking self-esteem reinforcement from the supervisory relationship, and the supervisors may be unable to provide the amount of emotional support needed. Conversely, supervisees with avoidant attachments may believe that their anxious supervisors are overbearing. Anxious supervisors may believe their avoidant supervisees are not invested in the supervision process. Most research regarding supervision and attachment focuses on supervisee attachment and disregards supervisors' attachment patterns and the interaction among the two. Kim and Birk (1998), in their research on supervisee attachment, found the secure attachment of the supervisee predictive of a positive view of the supervision relationship. Supervisees with a positive self-image were more likely to be satisfied with the supervisory relationship than supervisees with anxious or preoccupied attachments. However, Kim's and Birk's lack of emphasis on supervisor attachment orientation leaves some unanswered questions about contributing variables to an effective supervisory working alliance.

References

Ainsworth, M. D., Blehar, M. C., Waters, E., & Wall, S. (1978). *Patterns of attachment*. Hillsdale, NJ: Erlbaum.

Bernard, J. M. (1997). The discrimination model. In C. E. Watkins (Ed.), *Handbook of psychotherapy supervision*. New York: John Wiley & Sons.

Bowlby, J. (1969). *Attachment and loss: Attachment* (Vol. 1). New York: Basic Books.

Bowlby, J. (1980). *Loss: Sadness and depression* (Vol. 3). New York: Basic Books.

Bowlby, J. (1988). *A secure base: Clinical applications of attachment theory*. London: Routledge.

Fraley, R. C. (2003). Information on the experiences in close relationships—Revised (ECR-R) adult attachment questionnaire. Retrieved October 6, 2003, from http://tigger.uic.edu/~fraley/measures/ecrr/htm

Fraley, R. C., Waller, N. G., & Brennan, K. A. (2000). An item-response theory alliance of measures of adult attachment. *Journal of Personality and Social Psychology, 78,* 350–360.

Hazan, C., & Shaver, P. R. (1994). Attachment as an organizational framework for research on close relationships. *Psychological Inquiry, 5,* 1–22.

Hill, E. W. (1992). Marital and family therapy supervision: A relational-attachment model. *Contemporary Family Therapy, 14*(2), 115–125.

Horvath, A. O., & Greenburg, L. S. (1989). Development and validation of the working alliance inventory. *Journal of Counseling and Development, 36,* 223–233.

Kim, S. H., & Birk, J. M. (1998). *Influence of trainee attachment on counselor supervision*. Paper presented at the American Psychological Association, San Francisco, CA.

Note how the literature review funnels from a broad-based review of the attachment literature down to the specifics of attachment in counseling and supervision.

Note the gap in the literature, which provides rationale for the current study.

Review the references for consistency with APA style. Note the various types of references included (e.g., books, book chapters, journal articles, and Web-based resources. Is there anything missing?

Summary

Now that you have read through the chapter on conducting a review of the literature, you should be able to recognize how an author can use past and current research to identify an area in need of further exploration. Writing a quality literature review requires competency in searching for related information, an understanding of the essential components, and a mastery of APA style. To tie these things together effectively, you will need some constructive feedback on your work and a degree of patience for the editorial process. In order to become more proficient in writing a literature review, we suggest spending time reading and critically evaluating a number of published examples. Bibliography creators like those we suggested may be helpful in honing your literature review skills.

Review and Discussion Questions

1. Take some time to identify a topic of interest for a research study. Develop a list of keywords to begin your search of current counseling databases. How will you limit your search? What types of articles will you consider for your review?

2. Take some time to edit the following sentences for APA errors:
   a. Since the research design was cross-sectional in nature (see Gall, Gall, & Borg, 2006), it was assumed that subjects differed only in that they were beginning and ending counselor-trainees.
   b. Subjects were randomly assigned to one of 4 groups: micro-skills, didactic, experiential, and control.
   c. Doctoral students were administered the Minnesota Multiphasic Personality Inventory-2 (MMPI-2).
   d. Prejudice has been evident throughout the existence of mankind.

3. Did you find these issues? Are there any other changes you would make?
   a. Because the research design was cross-sectional (Gall, Gall, & Borg, 2006), it was assumed that participants were beginning and ending counselor-trainees.
   b. Participants were randomly assigned to one of four groups: (a) micro-skills, (b) didactic, (c) experiential, and (d) control.
   c. The Minnesota Multiphasic Personality Inventory-2 (MMPI-2) was administered to doctoral students.
   d. Prejudice has been evident throughout the history of humanity.

Helpful Resources

APA Online
   http://www.apastyle.org

Using APA Format: Purdue University Online Writing Lab
   http://owl.english.purdue.edu/handouts/research/r_apa.html

Tips from Temple University's Writing Lab
   http://www.temple.edu/writingctr/student_resources.htm

Software for Formatting and Bibliography Management
   http://www.styleease.com
   http://www.endnote.com

Getting Started with General Search Engines
   http://www.googlescholar.com
   http://www.google.com
   http://www.yahoo.com
   http://www.askjeeves.com

CHAPTER 4

Methodological Issues

Susan H. Eaves, *Weems Children and Youth Services*

OBJECTIVES
After reading this chapter, you will:

- Be able to understand the various ways of categorizing variables.
- Be able to understand the difference between defining variables for conceptual and operational purposes.
- Be able to understand the importance of variable identification in a study.
- Be able to understand the definitions of target and accessible populations.
- Be able to identify factors to consider when determining a sample size.
- Be able to select a representative sample.
- Be able to understand the importance of diversifying samples to include underrepresented groups.
- Be able to identify issues to consider when selecting an instrument.
- Be able to understand the different types of instruments and where to find them.
- Be able to understand sample bias, researcher bias, and participant bias—and how to decrease them in your study.

OVERVIEW

Once you have determined a research problem, reviewed the literature, and formulated hypotheses, you can turn your attention to planning your methodology. The methodology of a study determines the exact steps to be taken to conduct the research. To clearly plan your methods, you must often play the devil's advocate in order to consider all possible scenarios, pitfalls, and sources of error. You must have a clear plan and a rationale for why you are doing what you are doing. By reading this chapter, you will become aware of some of the common issues inherent in the methodological process and gain the necessary knowledge to develop a methodological plan pertaining to (a) variable selection, (b) population sampling, (c) instrumentation, and (d) bias reduction.

Imagine that you want to plan a trip to Italy. To plan such a trip, a number of decisions must be made. For example, which parts of Italy would you like to see? The wineries and vineyards? The countryside? The historical regions? Would you like to go for a day? A week? A month? How will you get there? What airline will you use? When would you like to depart? Will you rent a car once you are there? Where will you stay? A cottage? A luxury hotel? Will you go alone? Will you take someone with you? Who would you take with you? What would you do while you are there? What will you pack for the trip? How much money will you need? What other necessary items will you take? What will the weather be like during your stay? Are you beginning to wonder if you still want to go to Italy for vacation?

Deciding between qualitative and quantitative research methodology can be just as overwhelming for some people. Beginning researchers often find themselves feeling confused and unprepared. Does that mean you should never undertake research? Absolutely not. It simply means that you have some groundwork to do. Methodology is the itinerary to guide you successfully to where you want to go. Except where noted, the remainder of this chapter can be applied to both quantitative and qualitative research.

Suppose that during class last week, a counselor from the university outreach center came and spoke to your Introduction to Counseling class. During the discussion, the counselor talked about the prevalence of promiscuous sexual behavior on college campuses and its negative physical and emotional consequences for many students. Since the talk, you have been thinking about this issue and wondering why some students are sexually promiscuous and others are not. This is a possible research *idea.* Perhaps you suspect that differences in sexual promiscuity have to do with intrapersonal characteristics that could be the focus of counseling. This is a *hunch* (Babbie, 1992). So you take it a step further and begin to search the current literature on the topic (as will be discussed in chapter 5) to see what others in the field have had to say. You may find that others have studied sexual behavior, although not exactly in the manner as what you may be planning. Many great research ideas begin just this way. Before you decide to proceed in developing a research study, you must ask yourself if this idea can actually be scientifically investigated. Can it be broken down into manageable and doable steps? Can this topic be studied effectively? What variables are you investigating specifically? How will you measure the variables? From whom will you collect data? Are they the best population to sample? Can you gain access to this group? Does your study, if completed, have real-world applicability?

DEFINING THE VARIABLES

If your idea is to progress, you must first determine the variables you intend to study. A *variable* is any trait, attribute, or characteristic that varies. It can vary within each person over time or be constant within a person but vary across individuals (Furlong, Lovelace, & Lovelace, 2000). To explain, a person's age, weight, talkativeness, mood, net worth, and energy level are all examples of characteristics that change, or vary, relative to a person over time. Your age this year is different from your age last year or a year from now. How much energy you had at a given moment on last Friday was probably different from how much you had earlier that same day or might have had later that same night. Because of this, these characteristics are considered to vary within an individual over time. Certainly these traits vary across individuals as well; your energy level is different from that of another person's, as is your age. However, there are other traits or attributes that will remain constant within a person across time. Eye color, native language, birthplace, and childhood experiences are all examples of traits that are constant for each individual but vary across individuals.

Not only are there constant and variable traits, but variables can be of a numerical or categorical nature. Variables are also considered *independent* or *dependent,* and within the category of independent variables, there are *manipulated* and *selected* variables. Here is a pictorial diagram to help you conceptualize this more clearly.

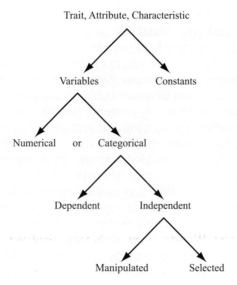

Ways to Classify Variables

NUMERICAL OR CATEGORICAL   Now that we understand that a variable is a trait or characteristic that varies within an individual or setting and/or across individuals or settings, let us look at the various ways to classify or think about them. First, variables can be either *numerical* (oftentimes referred to as *quantitative*) or *categorical* (otherwise known as *qualitative* variables). The difference here is in how the characteristic is measured or categorized. Variables of height, weight, and test score are easily categorized with numerical values and show differences in amounts. They can usually be plotted along a continuum to show how much of the variable they represent. Variables of religion, gender, and ancestry are instead categorized along type and show more qualitative differences (Furlong et al., 2000). If we wanted to know more about a person's religious lifestyle, we could not only document their religious affiliation (categorical variable—i.e., Catholic, Episcopalian, Jewish, Buddhist, etc.) but also how often they attended religious services (numerical variable—i.e., once a year, once a month, once a week).

DEPENDENT OR INDEPENDENT   Another way to categorize research variables is to classify them as independent or dependent. In other words, the dependent variable *depends* on the independent variable. This means that the independent variable (IV) causes changes to the dependent variable (DV). All research has at least one of each (although there is no limit to the number of variables you can have), and the purpose of research is to understand the relationship between the two. Various texts (Fraenkel & Wallen, 2006; Patten, 1997) talk about the relationship between variables in various terms:

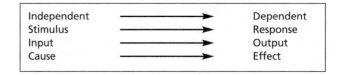

By way of example, suppose we wanted to examine how clients with depression responded to cognitive-behavior therapy. Depression would be the dependent variable, while cognitive-behavior therapy would be the independent variable. In other words, we would want to see how depression (the dependent variable) was affected by, or responded to, cognitive-behavioral therapy (the independent variable).

MANIPULATED OR SELECTED   In the preceding example, the independent variable, cognitive-behavior therapy, could either be manipulated or selected. If it is manipulated, the researcher selects participants to be exposed to this type of therapy. If it is selected, the researcher selects clients who are already being treated with this form of therapy. Said another way, manipulated variables are controlled, created, applied, enforced, or enacted by the researcher, while selected variables are observed as they occur or after they have occurred without researcher intervention. The reason this distinction is important is because oftentimes, when one is conducting research, it is not possible or ethical to manipulate the independent variable (Fraenkel & Wallen, 2006; Isaac & Michael, 1997; Patten, 1997). For instance, if we wanted to observe the effects of alcohol use on sexual behavior (getting back to our original research idea), we might observe college students' behavior at a party where there is alcohol, making note of how increased alcohol use affects sexual behavior. We might also want to survey college students about their drinking habits and their sexual behavior. Both of these examples involve selected independent variables because we are observing or surveying behavior that has already occurred or is occurring without the researcher's involvement. Would it be possible to manipulate the independent variable of alcohol use? Yes! Would it be ethical? Probably not.

Before moving on, let us review what you have learned thus far. You should now understand that traits can be changeable or constant, for any one individual at a particular time, across time, or across individuals. You also know that every variable will either be categorical or numerical, depending on whether it differs in type (gender) or in amount (test score). In addition, you have learned that all research has a dependent variable and an independent variable, with the former being the resulting change and the latter being the impetus for that change. Finally, you understand that an independent variable can be either manipulated or selected by the researcher, according to the purpose and needs of the study.

Here is a scenario to test your understanding of variables in research. Suppose we took your idea regarding sexual behavior and decided to actually incorporate it into a research study. Based on your readings in the literature and your understanding of previous research, your research question would look something like this:

> The aim of this study is to determine why some college students are sexually healthy and responsible, while others are not. In an effort to do this, I will explore the effect of attachment style (a pattern of relating to others), self-worth, and peer norms on sexual behavior. Specifically, I will collect data on age at first intercourse, number of sexual intercourse partners, frequency of cheating behaviors, and number of one-night stands.

First, consider the following list of all the possible variables:

1. Attachment style.
2. Self-worth.
3. Peer norms.
4. Age at first intercourse.
5. Number of sexual intercourse partners.
6. Frequency of cheating behaviors.
7. Number of one-night stands.

Next, determine whether each possible variable is indeed a variable or a constant, whether it is categorical or numerical, independent or dependent, and likely to be manipulated or selected.

Each possible variable is, in fact, a variable. While several of them are relatively constant within any given individual over time, they are all considered to vary across individuals. Of these seven variables, which are categorical and which are numerical? Attachment style is considered categorical because a person can fit into one of three types of attachment categories. Self-worth is numerical in this study because each participant will self-report his or her level of self-worth along a numerical continuum from low to high. Peer norm is also numerical in this study because the participants will report perceptions of their peers' behavior along a numerical continuum. What about sexual behavior? Age at first intercourse, number of sexual partners, frequency of cheating behaviors, and number of one-night stands are all numerical variables as might be implied by the words *number, age,* and *frequency.*

Now consider which variables are independent and which are dependent. Remember that the independent variable should lead to your dependent variable. For the purposes of this study, we want to examine whether changes across participants on the variables of attachment style, self-worth, and peer norms predict changes in sexual behavior. Therefore, attachment style, self-worth, and peer norms are the independent variables, and age at first intercourse, number of sexual intercourse partners, frequency of cheating behaviors, and number of one-night stands are our dependent variables. Lastly, the independent variables of attachment style, self-worth, and peer norms are selected rather than manipulated because these are traits that will already be in place for each individual.

Why Are Operational Variables Important?

def. variable + how it will be measured.

A few years ago a group of researchers in obesity reported results claiming that far more Americans were obese than had originally been thought. Obesity, they claimed, was becoming an epidemic! For the purposes of their study, these researchers had defined the variable of obesity slightly differently than normal. Rather than considering obese participants to be individuals with a Body Mass Index (BMI) of 30 or above, the researchers defined those with a BMI of 29 or above as obese. Such a tiny detail should not cause a stir, right? This one small adjustment in the operational definition of obesity resulted in an additional 10 million Americans being classified as obese, setting off alarmists all over the country.

Once variables are selected for study, you must get very specific about what the variables mean for the purposes of your study, what they do and do not include, and how you are going to identify and measure them. Measuring the wrong things or measuring them in the wrong way can change the entire purpose of the study, sometimes even making your results invalid. Variables cannot be measured or manipulated in a meaningful way if they cannot be defined. However, it is important to understand that a variable can be defined conceptually without being *operationalized.* What this means is that we can assign it a dictionary-type meaning, without defining it for the purposes of the research. Although it is important to define it in both ways, we should understand the difference. When we operationally define a variable, we not only state its definition for the purpose of the research study at hand, but we also state how it will be identified and measured (Blaikie, 2003; Furlong et al., 2000; Patten, 1997).

Recall the scenario discussed earlier regarding depression and cognitive-behavior therapy. How do you go about operationalizing a concept like depression? How will it be identified? How will it be measured? For some, depression may be a feeling of sadness. For others, it may consist of apathy and thoughts of suicide. Still for others, it may consist of hopelessness and changes in appetite. You may, for the purposes of your study, decide to operationalize your own definition of depression based on these and other symptoms. Or you may select participants on the basis of a documented clinical diagnosis of depression. Still another option would be to administer a depression inventory to measure and identify depression. The important point to remember is that you must document how you go about this process so that others can replicate your research if they choose. It is also important because others will interpret and understand your results in light of how you defined the variables. Consider the research report that claims fruits and vegetables decrease heart disease. For some, an apple pie and an order of French fries may constitute that fruit and vegetable.

POPULATION ISSUES

Why Are Population Issues Important?

I've often heard it said that redheads are mean, blondes are unintelligent, and men with mustaches are more likely to come on to you. I am guessing you may have heard this as well. On the positive side, I have also heard that redheads are assertive, blondes are pretty, and that men with mustaches look like Tom Selleck. Why is it that neither set of statements seems quite right? What is the problem here? The problem is that I am taking statements that were probably based on a few experiences with a few people and applying them to every person that meets those criteria. I am generalizing this information to *all* redheads, blondes, and men with mustaches, when, in fact, the sample this information is based on was not adequate or representative of *all* redheads, blondes, or men with mustaches.

In chapter 2, a brief overview of the importance of sampling and generalizability was given. From that discussion, you learned that it is important to obtain a sample that is representative of the population you want to generalize to, in quantitative research. Here, we discuss the many issues that must be considered with regard to sampling the intended population. Although it has been said about the other areas of methodology, it bears saying again. Selecting a sample is one of the most important steps in designing both quantitative and qualitative research studies. While the goal of quantitative sampling is to obtain a representative, random, and generalizable sample, sampling within qualitative research is typically done to highlight a specific case example.

Let us consider our sexual behavior study in an effort to understand the different terminology within this section. If you recall, we are interested in studying the sexual behavior of *college students*. College students make up our population. All college students within the United States is our *target population,* also called our *theoretical population.* More often than not, conducting a research study that includes your entire target population is difficult if not impossible. It is for this reason that we need to define our *accessible population.* In the sexual behavior study, the accessible population was identified as all college students at Mississippi State University. From the accessible population, we identify our sample, which is the actual group of people we will contact and rely on to gain information. For our sexual behavior study, the sample was comprised of 998 college students at this university. If the sample is to be applicable (generalizable) to the accessible population, it must be representative (the same as) of it. If the findings are to be applicable to the target population, they must be representative of it. With that said, the best way to do this, even with a representative sample, is by repeating the study several times (replication). Every effort should be made to give a detailed description of the population and sample so others can decide for themselves if your findings apply to them and also so that replication can take place. Not giving a detailed enough description of the procedures has been cited as one of the most common problematic issues found in research (Fraenkel & Wallen, 2006; Martella, Nelson, & Marchand-Martella, 1999).

The following write-up shows how these sampling issues are addressed:

> The participants for the proposed study consisted of undergraduate students attending a medium-sized university, granting approximately 3,000 degrees each year. Located in the southeastern part of the United States in a community of nearly 25,000, approximately 16,000 students were currently enrolled at this university, with 12,500 undergraduates. Males made up roughly 55% of the student body, with females accounting for 45%. Further, the student body was made up of 19% African Americans, 1% Hispanic, 1% Asian, 5% Native American, and more than 70% Caucasian. The sample being used for the study was comprised of approximately 44.2% males and 55.8% females, further broken down as 26.5% African Americans, 0.9% Hispanic, 0.9% Asian, 0.2% Native American, 70.3% Caucasian, and 1.1% other. Further exclusionary criteria were used to clearly define potential participants. The resulting sample consisted of 855 participants (Eaves, 2006).

Sample Size

One of the most worrisome issues in designing a quantitative research plan is deciding on sample size. Quantitative research is primarily concerned with discerning relationship, effects, and predictions. When your research is qualitative in nature, you are assuming that meaningful experiences can be interpreted. Prediction and randomness are not key elements in discerning what these experiences signify because you are not trying to predict future events based on a single event, nor are you trying to say that one's experience is indicative of other's experiences.

With regard to quantitative research, you will want to determine how many participants you need in order to find significance that exists—without reporting significance that should not be detected. At what point does a small sample become too large? The reason these issues are so worrisome is because there is no definitive answer—which most of us just hate! There are, however, several ways to go about deciding this number, and a combination of these ways is suggested. First, consider whether you anticipate finding a large-effect or a small-effect size. When a strong relationship between the variables is suspected (or a large effect), it will be fairly easy to find, and therefore can be found with fewer participants. Finding smaller effects generally requires a larger sample size because differences and relationships are not as easily detected.

Another useful practice for determining how many participants you need in your sample is to review previous studies similar to the one you are designing. It is important to choose studies that not only have variables in common with your study, but also ones using similar statistical methods to those you intend to use. By looking at others' research, you can get a general idea of both the range and the average number of participants used. Finally, pay careful attention to limitations of these studies related to sampling and sample size, which you will want to consider.

The type of statistical analysis will also influence the sample size you need. Fraenkel and Wallen (2006, p. 104) had this to offer:

> There are a few guidelines that we would suggest with regard to the minimum number of subjects needed. For descriptive studies, we think a sample with a minimum number of 100 is essential. For correlational studies, a sample of at least 50 is deemed necessary to establish the existence of a relationship. For experimental and causal-comparative studies, we recommend a minimum of 30 individuals per group, although sometimes experimental studies with only 15 individuals in each group can be defended if they are very tightly controlled; studies using only 15 subjects per group should probably be replicated, however, before too much is made of any findings.

Blaikie (2003, p. 166) states, "My rule of thumb when advising students is to say that 300 may be adequate, 500 would be better and 1000 would be even better." He goes on to add that nominal data require much larger sample sizes than ordinal and far larger samples than interval data, while metric-level analysis can utilize very small sample sizes. The differences here are based on the types of analyses used with various types of data. Blaikie also offers his own guidelines that encourage larger samples for more diverse (heterogeneous) populations and when incorrect results would lead to more serious consequences. (Blaikie gives the example of being wrong as to the average age of the population versus being wrong as to the safety of a drug. A mistake about the safety of a drug could have much more serious implications.) Patten (1997) suggests that sample sizes are smaller if they are expensive to obtain or require too much time, while they must be larger if the variables you are studying are rare. You should consider the sensitivity of your topic when deciding what sample size is warranted. I conducted a pilot study on marital infidelity and observed a hesitancy to participate due to the nature of the questions. If you realize that participant sensitivity to the research may affect response, you should take this into consideration when deciding your initial sample size. You can see that opinions are varied on this topic and that there are no clear-cut answers, or even agreed-upon guidelines. Indeed, with the exception of sample size related to exact statistical analyses, words such as *large* or *small* are generally used both relatively and ambiguously.

Tabachnick and Fidell (2001) cautioned against too many participants. As the number of participants increases, so too does your risk of finding significance where it should not have been found. Because of this, it seems most appropriate to measure the smallest number of cases that has a reasonable chance of revealing significance, while ensuring a representative sample. Last, have a rationale based on scientific reason for your choice of sample size. Consultation with a statistician is often helpful.

Underrepresented Groups

An ongoing issue in research is the lack of adequate representation of minority groups. A large percentage of the existing counseling literature is based on white, middle-class, educated participants. The problem this causes is that we cannot always say that results are applicable to minority groups or groups that are not white, middle class, or educated. According to the U.S. Census Bureau (2006), approximately 33% of the U.S. population is nonwhite. Only 25% have a bachelor's degree, while 12.5% are below the poverty level. Within the field of counseling, the omission of such members of the population can be especially troubling because many of our theories of development, personality, and therapeutic intervention are based on only a portion of those who present themselves for counseling services.

When you undertake a research study, you are making an effort to contribute to your field in an important way. You can do even more by making additional efforts to increase the diversity of a sample by oversampling minority groups in order to have an adequate representation of them. Minority groups include gays, lesbians, various religious groups, females, older persons, persons with disabilities, and various racial and ethnic minorities. Such efforts to include these individuals in greater numbers will not come easily, however, and will certainly entail greater time, effort, and resources. There is a reason why these groups are under-researched. As a researcher, you have the ability to give a voice to those who have been previously overlooked in the scientific literature, and you are strongly encouraged to do so.

INSTRUMENTATION

Now that you know what you are going to study, exactly what your variables are, and whom you are going to sample so that you can generalize to your target population, you must consider what kind of information you intend to collect and how it will be collected. Whatever mechanism you choose to collect data is called an *instrument*. This entire process of data collection, from instrument selection to instrument administration, is called *instrumentation*. Fraenkel and Wallen (2006) offer several questions to consider, including: (a) Where will you collect your data? (b) When will you collect your data? (c) How often will you collect your data? (d) Who will collect your data? I would add, (e) "Why?" I agree that the first four questions are of great importance and that they need to be answered while planning your research. I also believe that many beginning researchers are not able to give a rationale for *why* they would answer the way they would answer, or that they would not realize that their answers might be less than scientific. All too often, researchers make methodological decisions based on convenience rather than methodological rigor. If your answer to *why collect the data* is related to convenience, you may need to rethink your answers to *where, when, how often,* and *who.*

Considerations for Instrument Selection

Choosing appropriate measurement devices is one of the most important steps you will take to ensure a high-quality and relevant study. Something that is not done often enough by beginning researchers is familiarizing themselves with the wealth of instruments available to them. It is important to do this because knowing what is available will make you more likely to choose the most appropriate and applicable instrument for your study. It will also make you less inclined to develop your own instrument, something that is typically discouraged due to the time and effort required to develop a valid and reliable instrument. Several sources exist with lists of instruments, complete with reviews that will provide you with invaluable information. Perhaps the most comprehensive list of instruments and testing resources is the ERIC database, available at ***http://www.eric.ed.gov***.

Through keyword search, this site provides an excellent way for you to narrow down your choice of instruments to those directly applicable to your study. *The Mental Measurements Yearbooks* is another valuable source of information with test reviews for more than 4,000 instruments (available at ***http://www.unl.edu/buros/***). One other source is the website of the Association for Assessment in Counseling and Education, a division of the American Counseling Association. In addition to select test reviews, this site (***http://www.theaaceonline.com/home.htm***) offers *codes of fair test practices*, *standards for multicultural assessment*, *test-taker rights and responsibilities*, as well as resources on additional competencies, responsibilities, and qualifications. While many of these are aimed at those who test for the purposes of diagnosis, treatment, admission, and placement, the information still applies when the purpose is data collection for research.

Scanning lists of assessment instruments and reading selected test reviews are both excellent ways for you to become more familiar with the large number of assessment instruments available to you. However, so is reviewing previous studies in the literature to consider the instruments chosen by other researchers studying the same variables you intend to study. In fact, this may be the most appropriate place to begin. As you read through the relevant literature, take notice of instrument descriptions and the appropriateness of the instrument. To explain, unless a researcher is using an instrument that is common and well known enough to not need further explanation, a thorough description of the instrument should be given. When the instrument is a household name (for example, the Strong Interest Inventory), it is impossible and unnecessary to try to summarize all the information available on the instrument, and referring readers to relevant sources will suffice. When the instrument is less common, a discussion of the instrument should, at a minimum, include a description of the constructs and variables it measures, how it is laid out in format, how it is scored, what different scores mean, and information about its reliability and validity. This information is especially helpful to you in evaluating whether this is an instrument you will use in your own research (Heppner & Heppner, 2004; Martella et al., 1999). Consider the following example from Sim and Ng (2007):

> Mother attachment and father attachment. To measure how attached the adolescent was to his or her mother and father, we used a shortened 24-item version of Kenny's (1987) Parental Attachment Questionnaire (PAQ). The PAQ was developed particularly to be used in the context of the higher learning institution and has been used extensively with diverse samples in this setting, including African Americans (Hinderlie & Kenny, 2002) and missionary children (Huff, 2001). Notably, the PAQ has been used with Asians (Kenny & Perez, 1996; Klasner & Pistole, 2003). To ensure sufficient content coverage of Kenny's formulation, we adopted items from all three of the dimensions of affective quality of relationship (Affective Quality of Relationships scale, 11 items), fostering of autonomy (Parents as Facilitators of Independence scale, 8 items), and provision of emotional support (Parents as Source of Support scale, 5 items). . . (pp. 469–470)

Heppner and Heppner (2004), along with Fraenkel and Wallen (2006), also offer a few additional thoughts on instrumentation. When selecting an instrument, consider how long it is and how long it will take to complete; its readability, and if your sample can understand the language and words used; if you will have to make any changes to the instrument and if so, how; the appropriateness of its administration procedures; its appropriateness for answering your research questions; its psychometric properties; and if it has been validated for the specific sample you are using. In addition to these suggestions, also consider whether directions for administration and scoring are clear; the cost, if any, to use the instrument; if equivalent forms exist; if it requires you or someone else (a teacher, parent, counselor) to report information; if it is a paper-and-pencil version or based on performance behaviors; and if others have reported problems associated with its use.

Types and Definitions of Instruments

The following is a list of measurement types and defined terminology involving direct observation by the *researcher:*

- *Rating scales.*   Rating scales are used to provide a score in relation to how a person behaves. Rating scales differ from an observation in that they imply a judgment rather than just an acknowledgement.
- *Interview schedules.*   An interview schedule is a list of questions to be asked orally of a participant.
- *Observation forms.*   Observation forms contain specific behaviors for the researcher to observe and evaluate and provide a place to document the frequency of such observations.
- *Flowcharts.*   A sheet for recording frequency counts of a behavior, as well as the intended direction of the behavior.
- *Performance checklists.*   A checklist to record if, not how well, a person is engaging in behaviors typically associated with performing a particular task.
- *Anecdotal records.*   Records containing specific and factual recordings, usually in paragraph form, of observations deemed important to the researcher.
- *Time-and-motion logs.*   Logs are very detailed observations of a person or group that occur over a specified period of time in an effort to understand underlying reasons for behavior.

The following is a list of measurement types and defined terminology for instruments completed by *research participants:*

- *Questionnaires.*   A questionnaire includes a list of questions that the participant answers in writing or by marking the appropriate response.
- *Self-checklists.*   A list containing characteristics or activities for the participants to check if it pertains to them.
- *Attitude scales.*   These scales have a set of statements that represent certain attitudes, depending on which ones the participant endorses.
- *Personality inventories.*   Personality inventories measure the characteristics and traits of the participant.
- *Achievement and aptitude tests.*   These tests measure a participant's knowledge, ability, or propensity to achieve.
- *Performance tests.*   This test measures a participant's ability to perform on a certain task. (Fraenkel & Wallen, 2006)

As you can see from these lists, there are many options for you to consider when choosing a method for collecting data.

SAMPLING, PARTICIPANT, AND EXPERIMENTER BIAS

Why Is Participant and Experimenter Bias Important?

Several years ago, just days before a presidential election, I heard a conservative radio station announce that the results of a poll it had conducted revealed that the Republican candidate for president would win by an overwhelming majority of votes. On the evening of the election, I was awake and glued to the television well after midnight, awaiting the final results of the election. The resulting votes were so close in number that the outcome began to hinge on just a few states. What happened? How did this radio poll get it so wrong? Well, the participants in its survey were pulled from its listening audience. Because it is a conservative radio program, its listening audience is likely to be predominantly conservative. Its listening population was in no way representative of the voting population.

One of the most important methodological issues in research concerns *bias,* which unfortunately is an inherent part of any research. Biased results can come from unintentional errors related to how responses are elicited, how observations are recorded, the social desirability of participants, the purpose of the study, and expectations of the experimenter, just to name a few. Some feel that bias is more probable in qualitative research due to its nature. Regardless, bias can and does occur in both qualitative and quantitative research, so this next section is particularly important in that regard. Your responsibility as a researcher is to understand how these and other biases can occur, to use that knowledge for prevention through a well-thought-out methodological plan, to then be aware of the bias within your own study that is bound to occur despite your best efforts, and to take that into account when examining your results. Now, in order to do all that, you must first have the necessary knowledge.

Sampling Bias

Random sampling was briefly discussed earlier. As a reminder, in random sampling every member of a population has an equal chance of being included in a sample. Ideally, a sample should *mirror* the population it is intended to represent. However, rarely can we actually give every member of a population an equal chance of being included, oftentimes because we cannot even identify, much less have access to, every member of a population. Nevertheless, this inability to identify and gain access is a source of bias. The result is that certain members of the population of interest are underrepresented or overrepresented, meaning we have too few or too many of them. For instance, if you are conducting a study to explore the personality characteristics of persons with addictions, you may be able to identify those who are currently receiving treatment, who attend support meetings, or who have come to the attention of public service agencies. However, you have no way of identifying other members of the addicted population. Typically in this scenario, the resulting bias is not caused by your lack of effort.

Similar outcomes occur in other forms of sampling, though perhaps for different reasons. Unrepresentative and therefore biased samples can also result from convenience sampling methods. As mentioned previously, convenience samples are used, well, for convenience. Perhaps you want to investigate the anxiety levels of college students today. You decide to stand outside the library the week before final examinations and poll students as they are entering or leaving the library. Not only does your choice of location (the library) bias your results, but so does your timing (the week before finals). Obviously, anxiety levels might be higher for these students at this time than might otherwise be expected. Consider another example. Say that in regard to our sexual behavior study, we want to get a prevalence rate of how many students are sexually active. Would there be a difference in our numbers if we collected data at a popular college bar versus a church near campus? Of course there would. We know from past research that alcohol use is positively associated with sexual behavior (as the use of alcohol increases, so too does the likelihood of being sexually active), while church attendance is negatively associated with sexual behavior (as church attendance increases in frequency, the likelihood of being sexually active decreases). Where we collect our data makes a difference and can bias our sample.

Volunteerism is yet another major source of sampling bias. As is true for all research, participation is voluntary. I once carried out a study on infidelity among married couples. When potential participants were contacted and given the option to voluntarily participate, naturally some agreed while others refused. Why is this important? Those who volunteer are qualitatively different from those that refuse. This and the following issues are of equal concern to both qualitative and quantitative research.

Participant Bias

HAWTHORNE EFFECT   The Hawthorne effect refers to the generally accepted notion that participants are motivated to perform better when they know they are being studied for research. During the 1920s, research testing the effects of lighting on productivity level was conducted at the Hawthorne plant of Western Electric in Chicago. Regardless of what the researchers did to the lighting, worker productivity continually increased. From this, the researchers considered that it was not the lighting that was increasing productivity, but rather their presence and focus on the workers. Any time participants are aware that they are being evaluated, there is the potential for effects to be due in part to the increased attention, rather than to the treatment variable. Control groups receiving the same amount of focus and attention, but not receiving the treatment of course, must be used to decrease the potential for results to be biased because of the Hawthorne effect (Holden, 2001; Isaac & Michael, 1997; Martella et al., 1999).

JOHN HENRY EFFECT   Whereas the Hawthorne effect pertains to participants in an experimental group, the John Henry effect refers to participants in a control group. The John Henry effect was discovered during a study of student performance and teacher contracting and was then named after a mythological figure by the name of John Henry, who attempted to compete with and outdo the work of new machinery in laying railroad ties. With rivalry and competitiveness as the motives behind the behavior, participants identified as *controls* in a study are motivated to not only increase their performance, but to outperform the participants in the experimental group. Because of this, results are biased due to participant competitiveness (Holden, 2001; Isaac & Michael, 1997; Parker, 1993).

Experimenter Bias

EXPERIMENTER EFFECTS   Experimenter bias occurs when a researcher unintentionally influences participant behavior, participant ratings, or study outcomes in some other way. One such example of this is referred to as *experimenter effects*. Within an experiment, when the independent variable is, in fact, being implemented, results may be obtained that have more to do with the experimenter than the variable. In other words, these same results would not occur if a different person implemented the variable. For instance, earlier we considered the possibility of examining how clients with depression responded to cognitive-behavior therapy. Assume that you implemented this type of treatment, assessing for depression levels prior to, during, and at the conclusion of therapy. Because counseling effects are due to a host of factors, it might be difficult to know whether results were due to the treatment implemented or had more to do with intrapersonal characteristics of the counselor. To reduce the effects of the experimenter, multiple experimenters (in this example, multiple counselors) should be used.

EXPERIMENTER OR OBSERVER EXPECTANCIES   Whether we are aware or not, we tip people off as to what our expectations are. These cues may come in verbal or nonverbal form, but regardless, people pick up on them and typically perform according to them. Terms such as *self-fulfilling prophesy* and the *Pygmalion effect* are used to describe this phenomenon. These same ideas apply to research studies in that experimenter expectancies may influence participants' behavior and outcomes. Not only do these expectancies influence participant performance, but they *shape* data in the direction the experimenter chooses. Oftentimes, humans see what they want to see. We filter information through preconceived notions and take due notice of anticipated findings while ignoring others. Intentional shaping is highly unethical but may be unintentional. Having said that, the likelihood of this type of bias can be reduced by using objective individuals who do not know the purpose of the study or what the experimenter hopes to find (Isaac & Michael, 1997; Martella et al., 1999; Parker, 1993).

HALO EFFECT   The *halo effect* is another form of experimenter bias, and simply refers to the tendency to allow one trait (usually irrelevant to the purposes of the research) of a person to influence how you view other traits (usually relevant to the research) of a person. Typical irrelevant traits are attractiveness, sex, race, and social class. When an experimenter is making several observations, this can become a problem and bias the results of the research. It is not uncommon for a strong first impression, either positive or negative, to influence subsequent ratings and observations. When variables are defined vaguely or in abstract terms, the halo effect has more potential to cause bias. However, being very specific and operational in defining your variables of study can reduce the likelihood of the halo effect, as can increasing your familiarity with rating scales (Isaac & Michael, 1997; Pike, 1999).

COMMON METHODOLOGICAL ERRORS

Common mistakes made by beginning researchers include:

1. Selecting a topic for study that is too broad or vague.
2. Failing to clearly define the research population.
3. Not collecting a large enough sample.
4. Using the most convenient method of data collection rather than the best.
5. Attempting to go through all stages of the study within one semester.
6. Using inadequate or inappropriate instruments.
7. Generally lacking a well-thought-out methodological plan of action.
8. Over-generalizing, or generalizing to a population different from the one sampled.

Summary

This chapter reviewed various methodological issues related to variable selection, sampling, instrumentation, and bias. Because research methodology can be overwhelming, it is important to be knowledgeable regarding the potential issues and concerns inherent in this process. When well thought out and carefully planned, methodology will serve as the guide to successful research.

The importance of variable selection was discussed, beginning with the different types and categories of variables, including the difference between variable and trait, categorical and numerical, independent and dependent, and manipulated and selected. Variable selection is the foundation of methodology, and you must get very specific about what the variables mean for the purposes of your study. If not, you risk measuring them in the wrong way, possibly changing the entire purpose of the study.

The differences among a population, target population, and an accessible population were reviewed. Recall that in order for the sample to be applicable (generalizable) to the accessible population, it must be representative (the same as) of it. If the findings are to then be applicable to the target population, they again must be representative of it. With regard to quantitative research, you will also want to determine how many participants you need in order to find significance that exists, without reporting significance that should not be detected. Because there are no definitive rules for sample size (although a number of researchers offer their own guidelines), you must take into account the type of statistical analysis you intend to use, the effect size you desire, and the sample sizes used in previous studies.

Instrumentation is important with regard to data collection, instrument selection, and instrument administration. It is necessary to familiarize yourself with the wealth of instruments available to you. It is important to do this because knowing what is available will make you more likely to choose the most appropriate and applicable instrument for your study.

Finally, sampling bias, participant bias, and experimenter bias were reviewed. Such biases can result from unintentional errors related to how responses are elicited, how observations are recorded, the social desirability of participants, the purpose of the study, and expectations of the experimenter. As a researcher, your responsibility is to understand how these and other biases can occur; to use that knowledge for prevention through a well-thought-out, methodological plan; to then be aware of the bias within your own study that is bound to occur despite your best efforts; and to take that into account when examining your results. For further information on methodological issues and report writing, refer to Onwuegbuzie and Leech (2005) as well as to Heppner and Heppner (2004).

Review and Discussion Questions

1. Describe the difference between a trait and a variable, and discuss how each can change or remain constant across time, setting, and individuals.

2. What is the difference between an independent and dependent variable? What examples can you think of that could be interchangeable depending on the research question you wanted to answer?

3. If you wanted to measure someone's academic functioning, what are some ways to do this through categorical and numerical variables?

4. What specific situation can you think of that might show the importance of operationalizing variables?

5. Why is finding a representative sample that is generalizable to the larger population not important in some research?

6. When would a sample be too large, and what problems would it create?

7. What are some of the considerations you should reflect on when choosing an instrument?

8. For what reasons does sampling bias occur?

9. Describe the differences between the Hawthorne effect and the John Henry effect.

10. Is it possible to prevent experimenter bias? What are some safeguards that can be taken to reduce the likelihood of this?

11. Which common methodological errors do you think you would be most likely to commit?

CHAPTER 5

Experimental Designs

Richard S. Balkin, *Texas A&M University–Corpus Christi*

OBJECTIVES
After reading this chapter, you will:

- Be able to understand the underlying principles of experimental research design.
- Be able to understand how variables are manipulated or controlled.
- Be able to understand models of experimental design.
- Be able to understand threats to experimental validity.
- Be able to understand the implications of these issues to the counseling profession.

OVERVIEW

Experimental design is the blueprint for quantitative research and serves as the foundation of what makes quantitative research valid. Too often, consumers of research may focus on the rationale for a study and the discussion of the results. However, without proper methods, a quantitative study has no meaning. Instead of merely focusing on the statistical test, the end result so to speak, a quantitative study is based on a strong foundation of a generalizable sample, reliable and valid instrumentation, and appropriate research design (see Figure 5.1). By reading this chapter, you will gain a foundation in the central ideas related to an experimental study: (a) how variables are manipulated or controlled, (b) models of experimental design, (c) threats to experimental validity, and (d) the implications of these issues to the counseling profession.

CHARACTERISTICS OF A RESEARCH STUDY

Consider the following research idea:

A school counselor wishes to improve upon a program for students with low academic achievement. Currently, the school counselor leads a psychoeducational group on study skills. Based upon the responses from the participants, the school counselor believes that students with academic problems are having difficulty in areas outside of study skills. The school counselor decides to implement a group counseling program in addition to the study skills program and wishes to investigate whether group counseling would have a greater effect in increasing academic achievement among the participating students.

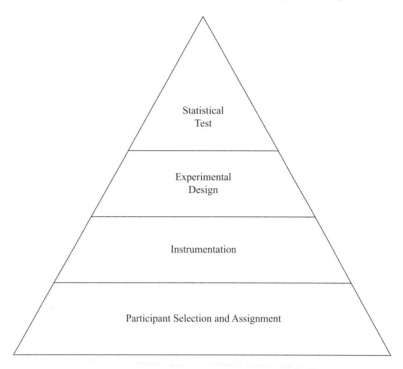

FIGURE 5.1 Foundation of Quantitative Research

To determine the effectiveness of a program or intervention, appropriate methods for sampling, measuring the outcome, and establishing the validity of the findings are necessary. *Experimental validity* refers to the process in which results are generalizable because the factors that have been tested or manipulated (e.g., the independent variable) truly effect a change in an outcome (dependent variable), and the results of the study can be applied to settings outside of the experimental setting (Best & Kahn, 2006). The generation of a generalizable sample was discussed in chapter 2. A random sample is pertinent in establishing the validity of an experimental design, although there are methods to establish experimental validity when random sampling is not possible. Experimental validity is discussed in more detail later in this chapter.

A researcher also needs to consider how a program or intervention is deemed effective. Think about the school counselor's research idea. If the participants obtaining group counseling and study skills interventions are performing better, can the school counselor conclude that it is due to the program? Progress could be due to either intervention, the combined intervention, or another variable not measured. The mere passage of time could be a reason for improvement. Kelly, Halford, and Young (2000) provided an example of the difficulty that researchers could encounter in determining the impact of different variables in a study. The researchers studied the effects of a short-term intervention related to alcohol abuse by assigning 16 participants to a treatment group and 16 participants to begin the intervention after one month (control group). After the initial month, the researchers reported that the treatment group had made statistically significant progress in reducing alcohol and depressive symptoms. The control group did not show any progress with respect to alcohol abuse but did show a statistically significant reduction in depressive symptoms. Thus, the researchers could not conclude that the intervention was more successful in treating depressive symptoms. Depressive symptoms appeared to diminish whether or not an intervention occurred. To determine whether a program or intervention is effective, experimental conditions are required. These conditions may include the implementation of treatment and control groups, random assignment, and measures to ensure experimental validity.

METHODS OF CONTROL IN EXPERIMENTAL RESEARCH

Treatment and Control Groups *(handwritten: (I Vs)*

(handwritten in left margin: treatment/ control)

In chapter 4, designing and evaluating the independent and dependent variable was discussed. Recall that the dependent variable is the variable that is being measured. The independent variable in classical experimental design is the variable that is being manipulated. In the Kelly et al. (2000) study, there were two dependent variables discussed: (a) change in alcohol consumption and (b) change in depression. There was also an independent variable: the group. Participants were either in the treatment group or the control group. Participants in the treatment group received an intervention. The control group did not receive the intervention. Thus, the intervention is that aspect of the independent variable that is *manipulated*. In the group counseling example at the beginning of the chapter, participation in group counseling and study skills, study skills only, and no intervention are the various levels of the independent variable.

(handwritten in left margin: pre-test/ post-test (still need comparison gr.))

Some research designs do not include a comparison group. Progress is assessed only by looking at the treatment group and comparing it with some baseline score. For example, in the Kelly et al. (2000) study, the Beck's Depression Inventory (BDI) was used to measure change in depressive symptoms. The BDI was administered as a pretest before any intervention and then after one month. Both the treatment group and the control group showed a statistically significant difference in depressive symptoms. Without the presence of the control group, the researchers could falsely conclude that the intervention was effective in decreasing depressive symptoms. When a design does not include a comparison group, this is known as a *pre-experimental design*. Pre-experimental designs are subject to criticism because there is no way to tell if the independent variable was responsible for any change in the dependent variable. There was no manipulation.

Random Assignment   *(handwritten: Quest (1)? What is the difference btw control + comparison gr.?)*

(handwritten in left margin: control → no treatment comparison → diff. treatment?)

Random assignment refers to the equal likelihood that a participant will be assigned to a treatment, control, or comparison group. Random assignment is similar to random sampling. In random sampling, participants from an accessible population have an equal chance of being selected for a study. If it could be shown that the participants in a study are representative of the accessible population, and the accessible population is representative of the target population, the qualifications for generalizability are met (Gall, Gall, & Borg, 2006). In random assignment, each participant has an equal chance of being selected for a particular intervention or no intervention at all. Random assignment helps ensure experimental validity by providing a measure in equalizing groups. Random assignment protects against selection bias; no group is predisposed to a treatment or intervention. Random assignment also protects the influence of *extraneous variables*—variables and attributes that are not being measured but may influence the results of a study (Gall et al., 2006). By using random assignment, a confounding variable is theoretically dispersed equally across all groups. "Random assignment is meant to make control and experimental groups equivalent" (Vogt, 2007, p. 96). For example, if random assignment is not used in the Kelly et al. (2000) study, then selection bias can occur. The treatment group could end up with fewer depressive symptoms than the control group (or vice versa), making it more likely for one group to show more progress than the other group. This would lead to an inaccurate conclusion that one group made more progress than the other group. When random assignment is used, equivalent groups are more likely. In the group counseling example, the school counselor would want to randomly assign participants to group counseling and study skills and study skills only. The school counselor may opt to also include a control group (i.e., no services), but this should be handled carefully because there are ethical issues in denying or delaying services. Experimental designs that utilize both random assignment and comparison groups are known as *true experimental designs*.

As mentioned earlier, classical experimental design utilizes an independent variable that is manipulated. However, in the social sciences it is common to examine independent variables that cannot be manipulated. For example, if gender is used as an independent variable, participants *b/c IV not manipulated.*

cannot be randomly assigned male or female. The same is true when examining differences based on ethnicity, or socioeconomic status. When comparison groups are used without random assignment, the design is known as *quasi-experimental*. When implementing a quasi-experimental design, extra care should be taken to make certain the groups are equivalent (i.e., scores are similar at the onset of the study for males and females or various ethnicities). Researchers may choose to conduct a statistical test to ensure equivalent groups at the onset of the study. If the groups are not equivalent, statistical tests may be conducted to control for the differences between the groups, assuming the researcher knows what variable needs to be controlled.

In summary, there are three major types of experimental design: (a) pre-experimental, in which there is no random assignment and no comparison group; (b) quasi-experimental, in which a comparison group is used but no random assignment; and (c) true experimental design, in which both random assignment and a comparison group are utilized. Pre-experimental designs are easy to implement, but the findings may not be reflective of what is being measured because of the absence of a comparison group. The meaningfulness of a study utilizing a pre-experimental design should always be questioned because the conclusions cannot be generalized. In a pre-experimental design, participants would be placed in both study skills and group counseling. The school counselor would evaluate whether or not academic performance improved as evidenced by changes in grade point average, standardized test scores, or other variables. Quasi-experimental designs are very common in social science research because of the use of nonmanipulated factors, which prevent random assignment of the independent variable. Special attention to ensuring group equivalence is pertinent. When group equivalency is demonstrated, results can be generalized because the effect of the independent variable can be evaluated. In a quasi-experimental design, participants would be assigned to study skills and group counseling and study skills only, but the assignment would not be random. For example, the school counselor could use intact groups based on their class schedule. Before the school counselor evaluates whether or not academic performance improved as evidenced by changes in grade point average or standardized test scores, statistical analyses should be performed to make sure that neither group has significantly higher or lower test scores or grade point average, because this could bias the results. True experimental designs are more complicated to implement, but the results are generalized more easily because random assignment promotes group equivalency, and the effect of the independent variable can be ascertained more easily due to the presence of a comparison group. In a true experimental design, participants would be randomly assigned to study skills and group counseling and study skills only. Thus, all participants would have an equal chance at being selected for study skills and group counseling or study skills only. The school counselor would evaluate whether or not academic performance improved as evidenced by changes in grade point average or standardized test scores.

external val. - can be generalized to other settings

EXPERIMENTAL VALIDITY

Before examining models of experimental design, it is important to understand that these models exist to substantiate experimental validity. There are two types of experimental validity. *Internal validity* is the extent to which the independent variable(s) truly effect the change in the dependent variable. *External validity* is the extent to which the study can be generalized to other settings and populations (Best & Kahn, 2006).

internal val. - I.V. truly impacts D.V.

Threats to Internal Experimental Validity

Threats to internal validity are due to extraneous variables; that is, any variable that is not controlled, for that can affect the outcome. In the social sciences, it is impossible to control for every conceivable extraneous variable. However, true experimental designs can minimize the effects of extraneous variables. To understand the effect of an extraneous variable, consider the group counseling example at the beginning of this chapter. Even if the groups were randomly assigned and participants in study skills and group counseling had greater change in academic performance than participants receiving study skills only, could the school counselor be certain that the change in academic performance was due to the added group counseling intervention? Campbell and Stanley (1966) identified nine factors that could threaten internal validity. Most of the threats listed in this section can be controlled for through random assignment.

Ways IV may not truly be △ing DV:

MATURATION   Maturation refers to the change in the participants over time. Participants may change simply due to time passing during the study. Other factors that may involve maturation are changes in emotional, intellectual, and/or physical functioning or fatigue from participation in the study (LaFountain & Bartos, 2002). In the Kelly et al. (2000) study, participants in the control group exhibited a statistically significant decrease in depression despite not having any intervention. This would be known as a maturation effect.

HISTORY   Unplanned events that occur during the study can have an effect on the outcome. Participants may experience an event outside of the experimental setting that influences the outcome of the experiment (LaFountain & Bartos, 2002). For example, a researcher is doing a study on high school athletes and moral development. During the study, the football team throws a party to celebrate a great victory. The school principal receives a call the next day that several football players were intoxicated and a female student was sexually assaulted. Such an event was beyond the control of the researcher. However, if the event had the same effect on both treatment and control groups, the effect of the event may be equalized. Otherwise, results are confounded due to the unplanned event (Best & Kahn, 2006).

TESTING   This type of threat is common in designs that utilize a pretest. The actual pretest may affect future performance on a posttest. Participants may be more knowledgeable about how to answer so that progress appears more evident. For example, using practice tests to prepare for a standardized exam may improve scores because the participant is more familiar with the question format, as opposed to being more knowledgeable about the material. However, if both the experimental and control groups are affected similarly, then the effect of the pretest is controlled. When the same test is administered repeatedly, or a series of different tests, instruments, or observations are utilized, then the testing effect is sometimes referred to as a *sequencing effect*. The sequence of the administrations may affect the validity of the experiment (Creswell, 2005). The sequence of the treatments might be responsible for the change in the dependent variable rather than the treatments themselves.

INSTRUMENTATION   It is important that instruments used in a research study measure constructs accurately and consistently. Instruments that lack evidence of reliability and validity are more likely to lead to erroneous results. In the group counseling example, consider the implications if the measure of academic performance was changed to grade point average. Poor academic performance for students in remedial courses may be quite different from poor academic performance for students in more accelerated coursework. Thus, progress for a student in remedial math may mean something very different from the progress of a student who is in an advanced placement course. In this example, grade point average may not be a good measure of change in academic performance because each group member has a different set of courses. Problems with instrumentation may also develop when rating systems are used. Raters may have different standards or be influenced by other variables unrelated to the study. For example, Riniolo, Johnson, Sherman, & Misso (2006) examined the influence of physical attractiveness on student evaluations for professors and found that instructors perceived as physically attractive by students had stronger evaluations than professors who were not perceived as physically attractive. Variations in student perceptions of physical attractiveness affected professor ratings, despite the fact that raters are not asked to consider physical attractiveness in the evaluation of an instructor.

STATISTICAL REGRESSION   Statistical regression is a process by which baseline (very low scores) and ceiling effects (very high scores) tend to even out over time. This problem is often seen in studies where a repeated measure is used. For example, in the group counseling example, students with very low academic performance will likely score higher simply because repeated measures over time tend to move toward the mean. Consumers of research should utilize results cautiously when the participants are selected on the basis of very low or high scores (Best & Kahn, 2006). The key to preventing statistical regression, while never totally eliminating it, is to have variability within the sample (LaFountain & Bartos, 2002). Remember that baseline and ceiling effects occur when scores are at an extreme. If participants tend to score at one extreme or the other, groups should be divided and separate analyses may need to be conducted with participants at either extreme.

SELECTION BIAS   Selection bias is a common problem in pre-experimental and quasi-experimental designs in which random assignment does not occur or intact groups are utilized. In such cases, the experimental and control groups may not start at the same level or with similar scores or characteristics. Consider what might happen in the group counseling example if the participants receiving study skills only had an average grade point of 1.8 and participants receiving study skills and group counseling had an average grade point of 1.2. The group with the higher grade point average may fare better because they already have more skills. Even in cases where random assignment is used, there is no guarantee that the groups are equal. Researchers can assess the influence of selection bias in a study by utilizing pretests to ensure group equivalence at the beginning of a study. Researchers can also employ *matching groups,* which entails using a pretest and matching participants with equivalent scores. Participants are randomly assigned to separate groups in order to ensure equivalent groups (LaFountain & Bartos, 2002).

INTERACTION OF SELECTION AND MATURATION   This type of threat may occur due to different attributes among the various groups. For example, if students in the study skills group were mostly in third grade and students in the study skills and group counseling group were mostly in fifth grade, the results may be erroneous if the age of the students is not controlled.

Interaction with selection is a common problem in social science research. Demographic variables such as sex, ethnicity, and socioeconomic status are often studied, but such studies may lack random assignment. Group differences may not necessarily exist because of the variables being studied. In other words, simply the fact that group differences exist does not mean that the differences are due to belonging to a specific group.

MORTALITY   Participants in research studies may not complete a study. As a matter of fact, it is unethical to force or influence participants to complete the study if they wish to withdraw. Thus, if dropouts are occurring in one group more than another group, the researcher may need to consider whether the groups are still equivalent. If a large number of students in the group counseling and study skills group dropped out but the study skills only group remained intact, the equivalency of the groups may have been compromised. Attrition in long-term studies is expected. When attrition occurs in longitudinal research, comparisons with the initial sample may be compromised, especially if sample size is small. The remaining participants may not be representative of the original sample (LaFountain & Bartos, 2002).

EXPERIMENTER BIAS   Experimenter bias occurs when the experimenter predisposes participants to a particular treatment. Experimenter bias is likely to occur when random assignment is not utilized. If a school counselor, for instance, believed in the value of group counseling and did not use random assignment, the school counselor may select participants that he/she believes are good candidates for group counseling. Thus, the beliefs of the counselor affect the outcome of the study. Experimenter bias is difficult to eliminate in social science research, especially when participants are selected to receive an intervention based on need. It is difficult to ascertain the effectiveness of an intervention, such as individual counseling, when participants who receive counseling probably volunteered for it. Naturally, the intervention is likely to have an impact because the participant wants the intervention to work.

Threats to External Experimental Validity

When cannot be generalized to other pop./setting.

Threats to external validity are related to the artificiality of the experimental condition. For example, clients who are hospitalized in a residential setting may make considerable therapeutic progress to the extent that the client appears ready to be discharged. However, upon leaving the residential program, clients may regress back to their previous high-risk behavior. Despite making progress in the residential setting, the therapeutic progress may not have translated well to the realities of the real world and may have been more a result of being in a structured setting. Thus, the therapeutic progress did not generalize to other settings. Campbell and Stanley (1966) identified five factors that could threaten external validity.

INTERFERENCE OF PRIOR TREATMENT   Participants who have a prior history with the treatment condition could affect the outcome of the study, particularly if such a history is not equally dispersed throughout the treatment and control groups. Using the example given earlier, clients who have a history of receiving counseling services and are placed in an institutional setting may have an understanding of what they need to say in order to appear healthier. The client therefore is discharged, but the progress was very superficial.

ARTIFICIAL EXPERIMENTAL SETTING   Change may occur as a result of the setting of the research. For example, participants who receive study skills and group counseling may express desire to make changes in study habits because such disclosure is positively reinforced by the group. However, upon leaving the group and the counseling setting, the participant may find it difficult to change study habits once outside of the experimental setting, where support may be much less.

INTERACTION EFFECT OF TESTING AND TREATMENT   This is similar to the testing effect in threats to internal validity, in which the practice of taking a pretest affects later administrations. The pretest can sensitize participants to the study and have an unintended influence throughout the course of the study (LaFountain & Bartos, 2002). In an interaction of testing and treatment, the pretest may affect the treatment and control groups differently. For example, a researcher wants to study the effects of yoga on memory. The experimental group receives a memory test, two weeks of yoga, and then another memory test. The control group receives a memory test, no treatment, and then another memory test after three weeks. Even if the treatment group scored higher on the second memory test, it is important to note that the higher memory scores could be due to the participants in the treatment group attending more to the method of the pretest, rather than the higher scores resulting from yoga practice. Random assignment is a preventive measure for this threat.

INTERACTION OF SELECTION AND TREATMENT   Research in the social sciences is complex. Random sampling and random assignment are difficult to obtain. Social scientists depend on cooperation from external groups, such as schools, agencies, hospitals, and organizations. Thus, participants are often obtained by utilizing intact groups (e.g., all of the clients at a particular counseling clinic). Social scientists often develop relationships with external agencies in order to get cooperation in research. Sampling is often convenient, based on the rapport the researcher has developed with the external agency. For that reason, selection and treatment can compromise experimental validity. The researcher needs to be able to demonstrate that the participants in the study are truly representative of the target population. The reporting of demographic characteristics informs readers about the generalizability of the study to other populations. When studies are conducted on populations with specific characteristics, the study is generalizable to individuals with those characteristics. For example, Balkin and Roland (2005) reported on differences between males and females in therapeutic goal attainment for adolescents in acute care psychiatric hospitalization. The findings were limited to adolescents in crisis residence and should not be generalized to children, adults, or other therapeutic settings because the population and setting in this study was specific.

INTERACTION OF TREATMENT IMPLEMENTATION When developing interventions across groups, it may be difficult for a single researcher to deliver the same intervention in the same manner. For example, a school counselor may wish to use a colleague to provide study skills psychoeducation (i.e., methods of focusing your attention) to one group, while the school counselor provides study skills psychoeducation and group counseling to another group. Even if the study skills are taught using the same materials, the presentation of the information may be qualitatively different. Researchers need to have procedures in place to verify that a treatment or intervention was conducted properly (Best & Kahn, 2006).

MODELS

experiment has: random assign.+ comparison grs.

Models for experimental design may be classified as either *between groups,* in which outcomes are compared between two or more groups, or *within groups,* in which a single group is measured across time using two or more different treatments. The models discussed assume utilization of a true experimental design—utilization of random assignment and comparison groups. However, random assignment is not always feasible, due to the categorical nature of the factors being studied (i.e., ethnicity, gender, or age). Therefore, when random assignment is compromised, the design is referred to as quasi-experimental. When a quasi-experimental design is utilized, the researcher needs to address the potential threats to internal validity, which are often controlled when random assignment is used (Fraenkel & Wallen, 2006).

Between Groups

In a between-groups design, the effect of the independent variable on the dependent variable is based on examination of group differences. In a true experimental design, one group receives a treatment or intervention (known as the treatment group), and the comparison group typically experiences no treatment (the control group). However, studies can be conducted in which two separate treatments are being compared. For example, a counseling agency may wish to determine if counselors employing a person-centered approach have better outcomes than counselors using a cognitive-behavioral approach when working with clients diagnosed with posttraumatic stress disorder (PTSD).

POSTTEST ONLY Participants are randomly assigned to a treatment group and a comparison/control group. The treatment group receives some type of manipulation or intervention while a control group would receive none. A quantitative measure is then used to determine the effect of the intervention. In this case, the quantitative measure is the dependent variable and the presence or absence of the treatment is the independent variable.

Consider the following example: a counselor wishes to know whether a peer-mentoring program would be effective in assisting students who are at-risk for academic failure. The counselor utilizes the Youth Outcome Questionnaire (Y-OQ-SR-2.0) as a measure of program effectiveness. The Y-OQ-SR-2.0 is a youth survey designed to be repeatedly administered to adolescents to assess their ongoing progress in counseling. It has 30 items on a 5-point Likert scale. Internal consistency was assessed at .91 and is noted to have adequate validity (Wells, Burlingame, & Rose, 1999).

Using our example for a posttest-only design, the counselor would randomly assign students identified as at-risk for academic failure to receive peer mentoring over the next three months or to receive peer mentoring three months later, after the initial group has received the treatment.[1] The effect of peer mentoring is being evaluated for change in well-being, as evidenced by the score on the Y-OQ-SR-2.0, the dependent variable. The treatment group receives peer mentoring, the control group initially does not, and both groups are evaluated by observing their scores on the Y-OQ-SR-2.0 (Table 5.1).

---

[1] Institutional review boards may insist that withholding services to individuals is unethical. To protect participants, the researcher is requested to provide services at a later time after the study is evaluated.

TABLE 5.1   Posttest Only

Random Assignment	Group	Treatment	Posttest
	Treatment	Yes	Yes
	Control	No	Yes

TABLE 5.2   Pretest–Posttest Control Group

Random Assignment	Group	Pretest	Treatment	Posttest
	Treatment	Yes	Yes	Yes
	Control	Yes	No	Yes

The posttest-only design is easy to implement. Random assignment is very important to help ensure equality between groups at the onset of the study. Without a pretest, however, the researcher cannot be certain that scores from the Y-OQ-SR-2.0 are the same between the treatment and control groups at the beginning of the study. Even with random assignment, equal groups are not guaranteed. When random assignment is not used, any change in scores may not necessarily be attributed to the independent variable. A quasi-experimental study will not protect against threats to internal validity.

PRETEST–POSTTEST CONTROL GROUP   Participants are randomly assigned to a treatment group and a comparison/control group. A quantitative measure is then used to determine the effect of the intervention. Both the treatment group and control group receive a pretest. The treatment group receives some type of manipulation or intervention, while a control group would receive none. After the intervention, a posttest is administered. In this case, the groups are still compared based on posttest scores, but the researcher can be certain of the degree of equal groups at the onset of the study.

Using our example for a pretest–posttest control group design, the counselor would randomly assign students identified as at-risk for academic failure to receive peer mentoring over the next three months or to receive peer mentoring three months later, after the initial group has received the treatment. Each group is administered the Y-OQ-SR-2.0 as a pretest in order to ensure equality of groups. The treatment group receives peer mentoring, the control group initially does not, and both groups are evaluated by observing their scores on the Y-OQ-SR-2.0 posttest (Table 5.2).

The primary advantage of the pretest–posttest control group design is the assurance of equality at the onset of the study between the treatment group and control group. The use of a pretest makes this design more appropriate when the design is quasi-experimental. However, pretest–posttest control group designs are susceptible to testing effects. A limitation of this design is that participants who are exposed to a pretest may have an idea of how to answer on the posttest in order to appear that they made progress or lack thereof.

SOLOMON FOUR GROUP   Participants are randomly assigned to one of four groups: (a) a treatment group that receives both a pretest and a posttest, (b) a treatment group that receives a posttest only, (c) a control group that receives both a pretest and a posttest, or (d) a control group that receives a posttest only. Thus, only one treatment group and one control group are administered a pretest. Both treatment groups receive some type of manipulation or intervention while both control groups would receive none. After the intervention, a posttest is administered to all four groups. In this case, the groups are still compared based on posttest scores, but the researcher can be certain of the equivalence of the groups at the onset of the study and assess the impact of the pretest to ascertain whether or not a testing effect exists.

Using our example for a Solomon four group, the counselor would randomly assign students identified as at-risk for academic failure to receive peer mentoring over the next three months or to

TABLE 5.3   Solomon Four Group

	Group	Pretest	Treatment	Posttest
Random Assignment	**Treatment**	Yes	Yes	Yes
	Control	Yes	No	Yes
	Treatment	No	Yes	Yes
	Control	No	No	Yes

receive peer mentoring three months later, after the initial group has received the treatment. From the treatment group, those students are randomly assigned to be administered a pretest or no pretest. From the control group, those students are randomly assigned to be administered a pretest or no pretest. One treatment group and one control are administered the Y-OQ-SR-2.0 as a pretest in order to ensure equality of groups. The other treatment and control groups do not receive a pretest. The treatment groups receive peer mentoring; the control groups initially do not. The posttest scores from the two treatment groups and the posttest scores from the two control groups can be compared in order to ascertain whether the pretest contributed to differences in the scores. If the posttest scores for both treatment groups and the posttest scores for both control groups are similar, then the administration of the pretest had no effect. Assuming there is no testing effect, the posttest scores between the treatment groups and control groups can be compared to determine the effect of the intervention (Table 5.3).

The Solomon four group is a strong design because it ensures equality of groups, even in a quasi-experimental design. Additionally, the researcher can determine whether or not the administration of a pretest is affecting the change in the dependent variable as opposed to the actual intervention. The utilization of this design is limited due to the need for a larger sample size and cost. For example, sample size needs to be doubled in order to have equal representation in each group. Additionally, more instruments are required, and this adds to the cost of the study. Additional time needs to be spent conducting analyses on posttest scores between both treatment groups, posttest scores on both control groups, and posttest scores between treatment and control groups. Analyses can be quite complex, especially if the pretest is having an unintended effect on the dependent variable.

FACTORIAL DESIGNS   Factorial designs are an additional element to between-group designs. The purpose of a factorial design is to study change in the dependent variable across two or more independent variables. For example, instead of simply examining the effect of a peer-mentoring program, the counselor wishes to know whether sex plays a role. Is the degree of change in well-being different across a peer-mentoring intervention for males and females? In other words, two analyses will be conducted: (a) differences in Y-OQ-SR-2.0 scores across the treatment and control groups and (b) differences in Y-OQ-SR-2.0 scores across males and females.

When more than one independent variable is studied simultaneously, the statistical analysis can become quite complex because results may not be able to be generalized across both independent variables. This is known as an *interaction effect* when the change in the dependent variable is not the same across both independent variables. The best way to demonstrate this concept is to graph it.

When an interaction effect is not present, the results can be generalized across both independent variables (see Figure 5.2). Notice that the same pattern of scores exists for males and females across both treatment and control groups. In other words, males and females in the control group scored lower than males and females in the treatment group. Thus, the researcher can generalize the findings to both independent variables. The researcher could determine whether statistically significant differences exist between males and females and whether statistically significant differences exist between treatment and control groups.

When an interaction effect is present, the results cannot be generalized across both independent variables (see Figure 5.3). Notice in Figure 5.3 that the effect of peer mentoring on well-being for

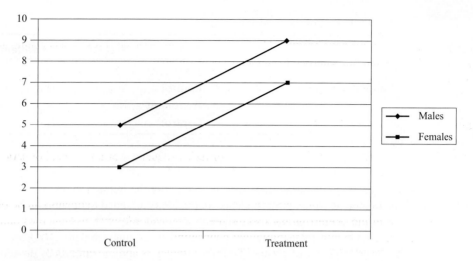

FIGURE 5.2 Nonsignificant Interaction Effect

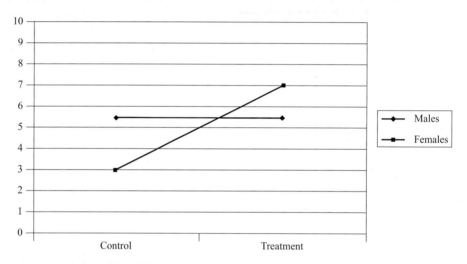

FIGURE 5.3 Significant Interaction Effect

females showed higher scores for the treatment group when compared with the control group. In contrast, scores for males were not affected by the peer-mentoring program. There were no differences in the treatment group and control group for males. In this case, the researcher would need to investigate males and females separately. An analysis between treatment and control groups across Y-OQ-SR-2.0 scores would be conducted to determine if there were statistically significant differences between the treatment and control groups for females only. A separate analysis between treatment and control groups across Y-OQ-SR-2.0 scores would be conducted to determine if there were statistically significant differences between the treatment and control groups for males only.

A factorial design can be applied to any of the experimental designs and has the added benefit of gaining more information because more than one independent variable is being examined. However, the addition of another independent variable creates problems related to sample size. Instead of needing a representative sample for a treatment group and a control group, a representative sample is necessary for males in the treatment group, males in the control group, females in the treatment group, and females in the control group. If a pretest is also added to the analysis or a Solomon four group design is utilized, sample size may need to be increased dramatically.

Within Groups

1 group measured across time

So far, we have examined how participants are affected across a dependent variable when either exposed or not exposed to an independent variable. Then, the change in the dependent variable can be compared between the groups. Change, however, does not occur only because of exposure to an independent variable. Change can also occur across time. A within-group design is utilized when a change in the dependent variable in a group is measured across time, or when participants in a group are exposed to two or more treatments simultaneously and the outcome of the treatments are evaluated across time (Leedy & Ormrod, 2005). Random assignment may be employed in some within-group designs. However, it is the different sequences of a treatment or series of treatments that is highlighted in a within-group design (Creswell, 2005).

CROSSOVER   In a crossover design, the effect of two treatments can be observed across a single group. Referring back to the peer-mentoring example, assume the counselor wishes to compare two treatments: individual counseling and peer mentoring. The counselor will still use the Y-OQ-SR-2.0 as a measure of progress, which is administered at the onset of the study and after each treatment. For example, a group of adolescents are administered the Y-OQ-SR-2.0, which is followed by four sessions of individual counseling, the first treatment. A second administration of the Y-OQ-SR-2.0 occurs to assess change after the first treatment, followed by the adolescents participating in a peer-mentoring program, the second treatment. The participants cross over to the other treatment halfway through the study. The study concludes with a third administration of the Y-OQ-SR-2.0 to assess change from the peer-mentoring intervention. Each administration of the Y-OQ-SR-2.0 is referred to as an *observation* (see Table 5.4).

Such a design allows the researcher to track progress across time, and differences can be assessed by comparing the various observations. However, because of the order effect of the treatments, the outcomes between the treatments cannot be compared. In other words, the researcher does not know if change occurs due to individual counseling, peer mentoring, both interventions, or the mere passage of time. The sequence of the treatments, the participants' history, and maturation may all be confounding variables. One way to control for these threats to internal validity is to counterbalance the crossover design (Creswell, 2005). For example, participants can be randomly assigned to receive the treatments with a different order. Group 1 receives the individual counseling followed by the peer mentoring. Group 2 receives the peer mentoring followed by individual counseling. This design has the advantage of eliminating the sequencing effect and allowing the researcher to compare observations and treatments (see Table 5.5).

LATIN SQUARE   A Latin square design is appropriate when three or more treatments will be measured across a group. When three or more treatments are investigated, the design can become quite complex, especially if the researcher wishes to provide a counterbalancing measure. When a

---

TABLE 5.4   Crossover Design

Observation$_1$	Treatment$_1$	Observation$_2$	Treatment$_2$	Observation$_3$

TABLE 5.5   Crossover Design with Counterbalancing

Random Assignment		Observation	Treatment	Observation	Treatment	Observation
Random Assignment	Group 1	Observation$_1$	Treatment$_1$	Observation$_2$	Treatment$_2$	Observation$_3$
	Group 2	Observation$_1$	Treatment$_2$	Observation$_2$	Treatment$_1$	Observation$_3$

counterbalancing measure and random assignment are employed with three or more treatments, not only does the design become more complex, but sample size must be quite a bit larger (Creswell, 2005). The Latin square design is ideal if the researcher has small sample sizes. For example, assume the researcher wishes to add a third treatment, psychoeducational group, to individual counseling and peer mentoring. Also, the researcher wishes to alternate which treatment is received first: (a) psychoeducational group, (b) individual counseling, and (c) peer mentoring. Generally, the intervention that is received first appears to be the most effective (Creswell, 2005). So, by alternating the initial intervention, part of the sequencing effect can be eliminated. Participants are randomly assigned to one of three groups, each with a different sequence of treatments. Using the previous example with the Y-OQ-SR-2.0 instrument, participants would receive the outcome measure initially and after each treatment. Group 1 may receive psychoeducation (treatment 1), individual counseling (treatment 2), and then peer mentoring (treatment 3). Group 2 may receive individual counseling (treatment 2), peer mentoring (treatment 3), and then psychoeducation (treatment 1). Group 3 may receive peer mentoring (treatment 3), psychoeducation (treatment 1), and then individual counseling (treatment 2) (see Table 5.6).

Rather than participants being randomly assigned to a treatment, participants are randomly assigned to a sequence of treatments. The sequence effect of the treatments is not entirely eliminated. Notice that while all treatments are alternated in the first spot, treatment 1 never follows treatment 2, which limits ruling out a sequencing effect. However, the purpose for running this design is to increase statistical power when small sample size is an issue. In other words, by running repeated tests with several different groups with small samples, the likelihood of finding a difference where one does not truly exist is increased. This is called a Type 1 error. So, the sequencing effect, although an important consideration, is less important because most of the order effects have been accounted for in this design (Creswell, 2005).

SPLIT PLOT   Sometimes, researchers wish to combine between-group and within-group methods. For instance, a researcher may be interested in knowing the effects of a peer-mentoring program as it applies to participants of different ethnic backgrounds. The researcher would administer the Y-OQ-SR-2.0 initially to establish a baseline measure for each of the participants and then administer the Y-OQ-SR-2.0 every 4 weeks for a period of 12 weeks (four administrations). The researcher might classify each participant according to his or her ethnic background to examine differences from a multicultural perspective.

A split plot design combines aspects of a repeated measures design and a factorial design. A participant is exposed to all aspects of the within-group variable (each administration of the Y-OQ-SR-2.0) but only one level of the independent variable (ethnicity) (Kerlinger & Lee, 2000). A researcher can track changes over time and compare various groups with respect to changes over time. However, the researcher cannot be certain that the independent variable (ethnicity in this example) is the reason for group differences. First, variables such as ethnicity and gender cannot be randomly assigned. The design in this case would be quasi-experimental. Such a design can detect group differences, but the researcher must be careful not to convey a cause-and-effect relationship. Furthermore, such designs can be complex to analyze due to the presence of an interaction, as previously explained in a factorial design. In other words, what is occurring within each ethnic group across administrations of the Y-OQ-SR-2.0 may not be uniform.

TABLE 5.6 Latin Square Design				
		Order of Treatment		
Random Assignment	Group 1	Treatment 1	Treatment 2	Treatment 3
	Group 2	Treatment 2	Treatment 3	Treatment 1
	Group 3	Treatment 3	Treatment 1	Treatment 2

APPLICATIONS TO COUNSELING

Research is essential to the profession of counseling. While not all counselors will be producers of research, they all need to be avid consumers of research. "Counselors have a responsibility to the public to engage in counseling practices that are based on rigorous research methodologies" (American Counseling Association, 2005, p. 9). Counselors need to understand the mechanisms of research in order to evaluate whether the research is generalizable to their clientele.

As you read through some counseling-related journals, it may be difficult for you to locate some of the research methods listed in Figure 5.1 (see the chapter overview). In fact, true experimental designs are less common in social science research. Many studies in counseling literature utilize intact groups and are quasi-experimental in nature. When reviewing a research study, particularly one that did not utilize a true experimental design, counselors should evaluate the degree to which internal and external validity were not substantiated. Threats to internal validity are most common when random assignment is not present. However, methods are available to evaluate group equivalence when random assignment is not feasible (i.e., pretests, matching groups, etc.). Counselors should assess the extent to which a study is meaningful to populations outside of the experimental setting. Particular attention should be paid to descriptive data, such as age, sex, ethnicity, and so on, to evaluate the extensions of the research to other populations and settings.

Summary

The goal of an experimental study is to test an idea using quantitative methods (Creswell, 2005). Generalizability depends on random sampling, instrumentation, experimental design, and statistical tests. Random sampling ensures that the participants in the study are representative of the target population. Instrumentation includes the use of accurate measures that are utilized appropriately for the study of particular phenomena. Experimental design is the blueprint for conducting the study. Through an appropriate experimental design, researchers can demonstrate that changes in phenomena are due to the treatments or interventions being investigated (internal validity) and applicable to settings outside of the experimental setting (external validity). Statistical tests demonstrate the likelihood of the results occurring outside the realm of chance and recurring again if the study were to be replicated.

This chapter focused on experimental design. Experimental models may be utilized to compare treat-ments, isolate treatments or treatment effects (between-group designs), and/or assess changes over time (within-group designs). Experimental designs contribute to generalizability when threats to experimental validity are minimized. Threats to internal validity call into question whether or not the independent variable truly had an effect on the dependent variable or whether the change was possibly due to an extraneous variable. Threats to external validity limit the generalizability of study outside of the experimental setting. Counselors should pay particular attention to the rigor of research designs. Lack of attention to issues of design may lead to the utilization of treatments and interventions that are inappropriate or unethical. Implementation of treatments and intervention that stem from rigorous research methods may enhance the practice of counseling and the well-being of the clients served in the counseling profession.

Review and Discussion Questions

1. Describe the various aspects that determine the generalizability of a study.
2. How does random assignment reduce threats to internal validity? Why do you think this happens?
3. What are some ways counselors can ascertain whether a study is generalizable outside of the experimental setting?
4. Compare and contrast true experimental designs, quasi-experimental designs, and pre-experimental designs.
5. A counselor selects ten adolescents to participate in eight sessions of group counseling. The counselor administers a self-esteem inventory on the first day of group. At the end of the eight sessions, the counselor administers the self-esteem inventory again. The counselor compares the scores at the beginning and end of the group counseling intervention and concludes that the adolescents' self-esteem

improved. Do you agree with this conclusion? Why or why not?

6. What are the two general models of experimental design? How are they different?

7. What are some advantages and disadvantages of using pretests in a study? Consider issues such as evaluating change over time, testing effects, and determining group equivalence.

8. Discuss how multiple treatments can be evaluated in a single study.

9. What are some ways to increase generalizability when quasi-experimental designs are used?

10. Review the *ACA Code of Ethics* (2005) and discuss the various ways comprehension, utilization, and production of research affects your professional responsibilities.

CHAPTER 6

Predictive Designs

Joshua C. Watson, *Mississippi State University*
Laura Simpson, *Delta State University*

OBJECTIVES

After reading this chapter, you will:

- Be able to describe the nature of predictive designs.
- Be able to describe the relationship between correlation and prediction.
- Be able to identify the various types of correlation coefficients, and explain under what conditions each should be used.
- Be able to interpret the magnitude and frequency of a correlation coefficient, and explain what they mean in terms of research design.
- Be able to define the terms *predictor* and *criterion.*
- Be able to explain the purpose of multiple regression and when it should be used.
- Be able to list the assumptions of a multiple regression analysis.
- Be able to explain the purpose of factor analysis and when it should be used.
- Be able to list the various forms of factor analysis, and explain how each affects the interpretability of your results.
- Be able to describe how predictive designs can be applied to counseling research.

OVERVIEW

This chapter provides you with a basic understanding of predictive designs and how to apply it in contemporary research. The statistical concept of correlation is presented along with an overview of the commonly used bivariate and multivariate correlational designs. Special emphasis is placed on the application of these techniques in counseling research.

PREDICTION IN RESEARCH

Predictive designs are a form of correlational research that use calculated information about the relationships between variables to forecast future outcomes. In a *predictive study,* researchers estimate the likelihood of a particular outcome by using a certain set of variables. To help illustrate this point, let us take a look at an example from student retention research. For the past 100 years, the student retention rate at postsecondary institutions has remained close to the 50% mark (Tinto,

1993). This means that nearly half of all students who enter college never finish or earn their degree. Consequently, several studies have been conducted to identify the factors related to successful student degree completion (Brawer, 1996; Eimers & Pike, 1997; Gerdes & Mallinckrodt, 1994; Martin, Swartz-Kulstad, & Madson, 1999). This research has shown that factors such as age at enrollment, socioeconomic status, parents' education level, ethnicity, and full-time student status are all predictive of student retention. This information becomes valuable to college counselors and student affairs personnel because they can now identify those students who might be at-risk and develop appropriate prevention programs. In addition to identifying the variables that will most accurately predict a given outcome, predictive studies may also be used to examine the validity of assessment instruments or treatment protocols. These types of studies allow practitioners to have confidence that the instrument or technique they are using is being implemented accurately. Hence, prediction studies are useful to researchers and have benefits for educators, counselors, and administrative personnel.

When designing a predictive study, it is important to first identify the variables to be used in the study. These variables are called the criterion and predictor variables. The *criterion* is the outcome variable being measured. In the preceding example, the criterion would be the institution's student retention rate. A typical predictive design includes a single criterion variable. The variables used to estimate the criterion are called *predictors*. Studies can be designed to include any number of predictor variables. Later, we discuss predictive designs using both bivariate and multivariate models. Once the predictors and criterion have been identified, the relationship between them can be examined. This relationship is most commonly explained using a statistical technique known as correlation.

CORRELATION AND PREDICTION

Correlation is a statistical technique used by researchers when they are interested in the degree of relationship between two or more variables. It forms the basis for almost all predictive designs. When a relationship is observed between variables we say that they are *correlated.* Correlations are based on the *covariance,* or degree to which two variables vary together (Howell, 2007). To calculate the correlation between variables, a researcher must first collect data on each variable in its natural state. Unlike the experimental designs introduced in chapter 5, correlational designs do not include any attempt to manipulate or control the variables. Consider the following example to help illustrate this point. A researcher is interested in the relationship between the use of open-ended questions and the number of issues clients bring up in session with their counselor. The research believes that clients will talk about more issues when the counselor uses more open-ended questions than closed-ended questions. To test this hypothesis, the researcher observes a series of counseling sessions. While observing, the researcher records the number of open-ended questions the counselor uses and the number of separate issues the client brings up in each session. You should note that the researcher does not manipulate either variable (type of questions asked or number of issues brought up); data are simply recorded as they naturally occur.

Once the researcher collects and records all data, a correlational analysis can be computed. The product of this correlational analysis is a statistic known as the *correlation coefficient.* The correlation coefficient, usually denoted by the letter r, describes the degree of relationship between two or more variables or sets of scores. When variables are found to be related, it means that they share a common variance. *Shared variance* refers to the fact that changes in the value of one variable will correspond to a systematic change in the value of the other. In our preceding example, the researcher hypothesizes that variation in the number of open-ended questions used by the counselor will coincide with changes in the number of issues the client brings up in the counseling session. By computing a correlation coefficient, the researcher is able to assess both the direction and degree of the relationship between the observed variables. These features can be found by examining statistical output or by viewing the representation of scores on a scatterplot.

Direction of the Relationship

The direction of the relationship is determined by the valence sign ("+" or "−" symbol) preceding the correlation coefficient value. A *positive correlation* (denoted by a "+" sign) refers to a situation in which both variables tend to move in the same direction. Let us assume we have two variables, *X* and *Y*. A positive correlation indicates that the two variables are related in such a way that they both trend in the same direction. In other words, as the value of variable *X* increases the value of *Y* increases, and when the value of variable *X* decreases the value of variable *Y* decreases as well. Researchers should note that it is not whether the scores on each variable increase or decrease that is important; rather, it is the fact that they change in the same direction that identifies them as having a positive correlation (Rosenthal, 2001). Figure 6.1 shows a scatterplot that depicts a positive correlation.

When the variables trend in opposite directions, a *negative correlation* (denoted by a "−" sign) exists. In a negative correlation, one variable increases in value as the other decreases. Continuing our illustration, when the value of variable *X* increases the value of *Y* decreases, and when the value of variable *X* decreases the value of variable *Y* increases (see Figure 6.1).

Degree of the Relationship

The degree, or strength, of the relationship is determined by the numeric value of the correlation coefficient. It provides a measure of consistency and predictability found in the association between two scores (Gravetter & Wallnau, 2006). Values for the correlation coefficient range from 0 to 1 in both the positive and negative direction. A value of −1.00 represents a perfect negative correlation while a value of +1.00 represents a perfect positive correlation. The strength of the relationship is determined by how close the correlation coefficient you compute is to the poles (−1.00 and +1.00), regardless of the valence sign. Because the strength is related to how close the correlation approaches −1.00 or +1.00, a correlation coefficient of −.90 indicates a stronger relationship than a correlation coefficient of +.85. A value of 0.00 indicates that there is no correlation between the two variables in question. Rosenthal (2001) provides a good reference chart for assessing the degree of relationship between variables. This chart is summarized in Table 6.1.

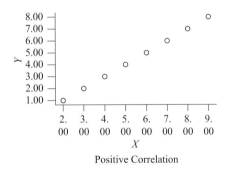

Positive Correlation

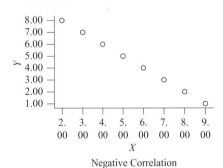

Negative Correlation

FIGURE 6.1 Scatterplots of Positive and Negative Correlations

TABLE 6.1 Descriptors of Association for the Correlation Coefficient

Correlation	Size of Association	Strength of Association
.10 – .29	Small	Weak
.30 – .49	Medium	Moderate
.50 – .69	Large	Strong
.70 and above	Very large	Very strong

Source: Rosenthal, 2001.

While the degree of relationship between two variables can be obtained from the correlation coefficient, researchers often prefer to go a bit further in their analysis and also compute the *coefficient of determination* (r^2). The coefficient of determination is a measure of the amount of variance in one variable that can be *predicted* from the other variable. It is computed by squaring the correlation coefficient. For example, assume that two variables (*X* and *Y*) are found to have a correlation of .70. The coefficient of determination for these variables would be .49 (.70^2). This means that 49% of the variance in variable *Y* can be predicted from variable *X*. The remaining 51% of variance is unexplained. The larger the coefficient of determination, the stronger the predictor is at estimating the criterion value. The coefficient of determination is a commonly reported statistic in most regression analyses (discussed later in this chapter).

Interpreting the Correlation Coefficient

You have just learned that the valence and value of a correlation coefficient provides researchers with a good deal of information about the relationship between variables. However, there are some additional issues that need to be considered when interpreting the correlation coefficient. The first issue is significance level. Sometimes an apparent relationship may exist yet this relationship may not be significant. For example, suppose a researcher conducts a study and finds a positive relationship between students' self-esteem and their grade point average in school, where the better students feel about themselves the higher their grade point averages (GPAs). On the surface there looks to be a true relationship between the two variables (self-esteem and GPA); however, we need to explore a bit further. The significance level of *r* provides a good measure of the consistency or reliability of the observed relationship. It tells the researcher how likely it is that the computed correlation value may be due to chance or sampling error. In our example, was the relationship found between self-esteem and GPA a chance finding, or could the results be replicated with other samples of students? When interpreting significance levels, it is important to consider the size of the sample from which the data were collected. Simply stated, the larger the sample size, the more reliable the correlation coefficient produced. When small sample sizes are used, the researcher runs the risk of finding spurious correlations. A *spurious correlation* exists when an apparent relationship detected between two variables is really due to an unintended or confounding variable. For example, our researcher might conclude that a child's poor performance in the classroom could be related to her or his level of self-esteem; however, upon further exploration, it may become evident that the child's difficulties are related to a learning disability or simply a lack of studying. To reduce the chance of finding a spurious correlation, a good rule is to use sample sizes that include at least 100 participants when conducting correlational research. This will help ensure that the assumption of normality (both distributions approximate the shape of the normal distribution) has been satisfied.

BIVARIATE PREDICTIVE MODELS

There are several types of bivariate correlational designs that can be used. The choice of design depends on the research questions the researcher is trying to answer and the type of data collected. In particular, researchers should pay attention to whether or not the data are quantitative (interval or ratio level) or categorical (nominal or ordinal level). Choosing the statistically appropriate correlation coefficient increases the interpretability of the results researchers obtain. Although the various correlation coefficients can be produced using current statistical software (e.g., SPSS or SAS), it is helpful to understand how they are computed. For this reason, the steps required to compute a correlation coefficient by hand are included in this chapter.

→ when both vars. are quantitative.

Pearson Product Moment Correlation Coefficient

The most commonly produced correlation coefficient is the *Pearson product moment correlation coefficient*. Often referred to as simply the *Pearson r*, the Pearson product moment correlation coefficient is computed when the data for both measured variables are quantitative in nature and a linear relationship between them is noted. A *linear relationship* exists when there is either a corresponding increase or decrease in value for each variable. In a scatterplot, a linear relationship is represented by a straight line.

In addition to describing the relationship between two variables, the Pearson *r* can also be used to make predictions. The numeric value of the correlation coefficient describes the amount of change in standard deviation units for one variable *(Y)* that can be expected when the other variable *(X)* increases by one standard deviation (Rosenthal, 2001). Suppose a correlational analysis between the variables of graduate record examination (GRE) scores and graduate (GPA) yields a correlation of *r* = .75. This means that a 1.0 standard deviation increase in GRE scores corresponds to a .75 standard deviation increase in graduate GPA.

There are several formulas that exist for computing the Pearson correlation coefficient. One of the most common involves the use of Z-scores. Z-scores are standardized scores that describe the exact position of every possible score in a normal distribution. They specify how much and in what direction a score deviates from the mean. Using Z-scores, our formula for the Pearson correlation coefficient is:

$$r_{xy} = \frac{\sum (Z_X Z_Y)}{N}$$

To solve this formula, use the following steps:

1. Convert each individual score on both variables (*X* and *Y*) to standardized Z-scores.
2. Multiply the Z-scores computed for *X* and *Y* for each participant.
3. Sum the products you obtain in step 2.
4. Divide the value you obtain in step 3 by *N* (the total number of participants in the study).

To illustrate the computations involved, let us revisit our earlier example exploring the relationship between the number of open-ended questions asked and the number of issues raised by the client in a single counseling session. After observing five counseling sessions, the researcher obtained the following data:

Session	Number of Open-Ended Questions *(X)*	Number of Issues Raised by the Client *(Y)*
1	9	4
2	13	5
3	7	1
4	15	6
5	11	4

First, we need to convert each raw score into a Z-score. The following table shows the computed Z-score (in bold) for each individual raw score.

Session	Number of Open-Ended Questions (X)	Number of Issues Raised by the Client (Y)
1	9 (**−0.63**)	4 (**0.00**)
2	13 (**0.63**)	5 (**0.53**)
3	7 (**−1.27**)	1 (**−1.60**)
4	15 (**1.27**)	6 (**1.07**)
5	11 (**0.00**)	4 (**0.00**)

Next, take the computed Z-scores and multiply them to find a product for each session.

Session	Number of Open-Ended Questions (X)	Number of Issues Raised by the Client (Y)	Product of XY
1	−0.63	0.00	0.00
2	0.63	0.53	0.33
3	−1.27	−1.60	2.03
4	1.27	1.07	1.36
5	0.00	0.00	0.00

Step three tells us to sum the products we just computed $(0.00 + 0.33 + 2.03 + 1.36 + 0.00 = 3.72)$. The final step is to then divide by N, the total number of sessions (3.72 by 5 = 0.74). This tells us that the correlation between the number of open-ended questions a counselor uses and the number of issues a client brings up in session is 0.74. Referring to Table 6.1, we can conclude that the relationship between these two variables is a strong relationship.

Taking our analysis one step further, we also can compute the coefficient of determination. Using the Pearson r just computed (0.74), we would produce a coefficient of determination of 0.55 (0.74^2). This means that 55% of the variance in variable Y (number of issues raised by client) can be predicted from our knowledge of variable X (number of open-ended questions used by counselor).

Spearman Rho Correlation Coefficient

Another type of correlation coefficient is the *Spearman Rho* (r_s) *coefficient*. The Spearman Rho is a special case of the Pearson r that is applied when measuring the linear relationship between two sets of data, one of which is recorded at the ordinal level. Ordinal data are rank-ordered based on either magnitude or frequency. In rank-ordered data, each score is assigned a ranking that indicates its place in a distribution of scores. When using the Spearman Rho, both sets of scores are assigned rankings from lowest to highest. Statistical programs such as SPSS compute this correlation coefficient using the difference in ranks between measures for each participant rather than the actual scores obtained. An example of a study where the Spearman Rho is appropriate would be an examination of the relationship between students' class rank and their ACT scores.

Point Biserial Correlation Coefficient

Another variant of the Pearson r, the *Point Biserial* (r_{pb}) is used when one set of data represents a continuous quantitative measure and the other a categorical or nominal measure. In this model, the categorical data is for a *dichotomous variable*. A dichotomous variable is one that has only two points and is either/or—such as male/female, graduate/undergraduate, counselor/client. When entering data for a Point Biserial correlation, the data for the dichotomous variable are recoded so that the two possible values are 0 and 1. Once the dichotomous variable has been coded, the same principles as the Pearson r apply. Both variables are treated as quantitative measures, and the linear relationship between them is measured. This approach would be used to address a research question interested in the relationship between gender and IQ scores. Let us say you are a researcher interested in the IQ scores of a group of 50 middle school students who have been referred to their school counselor for alternative school placement. One variable of interest you might explore is gender. Specifically, you may want to know if a difference in IQ scores exists between boys and girls. To address this relationship using a Point Biserial correlation, you would first collect the actual IQ scores of all 50 students. Next, you would code each student based on gender (e.g., boys = 0, girls = 1). Finally, compute a correlation between the two variables. Such an analysis would help you see if a relationship between gender and IQ scores existed among your sample of middle school students.

	Variable X $(-)$	Variable X $(+)$	TOTAL
Variable Y $(-)$	A	B	A+B
Variable Y $(+)$	C	D	C+D
TOTAL	A+C	B+D	A+B+C+D

FIGURE 6.2 Basic Contingency Table

Phi Coefficient

The *Phi coefficient* (Φ) is used when both sets of data are nominal, dichotomous measures. To compute the Phi coefficient, data from the two dichotomous variables are placed in a contingency table. *Contingency tables* are a visual aid for presenting the participant responses to one variable as a function of the other. A positive association is noted when most of the data fall along the diagonal cells (A and D). When the majority of the data points fall off the diagonal cells (B and C), we can conclude a negative relationship between the variables. Figure 6.2 shows the layout of a basic contingency table.

Once the contingency table has been constructed, a Phi coefficient can be computed. It is computed by comparing the product of the diagonal cells to the product of the off-diagonal cells. Figure 6.3 shows a contingency table created by a researcher who is interested in examining whether there is a relationship between gender and presentation for counseling services. In this example, the researcher hypothesized that males would be less likely to show up for counseling services following an initial referral.

While the preceding correlation models are useful in predictive studies when two variables are being used, additional methods are needed for situations in which multiple variables are examined. The following section details two such approaches that can be used when multiple variables are being measured.

MULTIVARIATE PREDICTIVE MODELS

Multivariate data analysis refers to any statistical technique used to analyze data that arise from more than one variable. This essentially models reality where each situation, product, or decision involves more than a single variable. The information age has resulted in masses of data in every field. With this much information, it is hard to determine which information is most appropriate to use. When available information is stored in database tables containing rows and columns, multivariate analysis can be used to process the information in a meaningful fashion.

Planning a Prediction Study

If two variables are highly related, it is possible to use one variable to predict a pattern. For example, college undergraduate GPA scores can be used to predict GRE scores for entrance to graduate school. Recall, the variable used to predict the outcome is called the *predictor* or *independent,* and the variable predicted is called the *criterion* or *dependent.* Prediction studies can serve a variety of purposes, including information regarding the extent to which a relationship can be predicted and to test theoretical hypotheses concerning variables believed to be predictors of a criterion. Predictive studies may also be used to examine the predictive validity of assessment instruments. The results of prediction studies are

	Counseling	No Counseling	TOTAL
Males	10	36	46
Females	35	19	54
TOTAL	45	55	100

FIGURE 6.3 Contingency Table for Gender and Counseling Usage

often used to suggest success. Performance in a particular class, for example, or the number of individuals likely to succeed in a particular training program might assist in determining a selection process for participation. Hence, prediction studies are useful to researchers, but they also have benefits for educators, counselors, and administrative personnel.

If more than one predictor variable correlates with a criterion, then a prediction based on a mixture of those variables will be more accurate than a prediction based on one of them. Let us say we are again attempting to predict performance on the GRE. A prediction of probable performance on the GRE based on a combination of factors such as cumulative undergraduate GPA, rank in graduating class, and scores on undergraduate entrance exams has the potential to be a stronger predictor than the use of any one by itself. While there are substantial differences between prediction studies and relationship studies, both involve determining the relationship between a variety of identified variables and a compound variable.

Data Collection

Subjects are selected from a population pertinent to the study and based on availability to the researcher. It is also important to choose instruments that are valid measures of the variable of interest. Surveys, standardized tests, questionnaires, or observational methods can be used to measure the predictor variables and the criterion variables. It is particularly important that the appraisal of the criterion variable be a valid one. The predictor variables must be measured before the criterion behavior pattern occurs. Otherwise, it cannot be claimed that the measure predicted the pattern. So, because we used scores on undergraduate admission exams and undergraduate GPA prior to application to graduate school, these variables are good choices for potential prediction of GRE performance. Finally, prediction of behavior that will occur in the near future is typically more precise than prediction of behavior that will occur in the remote future because there is more probability of predicting a behavior.

Data Analysis

In the primary method of data analysis for a prediction study, each predictor variable is correlated with the criterion. In the study we have been describing, GPA scores, ACT scores, and undergraduate class rank (the predictor variables) were each correlated with GRE scores (the criterion variable). Each of the predictor variables is effective in predicting students' GREs, but only moderately so. Students' ACT scores are a slightly better predictor overall.

Because a grouping of variables usually results in a more accurate prediction than any one variable, studies often result in a prediction equation referred to as a *multiple regression equation*. A multiple regression equation uses all variables that independently predict the criterion to create a more accurate prediction. Predictions made by multiple regressions are rarely perfect, which is not surprising because relationships are rarely perfect. Hence, predicted scores are typically paced in a confidence interval.

For example, a predicted GRE score of 1200 might be placed in an interval of 800 and 1600. Simply, students with a predicted GRE score of 1200 would be predicted to earn a score somewhere in the range between 800 and 1600. A graduate program that does not accept all applicants will probably have a cut-off score for admission, although it is very likely that even students who fall below the cut-off score could be successful if admitted. Although predictions for individual performance might be too high or too low, when examining an entire group of applicants, predictions are quite accurate on the whole; most applicants predicted to succeed will do so. Prediction equations may be formulated for each of a number of subgroups as well as for a total group.

Shrinkage

Prediction studies can produce initial equations that may be the result of a chance relationship that will not be found again with another group of subjects. This incidence of a prediction equation becoming less accurate when used with a different group is referred to as shrinkage. By definition, *shrinkage* is a decreasing trend in predictive validities due to the replication of a research study (Gall, Gall, & Borg, 2006). The likelihood of shrinkage also increases when the original sample size is small and the number of predictor variables is large. Thus, any prediction equation should be cross-validated. To do so, researchers validate data with at least one other group with variables that are not significantly related to the criterion measure removed from the equation.

MULTIPLE REGRESSION

Regression Analysis

The objective of regression analysis is to help predict a single dependent variable from the collected data of one or more independent variables. When the problem involves a single independent variable predicting a single dependent variable, the statistical technique is referred to as *simple regression.* When the problem involves two or more independent variables predicting a single dependent variable, it is referred to as *multiple regression analysis.*

Because a combination of variables typically results in a more accurate prediction than any single variable, prediction studies often involve multiple regression equations. In a multiple regression equation, variables that are known to individually correlate with the criterion are used to make a more accurate prediction. As a result, multiple regression analysis tends to be one of the more commonly utilized statistical techniques in educational research. This technique can be used with data representing any scale of measurement and can be used to interpret the results of experimental, causal comparative, and correlational studies. It determines the existence of a relationship and the extent to which variables are related, including statistical significance.

Additional independent variables are included in a study to improve the prediction of the dependent variable. This improvement is related not only to the way the independent variables correlate with the dependent variable, but also to the correlations(s) of the additional independent variable(s) already in the regression equation. Recall the example involving the prediction of performance on the GRE. Imagine the study with only rank in class as the independent variable. Now consider how the outcome was affected by the addition of the other independent variables of GPA and ACT scores. The addition of these variables improved the prediction of the dependent variables. *Collinearity* is the relationship, or correlation, between two independent variables. *Multicollinearity* refers to the correlation between three or more independent variables. It is common practice to use the terms interchangeably. Two variables are said to exhibit complete collinearity if their correlation coefficient is 1 and complete lack of collinearity if their correlation coefficient is 0.

Multiple regression shares all the assumptions of correlation: linearity of relationships, the same level of relationship throughout the range of the independent variable, interval or near-interval data, and data whose range is not truncated (Black, 1999; Hair, Anderson, Tatham, & Black, 1998; Heppner, Kivlighan, & Wampold, 1999). Specifically, in order to use multiple regression analysis to test hypotheses statistically, the following assumptions are made:

1. *Independence.*   The scores for any particular subjects are independent of the scores of all other subjects.
2. *Normality.*   In the population, the scores on the dependent variable are normally distributed for each of the possible combinations of the levels of the X variables.
3. *Homoscedasticity.*   In the population, the variances of the dependent variable for each of the possible combinations of the levels of the X variables are equal.
4. *Linearity.*   In the population, the relation between the dependent variable and an independent variable is linear when all other independent variables are held constant.

Steps in a Multiple Regression Analysis

The proposed strategy for conducting a multiple regression analysis entails a four-step process. Initially, the regression model will be determined through identification of the regression coefficients. The *regression coefficient* is the numerical value of any parameter estimate that is directly associated with the independent variables. The second step is determining the *multiple correlation coefficient (R)* and the proportion of *shared variance (R^2)*. The *correlation coefficient (R)* indicates the strength of the association between the dependent and independent variables. Computing the *coefficient of determination (R^2)* will measure the proportion of the variation of the dependent variable that is explained by the independent or predictor variable. The third step is the determination of the *statistical significance* of the *multiple R*. The coefficient can vary between 0 and 1. If the regression model is properly applied and estimated, the higher the value of R^2 the greater the explanatory power of the regression equation and therefore the better the prediction of the criterion variable. Finally, the significance of the predictor variables is examined. The individual regression coefficients will be tested for statistical significance. The combination that maximizes adjusted R^2 is considered identified as the optimum or best-fit model.

Types of Multiple Regression

There are a variety of approaches to multiple regression analysis. The most common types of multiple regression analysis are referred to as ordinary *least-squares regression.* Typically, these types of regression are utilized when the measure of the criterion variable is a continuous scale, the measures of the predictor variables are continuous or categorical scales, and the relationships between the predictor variables and the criterion variable are linear. These common variations include:

1. ***Step-up multiple regression.***   Also referred to as *forward,* the predictor that leads to the biggest increase in R is added to the existing group until the addition no longer leads to a statistically significant increase.
2. ***Step-down multiple regression.***   Also referred to as *backward,* all likely predictor variables are entered into the analysis first, then the variable that results in the least decrease in R is systematically removed until a statistically significant decrease occurs.
3. ***Stepwise multiple regression.***   In stepwise multiple regression, the step-up and step-down procedures are combined. Thus, each time a new predictor variable is added to multiple regression analysis, the statistical program determines if a predictor variable that was included at a previous step can now be deleted because it no longer contributes at a statistically significant level to the multiple regression equation.

A few of the multiple regression analyses to be considered depend on what circumstances apply, which include:

4. ***Discriminant analysis.***   Discriminant analysis is utilized, then the measure of the criterion variable is categorical and the predictor measures produce continuous scores.
5. ***Logistic regression.***   This regression is used when the predictor measures are continuous or categorical and the measure of the criterion variable is dichotomous.
6. ***Nonlinear regression:***   This regression is used if a hypothesis exists that suggests a *curvilinear relationship* between the predictor variables and the criterion variable.

A Research Example

The following example illustrates the application of multiple regression analysis as a predictive design. The use of multiple regression analysis is illustrated in a relationship study conducted by Simpson (2005). This study was conducted among volunteer participants to determine if a relationship exists between a counselor's level of spirituality and the development of secondary traumatic stress (STS) among counseling professionals. Pearson product moment correlations and a multiple linear regression were conducted to determine the best-fit model for predicting compassion fatigue among counseling professionals. Scores on a spirituality instrument were utilized as the predictor variable, with a measure of compassion fatigue serving as the criterion variable. The researcher hypothesized that five additional demographic variables had potential to play a role in the relationship between spirituality and secondary traumatic stress.

TABLE 6.2 Mean Scores of Instruments

	Mean	Standard Deviation	N
STS Score	27.95	11.92	223
Spirituality Score	131.35	15.70	223

Scores on the Spiritual Involvements and Beliefs Scale—Revised (SIBS-R) were utilized as the predictor variable. Scores for the respondent group (mean [M] = 131.35; standard deviation [SD] = 15.70) were slightly higher than norms for the norm referenced group (M = 113.1; SD = 20.9). Thus, the participants of the study had average scores that were higher than the sample used to set the norms for the scores on the test. The Compassion Satisfaction/Fatigue Self-Test for Helpers (CFST), a measure of compassion fatigue, served as the criterion variable. Participants scores (M = 27.95; SD = 11.92) were comparable to the norm referenced scores (M = 28.78, SD = 13.4). So, the study participants scored about the same as the sample used to norm the CFST. The mean scores for the spirituality and compassion fatigue instruments are presented in Table 6.2.

When data are transformed into new measurement variables with a mean of 0 and a standard deviation of 1, the term *beta coefficient* is often used to denote the regression coefficient. The exclusion of important causal variables or the inclusion of extraneous variables can markedly change the beta coefficient and the resultant interpretation of the importance of the independent variables (SPSS, 1999). When two or more independent variables are measured on different units (e.g., expenditures in dollars and education in years), standardized coefficients allow the researcher to compare the relative effect on the dependent variable of each independent variable. The final outcome of the variables included in the best-fit model is explained in the outcome of the regression analysis.

The author utilized a *stepwise selection model* of multiple linear regression for the research example. This method is the most commonly used regression method. The stepwise method is an alternative to the simultaneous approach. It involves entering the independent variables into the discriminate function one at a time on the basis of their discriminating power. This approach begins by choosing the single best discriminating variable. The initial variable is then paired with each of the other independent variables one at a time, and a second variable is chosen. The second variable is the one that is best able to improve the discriminating power of the function in combination with the first variable. The third and any subsequent variables are selected in a similar manner. As additional variables are included, some previously selected variables may be removed if the information they contain is redundant. Eventually, the independent variables are included from most important to least important. The stepwise method is useful when the analyst wants to consider a relatively large number of independent variables for inclusion in the function. By sequentially selecting the next-best discriminating variable at each step, variables that are not useful in discriminating between the groups are eliminated, and a reduced set of variables is identified. The reduced set is typically almost as good as, and sometimes better than, the complete set of variables. Because categorical variables with more than two levels were included in the multiple regression prediction model, additional steps were needed to ensure that the results were interpretable. These steps included recoding the categorical variable into a number of separate, dichotomous variables. This recoding is called *dummy coding*. Categorical variables with two levels were directly entered as predictor variables in the multiple regression model. The use of recoded variables in multiple regression analysis is a straightforward extension of simple linear regression. When the categorical variable of race had three levels, it was converted to two dichotomous variables. The categorical variable of occupation had four levels, and three dummy coded contrasts were necessary to use the categorical variable in a regression analysis.

The focus of the regression was to address the question of what best combination of independent variables (spirituality score, age, years of experience, race, gender, number of trauma victims on caseload) could be used to predict the dependent variable (score on the CFST). In regression, it is possible that not all of the independent variables fit in the final equation. Recall that when conducting a stepwise regression, predictor variables are entered into the regression one at a time based on statistical criteria. At each step in the analysis, the predictor variable that contributes the most to the prediction equation in terms of increasing the multiple correlation, R, is entered first. This process is continued only if additional variables add anything statistically meaningful to the regression equation. When no additional predictor variables add anything statistically meaningful to the regression equation, the analysis stops. Let us return to the research example to look at the regression model that best predicts the occurrence of compassion fatigue.

Results of Data Analysis

A Pearson product moment correlation analysis examining the relationship between participant's scores on the spirituality instrument and the compassion fatigue instrument reveals spirituality scores correlate negatively with STS ($r = -.129, p = .027$). This negative correlation implies an inverse relationship: as spirituality decreases, compassion fatigue increases.

A correlation matrix was calculated utilizing the six variables. Number of trauma victims on a counselor's caseload was found to correlate with STS at the 0.01 level with a significance value of .001. Spirituality scores showed negative correlation with STS scores at the 0.05 level with a significance of .027.

Remember that stepwise regression analysis attempts to take a large number of variables and find the combination with the greatest prediction potential. During this study, the author conducted an initial simple regression including all variables. Partial correlations were examined to assess the association between each independent variable and the dependent variable, while controlling for all other predictor variables. Again, the number of trauma cases was significantly positively correlated with STS scores while spirituality scores were significantly negatively correlated, suggesting that increased spirituality scores depress STS scores.

Next, the stepwise multiple linear regression was conducted to evaluate what combination of independent variables would maximize the probability of predicting the occurrence of secondary traumatic stress among counseling professionals. The combination of a counselor's level of spirituality ($\beta = -.147, t = -2.240, p = .026$) and number of clients served with a trauma history ($\beta = .213, t = 3.253, p = .001$) resulted in the highest adjusted R^2 (.053).

The correlations shown in Table 6.3 form the basis for multiple regression. Recall, the purpose of the multiple regression in this study is to determine which of the variables can be combined to

TABLE 6.3   Results of Regression Analysis with Partial Correlations

R			R^2		Adjusted R^2	
.285			.081		0.47	
	Standard Error	**Beta**	**t**	**Significance**	**Partial**	
(Constant)	10.678		4.129	.000		
Black	7.198	.155	.602	.548	.041	
White	7.004	.061	.238	.812	.016	
Private practitioners	4.610	−.128	−1.134	.258	−.077	
School counselors	3.826	−.146	−.952	.342	−.065	
Mental health counselors	4.074	−.134	−.954	.341	−.065	
Spirituality score	.051	−.157	−2.364	.019	−.160	
Trauma cases	.051	.224	3.368	.001	.224	
Years of experience	.090	−.025	−.370	.712	−.025	
Dependent variable: STS score						

form the best prediction of each criterion variable. The objective of multiple regression is to use the research participants' scores on some or all of the variables to predict their scores on each criterion variable. By contrast, each bivariate correlation coefficient represents the use of research participants' scores on one influence variable to predict each criterion variable.

A characteristic multiple regression will produce many statistics and equations. It is not unusual that only statistically significant data are in the published report of the study.

Cautions in Using Multiple Regression

One of the most common problems faced by researchers using multiple regression is confusing prediction with explanation. The existence of a predictive relationship is not equal to a causal relationship. Researchers must be careful if they hypothesize that certain predictor variables include causal significance to the criterion variable. If you wish to test a causal theory using multivariate correlational data, you might be better served by path analysis or structural equation modeling rather than multiple regression.

When choosing the number of predictor variables to be included in the study, it is critical to consider sample size. One suggestion is to increase sample size by a minimum of 15 subjects for each variable included in the multiple regression analysis (Gall et al., 2006). For example, you would select a sample of at least 60 individuals for a multiple regression analysis that includes four predictor variables.

FACTORIAL DESIGNS

A factorial experiment is a study in which the researcher determines the effect of two or more independent variables (i.e., factors), both singularly and interacting with each other on a dependent variable. The effect of each independent variable on the dependent variable is called the *main effect*. The interaction of the effect of two or more independent variables on the dependent variable is called the *interaction effect*. *Factorial designs* involve two or more independent variables, at least one of which is manipulated by the researcher.

The design and analysis of factorial experiments is a complicated matter. You can choose from many factorial designs. The choice of design depends on various conditions, such as the number of independent variables or factors, whether the factors are fixed or random, whether research participants receive repeated measures of the same variable, or whether each research participant is assigned more than one treatment. A *fixed factor* is an independent variable whose values will not be generalized beyond the experiment. For example, if gender is a factor in the experiment, there are two values, female and male. There are no other genders to which generalizations can be made. A *random factor* is an independent variable whose values will be generalized beyond the experiment. For example, if examining teaching methods, a researcher might select 10 teachers to use a method with the intent of having this sample represent a population of teachers. The distinction between fixed and random factors is important because it affects the statistical techniques used to analyze data resulting from the experiment. Because researchers often measure a large number of variables in a single project, factorial designs are commonly utilized techniques in multivariate research. *Factor analysis* is one example of a research approach used to study the patterns of relationships among many dependent variables with the goal of discovering something about the independent variables that affect them, although those independent variables are not measured directly. Factor analysis is more hypothetical than when independent variables are observed directly. The primary purpose of factor analysis is data reduction and summarization. It is one way to analyze the interrelationships among a large number of variables, and then explain these variables in terms of their common underlying dimensions factors.

In a factor analysis, the independent variables are referred to as *factors*. Factors are a linear combination of the original variables. Factors also represent the underlying dimensions (constructs) that summarize or account for the original set of observed variables. After a factor has been examined, it is often valuable to study it in combination with other variables or factors. Factor analysis can be a highly

	Type of Instruction	Type of Instruction
Week Intensive	Group 1	Group 2
Full Semester	Group 3	Group 4

	Type of Instruction	Type of Instruction	Type of Instruction
Week Intensive	Group 1	Group 2	Group 3
Full Semester	Group 4	Group 5	Group 6
Weekends	Group 7	Group 8	Group 9

FIGURE 6.4 An Example of Two Basic Factorial Designs

practical and influential multivariate statistical technique for effectively extracting information from huge databases. A typical factor analysis suggests answers to several questions:

1. How many factors are needed to explain the relationships among these variables?
2. What is the nature of those factors?
3. How well do the hypothesized factors explain the observed data?
4. How much purely random or unique variance does each observed variable include?

Because some variables work differently at different levels, factor analysis can illuminate relationships that might not be obvious from examination of the raw data alone or even in a correlation matrix. For example, a particular method of instruction may be more effective when teaching for 6 hours per day in a 1 week intensive class format, while another method may be more effective for a 3 hour class meeting once per week for a full-semester class format. Thus, each factor has two levels because there are two types of instruction, and the factor of class format has two levels, week intensive and full semester. As shown in Figure 6.4, a design with two factors that each has two levels is referred to as a 2 × 2 factorial design. The 2 × 2 is the simplest factorial design. It requires four groups, as the figure illustrates. Each of the groups represents a combination of one level of one factor and one level of the other factor. Using the same example, if the researcher uses two teaching method factors but three class format factors (such as week intensive, full semester, and weekends for one month) it would then become a 2 × 3 design. If the researcher examines three factors and two include three levels (three methods and three class formats) and one only has two (gender), it would be represented as 3 × 3 × 2.

Factor analysis provides a statistical procedure for reducing a large number of variables into a smaller number of distinct factors by combining variables that are at least moderately correlated with each other (Gall et al., 2006). Every set of variables that is pooled forms a *factor*, which is a statistical expression of the common facet in the variables that are combined. The primary purpose of factor analysis is data reduction and summarization (Hair et al., 1998). It allows the researcher to examine the interrelationships among an assortment of variables (teaching methods, test scores, questionnaire responses) and then explain these variables in terms of their common dimensions (factors). In other words, factor analysis assists the researcher in determining whether the effects of an experimental variable are generalizable across all levels of a control variable or whether the effects are specific to particular levels of the control variable. It is also useful in determining whether a variable that is not effective in a single variable experiment may interact significantly with another variable.

Let us return to our example of the two class formats. Figure 6.5 represents two possible outcomes for an experiment involving a 2 × 2 factorial design where the number in each box, or cell, represents the average posttest score of that group. Thus, in the top example, the week-intensive students under method A had an average posttest score of 80. In the top example, the mean of scores for week-intensive students was 60 when the scores for all week-intensive students were

Type of Instruction

	A	B	
Week Intensive	80	40	70
Full Semester	60	20	40
	70	30	

Type of Instruction

	A	B	
Week Intensive	80	60	70
Full Semester	20	40	30
	50	50	

FIGURE 6.5 2 × 2 Factorial Design with Interaction Graphs

averaged regardless of treatment. For full-semester students, the average score was 40. The average score for students under method A was 70 and for students under method B was 30. Looking at cell averages, method A resulted in higher posttest scores than method B for both week-intensive students and also for full-semester students. The inference can be made that the higher the posttest score, the better the instructional method. Thus, A was better regardless of class format; there was no *interaction* between teaching method and class format. The week-intensive class students in each method outperformed the full-semester students in each method. We could then predict higher scores in the future given these same formats, thus reinforcing this measure as a predictive design.

In the bottom example, for week-intensive students, method A was better. For full-semester students, method B was better. Even though week-intensive students did better than full-semester students regardless of method, how well they performed depended on which method they received. Which method was better depended on the class format. By using a factorial design, it was determined that an interaction appears to exist between the variables and that each method is potentially effective depending on the format of the class. The graphs illustrate the interaction.

While other types of multivariate techniques differentiate between variables (e.g., the criterion variable and the predictor variables), factor analysis works differently. It is an interdependence technique that simultaneously considers all variables. All variables are given equal consideration to function as a dependent variable that is a function of some theoretical set of factors. For example, a survey questionnaire may consist of 50 questions and each item will measure factors to a different extent. By using factor analysis, the researcher can identify the separate dimensions being measured by the same survey and determine factor loading for each survey item on each factor.

A Research Example

The implementation of factor analysis is demonstrated in a study conducted by Starkey (2005). The purpose of the study was to develop a questionnaire to assess perceived risk related to self-disclosure—the Interpersonal Risk Awareness Survey (IRAS)—and to examine the relationship between counseling students and other students' perception of risk as identified through the IRAS.

Factor analysis was used to identify commonalities in a pool of items written to measure perception of self-disclosure risk related to themes including body, money, and personality. Two factor analyses were conducted with *a priori* considerations. *A priori* considerations are used when the researcher has identified, prior to conducting the research, the factor model and the items anticipated to load on each factor based on theory and/or previous research (Heppner et al., 1999). A sample of students rated each item for its level of perceived risk. First, the IRAS factors and *item loadings* were compared to existing research themes. *Factor loadings* are the correlation between the original variables and the factors and the key to understanding the nature of a particular factor. Second, the IRAS factors and item loadings were compared with the four themes proposed by the researcher. Expanding the themes resulted in a 39-item instrument with four identified subscales. Four items did not load into a factor, but the remaining 35 loaded into the four subscales with no items sharing loading with other factors. The labels for the subscales and a sample item in each one are identified here:

1. *Body/appearance.*   Thinking about my body makes me feel . . .
2. *Money.*   The amount of income I receive is . . .
3. *Personality (internalized).*   The behavior I have engaged in that I am most ashamed of is . . .
4. *Personality (externalized).*   The emotion I find most difficult to control . . .

Factor Loadings and Factor Scores

The arithmetic of factor analysis involves seeking out groups of variables that are all correlated with each other. The individual correlation coefficients between factor scores and scores on a particular measure of a variable are referred to as the *loading* of each variable on the factor. Table 6.4 represents the factor matrix with corresponding item loadings.

Evaluation of the factor 1 loadings indicate that items 12, 14, 18, 22, 24, 26, 30, and 34 correlate moderately or highly with factor 1. The researcher is charged with interpreting the correlations to determine the conceptual meaning of the factor. In the case of this study, the researcher determined that the construct underlying factor 1 was body/appearance. The items in this subscale relate to how individuals present themselves to others and how that presentation is evaluated. The four identified factors represent the majority of the information contained in the larger correlation matrix. Each survey item can be treated as a variable with an associated score, called a *factor score*. The factor scores can be included in additional statistical analysis such as *t*-tests to determine if differences exist between groups on each of the factors.

Variations Within Factorial Analysis

There are several methods for conducting factor analysis. One of the first decisions in the application of factor analysis is determining the approach to use in calculating the correlation matrix. Two options follow.

1. *R factor analysis.* This is the most common type of factor analysis used. In this method, the factor analysis is applied to a correlation matrix of the variables, which results in a factor pattern demonstrating the underlying relationships of the variables.

2. *Q factor analysis.* In this method, the factor analysis is applied to a correlation matrix of the individual respondents, which results in a factor matrix that identifies similar individuals.

There are two fundamental models that can be utilized to obtain factor solutions. To select the appropriate model, the researcher must consider variance. *Variance* is a measure of the extent to which scores in a distribution deviate from the mean; it is calculated by squaring the standard deviation of the score distribution.

1. *Component analysis.* This is used when the objective is to summarize most of the original information in a minimum number of factors for prediction purposes. It is appropriate to use if the researcher is concerned with determining the minimum number of factors needed to account for the maximum proportion of the variance represented.

2. *Common factor analysis.* This is primarily utilized to identify factors that are not easily recognized. It is appropriate to use if the researcher seeks to identify underlying constructs represented in the original variables.

In addition to selecting the factor model, the researcher must determine how the factors are to be extracted. The extraction of principal components amounts to a *variance maximizing (varimax) rotation* of the original variable space. The choice should be made based on the particular needs of a research problem. Two options are available:

TABLE 6.4   **Factor Matrix for the Interpersonal Risk Awareness Survey**

Item	Factor 1	Factor 2	Factor 3	Factor 4
1		0.613		
2				0.480
3			0.611	
4			0.485	
5				
6				
7				0.585
8			0.458	
9		0.525		
10		0.531		
11			0.483	
12	0.433			
13				0.539
14	0.575			
15				0.501
16			0.551	
17		0.692		
18	0.648			
19				0.523
20				
21		0.580		
22	0.482			
23				0.414
24	0.551			
25		0.572		
26	0.512			
27				0.556
28			0.442	
29		0.567		
30*	0.658			
32			0.433	
33		0.521		
34	0.625			
35			0.619	
36			0.461	
37		0.604		
38				
39			0.460	
40			0.458	

* Item 31 was removed prior to data analysis.

1. *Orthogonal factors.* These are used if the goal is to reduce the original number of variables regardless of how meaningful the factors may be and how the resulting factors are uncorrelated. This solution is desirable if the researcher is seeking a set of factors that do not overlap with constructs measured by other factors.

2. *Oblique factors.* This is used if the goal of the factor analysis is to obtain several theoretically meaningful factors by deriving factors that correlate with each other. This solution is desirable if a researcher seeks to examine how factors relate to an underlying construct and a factor solution is computed so that the extracted factors are correlated.

Finally, *rotation* is the step in factor analysis that allows you to identify meaningful factor names or descriptions. It is the process of manipulating or adjusting the reference axes to achieve a simpler and more meaningful factor solution. Rotation serves to make the output more understandable and is usually necessary to facilitate the interpretation of factors. Rotation will alter the factor loadings, and because factor loadings are used to intuit the meaning of factors, this means that different meanings may be ascribed to the factors depending on the rotation. If factor analysis is used, the researcher may wish to experiment with alternative rotation methods to see which leads to the most interpretable factor structure.

Imagine if you plotted the factor loadings in a scatterplot. In that plot, each variable is represented as a point. If the researcher rotates the axes in any direction without changing the *relative* locations of the points to each other, the actual coordinates of the points, that is, the factor loadings, would of course change. *Factor loadings* are the correlation between the original variables and the factors, and the key to understanding the nature of a particular factor.

There are various rotational strategies that have been proposed. The goal of these strategies is to obtain a clear pattern of loadings, that is, factors that are somehow clearly marked by high loadings for some variables and low loadings for others. Some rotation methods include the following:

1. *No rotation.* is the default in SPSS, but it is a good idea to select a rotation method, usually varimax. The original, unrotated principal components solution maximizes the sum of squared factor loadings, efficiently creating a set of factors that explain as much of the variance in the original variables as possible. However, unrotated solutions are hard to interpret because variables tend to load on multiple factors.

2. *Varimax rotation.* is an orthogonal rotation of the factor axes to maximize the variance of the squared loadings of a factor on all the variables in a factor matrix, which has the effect of differentiating the original variables by extracted factor. Each factor will tend to have either large or small loadings of any particular variable. A varimax solution yields results that make it as easy as possible to identify each variable with a single factor. This is the most common rotation option.

3. *Quartimax rotation.* is an orthogonal alternative that minimizes the number of factors needed to explain each variable. This type of rotation often generates a general factor on which most variables are loaded to a high or medium degree. Such a factor structure is usually not helpful to the research purpose. The emphasis is on simplifying the rows of the factor pattern matrix.

4. *Equimax rotation* is a compromise between varimax and quartimax criteria. Rather than concentrating either on simplification of the rows or on simplification of the columns, it tries to accomplish some of each.

Cautions in Factor Analysis

Before choosing factor analysis, researchers must be aware that it is a complex statistical analysis. Research is inconsistent regarding which of the many techniques for conducting factor analysis is best. Because factor analysis has many subjective aspects—such as determining which factors to remove or which factor loadings are significant—researchers may have different opinions regarding interpretations of results.

Finally, the issue of reliability is critical with the use of factor analysis. The factors generated by a factor analysis are only as useful and meaningful as the variables entered into the correlation matrix. When the data change because of changes in the sample or the process used to gather the data, the results of the analysis also change. Thus, the results of any single analysis are imperfect. This problem is particularly salient because the outcome of a single factor solution may appear feasible. It is essential to highlight that feasibility is no guarantee of reliability.

APPLICATIONS TO COUNSELING

Predictive designs can be extremely useful to counseling researchers and practitioners. Their ability to predict future success or outcomes allows counselors to know the likelihood of the emergence of symptomology. As illustrated, a client who reports certain symptoms might develop a particular disorder, or it could be helpful in assisting clients who are at risk for secondary traumatic stress. They also allow counselors to estimate whether or not a certain treatment protocol would be successful for a certain type of client. In addition to the benefits for direct client interaction, predictive studies have also helped create many of the assessment instruments used today. These designs allow researchers and test developers to design their instruments so that they are structured and worded in such a way that they produce the most accurate results, which, in many cases, form the basis for treatment selection and diagnostic decision making.

Summary

In this chapter you were introduced to predictive designs and their usefulness in research inquiry. Predictive designs are based on the relationships, or correlations, between variables. These relationships can then be used to make accurate predictions about one variable based on the information known about the other. Predictive designs can be used in cases with any number of variables.

Approaches using such statistics as the Pearson r, the Spearman Rho, Point Biserial, and Phi coefficients are effective when two variables are being assessed and measured. When additional variables are added to the study, more advanced approaches such as multiple regression and factor analysis are warranted.

Review and Discussion Questions

1. What types of research questions would indicate to you that a predictive design should be used?
2. Why is the coefficient of determination reported and interpreted more often than the correlation coefficient?
3. Identify different types of research studies that would warrant the use of the various correlation coefficients.
4. How are predictors selected for a multiple regression analysis? How many predictors should be included?
5. How are factors determined in a factor analysis?

Helpful Resources

The American Educational Research Association
   http://www.aera.net/

Educational Research Newsletter
   http://www.ernweb.com/

Methods in Behavioral Research
   http://methods.fullerton.edu/noframesindex.html

Institute for Behavioral Research
   http://www.ibr.uga.edu/

Institute for Social and Behavioral Research
   http://www.isbr.iastate.edu

Galton, Pearson, and the Peas: A Brief History of Linear Regression for Statistics Instructors
   http://www.amstat.org/publications/jse/v9n3/stanton.html

Multivariate Statistics: Factor Analysis
   http://www.socialresearchmethods.net/tutorial/Flynn/factor.htm

CHAPTER 7

An Overview of Survey Research

J. Scott Young, *University of North Carolina at Greensboro*

OBJECTIVES
After reading this chapter, you will:

- Be able to describe the purpose of survey research.
- Be able to describe the types of survey methodology.
- Be able to explain various approaches to collecting survey data.
- Be able to identify the steps in completing a survey research project.
- Be able to understand the characteristics of high-quality interview, mail, or Internet surveys.
- Be able to identify the procedures for maximizing return rate.

OVERVIEW

Most readers are no doubt familiar with surveys as an approach to collecting data. We encounter surveys frequently in our everyday lives at restaurants, shopping malls, and other places of business. Yet there is much more to designing an effective survey and collecting meaningful data than you might expect. As with other forms of research covered in this text, a significant amount of effort is required to generate consequential survey research. Thus, the focus of this chapter is to introduce you to survey research methodology and to develop your skills in designing an effective survey, from conceptualization to completion.

Within the counseling field, surveys are commonly used by researchers both for the relative ease in which such studies can be conceptualized and for the directness with which data related to some aspect of human life can be obtained. For example, in a recently published survey study, American Counseling Association members were asked to rate their abilities to provide counseling services in accord with a set of competencies designed to guide counseling practice when addressing spiritual and religious issues. They were also asked to rate the importance of the competencies to overall counseling practice (Young, Wiggins-Frame, & Cashwell, 2007). This survey revealed that 53% of the 500 participants either agreed or strongly agreed that they could practice in accord with the competencies. Furthermore, the remaining half of respondents were less certain of their abilities and reported the need for additional training. This finding provides a sense of how practicing counselors view their work in relation to a set of theoretically derived competencies. In this case, there is both support for the competencies and evidence that more training is needed.

The fact that the basic ideas behind survey methodology are relatively easy to understand may cause many to fail to appreciate the science of conducting meaningful survey research. Subsequently, the quality of data collected from surveys varies widely. Yet, because survey research, if not well designed, may result in a low number of responses or generate data that are not particularly revealing about the topic under investigation, the need to design and execute a high-quality survey study is self-evident. By reading and obtaining mastery of the material in the chapter, you will come to understand that carrying out a high-quality survey study requires both careful planning and systematic execution.

PURPOSE OF SURVEY RESEARCH

Survey research is considered one of the most important methods of measurement in social science research (***http://www.socialresearchmethods.net/kb/survey.php***). This is due to the fact that the approach involves a systematic process for collecting data "straight from the horse's mouth," so to speak. In the case of survey research, knowledgeable participants provide information from their own experiences that is directly relevant to issues of interest to the researcher. The data collected by use of surveys are effective for exploring trends within populations, describing the relationship among variables, or comparing groups.

Survey research falls under the general category of *descriptive research.* The goal of such research is to describe or explain a participant's opinions or preferences related to some phenomenon the participant understands well. In contrast to experimental research designs, a survey does not compare the influences of one or more independent variables on a dependent variable, thereby determining if a causal relationship exists. Instead, survey methods are utilized to gather information about a group by either directly asking individuals for their feedback or by reviewing some documentation related to them. In the case of surveying documents, one might survey the mental health records of previous clients to look for trends in diagnoses or problems treated by counselors.

Survey studies are generally conducted for one of several specific purposes. Some may fall into one of the following categories:

- To describe an existing phenomenon by gathering detailed information about it.
  "60% of people with severe depression report taking three different antidepressant medications before finding relief."
- To identify people's problems or concerns.
  "90% of minorities living in rural areas report the number one barrier to their seeking out mental health services is transportation to and from the facility."
- To give good reason for and support current circumstances or practices.
  "75% of our college students surveyed reported that our counseling center provides services that 'exceeded my expectations.' "
- To make comparisons or evaluations.
  "70% of parents of Happy Times Elementary students report regularly reading to their child. The average for all schools in the state is only 60%."
- To determine what others are doing with similar problems or situations and benefit from their experience in making future plans and decisions. (Isaac & Michael, 1997)
  "According to a recent survey of administrators of rural psychiatric hospitals, 98% report the most effective means for increasing referrals to their facilities, is to buy lunch, at least once a month, for the Emergency Room nursing staff of towns within a 50-mile radius."

Regardless of the purpose of a survey study, data are generally collected by one of two formats: *questionnaires* or *interviews.* Questionnaires are self-administered by the participants using either pencil and paper or computer. By contrast, interview surveys are administered verbally by a trained interviewer (Hulley & Cummings, 1988). Both formats for survey research are used frequently and both require their own set of skills for successful data collection. However, a common mistake made by the novice researcher is to select a survey format before carefully considering the type of methodology that best matches the research goals of the study. Therefore, we now turn our attention to understanding the types of survey methodology or designs available to the researcher.

TYPES OF SURVEY DESIGNS

All survey research can be broken down into two basic design types: longitudinal and cross-sectional. The reasons for selecting one of these two designs depends on the researcher's questions of interest, the timeframe available for collecting data, access to participants, and cost.

Longitudinal Survey Designs

Longitudinal survey research occurs when data are collected over time (e.g., surveying a group of children every three years until they are adults). Needless to say, the proposition of conducting longitudinal survey research requires a significant investment of time and resources, because data will be collected at various points for a period of time. However, the advantage of this approach is that the data collected using the longitudinal method are richer and more detailed and, therefore, have the potential to provide insights about the questions under investigation in much greater depth.

Longitudinal survey designs fall into one of three basic varieties: trend, cohort, or panel.

TREND STUDIES   A trend study is used when a researcher is interested in understanding how a variable of interest changes over time within some general population. For example, suppose you are working as a school counselor and wish to better understand middle school students' knowledge of, and willingness to seek help for, academic or mental health concerns. You could decide to survey seventh-grade middle school students regarding their attitudes about seeking such services each year for five years to determine if their attitudes are changing. Even though you would be surveying different individuals each year, the same population (middle school students) would be surveyed. Subsequently, you would be able to report trends in the subjects' attitudes over the years. The advantage of this approach is that you will be able to gain access to the population of interest easily; all seventh graders are eligible to complete the survey. The disadvantage is that you obtain no knowledge as to the changes in the attitudes of specific individuals.

COHORT STUDIES   Another approach to conducting a survey utilizing a longitudinal design is a cohort study. Imagine that you are a counselor working in a mental health center and are interested in the effectiveness of your substance abuse treatment program for adolescents. Using a cohort design, you might select a group of clients who were between the ages of 12 and 14 years in 2008 when the program began and who had completed both the inpatient treatment and after-care programs. Two years later, in 2010, you would survey former clients who are now 14 to 16 years old, but not necessarily the exact same individuals, to gain information about their recovery progress. Likewise, two years later, in 2012, a group of former clients now 16 to 18 years old would be surveyed to determine their ongoing success with recovery. Using this approach, you would be surveying representatives of a group of individuals over time to follow the group's progress. The advantage of this approach is that you can survey any members of the population of interest without keeping track of specific individuals. The disadvantage is that although beneficial for understanding the overall group (i.e., the cohort), this approach reveals nothing about the recovery process of specific individuals over time, nor will you be able to know with certainty that variations in survey responses were due to uniqueness of the individual surveyed (recovery is going well for those who respond) or representative of true group differences (those who do not respond may have relapsed).

PANEL STUDIES   A panel design is the most rigorous of the three approaches to longitudinal survey research in that the exact same individuals are surveyed at each time of data collection. Using the preceding example, at the outset of the study you would select a group of adolescents to be your survey participants. Then, the same specific individuals in recovery from substance abuse would be surveyed in each of the three waves of data collection. The obvious advantage of this approach is that you obtain focused information about how specific participants are faring in their recovery from addiction. The primary disadvantage is cost. It is often difficult to locate specific persons across time. This fact requires that there will be greater costs involved in completing the research, because keeping close track of each individual in the panel, including searching for "lost" participants, is fundamental to the success of the study.

Cross-Sectional Survey Designs

The more commonly used design for survey research is cross-sectional methodology. In such studies, data are collected at only one point in time. For example, you might wish to survey the clients of a state vocational rehabilitation agency as to their perceptions of the effectiveness of the agency's counselors in helping them to secure employment. Within this cross-sectional design, you would collect data from a sample of clients and then use the results to make decisions as to the utilizations of agency resources to hire more counselors, to reduce counselor client load, to request more training for staff, or for any number of purposes.

Needless to say, such a design is advantageous in that the researcher is able to collect data quickly and generate research results in a timely manner. Furthermore, such designs provide information about participants' present-day attitudes, opinions, beliefs, and/or behaviors so that data obtained can quickly be used to make decisions about current situations. Common uses of cross-sectional survey designs include:

- A survey of current attitudes, beliefs, opinions, or practices (e.g., parents' practices of helping their children compete homework assignments).
- A survey to compare two or more groups (e.g., a comparison of the self-reported levels of depression among adults from a low socioeconomic status [SES] and adults from a high SES).
- A survey to measure community needs (e.g., a survey to learn the barriers to mental health services delivery for individuals living in a rural part of Mississippi).
- A survey to evaluate a program (e.g., gaining college students' opinions as to the effectiveness of the university career center in helping them identify potential jobs upon graduation).
- Statewide/national survey (e.g., in 1999, Holcomb-McCoy and Myers published the results of a national survey of practicing counselors' self- perceptions of their multicultural competence; they found that ethnicity was related to higher perceptions of multicultural competence but that program accreditation was not).

APPROACHES TO COLLECTING SURVEY DATA

After a researcher has determined the basic survey design (cross-sectional or longitudinal) that will be utilized to conduct a study, he or she must then consider the two basic formats employed for collecting survey data: the questionnaire and the interview. Both formats are utilized commonly, and each has variations as well as unique strengths and weaknesses. A detailed discussion of the types of questionnaires and interviews utilized in survey research are outlined next.

Data Collection Approach 1: Self-Administered Questionnaires

Regardless of the unique design elements, all self-administered questionnaires consist of a form that a participant completes and returns to the researcher by mail, electronically, or in person. Self-administered questionnaires ask participants to provide answers to a set of predetermined questions using either a pencil to mark or write a response or a computer mouse to click a response. Undoubtedly, most readers have personal experience completing surveys that have utilized these formats to survey data collection. To provide greater clarity as to how self-administered questionnaires are used in research, the two formats are explored in the following sections.

MAILED QUESTIONNAIRES   Self-administered questionnaires in which data are collected by mailing a survey to a sample of individuals, typically along with a letter of invitation to participate and a return envelope, is an approach that has been utilized extensively for research purposes.

Mailed surveys offer certain advantages in that they are relatively inexpensive to conduct compared with interviewer-based surveys, and they allow participants time to complete the questionnaire at their leisure before mailing it back to the researcher. Obviously, a significant disadvantage to this approach is that participants may not return the survey because there is no personal connection between participant and research. Undoubtedly, most readers have received a survey in the mail that they quickly discarded. Unlike interviewer-based surveys, with a mail survey there is no opportunity for the person completing the questionnaire to ask questions if he or she is uncertain as to the researcher's intentions or of the meaning of a particular survey item (Cherry, 2000). Therefore, to ensure the greatest likelihood that data collected from a mailed survey are meaningful; researchers should ask themselves the following questions:

- Are the directions for completing my survey absolutely and unmistakably clear?
  You must be certain that people completing the questionnaire will understand what they are being asked to do. Confusing or vague instructions can be devastating to the success of a survey.
- Are the items on my survey well-worded, such that their meaning is unambiguous? Researchers often believe the meaning of questions they write is clear, only to find that when someone else completes the questionnaire, items are interpreted in a manner different from what the writer intended.
- If included, are the scales used to mark items familiar to the respondents and easy to complete? For example, most people are familiar with Likert-type scales that ask them to rate their opinion related to some question, such as:

Strongly agree		Neutral		Strongly disagree
1	2	3	4	5

- Has careful attention been paid to designing the layout of the survey?
  If a questionnaire is difficult to read or to complete, or if it requires a long time to fill out, you will very likely obtain a lower response rate. A rule of thumb when designing a survey instrument is the simpler the better.
- How will you conduct follow-up requests to individuals who do not respond to the initial or secondary requests to participate?

Generally, it is unrealistic to expect that a large sample size will be obtained from only one mailing of a survey. Mail surveys are often conducted in two or more waves, with a wave consisting of one round of mailings to the sample. This would include an initial mailing to all members of the sample, and later, the follow-up mailings to those potential participants who have not returned their completed survey by the requested date.

ELECTRONIC QUESTIONNAIRES   Similarities exist between pencil-and-paper and electronic surveys, yet some unique considerations are required. Electronic surveys have grown increasingly popular in recent years due to the format's facility for reaching a large number of potential participants with one electronic solicitation. Electronic surveys are similar to pencil-and-paper questionnaires; however, the survey is set up using either a Web-based source (e.g., Surveymonkey.com) or an e-mail-based format. Individuals are usually requested by e-mail to take part in an electronic survey. A link to the survey is provided in the e-mail if the invitational e-mail does not contain the actual survey. Completed surveys are then e-mailed back to the researcher or are automatically stored upon completion and submission of the data by the participant.

A number of benefits to conducting surveys using an electronic format have been identified: (a) reduced cost, (b) ease and speed of administration, (c) the ability to provide anonymity, (d) access to samples that are larger and more diverse, and (e) if desired, to target minority and specialized populations that may be difficult to access using other means (Fox, Murray, & Warm, 2003).

Advantages notwithstanding, an important disadvantage of this format exists. As with mailed surveys, there exists no meaningful connection between the researcher and the participants. Therefore, motivating people to participate in electronic surveys can be challenging. As with mailed surveys, multiple requests and follow-ups to nonrespondents are to be expected.

Data Collection Approach 2: Interviews

A quite different approach to collecting survey data is the interview. The primary uniqueness of interview surveys is that there is a high degree of interaction between the researcher (or a trained interviewer) and the participant, which allows for a psychological connection to be established and the potential to gain depths of information that could never be ascertained in a written or electronic survey. The interview format has the possibility of creating in the participant a greater sense of obligation to complete a survey than does a paper form. An additional benefit is that the participant is able to ask questions or make comments to the interviewer that he or she may be unlikely to make in a paper or electronic format. In spite of the significant costs that can be involved with hiring and training interviewers, the benefits lead some researchers to go to the effort of collecting survey data person-to-person.

ONE-ON-ONE INTERVIEWS   In one-to-one-style data collection, the researcher or a trained interviewer asks a subject a predetermined set of closed-ended questions and records the participant's responses. A well-trained interviewer will be able to:

- Be polite to the interviewees and build goodwill for completing the survey.
- Provide instructions throughout the interview process.
- Ask the questions on the interview precisely as they are written to ensure consistency in responses.
- Complete the interview within the timeframe prescribed.
- Avoid interjecting their personal opinions into the interview.
- Maintain confidentiality.

Any time that multiple interviewers are used, it is important that they are well trained to collect data in a uniform manner. If not, it is more likely that bias will influence the data due to variations in the procedures used by the interviewers.

As mentioned earlier, a real advantage of one-on-one interviews is that an interpersonal bond may be built between the interviewer and subject. This creates the potential that greater time will be spent by the participant in completing the survey and that more honest responses will be obtained. A competing disadvantage is that, depending on the nature of the research, some people will be uncomfortable providing honest feedback about highly personal topics. There is no anonymity with face-to-face interviews; therefore, survey items related to highly personal topics such as sexuality, substance abuse, domestic violence, or finances may be difficult for a number of individuals to discuss openly with another person.

FOCUS GROUP INTERVIEWS   A focus group is an alternative to the one-on-one method of survey data collection in which a researcher brings together small groups of people who are selected as participants due to their knowledge about the topic of interest. All participants are allowed to express their opinions in response to questions asked by the interviewer so that a lively and varied discussion on a topic may result. Regardless of the uniqueness of some individuals' perspectives, all opinions are respected and recorded. A challenge of using the focus group is obtaining sufficient group consensuses pertaining to a question, so that the survey form may be marked appropriately by the interviewer.

TELEPHONE INTERVIEWS   Like one-to-one interviews, telephone interviews allow for interaction between the interviewer and subject. But unlike person-to-person interviews, telephoning allows for collecting data from persons widely scattered among different locations. Needless to say, a major challenge to this approach is that many individuals are reluctant to spend time answering long surveys or participating at all due to the intrusive nature of this method. Furthermore, there is no opportunity to observe the nonverbal behaviors of participants, and it is somewhat more difficult to form a bond with a respondent on the phone. In spite of these challenges, phone surveys are used effectively by counseling researchers as well as political groups and survey research companies.

STEPS FOR CONDUCTING A SURVEY RESEARCH PROJECT

Regardless of the specific purposes of a survey study or the methodology and format one selects, there are eight standard steps one will follow in completing any survey research project. These steps, if carefully executed, ensure that the resulting data will be of good quality and thereby of greater use to the researcher and other interested parties. The steps are as follows:

Step 1: Decide Up Front What You Want to Learn.

Earlier chapters in this book have discussed the importance of developing research questions when conducting any study. The research questions for a particular survey project should be carefully formulated before any items are developed. By taking the time to state the agenda of your project, you are more able to maintain a clear focus when it comes time to develop your questionnaire items. It is important to recognize that every possible item of interest cannot be included on a survey. Instead, by having clearly written research questions, you can decide what data are crucial to the success of the study and formulate items that indicate the essence of what you hope to learn. Also, by developing research questions, when the time comes to report findings of the study, you are able to state directly what results the research has yielded.

Step 2: Determine Your Population and Sample Selection Procedures.

After deciding what you are attempting to learn, you must carefully select the target population—the group of individuals you will survey to investigate the research questions. In most instances, it is neither realistic nor desirable to survey every member of a population. Instead, it must be determined how a sample will be drawn from the larger group. If, for example, you are interested in adolescents' views on issues that would cause them to seek out counseling services, you would likely decide that rather than trying to speak with every teenager in town, you would survey 250 of them (a sample) because this is easier and can also tell you important information about all teenagers who live in the area. By using sampling procedures, you would select a smaller subset of a larger group and then use the information gained from the survey of this smaller group of people to understand the larger population.

Regardless of sampling procedures used, you must determine how you will gain access to the sample you hope to survey. Novice researchers often develop an idea for a survey with little thought given to how they will obtain access to participants, and then discover they have little or no real means of making contact with the appropriate participants, making the project untenable.

There may be times when it is possible to survey every member of a population, such as surveying every employee of a mental health center to obtain data about employees' satisfaction with their jobs. This is ideal because you will be certain to have an accurate reflection of the population's perspectives. To complete a total population survey, you must organize a system to reach each member. In surveying the employees of a mental health center, you could speak with the human resources department and obtain a list of all the employees of the center. You then would develop a survey that asks about perceptions of working for the organization. Next you would give the survey to every employee along with his or her paycheck. By numbering the surveys and keeping a list of which number matches which employee, you could fairly easily obtain surveys from every employee of the mental health center. In this case, you would have sampled the entire population of interest (all employees of the mental health center). This approach is ideal because you can be assured that the data collected indeed represent the views of everyone involved.

Step 3: Determine the Survey Methodology and Data Collection Procedures You Will Employ.

As discussed earlier, there are two general designs for collecting survey data (longitudinal and cross-sectional). The decision as to which method will be used is determined based on the research questions the survey will address. Often, practical considerations related to the time, financial, and human resources allotted for the project will influence the methodological choice. However, when following good research procedures, a methodology is selected that most effectively answers the questions at hand.

Step 4: Develop a Questionnaire or Locate One That Has Been Used in Previous Research.

If you decide to develop your own survey instrument, it is important that you do so thoughtfully, obtaining feedback from others so that you will have created the highest-quality questionnaire possible. A discussion of how to develop a survey instrument appears later in this chapter.

Another possibility is to locate a survey instrument that has been previously developed for research and adapt it to your purposes. Finding a well-written questionnaire saves you time and ensures quality. You will need to conduct a literature review to locate survey research studies that had goals similar to your own. When such an article is found, you can contact the authors for permission to adapt their survey for your study. Many researchers are willing to share their instruments with other researchers.

Step 5: Pilot Test the Questionnaire.

Pilot testing means giving your survey a trial run to determine if it performs as you anticipate it will. The process involves having a small number of individuals complete your questionnaire and provide written or verbal feedback to the researcher regarding their impressions of its overall layout and the ease of completion. By conducting a pilot test, you gain invaluable feedback prior to the primary data collection. Indeed, it is much more efficient to learn through pilot testing that some questionnaire items are difficult for potential respondents to understand or that the time it takes to complete the instruments is much longer than anticipated. In short, there is no substitute for pilot testing.

I have frequently been asked by graduate students to look over questionnaires they have developed. More often than not, I will mark all over the questionnaires, making suggestions and asking questions about their intentions for various items. At times, students have appeared disappointed that their surveys were not given my stamp of approval without changes; however, it is the process of receiving objective feedback that makes any survey instrument more successful when used in research.

Step 6: Administer the Questionnaire.

Administering a survey can be a brief or long-term process, depending on the methodology selected. Nevertheless, survey research data are of the highest value only if administration procedures are followed carefully. As a researcher, you must strive to ensure that all data collected are of equal merit. Subsequently, the importance of providing clear verbal or written instructions, ensuring consistent means for survey completion, and keeping close track of all questionnaires returned, as well as those that are not, are of paramount importance to the integrity of your study.

Step 7: Analyze the Data.

After data are collected, you will analyze the results of the surveys using statistical procedures. A common approach is to use descriptive statistics (means, medians, modes, and percentages) to describe the sample you surveyed. For example, the mean age of your subjects or their median education level may be important to those who will consume the results of your research. It is also common to provide the percentage of respondents who support a particular idea or share an attitude.

Beyond using descriptive statistics to portray the sample, other statistical analyses may be used to examine relationships (i.e., correlations) among variables of interest to you. As discussed earlier, the relationships of interest are based on the research questions that drove you to conduct the survey. Chapters 14 and 15 on analysis, describe the mechanics of basic statistical procedures.

Step 8: Write the Report.

The final step of survey research involves creating a report that can then be shared with interested parties. Similar to writing the survey questionnaire, clarity and directness are important in writing the report of your findings. A well-written report facilitates readers in making decisions or gaining knowledge from your work. Subsequently, the appropriateness of decisions made will hinge on the writing you do (see chapter 16, on report writing, for a detailed discussion). A well-written survey report includes the findings of the study without overly stating weak relationships or minimal differences.

DESIGNING SURVEY ITEMS

Constructing items for a survey questionnaire is perhaps the single most important component in the overall success of a survey project. Although it may sound quite simple to develop a list of questions you would like participants to answer, formulating questions that are accurate, unbiased, and easy for respondents to answer is a scientific endeavor. There exist numerous books and studies that include discussions of the nuances of response types generated by various survey question designs. Interested readers can study in depth the subtleties of survey item construction in Dillman (2007). Suffice it to say, whether you choose to modify an existing survey or create one from scratch, it is imperative that you not underestimate the importance of creating tailored items that will result in meaningful data collection. Guidelines that will assist you in formulating effective questions are provided.

Open- and Closed-Ended Questions

The first consideration in writing a survey item is deciding on the basic question structure most appropriate for the survey under development. The two most rudimentary options for self-administered surveys are open-ended and closed-ended types of questions.

An open-ended survey question is one such as:

What led you to attend the University of Georgia?

_____

In this example, the respondent must determine, among all possible reasons for attending the University of Georgia, the one or two he or she will write about. Open-ended questions often result in inadequate responses from participants due to the fact that there is no interviewer available to encourage the in-depth disclosure, as might happen in an interview. Furthermore, many people find it burdensome to write long answers to generalized questions. Subsequently, many self-administered surveys rely on the closed-ended style of question.

An example of the closed ended style of survey question is:

Which *one* of the following factors most contributed to your decision to attend the University of Georgia?

- ☐ Proximity to where I live
- ☐ Reputation of the university
- ☐ Family members who attended the university
- ☐ The cost of tuition
- ☐ The programs of study offered

Obviously, closed-ended-type items are quicker for respondents to complete and, if well-worded, provide the information needed by the researcher. One important consideration with the closed-ended-type question is that responders are forced to make a choice among the options provided. This fact places greater responsibility on the researcher to deliberate possible response options that will generate results covering the spectrum of representative response opinions.

Question Construction

When faced with writing survey items, you must recognize that it is more difficult to ask a clear and concise question on paper or by e-mail than it might seem. There are many factors that go into the types of responses people give to survey items, including the length of the question, the sophistication of the language used, the educational level of the respondent, the overall length of the survey, the styles of the question, and the available options given for responding (to name just a few). Dillman (2007) offers guidelines for optimizing the effectiveness of survey items. The following list is adapted from his work:

- Write items using simple rather than specialized words.
- Ask questions using complete sentences.
- Ask a question in as few words as possible.
- Be sure questions are technically accurate.
- Avoid items that include more than one question.
- Ask questions for which the respondent has a ready-made answer (don't make them think too hard or too long).
- Soften the delivery of questions that some people may not wish to answer.
- Make certain that every respondent can answer all questions or provide options such as "Not applicable" or "If yes, answer the following . . . ."
- Do not include "check all that apply"–type questions because people tend to check the ones that appear first on the list.
- Avoid overlapping response options. For example, note the overlapping of answers to the following question:
  "What is your age?"

10 or less	_____
10–20	_____
20–30	_____
30–40	_____
40–50	_____
50 or more	_____

  Needless to say, the choices provided are unclear as to which range to select if your age is currently 30 years old.

MAXIMIZING SURVEY RESPONSE RATES

A researcher excitedly mails or e-mails what he or she believes to be an important survey, hoping that many completed questionnaires will be returned. Days and weeks go by, and the number of surveys returned is disappointingly small. Why did this happen, and how can it be avoided? In reality, there are many reasons that people do not respond to surveys. Nevertheless, it is of utmost importance to the overall integrity of the study that the return rate be as high as possible. The higher the number of questionnaires completed by the sample, the more confident the researcher will be that the results of the survey indeed reflect the attitudes, opinions, or experiences of the population under investigation. Therefore, obtaining a high response rate is always a great concern to survey researchers. Let us now turn to a discussion of means by which a researcher can secure the greatest number of returned surveys.

The total percentage of questionnaires returned is termed the *response rate.* A low response rate provides little assurance that the people who responded are indeed representative of the entire population and may lead to *nonresponse bias,* meaning that there are important differences between the people who responded and those who chose not to respond. Therefore, "What constitutes a sufficient response rate?" becomes an important consideration. In fact, this is a question that has received much attention among survey researchers, and there exist varying opinions as to its answer. Generally speaking, a response of 25% is considered low because three out of four people did not bother to complete the survey. When a low response rate is achieved, the researcher must assume that responders were more highly motivated, and, therefore, may be different from nonresponders in important ways, thus skewing the results. Conversely, a response rate of 75% or greater is usually viewed as a high response rate because the majority of people who received the questionnaire were motivated to complete it. Often, a response rate of 50% or higher is found among published survey research (Creswell, 2005).

To ensure a satisfactory response rate, giving attention to all procedural aspects of the data collection is paramount. This includes having a system for inviting people to participate, delivering the survey to the sample, having the survey returned, and following up with nonresponders. In fact, Dillman (2007) suggests that implementation procedures are more influential on response rate with self-administered surveys than are questionnaire design and an ease of completion. This means that as a survey researcher, you must be intentional about the number of contacts you make with the target population; the content of letters sent; the appearance of envelopes; any incentives that are offered; use of personalized contact (i.e., including the persons name, versus "You have been selected . . . "); and sponsorship of the study by an organization or individual to give it credibility.

To increase the response rate of a self-administered survey, you must think in terms of building goodwill. Every component of the process is an opportunity to make the respondent feel appreciated and respected for his or her contribution.

- Be certain that individuals targeted as participants are knowledgeable about the topic.
  The "shotgun" approach to data collection does not ensure a higher response rate. No amount of well-designed procedures, good survey layout, and well-constructed items will persuade someone to complete a survey that is perceived as irrelevant. Therefore, to maximize response rate, it is imperative that the individuals selected are persons who have knowledge of the area under investigation and are reasonably motivated to provide the information asked for.
- Pre-notify participants that they will soon be receiving a survey.
  A letter or e-mail explaining to the recipients that they have been selected to participate in your survey alerts the participants to be on the lookout for the forthcoming survey. Pre-notification also provides an opportunity to describe the importance of and purpose of the research and to give a specific timeframe for completion. If possible, use the potential respondent's actual name in your correspondence with him or her to provide a small psychological connection between the researcher and the participant.

- Provide a cover letter, either written or electronic, with the survey.

  With a self-administered survey, the cover letter is your primary psychological contact with the potential respondent. There are several goals of such letters. The letter should (a) encourage the person to complete the questionnaire, (b) explain the purpose of the study, (c) give informed consent to the participant, (d) assure the confidentiality of the person's responses, (e) include contact information about the sponsoring institution of organization, and (f) give specific information about the time it will take to complete the survey and procedures for returning it.

- Decide upon and systematically implement follow-up procedures.

  Typically, respondents to surveys are asked to complete the questionnaire and return it within a specific timeframe, say, two weeks. After two weeks, an additional copy of the survey is mailed or e-mailed to all nonresponders. Then, after another specific period of time, those who still have not responded are sent a third and final request to participate. Although this may sound time-consuming and arduous, such steps are necessary to ensure a higher response rate.

- If possible, use incentives to encourage participation.

  Although using incentives can be costly, research findings support the idea that providing someone with a small incentive of a dollar or two at the time he or she completes a survey is much more effective at increasing response rates than is the promise of a future payment after the survey is returned (Dillman, 2007). Although it may sound expensive to pay someone to complete your survey, the subtle psychological obligation that is provided by giving people a dollar when they open your survey envelope is effective. Even if funds are not available to pay for a completed survey, including any sort of small gift can be beneficial (a pen, a sticker, a coupon, etc.).

LIMITATIONS OF SURVEY RESEARCH

The decision to conduct survey research should be based on the research goals, resources, and time available to invest in conducting such a study. Undertaking a survey because it sounds easy or "just makes sense" will likely lead to results of diminished value to the researcher and the broader community. As with all approaches to research, surveys are not the correct choice for all research questions.

Survey research has limitations. As pointed out earlier in this chapter, although a survey can be utilized to describe relationships among variables, the approach is not useful for determining the cause of a phenomenon that respondents describe. For example, a survey might reveal a statistically significant relationship (i.e., a correlation) between the amount of time a child spends playing sports and the number of times a child is referred to the school counselor. However, this finding does not prove that playing sports causes a child to be referred to the school counselor. In fact, due to the nature of correlational statistics, you could use the same data to support the argument that the more times a child is referred to the school counselor, the more likely the child is to spend time playing sports. Neither of these arguments is supported by the data.

Second, survey studies rely on "self-report" data; that is, they depend on participants to truthfully and accurately report their attitudes, opinions, or behaviors. Yet, this does not always happen. For example, some respondents may deliberately answer questions incorrectly or flippantly. However, if a sample is selected so that the individuals responding feel knowledgeable of the subject and can easily provide answers, such respondent bias occurs less often. A bias that is nearly impossible to fully eliminate is that of subjects simply committing honest errors of omission, confusion, or false memory.

Third, survey studies are subject to well-known types of bias. For example, respondents often know they are being studied, and have at least some idea of *why,* which may lead participants, either consciously or unconsciously, to provide answers that show themselves in the best light or that conform to social norms. It is also possible for experimenters to deliberately or inadvertently write survey questions that bias people to respond in the manner preferred by the researcher.

Fourth, if conducted properly, a survey can accurately represent the opinions or behaviors of a population of people. However, this does not mean that the opinions obtained are "correct." Although survey data can be used to inform decision making, the results cannot substitute for expert judgments and analysis.

Finally, conducting a scientific survey is not a trivial undertaking. Scientific surveys require careful preparation; they are labor intensive; and they can take many weeks, months, or years to implement and analyze. In many cases, completing survey research is more labor intensive than an experimental research design would be. Therefore, the time and energy involved in such a study should not be taken lightly.

Summary

The purpose of this chapter has been to assist you in gaining the basic knowledge needed to effectively conduct a survey research study. You should now be familiar with the fundamental elements of methodology, item development, and survey procedures that are involved in this type of research. Survey research skills are best acquired through collaboration and practice. As a professor of mine said, "Any attempt is a victory." For the novice researcher, it is more valuable to attempt a survey project than to allow your lack of experience to prevent you from engaging in the exciting process of learning and the creation of knowledge.

Review and Discussion Questions

1. What are the various types of survey research methodology, and under what circumstances is each used?
2. What are the advantages and disadvantages of using a survey for conducting research?
3. What are the steps involved in designing and executing a quality survey research project?
4. What procedures would you include in the survey research process to ensure a maximum response rate?

CHAPTER 8

Time Series Designs

Edina L. Renfro-Michel, *Montclair State University*
Kimberly Hall, *Mississippi State University*
Kristen Johnson-Gros, *Mississippi State University*
Nicole Roberto, *Montclair State University*

OBJECTIVES
After reading this chapter, you will:

▪ Be able to describe the purpose of time series research.

▪ Be able to describe the types of time series methodology.

▪ Be able to explain various approaches to collecting time series data.

▪ Be able to identify the steps in completing a time series research project.

▪ Be able to understand the use of graphs to display time series data.

OVERVIEW

All research designs have their own terminology that allows for professionals to communicate and understand issues surrounding the type of design utilized. Single-subject design follows the same tenets as any research design. There is often a misconception about single-subject design, such as (a) it is only used to evaluate behavior modification techniques, (b) it does not permit causal conclusions, (c) it does not allow one to draw conclusions about generalization, and (d) it presents a perfect alternative to between-group designs. In this chapter, we discuss the most important common characteristics of time series designs. In addition, we define the terminology for each characteristic. With these definitions, a visual depiction is given to highlight the meanings of each characteristic.

PURPOSE OF TIME SERIES RESEARCH

To understand single-subject research, a primer on the terminology is needed for you to comprehend the designs that will be discussed throughout this chapter. Single-subject designs have been called or named several things, including *n-of-one studies, case studies,* and *intensive designs.* However, the most appropriate terminology to use is *time series designs*. The rationale is that many designs being discussed use more than one participant and intervention. The designs may not necessarily be intensive, but they all have one common characteristic: the design is carried out over time. Thus, throughout the remainder of the chapter, we use the term "time series design" to reflect all of the common terms.

Principles of Time Series Research

There are three guiding principles and goals in time series designs: (a) prediction, (b) verification, and (c) replication. *Prediction* can be defined as an awaited outcome of an unknown measurement either presently or in the future (Johnston & Pennypacker, 1980). *Verification* is a process by which a counselor can increase the probability that the change from one phase (baseline) to intervention is the reason the behavior changed (i.e., verify the veracity of the data). *Replication* is an important aspect of time series research in that it provides you with confidence that any change in behavior is due to the intervention or treatment. Replication also demonstrates the reliability of the behavior change.

With any experimental design, there is a *dependent variable* (i.e., the behavior of interest) and an *independent variable* (i.e., the intervention or treatment). Dependent variables can be expressed by rate, duration, latency, or a percentage. A few examples of behaviors measured in time series research are off-task, percentage correct on a test, or the number of times a person had negative thoughts throughout the day. In a time series design, the dependent variable is depicted by a datum point, a single measurement. *Datum* is a single data point representing one measurement of the person's behavior. *Data* are multiple measurements (e.g., repeated measurements, percentage of time off-task) of the person's behavior over time, which is called a series of data points. For example, a person displayed 60% off-task behavior on Monday, 65% off-task behavior on Tuesday, and 60% off-task behavior on Wednesday. This is a series of multiple measurements over time, thus, a series of data points.

As previously mentioned, behavior can be expressed in terms of rate, duration, latency, or percentage. *Rate* is defined as the amount of a behavior expressed over time (e.g., words a person reads correctly in one minute). *Duration* is defined as the length of time a behavior occurs (e.g., a child may scream continuously for five minutes). *Latency* is defined as the time from a stimulus being presented to the time the behavior is emitted (e.g., the amount of time between when the bell rings for class to start and when the child actually makes it to class). *Percentage* is defined as a fraction or a ratio.

In a time series design, a baseline phase (i.e., no treatment) is usually first; however, there are some designs that do not necessarily employ a baseline. The rationale for a baseline is to demonstrate the *natural* state of the behavior without intervention or treatment. The premise is to determine where the person is currently functioning and, therefore, to set a goal for treatment. Without a baseline, you cannot always show that a treatment ultimately worked. The baseline also serves as a control and only means that the specified treatment is not in effect. Thus, the first series of data points is usually baseline and generally noted as A (see Figure 8.1).

The next phase or condition change is a treatment or series of treatments. Each treatment is followed in the alphabet by the first intervention (B), the second intervention (C), and so forth. For example, if you were using an ABAB design, then you would know that it was baseline: one intervention (B), withdrawal of the intervention (A), and then a re-implementation of the intervention (B). Another example is A-B-B+C design. This would mean baseline (A) followed by one intervention (B) and finally the first intervention (B) with an additional intervention added to the first (C) (see Figure 8.1 for a depiction of the terminology and the components of a graph).

Graphs are used to illustrate data in a majority of time series designs. There are seven components to a graph that allow for communicating and facilitating decision making. The first is the horizontal, or *x*-axis, which represents the passage of time (e.g., sessions, days, weeks). The *x*-axis is numbered and labeled in equal parts such as day 1, 2, and 3. The vertical axis, or *y*-axis, is connected to the bottom of the left-hand *x*-axis. The *y*-axis depicts the behavior of interest by

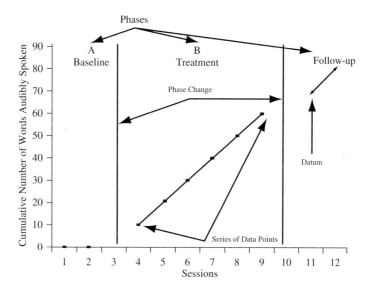

FIGURE 8.1 Depiction of a Time Series Design

Adapted from S. C. Hayes, D. H. Barlow, & R. O. Nelson-Gray. (1999). *The Scientist Practitioner Research and Accountability in the Age of Managed Care* (2nd ed.). Boston: Allyn & Bacon.

percentage, rate, or duration. Each tick mark upward represents a higher value with equal intervals. The third component is the phase or condition change lines, which are drawn from the bottom of the *x*-axis to the top of the *y*-axis. These lines demonstrate when a change has occurred. For example, a line would be drawn when there is a change from baseline to intervention. Other examples of when to draw a phase change line are when there is a change from one intervention to another or when the intervention is withdrawn.

The fourth element is phase or condition labels. Each phase change should have a label at the top of the graph, including baseline, intervention(s), or withdrawal. The fifth element is the data points. Data points represent two important aspects: (a) the target behavior that is quantifiable and (b) the time the measure was taken. The sixth component of a graph is the data path, which is discussed with types of data patterns. Finally, the last element is the figure caption, which is a brief statement that clarifies any observed unplanned event that may have affected the behavior (Cooper, Heron, & Heward, 2007).

Data Interpretation

In time series designs, interpretation of the data occurs through a visual inspection of graphs. Three important types of data patterns need to be considered when you make decisions: (a) level, (b) trend, and (c) variability. *Level* refers to the average, median, or general value of the measures. *Trend* is defined as the direction of the series of data points from the beginning to the end of the series. For example, if a student displayed 10, 12, and 14 out-seat behaviors across observations, you would have an increasing trend. *Variability* is described as the spread of data points around level and trend (see Figures 8.2, 8.3, and 8.4 for examples on level, trend, and variability).

Time series designs, similarly to group design research, need to be planned in detail before the study begins. The definition of the target behavior should be very specific, with an outside party being able to understand and measure the behavior based on your definition. For example, if as a counselor, you were interested in using a time series design to investigate the efficacy of a treatment protocol on the reduction of compulsive behaviors in a client, it would be necessary for you to clearly define compulsive behaviors in concrete and measurable terms. If, in this case, the client was diagnosed with trichotillomania and compulsively pulled his or

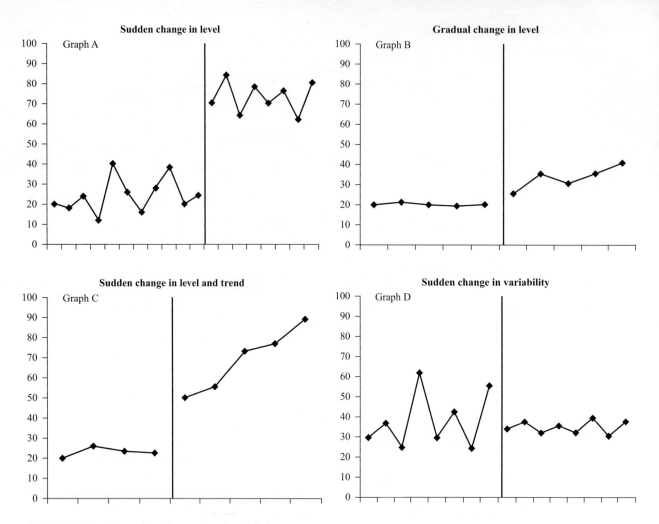

FIGURE 8.2 Depiction of Level, Trend, and Variability

Adapted from S. C. Hayes, D. H. Barlow, & R. O. Nelson-Gray. (1999). *The Scientist Practitioner Research and Accountability in the Age of Managed Care* (2nd ed.). Boston: Allyn & Bacon.

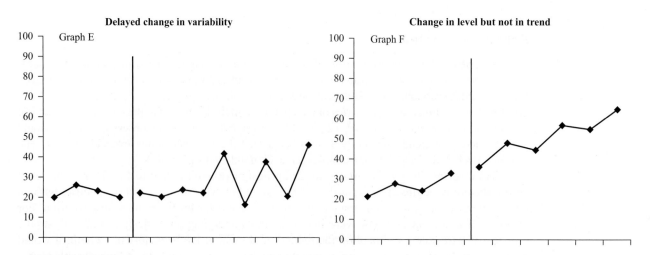

FIGURE 8.3 Depictions of Other Types of Level, Trend, and Variability

Adapted from S. C. Hayes, D. H. Barlow, & R. O. Nelson-Gray. (1999). *The Scientist Practitioner Research and Accountability in the Age of Managed Care* (2nd ed.). Boston: Allyn & Bacon.

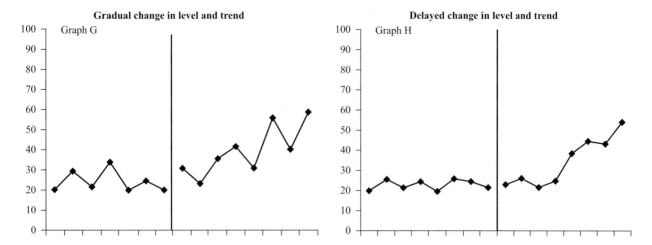

FIGURE 8.3 Depictions of Other Types of Level, Trend, and Variability (*continued*)

Adapted from S. C. Hayes, D. H. Barlow, & R. O. Nelson-Gray. (1999). *The Scientist Practitioner Research and Accountability in the Age of Managed Care* (2nd ed.). Boston: Allyn & Bacon.

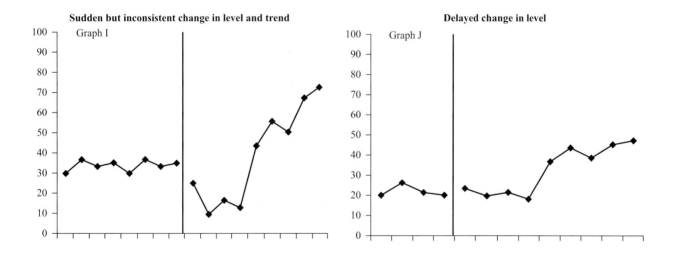

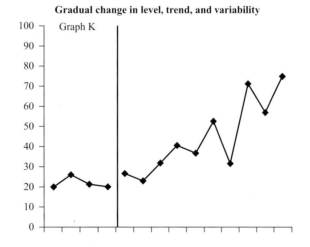

FIGURE 8.4 Continued Depictions of Level, Trend, and Variability

Adapted from S. C. Hayes, D. H. Barlow, & R. O. Nelson-Gray. (1999). *The Scientist Practitioner Research and Accountability in the Age of Managed Care* (2nd ed.). Boston: Allyn & Bacon.

her eyelashes out, it would be necessary for you to distinguish between the client rubbing the eyes and pulling eyelashes. In this case, compulsive eyelash pulling might be defined as any time the client grasps any part of the eyelash with the fingers. Often, clients are able to help provide specific definitions. The client might be aware of the mechanics of the compulsive behavior and thus might provide a more specific definition. By engaging the client in this process, more ownership of the process could occur, and the client might become more aware of the actual behavior.

Additionally, the research questions should be clearly defined. In the preceding example, the research questions could include:

1. How often does the client experience negative thoughts?
2. What situation is the client in when she/he experiences negative thoughts?
3. Which of the following treatments would reduce the negative thoughts: replacement with a positive thought or thought stopping?

These examples show that there are a wide variety of questions to be answered. Only after the target behavior and research questions are defined should the researcher determine the best methods for collecting data.

PAPER-AND-PENCIL VERSUS COMPUTER SOFTWARE DATA COLLECTION

After identifying the questions to be answered and the definitions of the behaviors, the time series researcher should determine the type of delivery for the assessments. Traditionally, paper-and-pencil assessments have been used, yet computer-administered or electronic assessments have gained popularity (Wijndaele et al., 2007). For the purposes of this book, we use the term *electronic* to refer to any assessment techniques that involve computer or web-based applications. When ascertaining the delivery system, it is important for you to consider the advantages and disadvantages of traditional and electronic assessments and current research.

Traditional Assessments

Traditional paper-and-pencil assessments provide the client with a familiar delivery system. The assessment can be administered in your counseling office or sent home, saving time during sessions.

The majority of assessments have been validated in their traditional form. However, it can take time to score and interpret the traditional assessments, requiring an additional visit from the client for interpretation and explanations. This latency may be crucial to a client's treatment.

Clients who are tracking their behavior or thought processes have the ability to carry paper check sheets or journals on their person and utilize them immediately. These assessments can be individualized quickly in session, over the phone, or through e-mail.

Computer Assessments

Computer-delivered electronic assessments have many advantages. They are less expensive, often requiring less effort to score and interpret, and results are instantaneous. Furthermore, electronic versions can require the completion of all questions, reducing errors due to omissions. Administration of computer assessments can increase the standardization of assessments by providing the same directions (verbally or visually) and including standardized answers to client questions. Computers may be programmed to detect hesitation, time between answers, changes in answers, and force of keystroke during an assessment (Skinner & Pakula, 1986). Clients have indicated positive reactions toward instant personalized feedback during computer assessments (Koski-Jännes, Cunningham, Tolonen, & Bothas, 2007).

Some researchers (e.g., Skinner & Pakula, 1986) indicate that clients are more likely to report sensitive issues, such as sexual history, on a computer than face-to-face. This increased reporting may be related to heightened perceptions of confidentiality when using a computer. As with traditional assessments, computer-based assessments are often completed in the counselor's office or on a home computer. However, a client who does not have access to a computer at home would be at a disadvantage with out-of-office computer assessments.

When discussing electronic assessments, computers are the general mode of delivery. As technology use increases, many other types of electronic devices may deliver electronic assessments. For example, clients may utilize electronic organizers to track their behaviors and thought processes. This system may provide benefits such as ease of use, being less conspicuous and bulky than paper-and-pencil checklists, and being easily downloadable to the counselor's computer. Personalized assessments can be created in a word-processing program or spreadsheet for ease of use.

While there are many assessments available in electronic form, most assessments have only been validated using their traditional paper form (Luce et al., 2007; Wijndaele et al., 2007). Until an assessment's electronic version is tested for reliability and validity, it may be prudent to use the traditional paper assessment.

Other factors are important when determining the type of assessment delivery system. Gender and age level may play a role in preference of the delivery of an assessment. There has been contradictory evidence that females tend to have higher anxiety and lower self-efficacy regarding computer use (Brosnan, 1998; Durndell & Haag, 2002; Joiner et al., 2005). Wijndaele et. al. (2007) discovered that younger participants (18–40 years of age) preferred computerized versions of assessments, 41- to 60-year-olds had no preference, and participants over 60 preferred traditional assessments. It is important to note that computerized assessments may be biased against clients with low socioeconomic status and education levels (Skinner & Pakula, 1986).

Additionally, there is some evidence that computer phobia may reach diagnosable phobia levels (Brosnan & Thorpe, 2006; Thorpe & Brosnan, 2007). Brosnan (1998) discovered that computer anxiety and self-efficacy of computer skills were directly related to correct responses during the navigation of a database. While participants with higher self-efficacy tended to take longer to complete their task, they utilized more complex methods and had higher scores. Thus, anxiety and self-efficacy may have an effect not only on the ability to complete an assessment accurately, but also on how much effort is placed into that completion. If a client has anxiety regarding computer use, then you should use more traditional methods.

RECORDING DATA

Unlike assessment instruments, observational data must be collected in vivo by observation or video recording. Observational data of the target behavior is recorded during these sessions. The definition of this target behavior is critical to ensure accurate data collection. The target behavior may be recorded in four different ways: (1) frequency or event, (2) duration, (3) latency, and (4) interval. The type of timing used depends on the research question. To determine the most appropriate use of timing for collecting data, an example of hand-raising behavior during a 10-minute math lesson will be used.

Frequency/Event Recording

QUESTION 1: HOW OFTEN IS THE CLIENT RAISING HER HAND DURING THE MATH LESSON?
With this question, you are requesting the frequency, or the number of times the client raises her hand during the lesson. If accurately defined, hand-raising behavior has a clear beginning and end and a relatively uniform duration. Additionally, the researcher is recording the number of occurrences (events) of hand rising. Therefore, frequency, or event recording, would be appropriate. If the behavior was a high-frequency behavior, event recording may not be appropriate due to observer drift.

Event Recording observation

Client: <u>Richard</u>   Date: <u>Monday April 5</u>   Time: <u>9:18–9:28AM</u>

Setting: <u>Math Class Room 203</u>

Behavior	1'00	2'00	3'00	4'00	5'00	6'00	7'00	8'00	9'00	10'00

Hand raising

| | | | I | | I   I | I | | |

Opportunities
presented by
teacher for
hand raising

   II   II   I   I

Calculation of rate per minute:

<u>   4   </u> / 10 minutes = 0.4 RPM

Percent of occurrence:

<u> 4 </u> / <u> 6 </u> × 100 = 66.7 %

FIGURE 8.5 Example of Event Recording

Hand raises during the entire 10 minutes could be tallied, or the 10-minute observation could be divided into smaller components to determine how often the hand-raising behavior occurs in the beginning, middle, and end of the lesson. It might be determined that the most effective way to measure the target behavior is to divide the 10-minute lesson into 1-minute segments. Data would be recorded each time the client's hand is raised within each time segment. See Figure 8.5 for an example of an event recording observation. To record these data on a graph as one observation session, the rate per minute (RPM) of hand-raising behavior should be calculated.

$$\text{RPM} = \frac{\text{Total number of occurrences of the behavior}}{\text{Total number of minutes of observation}}$$

Additionally, if you wanted to know hand-raising frequency in relation to the opportunities for the target behavior, event recording of discriminated operants would be utilized. For example, as an observer, you may record the number of times the teacher asks a question during the lesson. The calculation of these data would be a percentage rather than a rate per minute.

$$\text{Percent occurrence} = \frac{\text{Number of occurrences of behavior}}{\text{Total number of opportunities}} \times 100$$

Duration Recording

QUESTION 2: HOW LONG DOES THE CLIENT RAISE HER HAND BEFORE SHE (OR ANOTHER STUDENT) VERBALIZES THE ANSWER?   Determining the duration of the target behavior would require a different approach. You would use a stopwatch to record how long the client raises her hand. The duration of hand-raising is recorded until the client either calls out the answer uninvited, is called upon to provide the answer, or someone else provides the answer. If one of the objectives of the intervention is for the student to reduce the number of uninvited verbal answers, the terminating event should also be recorded.

Duration recording requires a target behavior definition that includes exactly when a behavior begins and ends. Generally, researchers use an average duration rather than the total number of minutes or seconds a behavior occurs.

$$\text{Average duration} = \frac{\text{Total duration of behavior}}{\text{Number of occurrences}}$$

Latency Recording

QUESTION 3: HOW QUICKLY DOES THE CLIENT RAISE HER HAND AFTER THE TEACHER ASKS A QUESTION?   The latency of the behavior would be collected similarly to the duration. Latency measures the elapsed time between the stimulus and the initiation of the behavior. You would start a stopwatch when the teacher completes a question and stop the stopwatch when the client's hand is fully raised (as determined by the target behavior definition). However, if the client raises her hand before the teacher finishes the question, you would need another approach. Thus, you would start the stopwatch when the teacher begins to ask a question and turn the watch off when the client's hand is raised. How would you know a question is about to be asked? Often teachers and observers create an unobtrusive code for such instances.

The preceding example demonstrates the need for the target behavior and the stimulus to be clearly defined. If the definitions are unclear, the latency recording would be inaccurate. For example, if you begin latency recording when the teacher finishes a question and end the recording when the client's hand is fully raised, elbow straight, and then end the recording when the client begins to raise her hand, the latency would be different for each observation. The inaccurate data collection could lead to differences in baseline and treatment designs, invalidating the data collection.

Latency is also recorded as an average:

$$\text{Average latency} = \frac{\text{Total latency of behavior}}{\text{Number of occurrences}}$$

Interval Recording

QUESTION 4: IS THE HAND-RAISING BEHAVIOR OCCURRING DURING THE LESSON? Generally, interval recording is used with continuous behaviors where the beginning and end are difficult to determine (i.e., tantrums) and have a variable duration. While hand-raising may have a definable beginning and end, it will be used for consistency. To determine the occurrence of the behavior, you would reduce the 10-minute lesson to smaller equal intervals. The length of the intervals is determined by the researcher but should be small enough to provide accurate data collection. Intervals are generally in 10-second increments, but they could be longer depending on the target behavior. It is not recommended that the intervals be shorter than 10 seconds. During each interval, you would record the occurrence or nonoccurrence of the target behavior.

There are two types of interval recording: (a) partial-interval and (2) whole-interval. During partial-interval recording, the observer records an occurrence if the behavior happens *at any time* during the interval. Nonoccurrence is recorded only if the behavior does not present *at all* during the interval. Partial-interval recording tends to overestimate behavior occurrence.

Whole-interval recording, on the other hand, tends to underestimate the occurrence of the target behavior. During whole-interval recording, the behavior is only recorded as occurring if the behavior presents during the *entire* interval. Otherwise, nonoccurrence is recorded.

Interval recording data are presented as a percentage of the occurrences of the target behavior.

$$\text{Percent of occurrence} = \frac{\text{Number of intervals of occurrence}}{\text{Total number of intervals observed}}$$

Momentary Time Sampling

Momentary time sampling (MTS) may be more accurate than interval recording (Murphy & Harrop, 1994). During MTS, the observer only observes the target behavior during selected intervals and records occurrence or nonoccurrence. The length of the observation interval and the number of intervals between observations is determined by the researcher. Using question 4, observations could be made during the first 15 seconds of each minute interval during the math lesson, during every other 15-second interval throughout the lesson. An advantage of MTS is the ability to record observations without taking away from observation time. Additionally, observers tend to focus more during MTS than during interval recording and have less observer attention drift. During MTS, behaviors are recorded as occurring if they occur *at any point* during the observed interval. Similar to interval recording, MTS is calculated as a percent of intervals.

Additional Considerations

It is important to note that often many observations over several days or weeks are required for you to develop an accurate representation of the target behavior. One observation would not be accurate due to the fluctuations in the environment or temperament of the client. In the preceding example, the client may be more energetic in the morning and thus tend to raise her hand more often. Observations only collected in the morning on Mondays, for example, would not produce an overall picture of the client's behavior. If the math lesson on Friday is in the afternoon, the client may not react in the same manner as she did Monday morning. As researchers, you should determine a variety of times and days for observations to ensure an accurate representation of the baseline or treatment.

Time series design lends itself to multiple target behaviors. Each behavior should be accurately defined and recorded separately. With the addition of multiple behaviors, the accuracy of the observational data may decline. You should determine the number of behaviors to be recorded before data collection begins and include only essential target behaviors.

Counseling researchers often use a timing aid to increase accuracy of observations. The observer uses headphones to listen to an audio tape with interval tones. In other words, the tape beeps at the beginning of each interval. This increases accuracy of observation because the observer does not have to check a watch, thus switching visual attention away from the client.

Increasing accuracy can also be obtained with multiple observers. With multiple concurrent observers, any inaccuracies in definitions, observer drift, or inconsistencies in recording would be readily apparent if there is low inter-observer agreement.

INTER-OBSERVER AGREEMENT

Because counselors are primarily interested in behaviors and social interactions that cannot be automatically measured, researchers developed a set of procedures to help measure behavior in the real world. With reliance on human beings to keep count of whether a behavior occurs or not, there is an increase in the possibility of human error. To reduce this error, you must take steps to monitor and evaluate the possible types of errors. By collecting inter-observer agreement data, you can monitor the consistency with which behaviors are being measured during a study. *Inter-observer agreement*, sometimes referred to as inter-rater reliability or reliability, helps establish the degree to which behaviors are being measured consistently.

To begin the inter-observer agreement data collection, you should train observers on the use of the same behavioral code and recording system. The trained observers then independently observe and record the specified behavior at the same time using the same procedures. A minimum of 20% (preferably 33%) of the total observations should be used to gather inter-observer agreement data (Kennedy, 2005).

By gathering independent recording of behaviors, you can obtain an objective comparison of how the behaviors are being recorded using the measurement instrument. You can then estimate the degree of agreement on what behaviors occurred or did not occur.

Occurrence/nonoccurrence agreement is the most rigorous and preferred method for calculating inter-observer agreement (Kennedy, 2005). This approach involves calculating two agreement coefficients: one for the occurrence of the response and one for the nonoccurrence of the response. The number of times that both observers agree on the occurrence of a behavior is tallied as well as the number of times the observers disagree. To calculate occurrence agreement, the number of agreements is divided by the total number of observations (Agreements + Disagreements) and then multiplied by 100.

$$\text{Occurrence agreement} = \frac{\text{Number of agreements}}{\text{Total number of observations}} \times 100$$

To calculate nonoccurrence agreement, the number of times that both observers agree on the nonoccurrence of a behavior is tallied as well as the number of times the observers disagree. To calculate nonoccurrence agreement, the number of agreements is divided by the total number of observations (Agreements + Disagreements) and then multiplied by 100.

$$\text{Nonoccurrence agreement} = \frac{\text{Number of agreements}}{\text{Total number of observations}} \times 100$$

Both percentages are reported separately with a minimum of 80% inter-observer agreement recommended by most researchers (Kennedy, 2005). The higher the degree of inter-observer agreement, the more consistent the observers were in using the measurement system. Therefore, changes in the behavior (or dependent variable) are more likely due to the intervention (or independent variable) rather than the variability of different observers.

Another method for calculating inter-observer agreement is by using the kappa (κ) statistic. Developed by Cohen (1960) and suggested for use in calculating inter-observer agreement by Hartmann (1977), the goal of using k is to provide a quantitative measure of the extent of agreement between observers. Kappa ranges from -1 to $+1$, where $+1$ is perfect agreement, 0 is chance agreement, and -1 is disagreement between observers. Table 8.1 provides a visualization of the interpretation of kappa (Viera & Garrett, 2005). The calculation of kappa is based on the difference between the extent of agreement between observers due to chance versus the extent of agreement actually present (Viera & Garrett, 2005). Fortunately, computer programs are able to calculate kappa.

TABLE 8.1 Interpretation of Kappa

Kappa	Agreement
<0	Less than chance agreement (disagreement)
0.01–0.20	Slight agreement
0.21–0.40	Fair agreement
0.41–0.60	Moderate agreement
0.61–0.80	Substantial agreement
0.81–0.99	Almost perfect agreement

MODELS

Time series designs employ many different types of intervention models to determine the effectiveness of treatments. The following sections are examples of the models most often used in time series designs.

Simple Phase Change

The simplest method for determining the impact of an intervention on a client is the simple phase change, or AB design, where A represents the baseline condition and B represents the intervention. Data collection during the baseline phase includes measuring the frequency, duration, and/or intensity of the client's targeted behavior(s) before the intervention. After baseline data are collected, the intervention phase begins. The target behavior is again measured repeatedly and recorded. Data from both the baseline and the intervention phase are compared to determine the effectiveness of the intervention.

COLLECTING BASELINE DATA   Baseline consists of repeated measurements of the target variable at equally spaced intervals over time. Considerations must be given to the type of measurement collected, how the measurements will be collected, the number of measurements obtained, and the time interval between measurements.

Measurements can reflect the magnitude, duration, frequency, or existence of a problem. *Magnitude* refers to the intensity or severity of beliefs, attitudes, moods, or emotions. *Duration* includes the length of time the problem occurs, while *frequency* is the number of times the problem occurs within the specified time period. Problem *existence* refers to the presence or absence of behavior, symptom, or problem (Tripodi, 1994).

According to Blythe and Tripodi (1989), measurements for baseline data can be obtained the following ways:

1. Observing and gathering measurements during problem assessment before any intervention.
2. Observing and gathering measurements on a specific problem while a separate intervention is being used to address a different problem than the one being baselined.
3. Reconstructing measurements based on archival data and available records, such as school grades, absences, and disciplinary referrals.
4. Gathering client's recollections concerning targeted problem through a questionnaire.

As a counseling researcher, you will need to ensure that enough measurements are taken during baseline to establish stability. A minimum of three points is needed to determine trends if the measurements are similar (Barlow & Hersen, 1984; Jayaratne & Levy, 1979). However, you should gather as many measurements as needed to establish horizontal stability of the target behavior. That is, the measurements should form a line that is parallel to the *x*-axis on a graph (see Figure 8.6).

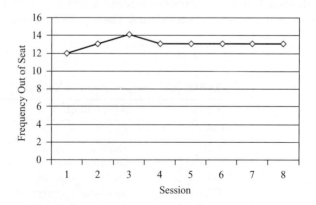

FIGURE 8.6 Baseline Data for Out-of-Seat Behavior Over 8 Sessions of Observation

However, if the targeted behavior is getting worse, you can end the baseline phase and begin the intervention without obtaining horizontal stability (Tripodi, 1994).

The decision for selecting the appropriate time intervals for measurement is based on your clinical judgment. The intervals should reflect a sufficient amount of time that would allow change to reasonably occur and should make clinical sense in relation to the client's problem (Tripodi, 1994). For example, if measurements are taken every day, then data should be collected for about one to two weeks to determine trends.

Baseline data can provide information for assessing specific problems and evaluating interventions. The severity and persistence of a specific problem can be clearly examined, thus providing information for problem assessment. Baseline data can also serve as a frame of reference for comparing measurements before, during, and after an intervention to measure its effectiveness (Bloom & Fischer, 1982).

INTERVENTION PHASE   Following the baseline phase, you would introduce an intervention designed to meet the objective for treatment. You may strive to achieve change through an intervention or may actually desire no change if the intervention is used as a prevention method. You should describe the intervention in detail, including such information as names of person(s) providing intervention, location, frequency, and duration of intervention, and a description of the actual intervention strategy (Tripodi, 1983). By clearly describing the intervention, you can ensure consistent implementation of the intervention as planned, thus increasing reliability and validity (Blythe & Tripodi, 1989). You can design a checklist of intervention guidelines to ensure consistent implementation (Blythe & Tripodi, 1989) or develop a client questionnaire to determine if you followed the guidelines (Tripodi, 1994).

Procedures for taking measurements during the intervention phase must be consistent with those of the baseline phase. The problem variables as well as the time between measurements should be identical to that of the baseline phase. The number of measurements taken during the intervention phase will vary, depending on the following: when you expect to observe changes (or lack of changes in the case of prevention) in the problem variable; the extent to which the severity of the problem variable deteriorates during intervention; or early attainment of treatment objective. The number of measurements taken during the intervention phase should demonstrate persistent achievement of the treatment objective when compared with a horizontally stable baseline (Barlow & Hersen, 1984). The absolute minimum number of measurements, however, should be the same number taken during the baseline phase (Tripodi, 1994) (see Figure 8.7).

During the intervention phase, you should examine the measurements to determine whether or not change occurs. If the problem variable does not change, then you need to determine the reasons

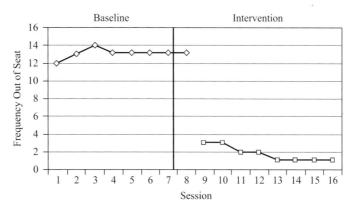

FIGURE 8.7 Baseline and Intervention Data for Out-of-Seat Behavior Over 16 Sessions of Observation

and whether or not to continue or modify the intervention. If the behavior changes after implementing the treatment, then there is strong evidence that the intervention changed the behavior. However, the simple phase change design does not necessarily demonstrate causation between the intervention and the target behavior, because other extraneous conditions may have influenced the behavior. You may either utilize an extension of the AB design, such as the ABA or ABAB, or replicate the intervention with another client to determine whether the behavior changed as a result of the intervention or due to extraneous conditions.

ABA Design

Counseling researchers may implement a third phase, which is referred to as follow-up, or ABA design. This phase involves the removal of the intervention to determine if the problem variable changes without intervention. Once the intervention phase has shown persistent achievement of the treatment objective, the intervention can be withdrawn and measurements for the follow-up phase can begin.

Measurements should include the same problem variable, the same counselor, and the same time interval between measurements as the baseline and intervention phases. The number of measurements taken, however, may vary. If the treatment objective indicates that the results of the intervention will last a certain amount of time, then measurements for follow-up are taken for that specified length of time. For example, if you expect treatment to last for a minimum of six weeks, then measurements are taken for a minimum of six weeks. If the treatment objective does not specify a length of time, then you should collect measurements until horizontal stability is established or for a minimum of eight measurements to detect any trend (Tripodi, 1994) (see Figure 8.8).

The ABA design can be used to determine if removal of the intervention leads to baseline behavior, which means the intervention was effective while being utilized. However, it is impossible to remove some interventions, especially if they include cognitive strategies that the client has learned and incorporated into his or her daily life. In this case, follow-up enables you to determine the lasting effects of a particular intervention and provide additional therapy as needed if the problem relapses. If the intervention is reintroduced, then the design becomes an ABAB design.

ABAB or Withdrawal-Reversal Design

The ABAB design is stronger than the simple phase change and the ABA design because it reintroduces the intervention phase after collecting follow-up measurements. This design controls many threats to internal validity (maturation, history, expectancy, and multiple treatment interference)

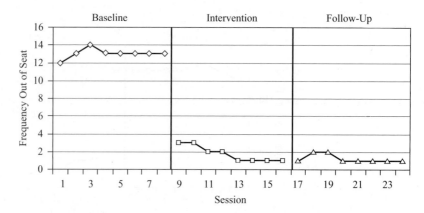

FIGURE 8.8 ABA Design: Baseline, Intervention, and Follow-up Data Collected Over 24 Sessions of Observation

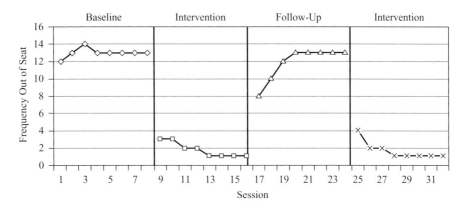

FIGURE 8.9 ABAB Design: Baseline, Intervention, Follow-up, and Intervention Data Collected Over 32 Sessions of Observation

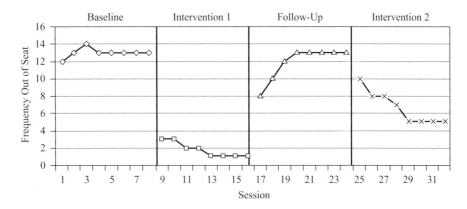

FIGURE 8.10 ABAC Design: Baseline, Intervention 1, Follow-up, and Intervention 2 Data Collected Over 32 Sessions of Observation

and more clearly demonstrates the connection between the intervention and the target behavior. Figure 8.9 provides an example of the ABAB design.

ABAC or Combined Simple Phase Change Design

Another extension of the simple phase change is the combined simple phase change design (ABAC). This design involves the comparison of two separate interventions. After implementing the first intervention strategy, you complete the follow-up phase and then introduces a new intervention (C). Measurements are taken during this phase and then compared with baseline, the first intervention, and follow-up phases. This allows you to determine if one intervention is more effective than another. Figure 8.10 provides an example of the ABAC design.

Conclusion

The simple phase change design and its extensions are extremely valuable for the practicing counselor. The simplicity of the design provides counselors with information for problem assessment as well as immediate feedback regarding the effectiveness of interventions for each client, thus making the counselor more effective.

However, the extensions of the simple phase change design require removal of the intervention phase, which may be unethical or impossible at times. For example, if a client was exhibiting severe aggressive behaviors, it would be unethical to withdraw an effective intervention. Similarly, it would be impossible to remove a cognitive strategy that a client has learned and incorporated into his or her daily life. Under conditions such as these, multiple-baseline design may be utilized.

MULTIPLE-BASELINE DESIGN

A multiple-baseline design is, in essence, a series of AB designs that are replicated by implementation (a) with the same person across different types of behaviors, (b) with the same person across settings, or (c) with the one behavior across different persons. This is considered an alternative to the ABAB design when it is not possible or ethical to withdraw a treatment (Foster, Watson, Meeks, & Young, 2002). In addition, counselors and researchers can collect data on several behaviors, or settings, or clients/students in comparison to centering on only one person, therefore obtaining a baseline for each setting, behavior, or person during the same period of time. You would apply the treatment at different points of time until all (behavior, setting, or individuals) are receiving the treatment. If the behavior change occurs only after the treatment has been implemented under each condition, the treatment is judged to be the cause of the change.

A multiple-baseline design across behaviors would be appropriate in the case of a student exhibiting several inappropriate behaviors in the classroom, and when you did not want to intervene with all behaviors for time efficiency, social validity, and treatment validity issues. An additional advantage of using a multiple-baseline design is that the intervention effects may generalize across behaviors, thus alleviating the need to intervene with each of the behaviors.

If several teachers are having similar problems with the same student, then multiple-baseline design across settings could be used. For instance, a student may be exhibiting disruptive behaviors in three different classrooms. In this situation, a multiple-baseline across settings design would be most advantageous for evaluating baseline and intervention. After collecting data in the baseline phase for all of the settings, treatment would then be implemented in the one setting with the most stability while baseline data continue to be collected in the other settings. The treatment could be that the student reduces the target behavior to an acceptable but obtainable goal to obtain a reward or activity at the end of the class period or time period. Intervention would be implemented sequentially in the second-most stable baseline setting.

The ultimate goal is to predict, verify, and replicate in the designs. For multiple baselines, these three goals can be accomplished and inherent within the design. As each baseline is changed at different intervals in time and the behavior changes reliably each time, we have then verified and replicated that the intervention was the reason for change in behavior. Finally, if the behavior changes in the desired direction, we have demonstrated prediction (Cooper et al., 2007).

As with the other designs discussed, multiple-baseline design has its advantages and disadvantages. The advantages are that the treatment or intervention does not have to be withdrawn. In addition, this design works well when the behavior is irreversible (e.g., learning has occurred). Finally, the design is relatively easy to understand. Although these are strong advantages, there are some limitations. First, a multiple baseline may be more time-consuming and may need more resources than other designs. This design is also weaker than a withdrawal design because experimental control is not always clearly present. Figure 8.11 provides an example of a multiple-baseline design.

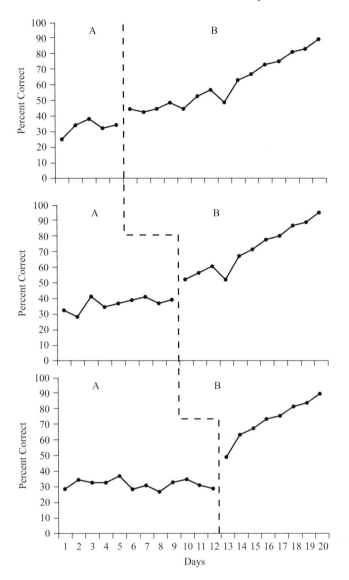

FIGURE 8.11 Depiction of a Multiple-Baseline Design Across Behaviors

Adapted from S. C. Hayes, D. H. Barlow, & R. O. Nelson-Gray. (1999). *The Scientist Practitioner Research and Accountability in the Age of Managed Care* (2nd ed.). Boston: Allyn & Bacon.

ALTERNATING TREATMENT DESIGN

There are times when you will want to answer the question: which intervention will work the best? The logic of an alternating treatment design (ATD) is a good alternative for examining two or more distinct treatments or interventions while examining the effects on the target behavior (Cooper et al., 2007). In contrast to other designs, the treatments are alternated regardless of the behavior response. Different treatments can be alternated in different ways, including (a) across days, (b) across separate sessions in the same day, or (c) within the same session. One of the key components is to counterbalance the treatments, which means that the treatments are never given in the same order. If you implemented the treatments in the same order every day or session, then the client could only be responding due to order effects. Thus, the confidence in the research results is diminished.

In an ATD, the ultimate goals of time series design—prediction, verification, and replication—are utilized. Each successive data point plays all three roles. The data predict future performance for each intervention, verify your previous prediction, and replicate the results that you previously obtained (Cooper et al., 2007).

The extent to which one can have confidence in the results of an ATD is the differential effects between treatments, which measure the vertical distance between the treatments. Obviously, a greater distance between the treatments produces larger confidence in the results. However, caution is noted because this depends on the target behavior. For example, two reading treatments were used in an ATD, and the target behavior was the number of words read correctly in one minute for a fourth-grade student. If the distance between the two treatments was three words, then the results may be somewhat powerful if you knew that children in the fourth grade only improve approximately one-half word per week.

Finally, there are several advantages of using an ATD. First, an ATD does not require a baseline. You can immediately examine the effects of multiple interventions or treatments. Second, when an intervention cannot be withdrawn due to ethical considerations or the treatment is irreversible because the student has learned, then an ATD is a good design. Third, a comparison of treatments can be observed quickly, which minimizes the sequence effects of other designs. Finally, an ATD can be used with unstable data.

However, with advantages there are always limitations. First, an ATD can feel artificial in nature by rapidly changing interventions in a counterbalanced order. Second, the design is limited in its capacity to examine other variables. Third, if the treatments do not diverge then the results are extremely limited.

Figure 8.12 gives you an example of an ATD with baseline and three treatments. The target behavior was number of digits correct per minute and number of errors per minute in mathematics. The intervention was how many trials (e.g., 3, 5, or 10) the child needed to be successful. As you can see, there was separation for 3 and 5 trials but some overlap with 10 trials. It appeared that 10 trials were going to be the most successful, but 3 and 5 trials had steady trends while 10 trials were more variable.

Once data are collected and inter-observer agreement calculated to ensure accurate data collection, you begin the next step of time series designs: graphing data.

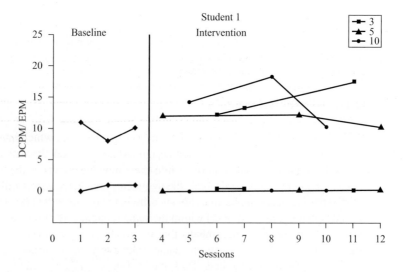

FIGURE 8.12 Depiction of an Alternating Treatment Design

GRAPHING: A HOW-TO PRIMER

Numerous authors have recounted the benefits of using graphs for interpreting and communicating results (e.g., Johnston & Pennypacker, 1993; Michael, 1974; Parsonson, 2003; Parsonson & Baer, 1978). In any time series design, the means by which the data are documented and a decision about behavior change is made through a graph. A graph allows for visual inspection of the behavior over time. *Graphing* is a relatively simply tool for organizing, storing, interpreting, and communicating results to others. There are several benefits to graphing, including that behavior change can be evaluated continuously; it requires little time, requires no special equipment, and is easy to learn; and it is a conservative method for determining change. Visual inspection is used to determine level, trend, and variability of the data over time to make decisions about the person's performance.

Graphing behavior can be executed through several different mediums. Only a few are discussed in this section. However, there are multiple software packages that can be obtained. The rationale for choosing the three that are discussed is that they are easy to obtain, free, and most people have access to them without having to purchase additional software. The easiest way is to use graphing paper to draw and number the axes, then plot the data. The phase change lines can then be drawn and the data plotting can continue. However, there are three other ways to graph behavior.

Two of these methods are to use graphs from Jim Wright at **http://www.interventioncentral .org/**, which has premade graphs that can be printed out. In addition, if charting academic progress, the data can be entered, and the chart will be automatically generated.[1] However, there are some limitations to using these resources. First, hand-graphed data do not look as professional as some other methods. Second, if entering the data on the website, several data points—or all of them— must be available at that time. This provides a limitation in visual inspection because you want to understand and inspect the data as they are collected. To make accurate and timely decisions, one needs to graph continuously and visually inspect throughout the process.

Finally, Microsoft Excel is one of the preferred choices because most people have access to the software. Carr and Burkholder (1998) provide an excellent primer on graphing different types of designs. The article takes a procedural perspective by giving step-by-step instructions.[2]

In the next sections, a discussion about types of designs to employ and the rationale to select each design is discussed as well as the strengths and limitations to each one.

ADVANTAGES AND DRAWBACKS

Single-subject research design has many advantages for the practicing counselor. The design can easily be built into your daily counseling practice and provide you with the tools for evaluating the effectiveness of interventions with individual clients, groups, or systems. Time series designs can be used to facilitate decision making regarding client assessment, treatment implementation, and treatment evaluation. You can gather data regarding specific client issues and interventions and develop models of empirically based interventions when working with specific clients. Clearly, single-subject research design makes clinical research compatible with routine clinical practice.

Single-subject research design also allows you to demonstrate accountability to clients and to the agency in which you work (Bloom, Fischer, & Orme, 2005). By using simple graphs, you can demonstrate change that a client has made as a result of a specific intervention. You can also begin to assess problems within your practice and can implement changes based on the results of those assessments.

---

[1] To understand more about graphing, please go to ***http://www.interventioncentral.org/.***
[2] To obtain more information about graphing in Microsoft Excel, please see J. E. Carr & E. O. Burkholder. (1998). Creating single-subject design graphs with Microsoft Excel-super (TM). *Journal of Applied Behavior Analysis, 3,* 245–251.

While single-subject research design has many advantages for the practicing counselor, the design also has some drawbacks. The cause-and-effect relationship is demonstrated for only one participant, which leads to concerns for external validity. If a client is aware that he or she is being observed multiple times, then client reactivity or sensitization could influence the responses, which leads to concerns for internal validity. The design also lacks statistical control, which could become an issue if graph results are ambiguous. Additionally, there are multiple ethical considerations you should address when developing and implementing single-subject designs.

ETHICAL CONSIDERATIONS

Your first duty as a counselor is to do no harm to your clients. Thus, ethical issues need to be taken into consideration when developing single-subject design studies. Many of the ethical concerns relate to any type of research, such as informed consent and Institutional Review Board consultation (for a thorough discussion of ethics in research, see chapter 17). However, there are several ethical issues specific to single-subject research. The ethical concerns are discussed in relation to the American Counseling Association's Code of Ethics (2005).

Independent Researchers (G.1.c.)

To protect the rights of the participant, all studies should be developed with the approval of an Institutional Review Board (IRB). However, if you are not affiliated with an IRB, then it is imperative that you seek consultation with someone familiar with IRB and single-subject design.

Informed Consent (G.2.a)

As with any research, all participants have the right to refuse to participate or to end their participation at any time. Each participant has the right to this information within the process of informed consent. With single-subject design, the consent should be specific in describing the methodology, including the fact that treatment may be halted, changed, or reduced during the study. Participants should be informed of limitations of confidentiality, dissemination of the research findings, and the benefits and risks of the study. Additionally, anyone participating in more than one study should be informed of each study and the implications of multiple studies on the participant's treatment and outcomes (Lackey, 1986).

Client Participation (G.2.d)

When a counselor decides to develop a single-subject design for use with a specific client, the client's best interests should always be taken into consideration. The study should not be conducted if the expected benefits to the client are minimal or if other treatments would be more beneficial.

Delay/Withdrawal of Treatment

Traditionally, treatment is delayed until an accurate baseline is collected. With a minimum of three data collections necessary, it may take several weeks before treatment begins. In counseling, it is unethical to withhold treatment from clients and it is often not in the client's best interest. Lundervold and Belwood (2000) recommend using this time to establish rapport while determining treatment options and conducting assessments. However, clients may change due to the relationship with the counselor. This chance of change should be taken into consideration when developing single-subject designs, because it may affect the baseline or treatments.

A unique situation with regard to single-subject design is that treatments are introduced, withdrawn, and often reintroduced. While this may occur in some instances in group design research, it is evident throughout single-subject design. When an effective treatment is withdrawn, the client could feel abandoned by the reduction in treatment (A.1.a.) or harm may be done to the client

(A.4.a.) (Reagles & O'Neill, 1977; Sterling & McNally, 1992). Should a treatment that is helping the client then be withdrawn to determine its effectiveness? The counselor conducting the research is ethically obligated to take the client's or participant's welfare into consideration, even if that means abandoning or altering the research study.

Confidentiality (B.1.c., B.1.d., B.7.d., G.2.e.)

When collecting data, all attempts must be made to keep the client's information confidential and private. This may be difficult in some settings. For example, in a school, the teacher may need to be informed as to which student you will be working with when observing the class. While you might not need to identify the student, your research procedures may reveal the participant's identity. For example, just sitting in a specific spot, focusing on a particular student when collecting data, or asking questions about the class schedule may inadvertently reveal your client's identity. Students are also perceptive and may guess your intentions. Additionally, when the results are published, the teacher and students may have access to the journal article, and thus have access to the participant's confidential information. It is your responsibility to inform the participant of possible inadvertent breaches in confidentiality before, during, and after the research.

APPLICATION TO COUNSELING OUTCOMES

Single-subject research design is considered to be "the best-kept secret" in counseling research (Lundervold & Belwood, 2000). This design encourages the counselor to focus on the individual client and evaluate the effects of an intervention immediately. Counselors can isolate the cause for behavior change(s) and objectively determine which intervention resulted in the most effective behavior change(s).

Single-subject research design is essential for bridging the researcher–practitioner gap. Counselors are ethically responsible for evaluating counseling effectiveness and contributing to the research base (American Counseling Association, 2005). However, many practicing counselors struggle with managing group research designs within their practice. Single-subject research design allows the counselor to focus on the individual client and still provide sound empirical data to demonstrate positive client outcomes.

Single-subject research design also provides information that counselors can use to make key decisions in practice. Issues of counselor effectiveness and accountability have become increasingly important. Empirical evidence is necessary to demonstrate effectiveness; the use of single-subject research design methods will allow counselors to demonstrate their accountability.

Summary

In this chapter, we provided you with the knowledge needed to effectively conduct a time series research study. You should now be familiar with the fundamental elements of methodology, the various types of time series designs, data collection procedures, and analysis techniques that are involved in this type of research. As is the case with any research process, the requisite skills for time series research are best acquired through collaboration, practice, and supervision. Because time series designs are so well-suited to the practicing counselor, it will be relatively easy for you to begin the process of conducting this type of research—you have ready made samples. Before taking on this task, we suggest that you immerse yourself in examples of current studies from peer-reviewed journal articles. Doing so will not only increase your understanding of time series methodology but also provide you with some insights for your counseling practice.

Review and Discussion Questions

1. Identify and explain the three guiding principles of time series designs.
2. List and explain the different ways behavior can be expressed.
3. Why would one determine the baseline before beginning research?
4. Which letters are used to identify different designs, and what does each letter represent?
5. What are the different elements of a graph, and how are they used?
6. What are the advantages and disadvantages of traditional and computer assessments?
7. What other factors should be considered when determining the type of assessment delivery system?
8. Describe and give examples of when each of the four types of timing would be used.
9. What measures can be taken to increase the accuracy of observations?
10. Why is it necessary to collect inter-observer agreement data?
11. What are the benefits of graphing research data?
12. Identify and explain two methods of graphing.
13. Compare and contrast the following design models: simple phase change, alternating treatments, and multiple baseline.
14. In what situations would you use each design model?
15. Identify and describe several advantages and disadvantages of single-subject research. After examining the advantages and disadvantages, do you believe single-subject research is an efficient research method?
16. Identify and explain why certain ethical concerns surround single-subject research.
17. Why is single-subject research considered the best-kept secret in counseling research?

CHAPTER 9

Grounded Theory Methodology

Matthew R. Buckley, *Walden University*

OBJECTIVES
After reading this chapter, you will:

- Be able to describe the importance of theory in a professional discipline.
- Be able to identify areas of inquiry that are best suited for grounded theory research.
- Be able to understand grounded theory as a qualitative research method.
- Be able to list the fundamental principals, methods, and rationale for conducting grounded theory research.
- Be able to recognize the importance of continually checking tentative conceptualizations to the data for goodness of fit.
- Be able to appreciate how bias within the researcher may enhance the research endeavor as well as influence the development of theory.

OVERVIEW

Imagine that you have decided to conduct research into marital dynamics of couples who are experiencing infertility. Immediately you will be faced with the challenge of deciding what variables to measure and how to measure them. You will need to locate or create assessment tools to measure the variables you select (e.g., communication, emotional closeness/distance, blame for the infertility, sexual difficulty, grief and loss, etc.). Furthermore, you will quickly encounter the frustration of realizing that many processes of human interaction cannot easily be reduced to observable or objectively measurable behaviors. So what would you do?

Out of this challenge, a group of nonempirical methods for investigating areas of interest to researchers were developed over the latter half of the 20th century. This group of methods that is utilized to develop in-depth understanding of human behavior is known collectively as *qualitative research methods*. In contrast to empirical research methods, which focus on the *what, when,* and *where* of human behavior, qualitative research investigates the *why* and *how* of human interactions. Subsequently, qualitative researchers identify a smaller focused sample (e.g., five couples with marital difficulty due to their inability to conceive) rather than a large random sample (250 women who have sought treatment at a women's hospital, some of whom are likely to be experiencing infertility). To collect in-depth data, qualitative researchers normally gather information by means of (a) detailed interviews of subjects, (b) participation in the setting where the phenomena exist, (c) direct observation of subjects, and (d) analysis of documents and other existing materials. Although there exist several classifications of qualitative research methodology (i.e., ethnography, narrative analysis, storytelling, and shadowing), the approach most relevant to the practice of counseling is known as *grounded theory*.

Grounded theory is a systematic qualitative methodology that emphasizes the generation of theory from data while in the process of conducting research. In this sense, grounded theory operates in a contrary manner to traditional research and at first may appear antithetical to the scientific method. Rather than beginning by choosing a theoretical framework, developing hypotheses, and applying a model to the studied phenomenon, in grounded theory a variety of data collection methods are the first step. After the data are collected, key points are marked or *coded* by reviewing the data. The coded data are then grouped into related concepts. From these concepts, categories are formed that become the foundation for the creation of a theory to explain the subject under investigation.

In this chapter, you will learn the foundational principles of grounded theory including methods of designing a study, procedures for data collection, methods of data analysis, and the implications for the counseling profession. In general, grounded theory is a qualitative research methodology that allows a counseling researcher to understand a topic of interest by investigating its existence within a real-world context. This method is utilized to formulate theories to explain phenomenon that can later be tested utilizing empirical methods. For this reason, grounded theory is often the research method employed when little is known about a subject related to counseling practice or training.

PURPOSE OF GROUNDED THEORY RESEARCH

The purpose of this chapter is to introduce counselors and other "helping" professionals to grounded theory methodology by laying a foundation for its use, and by describing the key concepts and how to conduct grounded theory research. The benefits and limitations of grounded theory methodology are discussed and an example of grounded theory study is presented (Buckley, 1997). Students will best approach this chapter by being open to how knowledge is a socially constructed phenomenon and how ultimately researchers affect and are affected by what they study. Qualitative methodology is a different way of looking at the world, and this perspective of inquiry has many parallels to how counselors are trained, how they develop, and how experience strengthens their view of the world.

Qualitative methodology develops rich descriptions of reality from the data by describing essential processes that capture aspects unattained by traditional quantitative methodology. For example, imagine that as a researcher you wanted to understand what the experience of attending counseling is like for individuals who are mandated by the court to obtain treatment as domestic abusers. If, after conducting a search of the literature, you learned that there is no research available on this topic, the most direct means to understand these clients would be to interview them. However, it is unrealistic to try to talk with a hundred such clients. Therefore, you might decide to conduct in-depth interviews with 8 to 10 such clients and their counselors, thereby beginning to develop a theoretical model about how best to treat them. In this example, you would be using qualitative research methods to formulate a theory based in counseling practice; hence, grounded theory.

Grounded theory uses data gathered from a variety of sources such as field observations, interviews, historical records, letters or journal entries, or activity logs. These allow respondents to describe their experience of a particular phenomenon, which yields vivid information and illuminates research problems for further inquiry (Haig, 1995). Grounded theory is unique in that the goal is to produce theory through a process that is grounded in "systematically analyzed data" (Haig, 1995, p. 1) through "constant comparative analysis" (Strauss & Corbin, 1994, p. 273). The researcher approaches a particular phenomenon of interest with theoretical sensitivity. This means the researcher has a solid conceptual and experiential base that allows him or her to know what questions to ask (Charmaz, 2006; Glaser, 1978). As data are gathered, analyzed, and repeatedly compared with what the researcher already knows, questions are refined and focused, and patterns emerge that illuminate important processes. These processes become the basis for a developing theory the researcher compares with the data and other existing theories. This constant comparison—checking and rechecking how the theory fits with the data—is how the theory becomes grounded.

Origins of Grounded Theory

Born in the science of sociology, grounded theory emerged through two seemingly opposing methodological research traditions developed by its founders Barney Glaser and Anselm Strauss. Glaser was a product of the positivist tradition at Columbia University, where quantitative research was regarded and promoted as the dominant research methodology. Conversely, Anselm Strauss trained in the tradition of qualitative field research at the University of Chicago, which holds a strong tradition in qualitative social science research. Strauss expanded the idea that participants were active in shaping their realities and not just passive observers of their respective worlds. He was also exposed to pragmatic data-gathering methods through getting out in the field among research participants, experiencing the world through their eyes, and describing their particular phenomenological worlds (Charmaz, 2006).

In the mid-1960s, Glaser and Strauss met at the University of California Medical Center in San Francisco and developed the methodology of grounded theory that focused on allowing data to drive the development of theory and creating specific and systematic processes for the analysis of data. Strauss and Corbin (1998) identified the beliefs and values that Strauss developed and were shared by Glaser. These values incorporate what grounded theorists believe about their work:

1. The need to get out into the field to discover what is really going on.
2. The relevance of theory, grounded in data, to the development of a discipline and as a basis for social action.
3. The complexity and variability of phenomena and human action.
4. The belief that persons are actors who take an active role in responding to problematic situations.
5. The realization that persons act on the basis of meaning.
6. The understanding that meaning is defined and redefined through interaction.
7. Sensitivity to the evolving and unfolding nature of events.
8. An awareness of the interrelationships among conditions (structure), action (process), and consequences. (pp. 9–10)

Grounded theorists do not seek to simply describe the events, conditions, and consequences of an area of study only for the sake of description, but consider it a critical responsibility to analyze and interpret these phenomena in the development of theory.

Characteristics of Counselors and Grounded Theorists

Qualitative researchers use their professional and life experiences to develop *theoretical sensitivity* (Morse & Field, 1995; Strauss & Corbin, 1998). Values, beliefs, perspectives, and experiences all influence and are influenced by the research process and analysis of the data. Strauss and Corbin (1998) described essential characteristics of a grounded theorist (see Table 9.1). Egan (1998) also described attributes of a seasoned helper or what he referred to as "helping wisdom" (see Table 9.1). As counselors gain practical experience, they develop sensitivity to what is effective with their

TABLE 9.1 Characteristics of a Grounded Theorist and an Effective Helper

Characteristics of a Grounded Theorist (Strauss & Corbin, 1998, p. 7)	Characteristics of an Effective Helper (Egan, 1998, pp. 19–20)
• The ability to step back and critically analyze situations	• The ability to "see through" situations; the ability to understand the meaning of events
• The ability to recognize the tendency toward bias	• Self-knowledge, maturity; the guts to admit mistakes and the sense to learn from them
	• Avoidance of stereotypes; holistic thinking; open-mindedness; open-endedness; contextual thinking; "meta-thinking" or the ability to think about thinking and become aware about being aware
• The ability to think abstractly	• The ability to frame a problem so that it is workable; the ability to reframe information
	• The ability to see relationships; the ability to spot flaws in reasoning; intuition; the ability to synthesize
• The ability to be flexible and open to helpful criticism	• The ability to embrace ambiguity and work with it; being comfortable with messy and ill-structured cases and, in general, the messiness of human beings; openness to events that don't fit comfortably into logical or traditional qualities
• Sensitivity to the words and actions of respondents	• A psychological and human understanding of others; insight into human interactions
• A sense of absorption and devotion to the work process	• The refusal to let experience become a liability through blind spots; the ability to take the long view of problems
	• The ability to blend seemingly opposing helping roles—being one who cares and understands together with being one who challenges and "frustrates"

clients, which guides their interventions (Buckley, 1997). The comparison of these two sets of characteristics strikingly underscores the notion that the training and experience counselors undertake to prepare themselves as counselors also aids them in becoming strong grounded theorists. Both Strauss and Corbin (1998) and Egan (1998) noted that these respective characteristics are gained through years of experience and are personalized by the researcher and counselor.

The Importance of Theory in Research

A comprehensive treatment of the function of theory is beyond the scope of this chapter; however, several concepts are important as a basis for the logic of grounded theory methodology. Theory provides the basis for action in an organized, logical sequence; accounts for consistency and variation within particular phenomena; and has explanatory and predictive power (Charmaz, 2006; Creswell, 1994; Glaser & Strauss, 1967; Marshall & Rossman, 1995; Morse & Field, 1995; Strauss & Corbin, 1998). A theory's *explanatory power* is its ability to accurately and completely describe a phenomenon and its process in such a way that the reader can draw conclusions and apply the theory in a variety of circumstances. A theory's *predictive power* is its ability to initiate action and predict causal relationships within key components and processes. Abstraction of a theory allows a broadening of its applicability within different contexts.

How theory is used in developing research also varies. In quantitative methods or the positivistic perspective (Charmaz, 2006), theory is used *deductively* to test hypotheses or research questions generated from the theory. Using carefully developed operational definitions and constructs, the researcher manipulates variables and quantitatively measures treatment effects.

Qualitative researchers, based in the constructivist perspective (Charmaz, 2006), use theory *inductively* by starting with a general area of interest, gathering data, asking questions, forming categories from the data, describing processes, and developing a theory or comparing what is discovered with existing theories (Creswell, 1994). Constructivist grounded theorists assume that data and their analysis are social constructions of reality; that researchers and what they study mutually influence each another; and that *reflexivity* is essential in helping put into perspective researchers' preconceived ideas, personal biases, and values as theory is constructed. *Reflexivity* occurs when researchers scrutinize the research process, decisions and interpretations, and the extent to which their "interests, positions, and assumptions influenced inquiry" (Charmaz, 2006, p. 189). Thus, how theory is conceptualized and constructed affects how it is used and interpreted within different methodological contexts.

Grounded theory is a way researchers think about the world and interpret their conceptualizations. "Theorizing means stopping, pondering, and rethinking anew. We stop the flow of studied experience and take it apart. To gain theoretical sensitivity, we look at studied life from multiple vantage points, make comparisons, follow leads, and build on ideas" (Charmaz, 2006, p. 135). Grounded theorists do not assume a "neutral" stance in their interpretation of the data but bring personal experiences, learning, influences, values, bias, and culture into the research endeavor to enhance the final product. The central purpose of grounded theory is theory creation; however, existing theories can also be expanded and their assumptions challenged. In grounded theory research, theory emerges from systematically gathered and analyzed data. Concepts, categories, and the eventual theory emergent from the data are constantly compared against the data for goodness of fit. Data collection and analysis, and theory generation stand in "reciprocal relationship" (Strauss & Corbin, 1998, p. 12) to one another. By comparing the emerging theory to the data that generated it, theory most closely resembles reality and is thus "grounded."

Grounded theory is especially suited for analyzing complex social processes between people and social structures and where no or inadequate theories exist about phenomena. Within the professions of counseling and counselor education, grounded theory has taken a greater hold and enhanced discovery in a variety of areas, including identity development in counselors-in-training (Auxier, Hughes, & Kline, 2003); how group counselors respond to group supervision (Christensen, 1999; Christensen & Kline, 2000); mutual influence between counselors and clients (Thorngren, 1999); how co-leader relationships develop (Okech, 2003; Okech & Kline, 2005); expert group leadership (Rubel, 2002); and students' perceptions of live supervision in individual, group, and couples and family counseling (Champe, 2004).

GETTING STARTED

As in any research endeavor, interest in a topic can develop from a number of sources. Personal interest in a particular area may stimulate further reading of the research literature. For example, a counselor may be interested in the concept of attachment in general (i.e., how relationships with caregivers develop in the formative years and affect future relationships) and specifically desire to investigate how attachment style affects career choice in adolescents. A divorced mother working on her counseling degree may want to examine unique stressors experienced by divorced, or single, working mothers. A volunteer counselor may be profoundly affected by his work with victims of natural disaster and develop an interest in expanding practical interventions with vulnerable populations. Developing these research interests may range from writing a paper for a class to being a member of a research team. How someone develops research interest is a varied and personal matter, and a process that could, itself, be a subject of inquiry. Marshall and Rossman (1995) also noted that intuition and imagination generate hunches within the researcher that will give substance and focus to the topic.

Quantitative methodology necessitates an exhaustive review of the literature in order to build an argument for one's hypotheses and to lay a foundation for the study. Grounded theory, in contrast, uses the review to develop an interest in the topic and stimulate questions that will start the data-gathering process. A balance of both approaches is necessary because researchers must be aware that immersion in the research literature may actually inhibit insights that may otherwise emerge during the process of analyzing data. Ongoing literature reviews are also often used as verification of concepts and codes developed during the data-gathering process. They may even guide sampling and the construction of interview questions. Accessing the literature numerous times during the research process can add context and richness to the emerging theory.

In an effort to illustrate the process of grounded theory research, I will refer to my dissertation on how counselors develop a personal counseling style beyond graduate training. My interest in the topic emerged because, at the time, I was a counselor with four years of experience working with clients in a variety of settings. This personal experience became the entry not only into the topic, but also my introduction to grounded theory methodology. What had become a significant, life-changing process within my own professional development evolved into a desire to understand others' experiences and perspectives within their own professional progress. As part of the dissertation research, an initial literature review was conducted to sensitize me to how counselors develop over the lifespan and what seemed to be the repetitive curative factors in working with clients. An experienced grounded theorist, Dr. William Kline, acted as a consultant throughout the research process and was invaluable in developing reflexive thinking and stimulating insights.

The primary question of study was:

"What was the process and experience that counselors engaged in when they decided what was therapeutic for clients?"

Related questions included:

1. What were the decisions counselors made about what to do or say with clients?
2. How did counselors arrive at their decisions?
3. What did counselors do or say?
4. What had counselors' experiences (professional and personal) taught them about what was and what was not effective in helping clients?
5. What did counselors believe were the most important therapeutic factors that effective counselors utilized in working successfully with clients? (Buckley, 1997, p. 17)

It was anticipated that these questions would begin to facilitate a discussion among counselors of why, how, and what they did when working with clients.

Selecting Participants and Data Gathering

Knowing how to gather data and how to select participants for a study are essential. As previously discussed, data collection can take a number of forms, and researchers must be intentional when deciding how to collect data (Charmaz, 2006; Creswell, 1994; Marshall & Rossman, 1995). Glaser held that "all is data" (Sacky Holdiness, personal communication, September 10, 2007) or, there is nothing that is *not* data that can be used to develop the emerging theory. Historical documents, case notes, journals, and data gathered for previous studies are available as nonintrusive forms of data collection. Observation data are generated from observing behavior within social contexts and recording in detail the observed behavior. Generally, data generated from participant interviews are the richest type of data because of the variety of perspectives from stakeholders (those involved directly in the phenomenon studied), who offer insights into their lives and direct descriptions of empirical events that stimulate insights into unseen but important processes. Reality is also viewed as a constructed phenomenon, which is at the basis of *symbolic interactionalism* (Blumer, 1969), a theoretical perspective that assumes people are dynamic, resourceful, and reflective and construct themselves, their roles, and society through interaction. Because reality emerges through interaction, these processes provide insights into how participants make sense of their experiences, and the participants are enriched by hearing themselves describe their experiences (Charmaz, 2006).

Because you as the researcher are invited to enter participants' worlds during data gathering, respect and sensitivity are important in facilitating trust and openness with participants as they share themselves through the data. The skills needed to do this include the ability to build trust, maintain good relationships, be sensitive to norms, obtain informed consent, remain ethical, be genuine, and preserve awareness of the importance of both physical and psychological entry into the research setting.

Using Focus Groups to Gather Data

Charmaz (2006) noted that qualitative researchers increasingly rely on "in-depth and focus group interviews" (p. 69) as indispensable data-gathering methods. Focus groups are composed of selected individuals that share similar characteristics and engage in a deliberate discussion about a particular topic area (Krueger, 1994). For example, focus groups were used to gather data in my dissertation study. Twelve licensed professional counselors (LPCs) practicing within a northwestern state (three males, nine females) were invited to participate in the study. I asked the counselors to share their experiences of what it was like for them to work as counselors, including how they approached their work with clients and how they made decisions regarding what to do in their work.

A review of the research literature drove my decision about sampling. Previous research on counselor development suggested that participants should have a minimum of three years' experience. Those with multiple years of experience were considered *individuation stage* counselors (Skovholt & Ronnestad, 1995). These counselors share similar characteristics and have sufficient distance from their professional training to "have continued to develop individually, and these individual paths have taken increasingly unique and separate ways." It was anticipated that these "individuation stage" participants would offer rich and important insights into their own process of development.

Two sets of focus groups of six members each were developed with two independent observers in each group. Two sets of raters were tasked to develop independent verification of the data between the groups and note potential differences. I acted as group facilitator and moderator. Participants' group interviews were taped and transcribed. These transcriptions constitute data. No identifying information would be included in the transcriptions except to identify each by their gender and a code number. Initial data gathering was conducted in the first round of focus groups. Analysis was conducted to develop ideas, themes, and concepts that would be used to refine further data gathering. This analysis involved categorizing the data through a process called coding.

CODING

Coding is the process of making sense of the data by succinctly describing what the data are telling the researcher. Coding involves labeling fragments of the data in such a way that each piece of data is categorized and summarized. Breaking down the data in this way helps the researcher begin to see nuances within the data and the complex relationships among *concepts, properties, and dimensions*.

Concepts are ideas that emerge from the phenomena being studied (Strauss & Corbin, 1998) in raw (unanalyzed) form. A variety of themes may be embedded in the specific language respondents use, how they describe their experiences, as well as what remains unspoken. These are concepts the researcher may cluster into categories. For example, from my research, a few concepts that emerged were *insight, efficiency,* and *intuition.*

Categories are general groupings of related concepts that help identify themes that emerge from the data. Categories emerging from my research might include "counselors celebrating client change," "client change expanding counselor self-efficacy," and "rewards of bring a counselor." Categories also have *properties* and *dimensions* that help further delineate richness of the particular category.

Properties are characteristics of the category that give it substance, richness, and meaning. These characteristics expand contextual understanding of a category and flesh out concepts. *Dimensions* constitute the range along which the properties of a category vary (Strauss & Corbin, 1998).

Charmaz (2006) described coding as generating the "bones" of a researcher's analysis and the eventual "theoretical integration" as assembling these bones into "a working skeleton" (p. 45). These coding structures all have specific uses, depending on the phenomenon being studied and the order in which they are used. As data are gathered, the coding process begins with two main phases: initial coding and focused coding (Charmaz, 2006).

Initial Coding

During initial or "open coding" (Strauss & Corbin, 1998), the researcher mines the data for all possible analytic ideas and theoretical avenues that have the potential to develop. Initial coding gives the researcher insight into areas that merit further exploration in follow-up interviews. This necessitates *theoretical sampling,* which is discussed later in the chapter. Data can be analyzed in detail by using word-by-word coding (Charmaz, 2006) or line-by-line coding (Charmaz, 2006; Strauss & Corbin, 1998).

Process observers are assistants who observe respondents and take notes in data-gathering settings. They get together with researchers to discuss hunches, meanings of words, and initial concepts. Word-by-word coding works best with transcribed data. A researcher taking notes in an interview is more likely to attend to data based on preconceived beliefs, values, and experiences and, thus, may code data within a narrowed scope. Although tedious, the detailed analysis of transcribed data can reap some important results. Documents or Internet data are also sources best suited for word-by-word analysis (Charmaz, 2006).

Line-by-line coding consists of naming each line of the dialogue to detect important processes within the data; it is where most grounded theorists begin their initial analyses. Lines of dialogue (i.e., larger segments of data) are analyzed much like word-by-word. The researcher takes care to label for action by using gerunds in place of their noun forms (Charmaz, 2006). A sample of line-by-line coding is located in Table 9.2.

TABLE 9.2 Sample of Line-by-Line Coding

Experiencing awe	F1: (speaking of a client) It was real profound and so I have to remember that with him I was truly the only one, who knew that he had positive attributes, and that he had something to look forward to. He really had nobody else in his life to really do that. So I think it's really powerful and I don't know how it happens. I truly don't know how that happened because I think it transcends—if somebody makes a small step forward, somebody made some progress . . .
Awareness of client's lack of social support	
Believing in client's potential	
Limited belief in client (from support system)	
Awareness of the power and mystery of the counseling process	
Awareness that small changes are significant	M2: You know it's really interesting that you used the word "powerful" because as you were describing this, I was thinking about how that's a worry . . . to many people . . . in the counseling profession, but sometimes it seems to me that it's all about power. It's about that good feeling that we have when we do our job, or when we believe we're doing our job well, that we have a certain kind of power, not omnipotent or spiritual, but some sense of power. It's almost like because that's such a rewarding feeling to us, when we see our client experience that feeling of having a certain amount of power or control in their lives, that it is just exhilarating when we see that they're sensing that they've done something they've chosen to do that's successful and it's something different and even they probably would describe it as power. They may describe it as building self-esteem or
Consensus about description of process as "powerful"	
Commenting on counselors' concerns (universal)	
Counselors trusting in counseling process (universal)	
Believing in self-efficacy	
Sensing power and influence with clients	
Rewards of being a counselor	
Witnessing clients' feeling their own power and control	

TABLE 9.2 Sample of Line-by-Line Coding (*continued*)

Vicarious satisfaction; excitement; accomplishment/success	the various words we use. But it is a very powerful feeling, both to know that you're helping someone. It's nice when your clients discover that awareness.
Describing clients' experiences; descriptors as "powerful" for similar experience	
Feeling successful in helping	<u>F1:</u> To see them walk a little taller.
Satisfying to see awareness	<u>M2:</u> Yeah.
Feeling satisfaction when clients discover their inherent power	<u>F1:</u> And you walk a little taller.
	<u>M2:</u> Yeah.
Both clients and counselors are uplifted—feeling proud	Moderator: Would you characterize that as kind of an awakening or kind of a sense of discovery for them when they have tapped into that hope that you're talking about or that belief that they can function?
Assessing meaning of client insight or hope	
Client self-efficacy	<u>F2:</u> Sometimes you want to describe it as the sun shining instead of clouds. Or something that causes them to wake up.
Describing metaphor of sun shining after a time of clouds; client awareness	Moderator: A shift in perspective?
Shift in clients' perspectives	<u>M1:</u> I think a shift; I think sometimes it's the "all or nothing" syndrome. That you can get clients to believe that the small steps are really, really important. It's like losing weight and if you don't lose 30 pounds, you lose five pounds this week, five pounds next week, then eventually you get there. And you reward and celebrate each step along the way.
Client belief in "all or nothing"	
Getting client to "buy in" to process of change	
Describing metaphor of losing weight related to change	
Change is incremental	<u>M2:</u> And it can come down to acknowledging that by the eye contact that you didn't have in a previous session. And it's what you're talking about. It's not just what they did at home or out, it's, "what's going on here?"
Celebrating each step	
Small changes manifest in relating; changing from session to session	
Being aware of, recognizing, and acknowledging client change	<u>F4:</u> "You're not looking at the wall any more." (laughter)
	<u>M2:</u> Celebrating that, I mean, really celebrating it.
Recognizing change, celebration; payoff for counselors; feeling powerful	<u>F4:</u> And just like with [F1], I've found that to be really powerful. That my client can look at me now or even smile occasionally. And I think that somebody here said that you had to be patient and you have to teach patience to your clients that they can't make these great big changes overnight, and that's hard because this is an instant society, you know. Right now. And everybody expects the thing right now.
Validating small changes	
Recalling other respondent's comment about teaching patience to clients	
Instilling realistic expectations; change conflicts with modern "instant" society	Moderator: That you're helping them see. Helping them measure their progress in the way that you've learned to measure their progress.
Helping clients develop a measure of progress	<u>F2:</u> And not forget that they're in the process of losing all those pounds, and of course she might gain a few back, but teaching them that it is a process and helping her to acknowledge that.
Helping clients embrace realistic view of change and trusting counseling process	

The line-by-line coding of this dialogue between counselors within a focus group illustrates what Charmaz (2006) referred to as "fresh, heavy, analytic work" (p. 68) on the front end of the analytic process. These respondents vividly described the elation they and their clients experienced when clients developed insight as an incremental process, a sense of their own efficacy, and a deeper trust in themselves and the counseling process. Numerous codes condense respondent action into bullet-like segments that act as material for further development. From this transcription, the line-by-line coding illuminates several concepts as potential categories: (a) counselors recognizing and validating change within clients, (b) clients recognizing change within themselves, (c) counselors using client change as validation for their work, and

(d) clients becoming realistic about change. These potential categories were used to develop follow-up questions and directions for further data gathering. These codes were also incorporated in multiple interviews. Researchers should code the second interview with the initial interview in mind and all subsequent interviews should be compared to the emerging theory (Sacky Holdiness, personal communication, September 10, 2007). Again, this comparison from interview to subsequent interview is consistent with the constant comparison process so integral to grounded theory.

Other coding processes within initial coding are important in analyzing data and include *incident-to-incident coding,* and *in vivo codes.* Some data, such as detailed behavioral descriptions of action where dialogue is minimal, are ill-suited to word-by-word or line-by-line coding. Behavioral descriptions of events are recorded in *field notes,* which are detailed annotations researchers make to themselves while gathering data. How the researcher approaches these descriptions is important. Charmaz (2006) points out: "Few novices have the eye and ear to record nuances of action and interaction . . . the mode of analysis matters. Comparative methods help [researchers] see and make sense of observations in new, analytic ways" (p. 53). Comparative methods include comparing events that are similar to others as well as those that are dissimilar. In vivo codes (Charmaz, 2006; Strauss & Corbin, 1998) are used to code specialized language respondents use during interviews. These terms and their meanings may be universally accepted to describe a concept or event or may be slang or "insider shorthand" (Charmaz, 2006, p. 55). Because words are important, respondents' language should be attended to and analyzed for meaning. In vivo codes should not be implicitly adopted as important concepts simply because they may appear unique and innovative. Often they are used to illustrate categories that capture more general but important processes.

Coding requires that researchers remain aware of the mutual influence of their own and their respondents' assumptions in the process of analyzing data and use language that accurately conveys the complexity of respondents' perspectives and experiences within the appropriate context.

Focused Coding

After initial coding is conducted, *focused coding* helps develop categories by grouping codes into larger segments based on emerging themes. Focused coding, also known as *selective coding* (Strauss & Corbin, 1998), begins to develop categories under which other concepts can be clustered. "Grouping concepts into categories is important because it enables the analyst to reduce the number of units with which he or she is working. In addition, categories have analytic power because they have the potential to explain and predict" (Strauss & Corbin, 1998, p. 113). Typically, one or two core categories will emerge that primarily explain the central process of the phenomenon of study.

As core categories emerge, they serve as the foundation of the emerging theory. Researchers should not be anxious to choose a core category, but allow the data to drive its development (Glaser, 1978). Allowing the data to drive the category is inherent in the concept of *theoretical saturation.* Theoretical saturation occurs when the analysis of data yields no additional conceptual strength to a core category. Once core categories are identified and saturated, the coding of unrelated data should cease and the process of integrating core categories should begin (Dick, 2005; Sacky Holdiness, personal communication, September 10, 2007). The integration of categories into a coherent explication involves a more abstract process referred to as *theoretical coding.* The researcher hypothesizes about relationships between categories that "not only conceptualize how . . . substantive codes are related, but also moves [the] analytic story in a theoretical direction" (Charmaz, 2006, p. 63).

Regardless of what emerges from the data in the process of open coding, researchers must take tentative categories and their dimensions and properties back and verify them against the data to ensure goodness of fit. Through synthesizing concepts, new ideas may emerge and either strengthen developing categories or take the researcher in new and unexpected directions (Charmaz, 2006).

In my study of how counselors develop a unique counseling style, line-by-line coding yielded some important tentative categories that led to theoretical coding. As I further analyzed the core category of *assimilating experience,* it became clear that as respondents evolved in their work with clients, they relied less on their graduate training as the primary source of their decisions and more on client responses as the primary standard by which to measure their interventions.

As beginning counseling researchers, it is important for you to know that you will begin to formulate some hypotheses about the nature of the qualitative data as you immerse yourself in the data and process of analysis. These insights can be invaluable and can help generate follow-up questions. Through the initial analysis, I discovered another core category related to the interaction between counselors and clients. *Relationship values,* which described the *beliefs about self* and *beliefs about clients* (subcategories), emerged from the data as preconditions respondents believed necessary to be effective in their work. These preconditions included a belief in the power of clients to change, trust in the counseling process, and counselors' trust in themselves and their own efficacy as subcategories.

From respondents' perspective, an initial property emerged within *relationship values* that described how counselors and clients experienced a parallel sense of their own efficacy and, occasionally, self-doubt. This corresponding process between counselors and their clients also related to the emerging subcategories of *mutual influence* and *mutual investment,* which initially were tentative categories but eventually clustered as subcategories under the dimension of *involvement effects,* which described how being involved in the process of counseling affected both counselors and clients in profound and meaningful ways. These concepts, subcategories, and core categories developed from this essential coding process would eventually be abstracted into a theory of counselor development. That abstraction took form from researcher memo writing, which permeated the data-gathering and analysis process and gave formal voice to hunches from the researcher and focus group observers.

WRITING FIELD NOTES, MEMOS, AND DIAGRAMMING

Recording impressions, insights, descriptions of what is seen in the data, connections between concepts, and follow-up questions takes place simultaneously with coding the data. Grounded theory researchers record these in the form of writing field notes, memos, and diagramming.

- *Field notes* constitute brief descriptions of what occurs during data gathering and initial impressions about what emerges from the data. Field notes can range from tentative but important insights to logistical lists of what the researcher needs to bring to the next interview. Note taking is also a way researchers converse with themselves about what they see going on in the situation being studied (Charmaz, 2006; Dick, 2005).
- *Memoing* is similar to field notes, but happens during the coding process and is comprised of the "products of analysis" that help direct the researcher to what is "analytical and conceptual rather than descriptive" (Strauss & Corbin, 1998, p. 217).
- *Diagramming* is memoing in visual form and depicts conceptual maps that help develop and delineate the emerging process. Diagrams are inherently dense conceptually and can capture an entire process at a glance. Diagramming also helps researchers begin to put together sequences of events within central and peripheral processes to form the emerging theory.

Respondents' direct quotes can also be included in memos and are often helpful in strengthening insights and ideas. "Providing ample verbatim material 'grounds' your abstract analysis and . . . permits you to make precise comparisons right in the memo" (Charmaz, 2006, p. 82). Memos often evolve into the final presentation of research results but do not, in themselves, have to be polished and in final form. Memos will, however, pull together concepts and become the basis for the final written research results.

During the research on how counselors develop their personal counseling styles, observers within the focus group sessions were instructed to record field notes regarding their observations. These observations were used to fortify emerging concepts and categories. At the end of one focus group session an observer noted:

> This is interesting. Just as members seem to really agree about the general themes being discussed they all seem to have different ways of saying or expressing it. Similar yet different. This is unique and personal to each group member. Their individual personalities came through in their answers and their interactions in group just as they profess about their own style of counseling and interactions with clients. Parallel. (Buckley, 1997, p. 210)

This observation strengthened the fundamental process of developing a unique counseling style—namely, that there are common experiences and nuances of style demonstrated in counselors' individualized expressions. It also underscored how descriptions merge in focus groups and that reality is socially constructed as participants described their common experiences as developing counselors.

During the third round of focus groups, another observer recorded a brief insight into how counselors and clients influence one another within the counseling relationship:

> Counselors read clues as to what clients are feeling/thinking. Clients come to know when counselors are getting a clear sense of what they are feeling. This enhances the counseling relationship. Going to "dark places" is a place counselors feel comfortable with in gaining client's trust after the relationship is built. (Buckley, 1997, p. 191)

These observer notes were a helpful source of triangulating the emerging themes in the data. *Triangulation* occurs when the researcher employs multiple sources of data collection and analysis to confirm his or her conclusions (Creswell, 1994). Observers noted that despite the respondents' unique processes, they were able to consensually define their emerging styles. This theme also emerged within each round of focus groups. The observer's field note regarding how counselors become adept at being sensitive to and reading clients' "clues" was another powerful piece of triangulation for the relationship effects between counselor and client. Consider a sample memo written about the emerging core category of "counselor validation" (see Table 9.3). This memo focused on the core category of how counselors learned from and were affected by their clients. This eventually emerged as a central category in describing how counselors validate their work.

Clustering is a technique in which researchers write down an idea and then branch out every conceivable association from the idea as a way of visually brainstorming and connecting categories. In its finished form, clustering looks much like a roughed-out diagram. *Freewriting* allows researchers to write in short bursts of time without the constraints of conventional form and parallels free association, encouraging writing down whatever bursts into researchers' consciousness (for a more in-depth description of these writing techniques, see Charmaz, 2006, pp. 85–91). The act of writing spontaneously or in notes, diagrams, or memos frees the researcher to think through—on paper or the computer—the connections emerging from the data in the moment. The developing theory is finalized through the process of theoretical sampling, saturation of core categories, and sorting.

TABLE 9.3 Example Memo About the Concept of Counselor Validation

---

Counselor Validation

Process: Counselors are describing a powerful process of learning from and being affected by their clients. To watch these counselors talk about their experiences is very compelling. Even the challenging (negative) experiences are somehow put into perspective when counselors share with each other their common, yet unique situations. They feed off of one anothers' comments in the group; it is not uncommon to hear them say, "Yeah, what you just said made me think of this," or "I see that, but I also see this too . . ." The group process is a very powerful validation for these counselors. It's like they don't even want to leave after the 2 hours are up. It speaks to the need of having counselors meet together often in a group to process their professional experiences: fears, struggles, successes, and failures. They are really hungry for it. I want to follow up with this idea of professional isolation and the need for connecting with other professionals.

Content: Counselors discuss developing a trust in their clients as they work with and get to know them. This trust is around the idea that clients are much stronger than they believe and counselors act on this assumption. One counselor talked about her concept of change in her own life and in the life of her client:

> F2: To me, the changes are kind of like you knock everything out of balance and then you have to readjust again and I think, in my own life, when I make changes I'm knocking everything out of balance; it turns everything upside down. And then everything has to readjust. And then you kind of put things back together and I think clients experience that there are those times when a client will come in and just be as angry as they can be at something that I have said, or something that I do say, and work through that. And leave angry and come back with all kinds of changes that have been positive. It's remarkable. I didn't do it. And I think that's one of my own belief systems, is that if things are going to change, things are going to have to get upside down first and I can't take responsibility for how they fall back in place because it's the client's strength that puts them back in place when they need to go back in place . . . .

This is representative of how other counselors speak about their clients and their beliefs about their strength and untapped potential. This idea of change being unbalancing within clients also parallels what occurs within counselors as they change and augment their unique counseling styles. There is being confronted with something that knocks them out of balance, seeking out solutions that may have worked in the past, consulting literature and past training experiences, seeking consultation, and relying on the strength of the counseling relationship.

THEORETICAL SAMPLING, SATURATION, AND SORTING

Theoretical Sampling

As researchers, you constantly compare your categories and concepts to the data through analyzing field notes, memos, and creating diagrams. This will help you detect which categories are thickly described and those that lack conceptual density. The terms *thick* and *dense* signify the need to layer emerging categories and interpret and describe complex processes and essential nuances in the data in abstract and meaningful ways. Conceptual density is achieved when the properties, dimensions, and processes of central categories are as fully and comprehensively developed as possible. Frequently, this requires researchers to collect more data through theoretical sampling (Charmaz, 2006; Strauss & Corbin, 1998). *Theoretical sampling* is intentional and induces the researcher to focus attention on samples representative of less than optimally developed categories. Through continued data collection in deficient areas, researchers can fill in the gaps, refine emerging categories, and discover new conceptual relationships. "Because theoretical sampling forces you to check your ideas against direct empirical realities, you have solid materials and sound ideas with which to work. You gain confidence in your perceptions of your data and in your theorizing about them" (Charmaz, 2006, p. 110).

Saturation

When a category becomes saturated, the gathering of new data fails to stimulate additional theoretical insights and adds nothing substantive to the emerging theory (Charmaz, 2006; Glaser & Strauss, 1967; Strauss & Corbin, 1998). Saturation is not the same thing as redundancy—repeatedly seeing the same pattern over and over again—but involves comparisons of incidents within the same category wherein no new properties occur. This outcome produces conceptual density and a rich and complete category (Charmaz, 2006). Like other aspects of grounded theory methodology, knowing when categories are saturated is sometimes difficult to determine. Because grounded theorists become immersed in the data and focused in analysis, they are in a prime position to determine when categories are saturated. Having other credible researchers with whom to reflect upon these issues and lend a critical eye to this process helps researchers assess saturation more concretely. Researchers are encouraged to examine their claims of saturation and the rationale for these claims. Proclaiming saturation is different from providing evidence for it (Morse, in Charmaz, 2006). Charmaz also pointed out that grounded theory shares the same vulnerability with other approaches in determining saturation. In the end, it requires researchers to tolerate ambiguity, work closely with their data, and be willing to reexamine prior assumptions when the concepts and categories do not match the data.

In studying how counselors develop a unique counseling style beyond graduate training, theoretical sampling was initiated to enrich *assimilating experience.*

Figure 9.1 illustrates the research process for the study (Buckley, 1997) with successive rounds of focus groups. Data sets were the transcribed focus group interviews from which the analyses were generated. From the first round of focus groups, I developed initial categories that were substantive and represented the data accurately but not comprehensively. Further sampling would include focused attention on *assimilating experience* as an important but underdeveloped category. Respondents shared that, as they gained experience in working with clients, their training experiences diminished in importance around what then became central to them—their work with clients. Clients became their primary source of learning, with aspects of their professional training being modified by what was learned from clients.

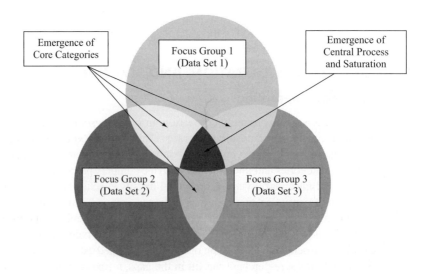

FIGURE 9.1 Phases of Focus Group Research for Counseling Style Development and Saturation of Categories

I initiated a third round of focus groups to saturate the emergence of what became well-developed categories and to further sample around the central process of *validation*: specifically, to see how counselors made decisions about what to do, how to intervene successfully with clients, and how to know their decisions were effective. After analyzing transcribed data from these focus groups, I determined the core categories were sufficiency saturated and analysis was shifting toward developing a theory that would describe the categories, their dimensions, and their properties within the frame of sequenced and interrelated events.

Sorting is a method researchers use to organize their analytical notes, memos, and diagrams into a logical sequence that stimulates the developing theory and organization of the written results of the study. Sorting, analyzing, and diagramming are interrelated processes that occur simultaneously within the analysis phase of research and are conducted for the sake of developing theory (Charmaz, 2006). During the analysis phase of the research on developing a unique counseling style, category names, properties, dimensions, and concepts were written on 3×5 note cards and color-coded for convenience. These cards also represented various memos that were written and catalogued for further analysis. These cards were spread out on a large table, sorted in a variety of configurations, and recorded in diagram form. An experienced grounded theorist was available to consult about various sorted configurations until a few tentative but parsimonious configurations were created that appeared to explain the data comprehensively. During the last sorting session, the cards were taped to the wall in an arrangement that created a framework for the entire body of data. A diagram was developed from this final sort to describe the process of validation. Categories were compared with the data through all phases of the analysis such that the diagram represented the process counselors engaged in as they decided what to do in their work with clients. This process also closely matched the empirical experience generated from data and observations (field notes) along with periodic literature reviews that triangulated the emerging theory. The sorted categories then drove the remaining final analysis as memos and notes were reviewed in this particular configuration and conceptualized theoretically. Constructing the theory became the end product of a rigorous, but rewarding journey.

THEORY CONSTRUCTION

Constructing a theory, writing the results of the research, and ensuring trustworthiness of the findings are the final steps in the grounded theory process. Thinking theoretically is an important function (Glaser, 1978) and is well practiced and finely tuned through the data-collection and analysis phases of the research. "A theory can alter your viewpoint and change your consciousness. Through it you can see the world from a different vantage point and create new meanings of it. Theories have an internal logic and more or less coalesce into coherent forms" (Charmaz, 2006, p. 128). Theoretical sensitivity is heightened and the researcher has literally become immersed in the data. This immersion makes the researcher sensitive to developing a theoretical perspective that will describe the phenomenon in specific and unique ways. Theory construction, like all other phases in the research process, is deliberate and should develop from the analytic work constructed through memos and diagrams.

The writing of the research should largely come from written memos. Although initially a tedious process, well-written memos have the benefit of making up the major building blocks of the formal publicized results. Because categories and fundamental processes have been meticulously developed, richly described, and refined, the final product is a matter of formalizing the results. This is not to say that writing is easy. Writing is a very personal endeavor and requires discipline in crystallizing the results and presenting them in a logical, persuasive, and interesting way. An excellent discussion of and practical advice for writing research results can be found in Charmaz (2006).

ENSURING TRUSTWORTHINESS OF THE FINDINGS

Validity in grounded theory is measured by the dependability of the conclusions on which the theory is based. Consistent with the analysis of any research study—whether qualitative or quantitative—is ensuring validity or trustworthiness of conclusions drawn from the analysis. Miles and Huberman (1994) described 13 strategies for testing the strength of findings in a qualitative study. These strategies overlap one another and enhance credibility of the findings:

1. Check for representativeness.
2. Check for researcher effects.
3. Triangulate findings.
4. Weigh the evidence.
5. Check for outliers.
6. Follow up surprises.
7. Look for negative evidence.
8. Make if-then tests.
9. Rule out spurious findings.
10. Replicate a finding.
11. Check out rival explanations.
12. Get feedback from informants.

An important perspective to maintain when checking for trustworthiness is to recognize that studied phenomena are context-based and time-bound. What enhances the richness of grounded theory research is the description of a central process and accurately rendering respondents' collective stories. Readers are then left to develop their own insights into the meaning of the findings. I used some of these tactics in my study.

VALIDATION: A THEORY OF COUNSELOR DEVELOPMENT

Throughout my research process, I constantly compared the data with emerging concepts and categories and the development of a central process. Through three rounds of focus groups, theoretical sampling was conducted, research questions were refined, and a final description of the process of how counselors progressed beyond their training and an elaboration of central concepts were developed.

Assimilating experience and *relationship values* were two categories that emerged prominently within the first round of focus groups. A second round of focus groups added *conceptual density* to these categories, and coincidentally, *validation* emerged as a third category. Figure 9.2 illustrates the distillation of coding into a final diagram of the central process of validation. Concepts related directly to the validation process are underlined in order to orient the reader to this process embedded within discussion of the theory. Other categories and concepts are *italicized* to alert the reader to the essential underpinnings of this grounded theory.

Assimilating Experience

Respondents described their beliefs and perceptions regarding what graduate training and postgraduate experience taught them about what was useful in working with clients. Properties related to the category of assimilating experience included training experiences, learning from clients, assimilating learning experiences, trusting in self, integrating experience, and developing intuition.

Assimilating learning experiences occurred as counselors built upon their training experiences by experimenting with new techniques and interventions not previously tested in graduate training. Respondents shared consistent perceptions that the process of assimilation felt risky. Risk

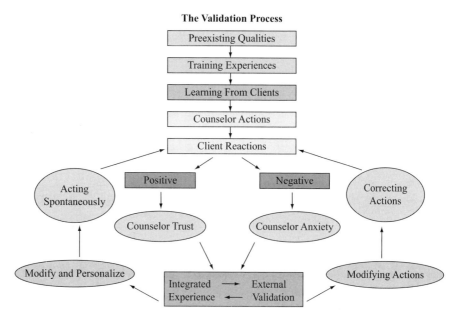

FIGURE 9.2 The Validation Process

occurred when respondents used techniques unfamiliar to them and became more immediate with clients by spontaneously sharing their perceptions. Client responses (i.e., client reactions) to these risks determined how respondents modified and/or confirmed their counseling style (see Figure 9.2). Assimilating learning experiences was a part of the process respondents employed to shape a personalized counseling style.

Respondents discussed arriving at a phase in their development where they felt comfortable integrating their experience into a personal counseling style. Expression of their personal style or counselor actions (see Figure 9.2) was supported by how clients responded. As clients responded in a positive manner to counselor interventions, respondents felt encouraged to employ more personalized techniques and interventions (see Figure 9.2). Integrating and assimilating were mutually influential processes. As respondents built upon their training experiences, their experimentation led to an expanded repertoire of techniques and interventions that became progressively personal in nature. Integrated experience was characterized by respondents feeling confident in their abilities and experiencing a high degree of trust (i.e., counselor trust; see Figure 9.2) in their own efficacy.

Developing intuition was also an important concept linked to integrating experience. Intuition is the ability to perceive client problems from deep insight precluding conscious cognitive processing. Intuition grew from experience. Respondents increased in intuitive ability when clients responded positively to their personal style. As respondents increased in their ability to sense client needs and verbalize their intuitive impressions, clients reciprocated with increased trust in the counseling relationship and counselor disclosure, willingness to try new behaviors and modes of relating in interpersonal relationships, and willingness to take personal responsibility for the condition of their lives.

Relationship Values

Relationship values described the values that respondents had regarding their work with clients. These values included beliefs counselors possessed that guided their actions in counseling with clients. The counselors employed personalized interventions based on their values and intuition.

Based on client responses, counselors experienced feeling successful or frustrated in their work. Client responses and counselors' reactions to those responses constituted involvement effects. Involvement effects were a primary source of validation for counselors in molding their personal counseling style.

Actions (i.e., counselor actions) that counselors initiated in the counseling relationship were connected to and guided by their beliefs and values. Actions included techniques, interventions, and roles that respondents employed to help clients. As respondents modified their actions based on client reactions, they also modified and confirmed their beliefs about the counseling relationship. As respondents modified and confirmed beliefs, they viewed themselves and their training experiences differently. Respondents developed the ability to be pragmatic in their work with clients based on the counseling relationship. They used what worked. Respondents also consistently described a process of personalizing techniques, interventions, and roles congruent with their personalities and values.

Counselors also consistently described experiencing involvement effects in their work with clients. They also believed that clients experienced effects from counseling based on their reactions to what occurred in the relationship. Clients reacted to the counselors' personalized styles as the counselors continued to utilize integrated experience (see Figure 9.2) in working with clients.

One involvement effect respondents described was anxiety. Counselor anxiety occurred when clients reacted in a negative manner to the counseling process (see Figure 9.2). Respondents described that as clients reacted negatively by withdrawing emotionally from the relationship and expressing resistance, fear, and frustration, clients were best served by counselors modifying actions by focusing on the counseling relationship and going back to basic relationship-building skills learned in graduate training (see Figure 9.2). Another aspect of anxiety was respondents realizing their own limitations and the limitations of counseling. Respondents recognized that they could not help every client and occasionally felt frustrated by this limitation. Respondents addressed their own anxiety by reverting to what worked. When clients reacted positively as evidenced by increasing disclosure and trust in the relationship, taking personal responsibility for problems, gaining insight, and incorporating behavioral changes based on insight, counselors felt more confident to shape and express their personal counseling style. Respondents engaged in correcting actions in the counseling relationship based on what they perceived helped clients (see Figure 9.2). Involvement effects were also a primary source of validation for counselors as they developed their personalized styles.

Validation

Validation emerged not only as a category but as another central process counselors utilized to form their individual styles. Validation occurred when respondents acted based on their values embedded in integrated experience, and clients responded. Respondents engaged in modifying actions based on internal validation that occurred within the counseling relationship and external sources of validation that included sources outside of the counseling relationship.

Internal validation primarily consisted of client reactions and respondents' internal responses to those reactions. Counselors believed that they learned from clients by being sensitive to client responses and sensitive to their own internal reactions in the counseling relationship. As respondents used their intuition, client reactions confirmed or disconfirmed counselors' perceptions and actions. If clients reacted in a positive manner, counselors' confidence increased in their ability as counselors to use spontaneous actions from their intuition, clients' ability to use counseling beneficially, and the efficacy of the counseling process. Counselors also became confident in their ability to modify and personalize their interventions within their work with clients (see Figure 9.2). When clients reacted negatively to counselors' intuitive verbalizations and interventions, counselors took action based on their experience. If negative client reactions were not beyond the scope of their experience, respondents experienced minimal anxiety. If negative client reactions were unexpected, respondents experienced higher levels of anxiety (i.e., <u>counselor anxiety</u>) and reverted back to assimilated and tested interventions. Counselors described this process as getting back to "those basic relationship building skills." Counselors were confident that when they focused on the counseling relationship, what was unclear about negative client responses would become clearer, and this type of internal validation was important in developing their personal styles.

Counselors also described seeking sources of validation outside of the counseling relationship. <u>External validation</u> included supervision, peer consultation, research literature, and professional workshops (see Figure 9.2). Respondents described utilizing external sources of validation when they experienced apprehension about their ability and efficacy. Respondents also used external validation to confirm that what they did with clients was effective. Respondents' reality tested their perceptions and interventions by comparing them with the experience of other professionals. Counselors consistently perceived that both internal and external sources of validation were essential to their development.

Assimilation of experience, relationship values, and validation were confirmed as essential elements in counselor development. They provided the framework for a grounded theory of counselor development in which validation surfaced as the overarching process respondents used to develop their personal counseling style.

As categories were developed and the theory took shape, meeting with respondents and describing the emerging theory was the primary form of ensuring the trustworthiness of the research results. Checking with respondents to ensure that the researcher is accurately representing their experiences and conceptualizing their process is essential in the constant comparative process, and makes certain that the grounded theory is valid (personal communication, William B. Kline, October 8, 2007). Literature reviews and subsequent interviews with experts in the area of counselor development also triangulated the results and confirmed the emergence of these categories and concepts from the data as accurate and meaningful.

Summary

Grounded theory starts with a research idea that is suited to this methodology, which is intended to discover process, to render a constructed reality from research participants' sharing, and to generate a theory that explicates how a phenomenon occurs within time- and situation-bound contexts. Grounded theory stimulates fresh insights and perspectives that lead to further discovery. Those training to become counselors have the opportunity to instill within themselves qualities (i.e., active listening, effective questioning, interpreting the relationships between phenomena, tolerate ambiguity, etc.) that can make them strong grounded theorists. Those who use grounded theory prize what emerges from the data and carefully, consistently, and meticulously compare concepts, categories, properties, and dimensions to the data from which they surfaced. Coding helps organize concepts within a usable frame. Note taking, memo writing, and diagramming serve to refine what occurs to the researcher, document the process of the developing theory, and provide the foundation for the written results.

The specific phases of the research are encompassed in sampling, data collection, and analysis, which mutually influence and enhance each other. Counselors constructed a described experience of themselves as a therapeutic instrument in the counselor–client relationship as they blended insight with intuition within the validation process.

As a counselor, it is my hope that you will participate in and utilize research to validate the success of interventions and theoretical approaches for specific populations with whom you work. It is an important perspective to maintain that "while the researcher may use a variety of instruments to gather data, the primary research instrument is the *researcher*" (Erlandson, Harris, Skipper, & Allen, 1993, p. 16). The future of grounded theory methodology will largely be determined by how counselors, counselor educators, and supervisors embrace this research perspective and utilize it in the service of discovering and explicating the varied processes that occur within our profession.

Review and Discussion Questions

1. What personal qualities and characteristics do you possess that might make you an effective grounded theorist?
2. How is a counselor's ability to attend to the verbal and non-verbal messages consistent with the gathering of *rich* data?
3. How is *theoretical sensitivity* developed within the researcher? What do you think the importance of theoretical sensitivity is within the research process when conducting a grounded theory study?
4. How would learning to tell stories be beneficial to a grounded theorist?

5. What do you believe are the areas of inquiry best suited for grounded theory studies? What research questions might grounded theory not be suited for?
6. How do grounded theorists determine when categories are saturated?
7. How do the concepts of validity and verifiability relate to the trustworthiness of the data and emerging theory within grounded theory research?

CHAPTER **10**

Phenomenological Designs:
The Philosophy of Phenomenological Research

Teresa M. Christensen, *Old Dominion University*
Kristy A. Brumfield, *Xavier University*

OBJECTIVES
After reading this chapter, you will:

- Be able to describe the importance of phenomenological research in counseling.

- Be able to identify areas of inquiry that are best suited for phenomenology research.

- Be able to understand phenomenology as a qualitative research method.

- Be able to list the fundamental principals, methods, and rationale for conducting phenomenology research.

- Be able to recognize the importance of continually checking tentative conceptualizations to the data for goodness of fit.

OVERVIEW

Phenomenology was initially proposed as a school of philosophy and appeared in the writings of Edmund Husserl (1859–1938), a German mathematician. Husserl (1970) offered one of the first definitions of pure phenomenological research as a question that starts from a perspective free from hypotheses or preconceptions and whose answer describes rather than explains. Miller and Salkind (2002) offered a succinct and clear description of phenomenology as a method that seeks to describe the meaning of the lived experiences surrounding those who are intimately involved or confronted with a concept or a phenomenon. According to Polkinghorne (1989), phenomenologists explore the structures of consciousness in human experience. Thus, *phenomenology* evolved into more than a school of thought rooted in philosophy and psychology; it is seen as a method within the realm of qualitative research that focuses specifically on the subjective experiences of individuals. While all qualitative research attends to individuals' experiences, phenomenology "seeks to understand the essence or structure of the phenomena" (Merriam & Associates, 2002, p. 93). In this chapter, you will learn the foundational principles of phenomenology research including methods of designing a study, procedures for data collection, methods of data analysis, and the implications for the counseling profession.

PURPOSE OF PHENOMENOLOGY RESEARCH

Phenomenological researchers view the person and his or her world as inextricably linked, thus they refrain from focusing on the world or individual as distinct entities and explore the essence of the meaning of their interaction. Phenomenology focuses on participants' perceptions of their experiences and circumstances (Creswell, 1998; Gay & Airasian, 2000; Merchant, 1997). Accordingly, the researcher's mission is to keenly observe the interaction and dialogue between person and world. As Van der Mescht (1999) proposed, "eavesdrop, as it were; to listen in, and capture the essence of what is perceived by the subject" (cited in Merriam & Associates, 2002).

The purpose of phenomenological research is to answer the question: "What is the meaning, structure, and essence of the lived experience of [a particular] phenomenon by an individual or by many individuals?" (Johnson & Christensen, 2004, p. 363). Thus, phenomenological studies pertain to questions about everyday, lived, human experiences. Examples of phenomenological studies by counselor educators and researchers include (a) African American parents' perceptions of play therapy and counseling (Brumfield, 2006); (b) the experiences of orthodox Christian students attending public, secular, or counseling graduate programs accredited by the Council for Accreditation of Counseling and Related Educational Programs (CACREP; Schaefer, 2006); (c) elementary school children's perceptions of play therapy (Green & Christensen, 2006); (d) supervisees' perceptions on childhood memories and receptivity to corrective feedback in group supervision (Alexander, 2002); counselor educators and qualitative research—affirming a research identity (Reisetter, Korcuska, Yexley, Bonds, Nikels, & McHenry, 2004); and (e) the death of a loved one (Johnson & Christensen, 2004). As these examples illustrate, the purpose of phenomenological research is to address questions that pertain to a lived experience whereby answers can be derived from participants who have lived through that particular experience. Patton (2002) describes phenomenology as a means or method of

> Exploring how human beings make sense of experience and transform experience into consciousness, both individually and as shared meaning. This requires methodologically, carefully, and thoroughly capturing and describing how people experience a specific phenomenon—how they perceive it, describe it, feel about it, judge it, remember it, make sense of it, and talk about it with others. (p. 104)

As such, phenomenology is interactive and relies on the relationship between the researcher and the participants (Merchant & Dupuy, 1996). The qualitative researcher invites the participants' feedback, acknowledging their "expertise . . . regarding their own experiences" (p. 540). This process is not unlike counseling, as the researcher gains the participants' trust, uses active listening skills, seeks clarification, and finds themes to deepen understanding of the material presented.

In fact, Merchant (1997) indicated the usefulness of qualitative methodology in the field of counseling. The skills and training common to counselor training programs are especially applicable in this process of inquiry. Both counselors and qualitative researchers must be aware of cues given by the client or participant, and both seek to empower the individual offering information.

Terminology

As noted by Newsome, Hays, and Christensen (2008), several key terms are associated with phenomenology. One such term is the German word *Lebenswelt,* which means *life-world.* Life-world refers to a combination of feelings, thoughts, and self-awareness experienced by an individual at any given moment in time (Johnson & Christensen, 2004). Phenomenologists seek to understand individuals' life-worlds at a deep level and to then describe that life-world as it applies to a particular experience. Phenomenologists must empathically enter the lived world of the research participant in order to gain a true understanding of the meaning of that world from the participant's point of view. In many ways, the role of the phenomenologist is comparable to that of the counselor who empathically and nonjudgmentally enters into the world of his or her client in order to provide therapeutic help.

Another term associated with phenomenology is *bracketing,* or the process of *epoche,* which refers to an intentional process whereby researchers attempt to extract their own biases and explain the phenomenon in terms of its own intrinsic system of meaning (Merriam & Associates, 2002; Newsome et al., 2008). Researchers *bracket* when they apply various steps to "set aside" their assumptions or beliefs about a phenomenon in order to reflect on how that phenomenon manifests itself in the lived world of the participant (Christensen, 2005). Bracketing occurs before the researcher enters the world of the participant and involves the researcher consciously exploring, documenting, and then setting aside any preconceptions, biases, or learned feelings about the phenomenon under investigation. For example, in Brumfield's study of African American parents' perceptions of play, play therapy, and counseling, she made efforts to expose characteristics about herself, such as gender, race, experiences as a researcher; beliefs about play, play therapy, and counseling; and assumptions about what participants might say (2006). Researchers are encouraged to explain specific steps they will take to refrain from allowing the influence of their experiences to interfere with data collection and analysis procedures. Likewise, researchers are encouraged to describe how they will gain an in-depth understanding of each participant's unique, lived experience.

In addition to understanding the unique experiences of the individuals in a phenomenological study, researchers also search for commonalities among experiences. The commonality of lived experiences is known as the *essence* of the phenomenon (Newsome et al., 2008). In other words, there are some universal, core elements of experiences that researchers attempt to determine. For example, grief and sorrow are core elements associated with the death of a loved one (Johnson & Christensen, 2004). Searching for the essence of an experience is one of the defining characteristics of phenomenology. While there are other terms that pertain to phenomenology, they pertain directly to data collection and analysis procedures and are discussed later in this chapter.

CONDUCTING PHENOMENOLOGICAL RESEARCH

Role of the Researcher

As noted previously, phenomenological researchers play a critical role in the research because they serve as the primary instruments for data collection and analysis (Merchant, 1997; Miles & Huberman, 1994). Therefore, the researcher is encouraged to be open to self-disclosure of biased values and beliefs as a primary step in bracketing his or her perceptions. Furthermore, the researcher is encouraged to validate the significance of participants' experiences by actively listening, attempting to understand from the participants' perspective, and illustrating this understanding regarding any given concept that a participant describes. Illustrations can include visual representation of themes, descriptions of findings, and the utilization of participants' words to define and describe concepts.

When it comes to methods to prepare qualitative researchers, Merchant (1997) noted that some of the preparation that counselors in training receive is synonymous with the training that qualitative researchers often undergo. Specific characteristics identified as being synonymous for good counselors and good researchers include, but are not limited to: (a) awareness of one's own worldview; (b) ability to enter the client's/research participant's worldview; (c) acknowledgment of polydimensionality, the contextual and nonlinear nature of human experience; (d) use of narratives and stories; (e) tolerance for ambiguity; (f) focus on process and content; and (g) empowerment as a goal (pp. 12–14). Furthermore, Reisetter et al. (2004) found that "worldview congruence, theory and skills congruence, research identity and professional viability, and holistic nature of perceptions and experiences" (p. 2) were among the themes that doctoral students used to describe their experiences when conducting qualitative dissertations in counselor education.

Participant Selection

Participants, who often are called co-researchers, are selected because they have experienced the phenomenon being studied and are willing to share their thoughts and feelings about it (Christensen, 2005). While the number of participants can vary, depending on the nature of the research

(Newsome et al., 2008), between 8 and 10 participants are recommended for most qualitative research (Creswell, 1998; Miller & Salkind, 2002). However, Polkinghorne (1989) indicated that researchers typically include groups of informants that range between 5 and 25 individuals. In contrast, Wertz (1985) noted that between one and six participants may be sufficient when conducting phenomenological research.

Purposeful Sampling

Sampling in qualitative research differs, both in purpose and in method, from quantitative research. In quantitative research, the researcher utilizes probability sampling in order to generalize about the broader population from which the sample was drawn. To accomplish this task, random samples are selected from the representative population (Newsome et al., 2008). In contrast, qualitative researchers typically do not engage in probability sampling; instead, they select purposive samples (Creswell, 1998) so that the research question can be explored most effectively. In phenomenological research, *criterion* sampling ensures that all participants are purposefully selected based on the fact that they have experienced a similar phenomenon—for example, elementary school–age children who receive counseling (Green & Christensen, 2006) or individuals who experience the death of a loved one (Johnson & Christensen, 2004).

Measures to Ensure Participants' Safety

Due to the fact that phenomenological research can reveal intimate details about research participants, special measures must be taken to ensure that participants are protected and that they remain anonymous. Before the onset of data collection, participants should be familiarized with the research process, informed about their rights, and warned about potential risks related to participating in any investigation. For example, in the case where the researcher interviewed participants who had lost a loved one (Johnson & Christensen, 2004), prior to the interviews, the researchers informed participants about the potential discomfort that they may experience as a result of discussing what they have been through and what counseling was like, if they, in fact, had sought such services.

In the case of phenomenology, participants should also be informed of their right to confidentiality as well as the limits associated with confidentiality in this type of study. Participants should be encouraged to select a pseudonym or have one assigned to them as a means to protect their identities. Finally, participants involved in a phenomenological investigation should be assured that they have a right to leave the study at any time, without consequence.

Participant Profiles

In many phenomenological studies, individual and group participant profiles are created to provide a detailed description of each member who agreed to participate in the study, thus sensitizing the reader to the participants' unique characteristics (Alexander, 2002; Brumfield, 2006; Schaefer, 2006). These profiles are compiled from information provided by participants in response to a demographic survey or specific questions that arise at the beginning of initial interviews, and from additional information gained both verbally and nonverbally throughout the duration of data collection. According to Seidman (1998), participant profiles serve as a way to present the data in the context of the specific participant. Thus, profiles help create a narrative about categories, themes, and patterns as they emerge.

INDIVIDUAL PROFILES   Individual profiles can be comprised of general demographic information about participants such as race/ethnicity, gender, age, religious affiliations, number of children, level of education, work experience, and geographic location. Additionally, individual profiles can be generated with information that is specific to the phenomena under investigation. For example, in a study about counseling with children affected by Hurricane Katrina, profiles might include information about where children evacuated, whether or not their homes were destroyed, whether or not their schools were destroyed, and whether or not they lost family members because of the hurricane.

GROUP PROFILES   Group profiles include a compilation of characteristics that pertain to all participants. The goal of a group profile is to present comparisons among all participants and to provide an overall picture of those who took part in the investigation at hand. Because phenomenological research explores not only the experience but the participants as they interact with the given experience, group profiles can illuminate characteristics that would not be revealed otherwise. Because of the magnitude of information that is presented in the typical group profile, phenomenological researchers might choose to create a table or some other form of visual representation that illustrates the group of participants as a whole. Table 10.1 provides an illustration that included the group profile of participants who took part in the study of African American parents' perceptions of play therapy and counseling (Brumfield, 2006).

TABLE 10.1   **Group Profile of Participants**

Participant	Pseudonym	Age	Gender	Marital Status	Educational Level / Occupation / [co-parent info]	Number of Children	Children's Age	Gender	Type of School Children Attend	Have children had previous counseling?
1	Tweety Byrd	35	F	Married	M.Ed.; college professor (doctoral student) [master's degree; administrator]	2	9 11	M F	Public	Y
2	Patrice	32	F	Divorced	M.S.; unemployed (counseling degree) [some college; head chef]	2	5 11	F F	Public (parochial before Hurricane Katrina)	Y
3	Mr. Jack	49	M	Married	Some high school; pastor, bus driver [college; LPN]	3	12 16 18	F M M	Public	N
4	Mrs. Brown	45	F	Married	B.S.; nurse [some college; police officer]	1	7	F	Public	Y
5	Shawanda Wilson	36	F	Married	Some college; administrative assistant [some college; small business owner]	2	12 14	F M	Charter (public before Hurricane Katrina)	N
6	Kimberly	28	F	Single	Some college (current student); administrative assistant [high school; self-employed]	1	5	F	Parochial	N
7	Mary	24	F	Single	High school; SAHM [no information given]	3	1 4 6	F M M	Charter (public before Hurricane Katrina)	Y
8	Marion	48	F	Married	High school; nurse assistant [high school; carpenter]	3 (2 grandchildren)	10 11 (grandson) 12 (grandson)	F M M	Parochial Public Public	Y

DATA COLLECTION METHODS

To enhance the credibility of findings, many qualitative researchers utilize multiple methods of data collection (Newsome et al., 2008).

Individual Interviews

According to many researchers, the typical method of data collection for phenomenological research involves long, semistructured individual interviews with participants who have experienced the phenomenon in question (Creswell, 1998; Newsome et al., 2008). Interviews may last from one to two hours, and participants may be interviewed more than once. In most cases, interviews are audiotaped and transcribed. Following transcription, the tapes are checked against transcripts for accuracy and are often then destroyed. According to many human subjects committees and the American Counseling Association's ethical guidelines (2006), original transcripts and other identifying information must be stored in a secure manner for a minimum of five years.

Interviewers need to be skilled at eliciting information that contains rich descriptions and concrete details (Newsome et al., 2008). An interviewer may begin by asking the participant, "Please carefully describe your experience with . . ." The interviewer needs to be able to actively listen, prompt when necessary, and encourage participants to elaborate and expand on their descriptions (Patton, 2002).

An interview guide can be developed based on the researcher's theoretical sensitivity toward the phenomena under investigation. Because data collection and analysis occur simultaneously in phenomenological research, each interview may facilitate the development, emergence, and verification of categories, themes, and descriptors of participants. Accordingly, data can be reduced into coherent units and used to generate questions for follow-up interviews. When this is the case, interview guides must be revised and updated to reflect the purpose of subsequent interviews.

Focus Group Interviews

While in-depth individual interviews are the most common form of data collection in phenomenological research, some researchers utilize focus groups in which some or all participants participate in a group interview. According to Atkinson, Heath, and Chenail (1991), the legitimization of knowledge involves a democratic process in which all stakeholders have an equal opportunity for input. Therefore, group interviews offer participants an opportunity to hear, clarify, and verify the trustworthiness or legitimacy of findings.

Observations

Many phenomenological researchers record their observations in a *reflexive journal*. The purpose is to record their thoughts and reactions to the research process and participant responses, as well as to document participants' nonverbal communication.

As Shank (2002) stated:

> Observation is both the most basic and the single trickiest skill for qualitative researcher to master. . . . As human beings, we are programmed to observe. We cannot ignore our surroundings or the activities that go on in those surroundings, unless we actually make a sustained effort to ignore these things. (p.19)

Consequently, it would behoove phenomenological researchers to access their natural tendencies to make ongoing observations regarding the participants involved in their studies and the phenomena at hand. Such observations are made while researchers conduct interviews and interact with participants within their natural settings as a means to place participant responses in context.

Merchant (1997) indicated the similarities among characteristics of a qualitative researcher and that of a counselor. The skills and training common to counselors is especially applicable to the process of data collection in qualitative research, particularly when utilizing interviews. Both counselors and qualitative researchers must be incredibly observant and aware of cues given by the client or participant, and both should seek to empower the individual by offering information.

According to Shank (2002), there are eight types of observers:

1. The embracer (experiences and documents so effectively that one gains the sense that he or she "re-experiences" the situation).
2. The photographer (overwhelmingly visual and drawn to the use of sight and watching to make meaning of experience).
3. The tape recorder (drawn to the sounds involved in the experience, i.e., human speech, conversation, words, voice intonations, etc.).
4. The categorizer (observes by sorting information and creating categories to organize his or her experiences).
5. The baseliner (organizes information according to some sort of temporal, or time, dimension).
6. The abstracter (tries to objectively organize or categorize but allows for the use of sensory motor input to assist in this process).
7. The interacter (sees observation as the study of people and their interactions with their setting and with others within their setting).
8. The reflector (focuses and reflects on those things that are universal and significant to other human beings).

While observations offer several realms of information for the phenomenological researcher, participants and the phenomena under investigation will determine whether or not observations can serve as yet another means for data collection.

Artifact and Document Reviews

Along with interviews and observations, phenomenologists have been known to utilize the study of documents and artifacts (pictures, music, poetry, etc.) to gather additional data. Artifact and document reviews involve the researcher's ability to objectively examine and explore specific artifacts and documents that directly pertain to the phenomena under investigation. For example, when exploring counselors' perceptions of working with children affected by Hurricane Katrina, pictures drawn by child clients while in counseling might spark specific memories for the participant as well as offer a visual representation of what takes place in the counseling process.

Documents can include anything written, such as case notes, journals, short stories, poems, and newspaper clippings. While some phenomenological researchers believe that it is not possible for participants to write about their complete experiences (Johnson & Christensen, 2004), it has been my experience that participant journals or other examples of reflective writing may offer valuable information about participants' perceptions about themselves and their experiences. Thus, a review of documents that pertain to participants' reflections and perceptions about any given phenomena they experience can offer additional insight.

DATA ANALYSIS AND INTERPRETATION

Miles and Huberman (1994) explained that phenomenologists extract participant experience in data analysis through several steps whereby researchers continually review data emergence and vigilance over the researcher's own presuppositions. Creswell (1998) and Newsome et al. (2008) also commented on the recursive nature involved in data collection and analysis. Due to the fact that qualitative research is philosophically grounded in postmodern premises and deductive reasoning, many phenomenological researchers possess their own unique way of analyzing data. Regardless of the researcher, all phenomenologists agree that there are several steps that make up data analysis. Accordingly, the following steps attempt to offer a comprehensive overview of the procedures that we have employed and that have been consistently documented throughout literature specific to phenomenological research.

Bracketing

While concepts related to the exploration of researchers' assumptions and bracketing were previously discussed during data collection procedures, researchers should continuously review their reflective journals in order to prevent their biases from interfering with their data analysis (Ashworth, 1999; Christensen, 2005). At this point, researchers might also explore how their perceptions have changed because of their experiences with participants and exposure to the phenomena under investigation. Phenomenological researchers are also encouraged to objectively explore how their perceptions might influence their data analysis and review the steps they used to bracket their biases and attend to researcher subjectivity at the onset of the investigation.

Data Review

According to Merriam & Associates (2002), the researcher (or research team) then listens to and transcribes the interviews. As researchers listen to the tapes and review completed transcriptions, they attempt to grasp participants' expressions and meanings in the broadest context (Reisetter et al., 2004).

Phenomenological Reduction

Next, the researchers engage in a process where they continually return to the essence of the experience to derive the initial structure or meaning in and of itself (Merriam & Associates, 2002). Significant statements or short phrases made by participants were then identified and summarized in order to capture the meaning of the phenomena being explored (Moustakas, 1994).

Extraction of Meaning Units

To elicit the essence of participants' responses, the researcher looks for overlapping or redundant significant statements. These statements are then grouped into "meaning units," which are listed and extracted into meaningful analyzable units (Atkinson & Coffey, 1996; Miller & Salkind, 2002). *Meaning units* are significant statements (words or phrases) that are relevant to the phenomenon being studied. Accordingly, researchers then find meaning units that pertain to how participants experience the topic. Researchers next list the significant statements that explain meaning units while being mindful to treat each statement as having equal worth, which is known as *horizontalization* (Merriam & Associates, 2002).

Finally, these meaning units are described in written units or narratives known as *textured description* of the experience—what happened—including verbatim examples. Direct quotations from the transcripts were identified and dissected for meaning. These units were then described to convey the analysis of their meanings. For example, in Brumfield's (2006) phenomenological study of African Americans parents' perceptions of play therapy and counseling, a meaning unit dealing with parents' perceptions about the developmental benefits of play and other African Americans' negative perceptions of counseling emerged. "Even though I think counseling and play therapy are beneficial, most African American's don't believe in it" (p. 98).

Identification of Themes

After constructing lists of meaning units, researchers then search for themes among the meaning units and develop an overall description of themes and the *essence* of the experience. The goal of this step is to determine the essence for the total group (Johnson & Christensen, 2004). In searching for themes, the researcher continues to maintain an empathic attitude, striving to leave his or her world behind so as to enter fully into the situations of the participants (Wertz, 2005). In Brumfield's (2006) study of African American parents' perceptions of play therapy and counseling, themes that emerged included a lack of education and exposure to play therapy and counseling, cultural influences, and the overall benefits of play.

Data Displays

Once themes are identified, data displays may be developed to offer visual representations of themes and the results of data analysis systematically. This assists the researcher in *imaginative variation,* or exploring the data from divergent perspectives and different frames of reference (Moustakas, 1994, p. 96). Essentially, data displays assist the researcher in data analysis and drawing conclusions (Miles & Huberman, 1994). Specifically, within-case and cross-case data displays are especially helpful when analyzing participants' experiences.

WITHIN-CASE ANALYSIS Within-case displays involved visual representations of each participant's perceptions regarding a specific cluster of meanings, relevant concepts, themes, direct quotes, data memorandums, and a brief summary of the relevance of data memorandums. There are no standard formats for the display of data; thus, the format used depends on the phenomena under investigation and the type of data provided by participants. The purpose of data displays is to facilitate the further exploration, description, and comparison of data that has emerged (Miles & Huberman, 1994).

CROSS-CASE ANALYSIS To deepen researchers' understanding, and to help find the essence of participants' experiences, cross-case analyses are often conducted (Miles & Huberman, 1994). A cross-case display was constructed comparing relevant concepts, themes, or categories across participant interviews. Displays that illustrate cross-case analysis vary but typically involve the presentation of consistent and relevant concepts and themes across all participants' responses. Thus, the goal of cross-case analysis is to offer an avenue to explore and address the similarities and differences among themes and all participants' responses.

All qualitative research involves a recursive pattern of data collection, interpretation, modification, and further data gathering as researchers and participants interact (Newsome et al., 2008). This process often involves reading between the lines in order to grasp the implicit dimensions of the complex experience being investigated. Therefore, qualitative researchers often repeat the steps that have been outlined throughout the data collection and analysis procedures until redundancy occurs. To ensure the "value" of the findings, qualitative data analysis also includes specific procedures to establish the trustworthiness of findings.

ESTABLISHING THE TRUSTWORTHINESS OF FINDINGS

In qualitative research, the soundness of all research is evaluated by its *trustworthiness.* Lincoln and Guba (1985) stated that trustworthiness in qualitative research refers to the investigation's credibility, transferability, dependability, and confirmability. In other words, qualitative researchers seek trustworthiness in terms of *truth value, applicability, consistency,* and *neutrality* as opposed to reliability and validity (Lincoln & Guba, 1985). *Truth value* pertains to the question, "How can one establish confidence in the 'truth' of the findings of a particular inquiry for the respondents with which and the context in which the inquiry was carried out?" (Lincoln & Guba, p. 290). *Applicability* refers to the extent to which the findings of an inquiry are applicable in other contexts (settings) and with other respondents (participants). *Consistency* pertains to questions about the replication and repetition of themes if the method of inquiry were applied with the same or similar research participants. *Neutrality* pertains to the question asked by many critiques of qualitative research: "How can one establish if the findings of the research are genuinely a reflection of the participants being studied and not merely a reflection of the researchers' biases, motivations, interests, or perspectives?"

Miles and Huberman (1994) shadowed the propositions made by Lincoln and Guba (1985) when they constructed three questions that help determine trustworthiness in qualitative research: (a) Do conclusions of this investigation make sense? (b) Do conclusions sufficiently describe the information received from the participants? (c) Do conclusions accurately represent the study at hand?

Because most qualitative data are collected and interpreted in a subjective manner, counseling researchers engaging in qualitative inquiry are challenged to reflect on how their conclusions "might be wrong" (Maxwell, 1996). Specifically, qualitative researchers in counseling must address specific threats to establish the trustworthiness of their study (Christensen, 2005). Validity threats may be a part of all aspects of research design, including data collection methods, data sources, researcher bias, research questions, study goals, and guiding research paradigms. For more than 20 years, numerous qualitative researchers provided guidelines and specific methods to establish and ensure the trustworthiness of qualitative inquiry. Methods focused on strengthening the study's *credibility, transferability, dependability,* and *confirmability* (Denzin & Lincoln, 2000).

Credibility

Credibility involves demonstrating the believability and assurance that conclusions make sense in a qualitative inquiry (Glense, 1999). Lincoln and Guba (1985) offered five elements (i.e., prolonged engagement and persistent observations; triangulation, transferability, dependability; and confirmability) that should be addressed to help ensure the credibility of findings.

PROLONGED ENGAGEMENT AND PERSISTENT OBSERVATIONS *Prolonged engagement and persistent observation* refers to a process that infers that the researcher invests enough time so that he or she establishes trust with participants and eventually learns about the culture, climate, and socialization process inherent in human nature and the phenomena under investigation. While "prolonged engagement offers scope, persistent observation provides depth" (Lincoln & Guba, 1985, p. 304). As such, persistent observation entails accessing multiple opportunities for the researcher to identify characteristics within various situations that are most relevant to the phenomena under investigation.

TRIANGULATION As mentioned earlier in this chapter, *triangulation* is the use of multiple and different sources, methods, investigators, and theories to gather information that is pertinent to the study and the participants and that can be used to support assertions and interpretations of the researcher (Christensen, 2005; Denzin & Lincoln, 2000).

- *Consultation with a peer debriefer:* Used for the purpose of providing an external check on the inquiry process and researchers' interpretations.
- *Negative case analysis:* or "revising hypothesis in hindsight." Refers to refining working hypotheses as more and more information becomes available until the hypothesis accounts for all known cases without any exceptions.
- *Referential adequacy:* Involves checking preliminary findings and interpretations against archived "raw data," previous literature, and existing research to explore alternative explanations for findings as they emerge. This can also lead to searching for rival hypotheses or different interpretations of findings based on existing knowledge regarding the phenomena at hand. Peer and expert consultants can be used to assist in this process (Creswell, 1994).
- *Member checking:* Ongoing consultation with participants of the investigation as a means to offer a direct test of the goodness of fit of findings and interpretations as they emerge. This serves as a "direct test of findings and interpretations with the human sources from which they have come" (Lincoln & Guba, 1985, p. 300). Therefore, phenomenological researchers may ask participants to review their interpretations and descriptions of the experience (Johnson & Christensen, 2004).

Transferability

Gay and Airasian (2000) defined *transferability* as the degree to which results could be generalized to other contexts and settings. However, many naturalists believe that transferability in qualitative research is very different from the concepts of external validity or generalizability (Lincoln & Guba, 1985). Thus, the charge for a qualitative researcher is to "provide only the thick description necessary to enable someone interested in making a transfer to reach a conclusion about whether transfer can be contemplated as a possibility" (Lincoln & Guba, p. 316). Therefore, qualitative researchers are encouraged to provide as many details and the widest range of information possible for inclusion in their interpretations of data and final reports of findings. Rich descriptions of the contexts in which interviews and observations take place; details about the process that unfolds throughout each interaction with participants; in-depth descriptions of participants (participant profiles); and the specific steps that researchers take while collecting, interpreting, and reporting the data (reflexive journals or memos) are just a few of the ways that researchers can offer a complete account of the research process.

Dependability

According to Lincoln and Guba (1985) and Miles and Huberman (1994), *dependability* involves the consistency of the results over time and across researchers. While the dependability of a given study is seemingly inextricably linked with the credibility of the study, qualitative researchers are encouraged to employ steps to establish the dependability of findings that go above and beyond those employed to establish the study's credibility. Consultation with a different or new peer debriefer throughout the analysis and interpretation of data can be a valuable way to add to the dependability of findings. Likewise, the utilization of research teams or multiple researchers who overlap one another or use similar methods of collecting and analyzing the data can enhance the dependability of findings. For example, in a study that was conducted by a counselor educator who had developed a model for training counselors to train teachers to identify and report suspected child abuse was also analyzed by the counselor educator and a qualitative researcher who was a teacher educator. While the counselor educator and teacher educator had very different perceptions of the model and the findings, when they synthesized the results of their data analysis, the final product was much more comprehensive and credible. Finally, qualitative researchers are encouraged to employ the services of an auditor, who can explore the researchers' reflective journal throughout the process of data collection and analysis but, at the end of the final report, ascertain whether or not the results of the investigation are dependable.

Confirmability

Confirmability assumes that the findings of the study are genuinely reflective of the participants' perspectives within the context of their natural environment. As such, confirmability directly addresses whether or not the researchers' biases and subjectivity interfered with data collection and analysis as well as the researchers' ongoing interpretations and final report. In terms of researcher bias, Creswell (1998) encouraged researchers to clarify their opinions, current life circumstances, and any potential biases or assumptions that might have an impact on the inquiry from the onset and throughout data collection and analysis. Accordingly, it would behoove qualitative researchers to state their perceptions regarding the following issues prior to the initiation of the investigation:

- Discuss any personal and professional motives and reasons for conducting the study at hand.
- Describe any personal or professional affiliations with the participants and/or the phenomena to be investigated.
- State any biases or assumptions that they have about the phenomena at hand.
- Based on their theoretical sensitivity (Glaser, 1978) regarding participants and the phenomena to be explored, describe what they think they might find. What does the researcher expect to find as a result of this investigation?

- Explore how the researchers' initial thoughts, feelings, and behaviors might interfere with the research process.

As discussed earlier in this chapter, the researcher is encouraged to keep an ongoing *reflexive journal* and *audit trail* throughout the duration of the investigation so that peer debriefers, peer consultants, and expert consultants can continue to explore how the researchers' biases may or may not interfere with the research process and findings (Merchant, 1997). Peer debriefers, peer consultants, and expert consultants are also encouraged to explore rival or alternative explanations for the researchers' findings. Likewise, researchers are encouraged to review their own reflexive journals and audit trails in order to explore how their own insights might interfere or contribute to data collection and analysis (Glense, 1999).

CONSTRUCTING THE NARRATIVE

At the conclusion of the study, the researcher writes a narrative report that includes descriptions of the research question, the participants, methods used to obtain information, the fundamental structure of the participants' experiences, and a discussion of the findings (Johnson & Christensen, 2004). The narrative often contains verbatim descriptions provided by the participants as well as the researcher's method of organizing data (Wertz, 2005). Findings are discussed with regard to their connection with previous research and theory, their practical implications, and their impact on participants. Also included in the narrative report are specific methods used by the researcher to establish the trustworthiness of the study.

DRAWBACKS

While phenomenological designs can be an excellent tool whereby qualitative researchers can gain an understanding of the true essence of an experience, like all research, there are some potential limitations or drawbacks. Because interviews are the primary means for collecting data in phenomenological research and because participants are the primary tools of data collection, drawbacks can pertain to the interview process as well as the influence of the relationship between participants and the researcher.

The Interview Process

One drawback might pertain to the setting and the researcher's inability to control for things that might interfere with the interview process or distract the participant during the interview. For example, Brumfield (2006) was forced to interview African American parents in a variety of settings (school closets, coffee shops, participants' homes, parks, etc.). Not only do these situations pose complications related to confidentiality, but the settings were not necessarily optimal for the effective facilitation of the interview process. Scheduling complications, unavailability of participants for follow-up interviews, and lack of participants' investment in the research process may be other drawbacks that phenomenological researchers face.

Influence of Relationship Between Researcher and Participant

There is the potential for participants to "overidentify" with the researcher (Christensen, 2005). If this is the case, participants may feel pressure to "perform/please" or give responses that they believe the researcher might want. For example, Brumfield (2006) was concerned that her participants might overidentify with her because she was an African American woman who was studying African American parents. Because she was a counselor, Brumfield attempted to address this issue by directly addressing the concern with participants, or as she stated, "I did exactly what I would have done in a counseling session with an individual who 'looks like me.' I talked about it in the initial interviews with each participant and explained that there were no 'right or wrong' answers and that I was truly interested in their perceptions" (p. 100).

Another potential drawback pertains to the influence of researchers' backgrounds and possible biases and preconceived assumptions. Despite the fact that researchers can use methods like *bracketing, member checks,* and *consultation with peers and experts in the field,* it is impossible to completely extract a researcher's assumptions and biases. Unfortunately, controlling for all of the variables that might influence participants' perceptions is virtually impossible.

Other drawbacks related to researchers may pertain to their ability and experience with conducting qualitative research. Inexperienced phenomenological researchers may not adequately utilize interviewing skills and may not know how to facilitate the interview process. Additionally, because the interview questions are such a vital component of phenomenological research, novice researchers may not ask the right questions to begin with. A final limitation, which exists in all research, is the researchers' own subjectivity. For example, as an African American female who grew up in the same geographic location where parents involved in her study resided, Brumfield (2006) had similar experiences and possessed a level of sensitivity that might have been detrimental to her ability to relate to participants objectively. She stated:

> While my race and "familiarity" with the geographic location might have positively influenced parents to be more open and candid throughout the interview process, these factors might have also inhibited my ability to be as objective as I would have hoped. (p. 101)

Other Complications

Yet one more potential drawback of phenomenological research is that it generates a large mass of information. The sheer quantity of words that is collected from interview transcripts, researchers' notes, documents, and artifacts can be overwhelming. Analysis of large volumes of information can be confusing, frustrating, and messy for even an experienced qualitative researcher. Data do not tend to fall into neat categories, and there can be literally millions of ways to link different parts of discussions or observations (Lester, 1999).

Lester (1999) also raised an important point that holds true with other forms of qualitative research but more so with phenomenological designs. As Lester stated, when it comes to the general public:

> People do not understand what it [phenomenology] is and they often expect similar parameters to apply as for quantitative research. A fairly common comment concerns sample size—it can be hard to get over to people that a single-figure sample is valid . . . . If the sample size is increased, a common misunderstanding is that the results should be statistically reliable or better. (p. 16)

Sheer ignorance about qualitative methodology and the power of empowering people to share their experiences can interfere with how some view the results of qualitative research.

ADVANTAGES

Despite the potential disadvantages of phenomenological research, there are numerous advantages. Specific advantages pertain to benefits to participants, benefits for the researcher, and the multitude of topics that can be explored via phenomenological research design. Because phenomenological research is interactive (Merchant & Dupuy, 1996) and relies on the relationship between the researcher and the participants, there are obvious benefits related to that relationship and specific to both researchers and those who are studied (participants). The following sections address advantages of phenomenological research for both participants and researchers, as well as the field of counseling in general.

Participants

One of the main advantages of phenomenology is synonymous with some of the efficacious effects of counseling. First, participants reap the benefits of having an opportunity to be heard and share their thoughts and feelings about their lived experiences. Data-collection procedures included in phenomenological research involve interviews where participants are invited to share their perceptions and offer feedback, thus acknowledging the value of their experiences and respecting their "expertise . . . regarding their own experiences" (Merchant & Dupuy, 1996, p. 540). This can be very empowering for participants—and again, is one of the same benefits of the counseling experience.

Participants involved in phenomenological research also gain a deeper understanding of their own experiences and the phenomena at hand. Because the process of data collection is not unlike counseling—where counselors use various skills and techniques to facilitate clients' willingness to share their experiences—as the phenomenological researcher gains the participants' trust by utilizing active listening skills, seeking clarification, and identifying themes, both participants and researchers enhance their understanding of the phenomena at hand. Likewise, participants often gain insight into themselves and their experiences.

Researchers

Researchers can dare to ask questions that have been neglected or avoided in research and the general public. As Lester (1999) stated: "Phenomenological approaches are good at surfacing deep issues and making voices heard . . . many organizations value the insights which a phenomenological approach can bring in terms of cutting through conventional wisdom, prompting action or challenging complacency" (p. 17).

Furthermore, phenomenology offers a methodological approach for researchers who are interested in studying the essence of phenomena that are difficult to explore. According to Gay and Airasian (2000), a qualitative approach is most appropriate when the researcher wishes to gain insights about phenomena of interest, particularly if such insights are not possible using alternate types of research. Creswell (1998) said that phenomenological research can capture a "complex, holistic picture" (p. 15). Furthermore, Creswell illuminated that qualitative research, specifically phenomenology, is typically focused more intently on fewer cases and more variables.

The Field of Counseling

Not only are such insights and increases in knowledge beneficial for participants and researchers, but this is also advantageous for the general public. For example, phenomenological research is an excellent way to explore phenomena about which little is known. Recall from the beginning of the chapter how Merchant (1997) indicated the usefulness of qualitative methodology in the field of counseling. Hopefully, you can now see that the skills and training common to counselor training programs are especially applicable to the process of inquiry involved in phenomenological research. We believe, like Merchant that counselor training is preparation for qualitative research.

As you explore the world of phenomenology, we hope that you can see how being aware of your own worldview and your clients' worldviews would be beneficial to your work as a counselor and qualitative researcher. Through the polydimensional lens you use to understand the multiple systems involved in your clients' experiences, you will be able to see the multiple perspectives in the narratives and stories of research participants' lives. By practicing the tolerance for ambiguity in the counseling process, you will be better able to explore research from a phenomenological perspective.

Because interviews and observations are the most common forms of collecting data in phenomenological research, skills specific to these tasks are most valuable. Both counselors and qualitative researchers must be aware of cues given by the client or participant. Just like counseling, phenomenology has a focus on process, content, and empowerment.

Multicultural Considerations

Furthermore, phenomenological methodology offers researchers an ideal means to explore diverse cultures, oppressed populations, and unique phenomena surrounding any number of concepts that arise in human existence. Merchant and Dupuy (1996) have recommended the use of qualitative research methodology for the examination of multicultural issues, citing quantitative research paradigms as based on Eurocentric worldviews, which is not consistent with other cultures' belief systems. According to Jackson and Meadows (1991), the European conceptual system

> Emphasizes a material ontology, with the highest value (axiology) placed on the acquisition of objects. External knowledge is assumed to be the basis of all knowledge (epistemology), and one knows through counting and measuring. The logic of this conceptual system is dichotomous (either–or), and the process is technology (all sets are repeatable and reproducible). The consequence of this conceptual system is an identity and self-worth that is based on external criteria (e.g., how one looks, what one owns, prestige, and status symbols). (p. 75)

> Similarly, Merchant and Dupuy (1996) have asserted that qualitative methodology, specifically phenomenology, aligns with African worldviews and may be more appropriate for research exploring non-European cultures, including the subcultures in America. According to Jackson and Meadows (1991), the African conceptual system

> Emphasizes both a spiritual and material ontology with the highest value (axiology) on interpersonal relationships between women and men. Self knowledge is assumed to be the basis of all knowledge (epistemology), one known through symbolic imagery and rhythm. Therefore, the primary emphasis of the counseling pair should be building the relationship and recognizing the importance of the knowledge that the client has within himself or herself. The logic of this conceptual system is *diunital* (union of opposites), and the process is *ntuology* (all sets are interrelated through human and spiritual networks). The consequence of this conceptual system is an identity and self-worth that is intrinsic. (p. 75)

While this section was specific to the African American culture, implications pertain to many other cultures and emphasize the fact that phenomenological research offers a means that is multiculturally sensitive.

Summary

This chapter offered an initial introduction to the qualitative methodological approach known as phenomenology. The history, philosophy, and rationale for the use of phenomenological research design was presented at the beginning of the chapter. This was followed by a detailed description of participant selection procedures, data-collection data analysis, and verification procedures. Finally, disadvantages and advantages were presented. Implications pertained specifically to counseling research to illustrate how phenomenology has become an effective and practical means to study phenomena related to counselors, clients, and the field of counselor education.

Review and Discussion Questions

1. What other advantages might exist that pertain to the use of phenomenological research design when studying any phenomena that pertain to counseling, counselor education, and supervision?

2. What other disadvantages might exist that pertain to the use of phenomenological research design when studying any phenomena that pertain to counseling, counselor education, and supervision?

3. How does phenomenology differ from other forms of qualitative research designs?

4. How is phenomenology the same as other forms of qualitative research designs?

5. If you were going to conduct a phenomenological study, what would your research question be, and why do you think phenomenological research design fits your question?

6. What are specific verification procedures that phenomenological researchers might utilize to enhance the credibility of their investigations, and how would you describe each verification procedure?

7. What is trustworthiness, and why is it important in qualitative research?

Narrative Research:
Interpreting Lived Experience

April Whatley Bedford, *University of New Orleans*
Sandra Trupiano Landry, *University of New Orleans*

OBJECTIVES
After reading this chapter, you will:

- Be able to identify the underlying principles of narrative research.
- Be able to understand the concept of naturalistic investigation.
- Be able to understand the process of conducting narrative research.
- Be able to interpret narrative inquiry.
- Be able to understand the basic forms of narrative inquiry.
- Be able to understand how to interpret people's lived experiences.
- Be able to understand how to evaluate the quality of a narrative study.
- Be able to understand how to apply narrative research to the world of counseling.

OVERVIEW

"Tell me a story." We all recognize this request so frequently made by children from the time they learn to speak. Riessman (1993) suggested, "Telling stories about past events seems to be a universal human activity, one of the first forms of discourse we learn as children" (p. 3). As adults, some of us have perfected the art of storytelling, and almost everyone, regardless of age, enjoys a good story. Narrative research, at its purest level, is simply a good story. Within the past two decades, researchers from a variety of fields have heightened their exploration of this powerful tool. Inquirers interested in the study of lived experience have turned with increasing frequency to the collection of stories in order to understand the lived experiences of individuals.

In this chapter, you will learn the foundational principles of conducting narrative research including methods of designing a study, procedures for data collection, methods of data analysis, and the implications for the counseling profession.[1]

---

[1] The examples and personal reflections provided throughout this chapter are from the voice of the first author (Bedford).

FOUNDATIONS OF NARRATIVE THERAPY

Narrative inquiry has been growing in popularity since the 1980s. However, in spite of considerable interest in narrative research, methods of qualitative inquiry are still being developed and are infrequently discussed in the literature. The literature we reviewed for this chapter included a sizable number of articles written in the late 1980s and through the 1990s describing narrative research—with varying degrees of specificity—but all calling for more thorough explications of *how* to conduct narrative research. Since that time, a number of narrative studies have been published, but explicit descriptions of the researchers' processes seem to be lacking. In their book entitled *Narrative Inquiry,* Clandinin and Connelly (2000) stated that "narrative inquirers describe lives, collect and tell stories of them, and write narratives of experience" (p. 25). While this definition seems broad enough to include many approaches to narrative research, it does not universally fit all narrative inquirers. The need for meticulous detailing of how to conduct narrative studies and the desire to retain the experimental nature of narrative work create ongoing tension in the field of narrative inquiry.

Disciplinary Approaches to Narrative Inquiry

The ambiguity surrounding narrative arises in part from the fact that a number of disciplines have shaped the practice of narrative research. In fact, narrative inquiry is used across anthropology, history, sociology, psychology, sociolinguistics, literature, and education. The ethnographic approach to research practiced by anthropologists is perhaps the best-known strain of narrative methodology. Historians have always collected stories to construct an account of a specific past. Sociologists are concerned with how such stories are shaped by culture. Linguists emphasize the analysis of speech patterns in an oral history or an interview. Folklorists examine the role of storytelling as performance. Literary theorists use textual analysis to examine those forms of narration, such as biography or autobiography, that have traditionally been presumed to be true (Gluck & Patai, 1991).

Storytelling is part of psychoanalytic heritage. Thus, narrative inquiry is a particularly fitting methodology for counseling because it focuses on the construction of life stories in the development of individual identity (Howard, 1991). In the early 1900s, Henry A. Murray, physician and director of the Psychological Clinic at Harvard, expressed that the narrative form of case study, which had been central to the growth of medical science, was also essential for the development of psychology. A few years later, William Stern, who proposed the term *individual psychology,* found that statistical analysis alone did not provide a complete picture of personality traits; he advocated for the inclusion of personal biographies in the study of personality. Freud made extensive use of narratives and narrative analyses. Between 1920 and 1945, there was significant growth in the study of the biography of individual lives. However, just as in other disciplines, after 1950 and Sputnik, psychology turned almost exclusively to positivist theories of formal science and limited studies to overt behaviors and publicly accessible data, excluding the type of data narratives provide. By the 1970s, the works of Bruner and others prompted a renewed awareness of the shortcomings of the positivistic approach to psychological research.

Researchers in the field of psychotherapy looked for research methodology that would give specific data about individuals, offer a systematic way of approaching data, and broaden the perspective beyond that of the therapist, a shortcoming of the commonly used case study research report. Additionally, such a methodology would need to stand up to the complexity of the therapeutic process. Narrative provides specificity, complexity, and systematic data analysis, and, because narrative utilizes the research interview as the main data collection instrument, narratives provide a window into cognitive processes of the individual (J. Bruner, 1986).

Variations of Narrative Inquiry

The theoretical orientation of the narrative inquirer often influences which of the many written forms a narrative will take. For example, in education, narrative researchers typically develop life histories to inscribe their findings. Casey (1995/1996) provided an extensive list of forms of narrative research, including the following:

- Autobiographies.
- Biographies.
- Life writing.
- Personal accounts.
- Personal narratives.
- Narrative interviews.
- Personal documents.
- Documents of life.
- Life stories and life histories.
- Oral histories.
- Ethnohistories.
- Ethnobiographies.
- Autoethnographies.
- Ethnopsychologies.
- Person-centered ethnographies.
- Popular memories.

Researchers from various cultures craft narrative studies specific to their cultural norms for story-telling, such as Latin American *testimonios,* heroic life stories of poor, often illiterate indigenous women militants; and Polish *pamietniki,* or memoirs (Casey, 1995/1996). However, these different forms can be difficult to categorize. To further complicate categorization, narrative researchers are continually experimenting with new forms of narrative research and coining new terms, such as "collaborative autobiography," to more accurately portray the type of inquiry in which they are involved (Butt & Raymond, 1989). What then unites this multitude of forms and approaches to narrative? Cortazzi (1993) asserted that narrative inquiry includes an interest in personal reflection, in what people know, and in empowering people to talk about their own experiences. The same story may be told orally, in writing, through painting, through dance, or through film. The essential element that links narrative researchers from diverse fields is "an interest in the ways that human beings make meaning through language" (Casey, 1995/1996, p. 212).

Clarifying Terms

If an interest in meaning-making through language is the heart of narrative inquiry, then the evolution of a number of linguistic terms related specifically to narrative research is not surprising. Particular meanings of these terms within the context of narrative research include the following:

- *Story:* "narratives told orally to recall events and describe experiences about people in a setting doing something for a purpose" (Ollerenshaw & Lyons, 2002. p. 3).
- *Narrative:* both the methodology in which researchers engage and the texts they create (Clandinin & Connelly, 2000).
- *Plot:* "the narrative structure through which people understand and describe the relationship among the events and choices of their lives" (Polkinghorne, 1995, p. 7).
- *Restorying:* a retelling of stories collected in narrative research organized around literary elements such as problem, characters, setting, actions, and resolution (Creswell, 2005).

INTERPRETING EXPERIENCE

Issues of interpretation are present at every phase of narrative inquiry and are discussed throughout this chapter. Clarifying your philosophical stance toward particular concepts (i.e., *self, truth,* and *experience*) is a necessary precursor to conducting narrative research. While self understanding is important, it is also essential that you, as a narrative researcher, consider the cultural and social elements that impact a participant's story.

Conceptions of Self

Narrative researchers reject the notion that an individual possesses "a unitary self, a singular, cohesive, and essential identity," or "an authentic core or pure essence" (Britzman, 1992, p. 25). Josselson (1995) asserted that the many selves of a research participant are engaged in an internal dialogue during the construction of any narrative as it is being told to a researcher:

> If we wish to trace the growth of whole people, we must cease to regard people as finished entities and, somewhat paradoxically, we must find those places within narrative where the self is most clearly in dialogue with self. . . . In these dialogic moments, where the planes of self meet, the challenge to empathy and to our capacity to narrate is greatest and is also where our learning about the other is maximized. (p. 37)

This conception of self applies not only to participants in a study but also to the researchers who design and conduct the study and to the various readers of a study.

Conceptions of Truth

Narrative researchers also accept narratives as being open to interpretation and analysis, although their beliefs about narrative truths seem to fall along a continuum. Members of the Personal Narratives Group (1989) offered this interpretation:

> When talking about their lives, people lie sometimes, forget a lot, exaggerate, become confused, and get things wrong. Yet they are revealing truths. These truths don't reveal the past "as it actually was," aspiring to a standard of objectivity. They give us instead the truths of our experiences. (p. 261)

Phillips (1994) provided a note of caution that is particularly relevant for counselors who are narrative researchers when he stated that there are times when researchers and readers of research need to know whether the events recounted in a story actually happened.

Conceptions of Experience

Narrative research is a prime method for learning about an individual's experience. Typically, in narrative research, respondents tell stories of their experiences that provide a lens for greater understanding. In essence, individual stories provide a package for people's lived experiences (Shuman, 1986). However, experience alone has no meaning. Instead, experiences become meaningful in retrospect and through reflection. Like *self* and *truth, experience* is a narrative construct, one that is likely to change throughout an individual's life. Recognizing and valuing the experiences of all people is one of the primary arguments for narrative research.

Influences of Culture

Researchers and respondents are products of the culture, time, and place in which they live, and this must be acknowledged in a discussion of interpretation. Some writers contend that imposing a narrative structure upon fragmented life events is a cultural practice designed to make sense of disordered or fragmented reality. Because the symbols of storytelling are culturally based, we must understand narrative inquiry "as not being the production of a unique, free-willed individual but as a cultural being living in specific ways within cultural bounds" (Blumenfeld-Jones, 1995, p. 30). Therefore, it is imperative for narrative researchers to be highly knowledgeable about the cultural contexts that shape their participants and themselves.

PHASES OF NARRATIVE INQUIRY

All research studies, both qualitative and quantitative, share common design elements, including choosing a research problem; selecting research participants; reviewing relevant literature; collecting, analyzing, and interpreting data; and writing the research report. After proceeding through these phases of the research process, a study is then subjected to evaluation from readers and experts in the field to which the research applies. Each type of inquiry offers unique strengths—as well as drawbacks—that must be considered. Although narrative is a form of qualitative research and, as such, shares many characteristics of qualitative research in general, it is also a distinct form of inquiry, with unique characteristics at each stage of the research process.

Riessman (1993) proposed a model for representing experience—the essence of narrative research—that includes five levels: *attending, telling, transcribing, analyzing,* and *reading*. We discuss each of these levels as they relate to narrative study, and we add a sixth level, *writing,* inserted between analyzing and reading.

Attending to Experience

Inquirers attend to those experiences they wish to study as they design and carry out narrative research, and informants must attend to particular experiences on which the research focuses and at the request of the researcher. Therefore, attending to experience begins in the design phase of a narrative study and flows into the collection of narrative data.

BEGINNING WITH THE INQUIRER   A researcher's own experiences and beliefs are what attract an individual to narrative inquiry in general as well as to particular research questions. Certain types of researchers are drawn to narrative inquiry because of its literary form. This is exactly why I like to read, conduct, and write narrative research, although I continually worry about my ability to write with enough literary flair—an anxiety shared by many narrative researchers.

I am also drawn to narrative research because of its acknowledgment of the researcher's experiences with the topic being studied. Although I agree with Riessman (1993) that every research project is affected by the researcher, the narrative researcher makes his or her autobiographical connections to the research question explicit. Writing this autobiographical reflection is one of the first steps in the attention to experience requisite to narrative study. Where to include the researcher's own story and how much of it to include are questions that are often debated among narrative scholars. Unless a study is an autobiography, inclusion of so much of the inquirer's story that it overshadows the stories of participants is self-indulgent and inappropriate. However, most beginning researchers are hesitant to include much self-disclosure in their research reports because this is traditionally not done in the types of research with which they are familiar. As a reader, I always want to know what experiences prompted a researcher to undertake a particular research study, and I encourage my students to include self-disclosure at several points in their research reports.

Naturally, researchers drawn to this type of study will likely be drawn to questions that lend themselves to narrative exploration. Questions appropriate for narrative inquiry should focus on exploring the personal and social experiences of one or more individuals. Specific examples of narrative studies I have designed, or to which I have contributed, include a study of adoption, including informants with a variety of perspectives; a life-history study of female teacher educators and their personal visions of education (my own dissertation research); a small-scale study of gay and lesbian elementary teachers; a large, grant-funded study of child abuse education in an urban school district; and personal experience narratives of survivors of Hurricane Katrina. Specific elements of each of these studies are described in subsequent sections of this chapter.

The monitoring of biases and subjectivities remains a crucial and ongoing task of the narrative inquirer. Although this is true for all qualitative researchers, it is perhaps more necessary for narrative researchers because narrative is a highly personal form of inquiry (for detailed descriptions of monitoring researchers' subjectivity, see Peshkin, 1988).

SELECTING RESEARCH PARTICIPANTS   A narrative researcher must also attend to relevant characteristics or experiences of respondents and then purposefully select individuals who meet the criteria and have stories to tell that are relevant to the chosen research question. Creswell (2005) said that narrative research usually focuses on a single participant, but I have not found this to be true of narrative studies in education and counseling. However, it is true that narrative researchers typically select fewer participants than other types of qualitative researchers because of the breadth *and* depth of information collected from each participant. When I (Bedford, formerly Kemp) was designing my dissertation research, I wanted to compare the experiences of a variety of female teacher educators rather than focus on the experiences of only one. I selected five participants for that study, which seems to be at the high end of number of participants in a narrative study (Kemp, 1997).

REVIEWING RELEVANT LITERATURE   The necessity of a literature review within a narrative study is open to debate among researchers. As is the case with most qualitative inquiry, literature review plays a small role in narrative research. However, as students you should be aware that many academicians expect to see a substantial review of literature, even in narrative studies. With this in mind, it should be noted that much of the literature used to support a narrative study is methodological. In dozens of narrative studies I reviewed from the social sciences, I found fairly lengthy descriptions of what narrative research is and why narrative was an appropriate fit for a particular investigation. The majority of studies I reviewed included some type of literature review, but I found that narrative inquiry allows for inclusion of academic literature in playful or experimental ways.

   The literature review requires the narrative researcher to attend to particular theories and not to others. Narrative research allows for a more personal connection to literature than other types of inquiry. In my own dissertation, I reviewed the literature that shaped my life, literature for which I felt a biological affinity that fostered beliefs that influenced my study. While much of this literature was scholarly, some of it was literary, including my childhood reading of particularly influential children's literature.

   All researchers subscribe to theoretical perspectives that will shape their research. This creates an interpretive dilemma for the narrative researcher seeking the personal meanings of informants' experiences, because research participants might not attach the same significance to sociohistorical and theoretical perspectives as a researcher might (Blumenfeld-Jones, 1995). Thus, narrative researchers must continually strive to balance their theoretical influences with the interpretations provided by their informants.

ADVOCATING FOR RESPONDENTS   Across the disciplines that employ narrative inquiry, particular theoretically oriented narratives enable researchers to attend to the stories of specific groups or individuals and to advocate for their research participants. For example, feminist, Marxist, and critical theorists are often activist narrative researchers who hope to provide "a 'voice' for individuals whose voices may not be heard in the research literature" (Creswell & Maiette, 2002, p. 149). However, Riessman (1993) cautioned that narrative researchers must continually interrogate and acknowledge their presence in every phase of the research process. She stated, "We cannot give voice, but we do hear voices that we record and interpret" (p. 8).

   Finally, theoretically oriented narratives can be combined with other narrative forms. Although I did not assume the role of advocate in my dissertation research, I combined forms by collecting life-history narratives of teacher educators from a feminist perspective. In the study that I conducted with gay and lesbian elementary teachers (Bedford, in press), I was speaking for and with individuals whose voices are often silenced—one of the reasons for doing the study—and narrative inquiry offered an appropriate opportunity to do so.

ELICITING STORIES   While designing narrative studies, researchers must attend to *how* they want to gather the stories that are the heart of narrative inquiry (typically called "data collection" in other types of research). For the narrative researcher, three basic methods of gathering stories are available: interviews, observations, and review of public and/or personal documents. Each of these basic methods can be applied in a variety of ways and can be used individually or in any combination. Whether they are called *research interviews, conversations,* or *oral histories,* interviews seem to be the method of choice of most narrative researchers for collecting data.

A key issue for narrative researchers to consider when designing a study that includes interviews is what initial question to ask participants. I call this the *eliciting question,* a broad question designed to elicit stories that will ultimately lead participants to the overall research problem. You should note that stories are different from reports in that *stories* communicate a message that is chosen by the narrator and *reports* usually provide information primarily of interest to the recipient. Narrative researchers should ask a minimum of broad questions related to participants' experiences and be as nondirective as possible.

In my study of female teacher educators, I was interested in knowing about the participants' life experiences that influenced their visions for education. Instead of starting the interview with, "Tell me your vision of education" (the type of sociological question that might elicit a report rather than a story), I began by explaining the problem I was interested in exploring, and then prompted each participant: "Tell me your life story." This allowed my respondents to begin our research together by attending to those particular life events they found meaningful and communicating those meanings through telling stories. This eliciting question also offered opportunities for data analysis and interpretation that would not have been gained through more tightly focused questions. Broad-based, open-ended eliciting questions allow for themes to truly emerge as stories are collected, analyzed, and interpreted.

Telling About Experience

Language is often viewed as "a transparent medium, unambiguously reflecting stable singular meanings" (Riessman, 1993, p. 4). Most narrative researchers believe that language not only describes reality but also creates it, so research participants are often creating their identities as they tell stories about their lives (Riessman). Research participants' stories (i.e., personal narratives) are "constructed, creatively authored, rhetorical, replete with assumptions, and interpretive" (Riessman, p. 5). Narrative researchers need to explicitly acknowledge their own roles in constructing these stories. The researcher should not only listen to the stories constructed by the respondent but should also actually participate in the conversation.

The relationship between the researcher and the informant will heavily influence how their narrative is jointly constructed during the telling phase. In every research study the informant is participating at the request of the inquirer, and in most cases the researcher is in a position of greater authority than the informant. In such cases, the tension created by unequal power must be mediated. Especially in cases where the researcher and the informant are of different genders or different cultural, economic, or linguistic backgrounds, there may be discrepancies between the words a respondent speaks and the emotion behind those words. In such cases, researchers should explicitly question participants in order to clarify their meanings and the emotions attached to their words—particularly when participants appear to be struggling with their responses. When a storyteller entrusts his or her story to a researcher, the researcher has a responsibility to accurately convey the story and to preserve the dignity of the storyteller.

Narrative research involves close collaboration between researchers and participants. Continual negotiation is usually required throughout a study as the relationship between researcher and informant evolves. As narrative inquirers, you should actively involve participants in every phase of the inquiry process; such involvement by respondents might include helping to shape the questions asked, searching for data to support stories, working with you to analyze information, and interpreting their own narratives (Clandinin & Connelly, 2000).

In other types of qualitative research, the task of interpretation typically falls to the researcher (Chase, 1995). However, meaning-making in narrative inquiry requires a shift in focus. Stories in narrative research are constructed, analyzed, interpreted, and reported. Narrative researchers and participants are often profoundly affected by the experience of participating in a study, and the relationships fostered by narrative research can make both researchers and informants vulnerable. The very personal sharing demanded by narrative inquiry, however, also makes engagement in the research process satisfying for inquirers and participants alike.

CREATING FIELD TEXTS In narrative research, the primary method through which participants communicate their lived experience is oral storytelling. However, narrative researchers may both examine and create a number of types of texts (or data), such as journal entries, field notes, and photographs, during a study. Field texts may take many forms; Clandinin and Connelly (2000) provided a thorough overview of these:

- Oral histories.
- Research interviews.
- Conversations.
- Family stories.
- Annals and chronicles.
- Autobiographical writing.
- Journals.
- Diaries.
- Letters.
- Field notes.
- Photographs.
- Memory boxes.
- Personal and family artifacts.

In many of these field texts, participants tell their stories through writing rather than orally. Written field texts may be produced by research participants spontaneously, at the request of a researcher, or in collaboration with the researcher. In particular, letters to or from a research participant or journals kept by participants might be examined by a researcher, but the researcher might also prompt participants to write letters to other participants or to the researcher, or to keep a journal during the course of the research study. Artifacts such as photographs, memory boxes, scrapbooks, or trinkets—to which participants attach special meaning—also have stories to tell because they become triggers for particular memories and can provide researchers with valuable insights into the lives of their participants.

In my dissertation study (Kemp, 1997), I conducted repeated, in-depth interviews with each participant, elicited written texts from each participant based on specific questions that emerged from the interviews, and examined documents the participants selected and provided. I examined artifacts, and I asked each of the participants to share with me any items that might represent their educational vision. All of them chose to share written documents, and two shared photographs and physical objects as well. In three of the five cases, they chose to show me the personal portfolios they had created for the promotion and tenure process.

Any artifacts participants choose to provide will help researchers gain a greater understanding of their respondents. I have several suggestions for narrative researchers hoping to collect personal documents and artifacts from respondents. These items could be already created or could be created specifically for research purposes. First, some items, because they have sentimental value, might be too personal or sensitive for participants to share. Also, participants might not have direct access to such items. It is important for researchers to ask informants, "Are there any documents, photographs, or other artifacts that you would like to share with me that might better help me understand the experience I'm exploring?" Although discussion about personal items might create triggers for unresolved grief, loss, or other psychological issues, they hold no special meaning for researchers without the verbal reporting of their meaning by their owners. Finally, as researchers, we must keep in mind the demands on participants' time. Just participating in a research study is time-consuming; creating additional artifacts like journals or letters might be more than individuals are willing to do.

Narrative researchers should never pressure informants to share or create items, and the nature of the research relationship should alert researchers to this sensitive issue. While personal documents and artifacts can add depth and richness to a narrative study, researchers might not gain access to the items for which they were hoping.

TRIANGULATING STORIES   Narrative researchers rely heavily on self-reporting from informants and must trust that informants are being honest with them in order to preserve the research relationship. *Triangulation* (i.e., the use of multiple sources of data, multiple methods of data collection, or multiple investigators to confirm the accuracy of findings) is a strategy recommended by most qualitative inquirers but discussed infrequently in the literature on narrative research. The traditional rationale for using triangulation in research studies is based on two assumptions: (a) multiple sources reduce overall bias, and (b) researchers are more likely to develop a true understanding of a sociological phenomenon (Mathison, 1988). Even when triangulation is used, convergence upon a single conclusion is not always the outcome. More frequently, inconsistent findings or even contradictory findings will result (p. 15). Mathison suggested using multiple methods or sources of data to provide a detailed picture of the phenomenon under investigation so that all possible findings—convergence, inconsistencies, and even contradictions—can be understood and explained.

Transcribing Experience

The third level of representing experience is transcribing stories collected orally into written documents. The transformation of experience from oral to written language is a tremendous undertaking; at this level, the task of representing and transforming experience shifts from the informant or the collaborative efforts of informant and researcher to the researcher alone.

Riessman (1993) is one of the few narrative researchers who discuss in detail the processes and implications of transcribing in narrative research. One of the processes involves translating ideas from one symbol system (oral language) into another symbol system (written language). The translation across symbol systems is a cognitive process known as *transmediation.* As you may see from this one process, transcribing stories places complex intellectual demands on researchers.

Like most qualitative researchers, narrative researchers usually preserve interview conversations on audiotape and then transcribe the tapes. Transcripts are often considered raw data. The experiences represented in transcripts are transformed across four levels: lived experience of the narrator, details selectively attended to by the narrator, telling of the experiences by the narrator in conversation with the researcher, and the written transcript created by the researcher. However, oral stories must be transformed into written texts in order for analysis to occur. Because of the complexity of the transcription process, narrative researchers cannot delegate this task to professional transcribers (Riessman, 1993).

A written transcript can never be an exact replication of a spoken conversation; the task of transcribing necessarily involves selection and reduction. Riessman (1993) compared the task of transcribing discourse with the task of photographing reality. Both are interpretive practices, and in each case the researcher or the photographer places boundaries around the experiences available to the reader or viewer. For example, researchers must decide whether or not to include conversation fillers like "ah" and "um" and how to indicate gestures, tone of voice, and emotion conveyed during data collection. These might seem like unimportant decisions, but they have implications for how a reader will understand the narrative. Neglecting nuances in speech can alter the reader's understanding. Riessman also believes that narrative researchers must be much more forthcoming about their procedures for transforming experience through transcription when they write their final research reports; but such descriptions were not present in the majority of narrative studies I reviewed for this chapter.

Specifically, Riessman (1993) recommended creating a first draft of an entire interview in order to record the words and "other striking features of the conversation" on paper (p. 56). She then recommended going back and "retranscrib[ing] selected portions for detailed analysis" (p. 56). Transcribing will probably require listening to interview tapes a number of times in order to gain awareness of linguistic features such as intonation; rising and falling pitch; pauses; discourse markers such as *like, well,* and *so;* and nonlexical expressions like *uh.*

For me, transcribing data is usually where my narrative analysis begins. I type questions, comments, and impressions about an interview directly into a transcript when they occur to me, signifying these additions with brackets. Often, these notes lead to follow-up questions with participants in subsequent interviews. On typed transcripts, I identify and mark where individual stories begin and end. As with other aspects of narrative research, the ways in which experience is transformed during transcription will be unique to each researcher; however, these practices should be explicit in their research reports.

Analyzing Experience

The fourth level of transforming lived experience is analysis. *Analysis* is conducted primarily by the researcher, with continual input from research participants. While much of the literature on narrative inquiry has focused on procedures for collecting stories, less attention has been paid to how those stories are analyzed. This lack of attention to analytic strategies is a major criticism of qualitative inquiry in general and narrative inquiry in particular. There is no recipe or prescription for analyzing narrative data; indeed, most narrative inquirers strongly resist any movement toward uniform procedures for data analysis. Narrative analysis is a highly individual and idiosyncratic process. However, regardless of its personalized nature, each researcher's individual research process should be thoroughly explicated in any narrative study.

Narrative inquirers can contribute much to the body of scholarship on narrative research by clearly and comprehensively detailing their methods for analyzing data.

Creswell (2005) asserted that narrative research includes four analytic processes: (a) retelling an individual's story, (b) identifying themes, (c) situating the story within a specific setting, and (d) placing an individual's life events in chronological order. Again, narrative inquiry does not always seem to fit such neat categorization. Not *all* narrative inquirers apply all four of these analytic processes to their studies, and those who do may not devote equal amounts of time or space to each process. Retelling an individual's story, placing that story in chronological order, and situating the story within a larger context tend to be the typical processes of most narrative studies.

Within the field of psychology, Gregg (1991) uses life narratives to study the relationship between different levels of self-representations that he terms *metaphorical, indexical,* and *ontological.* His description of his analytic process involves delving deeper and deeper into a text through repeated readings that focus on different aspects of the text. First, Gregg focuses on the *foreground* of the text, or as Gregg terms it, the client's cover story. He then rereads specifically to uncover the background of the text—or the abstract concepts, the concrete symbols, the metaphors used at critical turning points, and the affective states that build the story. Gregg divides the total hours of conversation between counselor and client, transcribed verbatim, into individual story segments and analyzes each one for text (foreground) and affect (background). In one example, 14 hours of conversation yielded 143 separate stories.

The core of the analysis occurs in the middle ground. This is the space where the affective states are organized into a *kernel* structure of *intentional* relations. At this stage of the analysis, the stories are reviewed as a whole narrative from the original sequence and context. The kernel structure—textual structure at the middle level—represents an effort to bring order to chaos and stability to change in the client's story (for a thorough description of this methodology, see Gregg, 1991).

A different type of analysis particularly relevant for counselors involves *listening to voice* in the narrative (Brown & Gilligan, 1991). Brown and Gilligan described listening to a client/participant's collected story four different times in four different ways: (a) for understanding of the story, (b) for self in the story, (c) for relationships in the story, and (d) for cultural frameworks in the story. An example of this methodology is explained through the narratives of Tanya, a 12-year-old girl who stands up to a camp counselor who will not allow her homesick 7-year-old cousin to call home. This narrative reflects the voice of a confident and intelligent young woman, whose relationship with her young cousin was more important to her than her fears of the counselor. When the same young woman tells her present life story a year later, the counselor, Gilligan, hears a voice filled with ambivalence, insecurity, and confusion. Gilligan hears fraudulent relationships and a desire not to hurt or upset anyone. Tanya is unable to speak of her feelings. She has assumed the authoritarian voice of the culture. Her loss of voice, her loss of self-authorization, her move from real to idealized relationships, and her move to model herself on the "perfect girl" present many messages to the psychologist about the enculturation of young women into our society.

Thematic analysis, which Polkinghorne (1995) called *analysis of narratives,* is not always presented in narrative studies. In conducting *analysis of narratives,* stories are collected as data and researchers analyze these stories for themes common across stories. The researcher turns these data into a story by asking questions like "How did this happen?" or "Why did it happen?" and then searching for pieces of information that will contribute to a story that answers these questions.

I propose a third type of narrative research. I have collected stories and then *restoried* them through analysis. Polkinghorne discussed collecting data as stories and analyzing them for themes *or* collecting descriptive data and transforming them into stories through analysis. Although the data I collected were in the form of stories, the process I went through to restory them involved both analysis and synthesis.

RESTORYING NARRATIVE DATA   *Restorying* is a term applied to narrative research that describes the process of turning data collected into a coherent story (Creswell, 2005). These data may or may not have been originally collected as stories. Even if stories are collected, the narrative researcher must still engage in restorying in order to merge data collected from multiple sources or multiple encounters with a research participant. Restorying includes placing data in a selected sequence and describing a rich context for the story, including time and place. Restorying begins after some amount of data have been coded.

ORDERING EVENTS IN SEQUENCE   For Cortazzi (1993), the sequence of narrative research distinguishes narrative from other genres of qualitative research. However, organizing data sequentially can be extremely taxing for narrative researchers. Participants in narrative research often do not tell stories of their lives in a particular order. Riessman (1993) suggested three types of sequences that might be applied to narrative data: chronological sequencing—one event after another; consequential sequencing—one event leading to another; and thematic sequencing—ordering events by theme rather than time or causal link. In a life-history study, codes are typically sequenced chronologically, and this ordering is a fairly simple and straightforward process. Narrative researchers employing consequential sequencing should analyze data carefully in order to distinguish between explicit and inferred causes of events. Whenever possible, narrative researchers should ask participants specifically about cause-and-effect relationships in the stories they tell of their lives, and they should make clear in their research reports whether causality was attributed by the researcher or the participant.

Most complex is the sequencing of themes. Themes generally do not fit within a hierarchical structure, so deciding a logical order in which to present them can be a time-consuming analytic task. Different researchers might report the same elements in a different sequence.

In my dissertation study, I ordered each participant's individual life story chronologically. This involved merging details from all of the field texts collected into a coherent sequence. I then organized themes that emerged across the narratives of all participants in an order that made sense to me.

ORGANIZING BY PLOT   All stories have a beginning, middle, and end, and narrative researchers must place boundaries around the sometimes overwhelming amounts of data collected for their studies. Stories also have plots. Plots not only specify the beginning and end points of a story; they also provide criteria for the selection of events to be included in the story, they order events into an unfolding movement toward a conclusion, and they clarify or make explicit the meaning each event contributes to the whole (Creswell, 2005).

The first step in plotting data is to determine where each story begins and ends. Riessman (1993) urged narrative researchers to listen for "entrance and exit talk" (p. 17) by participants that will alert researchers to the boundaries respondents are placing around their own stories. She cautions, however, that the inquirer should make explicit his or her role in where to begin and end the narrative. Participants' responses to eliciting questions offer interesting opportunities for beginning analysis. For example, when I asked participants in my dissertation to tell me their life stories, analyzing where they chose to begin their stories was intriguing. Of the five women I interviewed, four of them began with their births; of these, two located themselves in relationship to their siblings while the other two mentioned the names of their parents in their opening statements. The fifth participant began her life story at the point when she learned to read, signifying the important role of reading in her life.

When I asked a married couple to tell me their son's adoption story, the husband and wife each began with different events, included and excluded different details, and attached different meaning to different events. The birth parents would tell the same story in very different ways, although all four individuals would basically be telling the same story that includes many of the same major events. When I have been asked a similar question about my son, I sometimes begin with the call saying he was born; sometimes I start with seeing him for the first time. Occasionally, I begin further back in time with the infertility treatment and the surgery that prompted my decision to adopt. Some of my answers would depend on what I knew the researcher was hoping to learn. All of these examples support the idea that although we tell our lives in story form, we do not necessarily live our lives in storied ways. We all actively construct our stories based on our unique perspectives as well as our audience in a particular place at a particular time. This is true of both the respondents during a research study and the researcher who is crafting the study.

Not all data will be needed to tell the story. Although the researcher determines what data are or are not pertinent to the story—in collaboration with respondents—data that contradict the main storyline cannot be left out. Leaving out some data elements that are not necessary is acceptable; this is called *narrative smoothing* (Spence, 1986).

Determining significance of individual events to the whole story is accomplished through a causal link to a prior event with a subsequent outcome, according to Polkinghorne (1995). One event leading to another is the essence of plot—as opposed to one thing *after* another, which is episode. Attributing causality is typically cautioned against in qualitative research, but plot is essential to narrative analysis. When striving to interpret the meanings participants attach to stories about their own lives, narrative researchers must recognize that memory is selective and produced from the present perspective of the respondent. Thus, the significance of an event recalled may differ from its effect at the time of the original experience (Polkinghorne). In telling stories of their lives, participants frequently link one event to another. Much interpretation, then, occurs during analysis as the narrative researcher attempts to order an experience—not necessarily in the chronological order in which it actually happened but in the order in which it makes sense to the storyteller. "Reality does not carry meaning with it," argued Blumenfeld-Jones (1995). "Meaning is derived from reality by this act of ordering" (p. 29).

Based on the events selected for inclusion, the sequential ordering of events, and the linking of related events, the narrative researcher develops an intellectual construction (e.g., plot outline) that the researcher begins to fill in with data. As the plot outline is filled in, gaps or weaknesses in the data are revealed. Ideally, the researcher will gather additional data to fill in the holes. As in all qualitative research, narrative analysis requires recursive movements from the data to analysis to further collection, and back and forth from part to whole repeatedly. Researchers often begin crafting plot outlines at various points, such as starting with the end of the story and then determining the events that led to this ending or made it possible (Polkinghorne, 1995). When analyzing narrative data, researchers must remember that the same data can be organized into more than one plot.

ANALYZING NARRATIVE DATA THEMATICALLY   According to Creswell (2005), narrative researchers usually present themes from an individual's story or across participants' stories after retelling the individual stories. This is what I did in my dissertation study and, to a lesser degree, in all the narrative studies of which I have since been a part. Polkinghorne (1995) said that two types of thematic, or paradigmatic, analysis are possible: (a) imposing a previous framework upon gathered data and (b) deriving themes inductively from the data. The second method is most common in narrative research. Coding for themes happens in most qualitative inquiry; in narrative research, "the identification of themes provides the complexity of a story and adds depth to the insight about understanding individual experiences" (Creswell, p. 482). Creswell urged narrative researchers to identify five to seven themes, depending on the length of the study, but most narrative research I have written as well as reviewed includes discussion of three to five themes.

EXPLICATING ANALYTIC PROCESSES   In an attempt to address the criticism frequently aimed at narrative researchers for not explicitly describing their own analytic processes, I include here the procedures I developed during my dissertation study, the most extensive study I have produced. I have continued to refine these strategies during subsequent studies. Recall that Creswell (2005) identified four analytic processes used by narrative researchers. In my dissertation study of female teacher educators, I applied all four processes but I presented the findings in two different ways. I analyzed the life narratives collected from multiple interviews with each participant by placing them in chronological order and situating them within historical and geographical contexts, and then I presented an individual biography of each participant. I also analyzed the stories collected for themes that emerged across narratives and presented these themes within a theoretical and metaphorical framework.

For me, analysis typically begins when I have transcribed one interview or received or created one field text; at this point, I code the field text for the first time. Although some researchers may collect more than one field text before beginning the coding process, I try to code a single field text before collecting another because coding points me in the direction of what to collect next. The coding process is highly individualized, although various narrative researchers offer recommendations for how to code interview transcripts and other field texts. Creswell (2005) called the coding process in narrative inquiry *retranscribing*. In working with narrative data, codes may be related to chronological sequence, to literary elements, or to themes, to name a few from a vast array of possibilities. I always mark handwritten codes on a hard copy of a field text, keeping a clean copy of each field text stored in my computer.

Generally, my initial codes focus on breaking large chunks of text into individual story segments. For example, in my dissertation study, the women I interviewed told stories of their childhood, of their college experiences, of their marriages, of their teaching careers, and of many other areas. I also began to note words, phrases, or emotions that were expressed repeatedly. In particular, I highlighted unique phrases that characterized an individual participant. For example, one teacher educator I studied had aspirations of being a professional actress, but she stated, "Teaching is my Broadway!" To me, this phrase captured the exuberant essence of this participant as well as her feelings about teaching, and I used it as a subtitle when I wrote her individual biography. My initial coding of a field text is usually broad and includes codes related to anything that strikes me as important or interesting. During the first coding, I write notes and codes in the margin of a transcript.

Without exception, transcripts and other field texts I create will be coded several times. Generally, when I read a field text a second time, I am looking for information related to a specific concept—for example, a participant's elementary school experience—and I highlight this information in the same color throughout the field text. On a third reading, I highlight in a different color. By a fifth reading of an interview transcript, the hard copy might include notes to myself typed into the transcript and contained within brackets; broad, initial codes written in the margins indicating ideas of interest or importance; and highlighted segments in four different colors (sometimes overlapping), with a key at the top of the transcript identifying the focus of each colored highlight.

I do not begin coding for themes until I have collected at least two field texts. Sometimes these are both from the same participant; sometimes they are from different participants, depending on the study. Each time I code a new field text, I return to previously coded texts and reanalyze and recode them based on ideas that emerged from the new field text. I do not read each field text a specific number of times, but I read each field text repeatedly as new ideas emerge from data that are newly collected or newly analyzed. During this process, data analysis leads to further data collection, which leads to further data analysis—the recursive nature of all qualitative inquiry.

For me, personally, thematic analysis is always the most cognitively complex task in which I engage as a narrative researcher. Polkinghorne (1995) stated, "The final story must fit the data while at the same time bringing an order and meaningfulness that is not apparent in the data themselves" (p. 16). The search for this order and meaningfulness is, for me, an intellectual struggle. As often as possible, I try to identify themes that emerge from the language of the participants themselves. In my dissertation study, for example, a participant frequently used the terms *generate, generative,* and *generativity.* While none of the other participants used these terms, I found that much of the work they described as "teacher educators" fit the notion of generativity, and so I chose this as a label for one of the themes I identified.

I repeatedly find that themes I have identified are interrelated and overlapping, and deciding which example best represents which theme is taxing. Beginning with my dissertation study and applying it to subsequent studies, I have printed all field texts collected from an individual participant in the same color and assigned a different color to each participant. I then cut these colored documents into sections including only one code (the code I have, through repeated rereadings and recodings determined to be the most relevant to that particular segment of data). Next, I lay the various slips of colored paper on poster board or index cards labeled with each emergent theme and subtheme. At this stage of analysis, the physical manipulation of the data and the visual representation of a different color assigned to each participant help me not only to order the themes but also to change themes, subsume some subthemes under a broader heading, or add an additional level of subtheme. This is my process. It is definitely idiosyncratic.

The sharing of my analytic processes suggests several possible explanations for the lack of attention paid to data analysis in discussions of narrative research. First, I think it is likely that narrative researchers do not pay close attention to their own analytic processes. Narrative data analysis is often messy, unorganized, intuitive, and far from systematic, as depicted in the description of my own processes. Unless researchers make a conscious effort to record the ways in which they analyzed data, they may be unable to remember and describe their processes in detail after the analysis is concluded. I recommend keeping a dated log of all analytic processes with specific descriptions of activities in which the researcher engaged. Simultaneously recording procedures for analysis, while engaging in analysis, is both difficult and time-consuming for narrative researchers. However, combining these efforts will ultimately make narrative studies stronger. Because there are no prescribed models for analyzing narrative data, I think some researchers may be hesitant to describe their own processes because they fear they are not analyzing data correctly. Certainly, describing one's own unique strategies for analyzing data makes a narrative researcher vulnerable to criticism; I must admit that I feel extremely vulnerable by including detailed descriptions of my own processes in this chapter, but I hope that narrative researchers will take the risk to reveal their procedures for analysis in narrative studies they publish. I think that such explicit descriptions are necessary to answer the critics of narrative research as well as to encourage conversation about techniques of data analysis within the community of narrative inquirers.

CHECKING EVOLVING ANALYSIS   Most narrative researchers recommend giving both interview transcripts and emerging interpretations to participants to allow them to recheck for meaning. This process, called *member checking* (Guba & Lincoln, 1981), allows narrative researchers to validate informants' responses to the written research report and to mediate distortion arising from interpretation. Merriam (1988) defined member checks as "taking data and interpretations back to the people from whom they were derived and asking them if the results were plausible" (p. 169). I did this with all five respondents continuously throughout my dissertation study, both verbally and in writing, beginning with my initial interview transcripts. While transcribing, I jotted questions about any statements made by participants that I did not fully understand and began subsequent interviews by asking these questions. I also returned all completed transcripts to participants and asked for their feedback. As I began to analyze the data and write the final research report, I frequently contacted individual participants via telephone or e-mail to check my emerging interpretations. Finally, when I had completed a first draft of the dissertation, I constructed a summary of the themes I identified across the narratives of all five participants and e-mailed this summary to each participant with the following query:

> I hope that you can see yourself in this framework. Would you let me know if there are places where you don't see yourself fitting in or places that especially resonate for you? I want to make sure that your own interpretations are included in the final write-up.

While I hoped that participants would recognize their own experiences somewhere within the framework I crafted, I did not expect it to apply equally to all of them because, as Riessman (1993) pointed out, validating themes across multiple narratives cannot be expected of individual narrators. In subsequent studies that I have conducted or supervised, my co-researchers and I always attempt to elicit participants' interpretations at various stages of the research process. Participants respond with varying degrees of feedback.

Mishler (1990) argued that such procedures help address the concerns about *rigor* voiced by skeptics. He believes that other investigators can make reasonable judgments about the adequacy of his studies. Mishler enumerated these visible elements as the field texts he collects; the tapes and full transcripts of interviews; the methods of transforming texts into data; and the direct links shown among data, results, and interpretation. He believes that other researchers who examine all of these elements will be able to determine how his findings emerge, and he urges all narrative researchers to be this explicit in describing their research processes.

Writing About Experience

I have added an additional level to Riessman's (1993) model of transforming lived experience: *writing*. The task of writing a narrative research report falls primarily to the inquirer, but different inquirers have included research participants in the writing of the report to varying degrees. We tend to think of art and science as mutually exclusive, especially in terms of research, but narrative researchers strive continually to blur the boundaries between science and art. However, art differs from science in that "the artist hopes to stimulate in a direction rather than dictate exact interpretations" (Blumenfeld-Jones, 1995, p. 31). In writing reports of narrative research, inquirers attempt to stimulate in a direction, and such writing requires talent and skill. Because the written result of a narrative analysis is a story, I think researchers with a literary proclivity are best suited to do this research. While the goal of narrative inquiry—just like all qualitative research—is to facilitate understanding, narrative researchers, in particular, tend to write in such a way that readers are prompted to reflect upon their own experiences and consider their own interpretations. Emihovich (1995) asserted that many research reports read as if they are the true accounts of lives and events. She says this occurs "either because we have excluded the evidence that contradicts our argument," or because "the style in which we have claimed the truth blinds people to the content that is missing" (p. 44). Narrative researchers must be vigilant in describing their own contributions to the construction of the research report so that readers are aware that the final write-up is not just a record but a *product* of research (Zeller, 1995).

EXPLORING LITERARY FORMS   Recently, narrative researchers in the social sciences have experimented with such writing models as new ethnography, literary journalism, creative nonfiction, poetry, and even fiction in keeping with the fundamental principles of qualitative inquiry

(Zeller, 1995). Emihovich (1995) called these varying forms of narrative research *impressionist tales,* and she sees an advantage to narrative researchers to be able to take dramatic license with stories collected as data by employing literary conventions such as allegories, scripts, poetry, or multiple perspectives. Barone (2001) studied a high school art teacher in Appalachia and his lasting impact on students by interviewing nine former students more than a dozen years after they were in high school. In his 2001 book detailing this study, *Touching Eternity,* Barone experimented with "textual formatting, language style, narrative tone, emplotment strategies, and other discursive features" (p. 35). Various chapters were presented as a monologue, poetry, a third-person narrative from the perspective of an informant, and a description and analysis of Barone's textual experiments. Ollerenshaw and Lyons (2002) adapted the musical form of the sonata to a textual format for their study of a professor and a pre-service teacher working in a reservation school. While some critics do not view exploration with such literary forms as "research," many narrative researchers pursue this type of scholarship precisely because of the exploration it fosters.

APPLYING LITERARY TECHNIQUES   In addition to experimenting with textual formats, narrative researchers frequently apply literary devices such as flashback, dialogue, and foreshadowing in their writing of narrative research reports (for an overview of literary forms and devices available to narrative researchers, see Zeller, 1995). When I teach doctoral courses in qualitative and narrative research methods, I encourage students to identify such literary devices in the published research they read and to try out similar techniques in their own research writing. In the fall of 2005, when the University of New Orleans resumed functioning after Hurricane Katrina, I focused a course on qualitative methods of data analysis on collecting, analyzing, and interpreting *Katrina narratives.* We began the class with each class member (myself included) posting the story of his or her own experiences with the storm to an online discussion board. Next, I asked the students to revisit their narratives and identify the literary devices they had (consciously or inadvertently) included in their written stories. For example, I chose to begin my written narrative with the following sentences: "When I kissed my husband goodbye in the driveway, I remember thinking briefly, 'Should we really be leaving without him?' Then in the next second, I convinced myself, 'We'll see him tomorrow.'" I wanted to foreshadow the beginning of what was to become a very traumatic week, and I wanted to demonstrate the use of foreshadowing for my students.

During this exercise, I was surprised both by how many students were unaware of the ways in which they had structured the telling of their own experiences and by how many students were resistant to analyzing their own stories. In response to my query about how they had organized their Katrina narratives, I received a number of statements like, "I told it this way because it happened this way." This highlights the idea that, as narrative researchers, we must continually refute the seeming transparency of the stories of our participants and ourselves.

Reading About Experience

The final level of representing lived experience discussed by Riessman (1993) is reading about experience. By the time the researcher has reached this level, lived experience has been transformed by the narrator's attention to particular details and the telling of the experience to an inquirer, and by the inquirer's transcribing, analyzing, and writing—with continual input from the narrator. Although a new participant—the reader—enters the research process at this stage, the reader's reaction is anticipated at every phase of inquiry by both researchers and respondents. There are three groups of potential readers of a narrative study: participants portrayed in the study, readers with an interest in the study, and experts in the field of narrative research.

RESPONDENTS AS READERS   As a narrative researcher, I am always conscious—from the beginning of any study—of how participants will feel about reading my interpretations of their stories. I have already described how I seek participants' feedback throughout the research process, and I have never published any portion of a respondent's story over his or her objections. In virtually every narrative study I have completed, published or not, the informal responses of the participants to reading the final draft have been fascinating. Many of them have described the unusual experience, as readers, of reading stories that are their own and not their own because they have been transformed through the research process. I have never written, recorded, or formally gathered these responses of research participants as readers, however, and I wish I had. I think this is an area ripe for further research; as Riessman (1993) argued, "The afterlife of a study can be as instructive as the formal research itself" (p. 66).

INTERESTED READERS   There is a second broad category of readers of narrative research that includes any individual with an interest in the study. This category includes readers who are scholars in the field in which the research is situated, but it may also include colleagues, friends, and family of the researcher. For this second group of readers, evaluative criteria tend to focus on what makes a compelling story. Among others, Dollard (1935), Blumenfeld-Jones (1995), Creswell (2005), Polkinghorne (1995), and Riessman (1993) have all suggested criteria for evaluating narrative research that I present as a set of questions for both the researcher and the reader to consider:

1. Does the story include a beginning, a middle, and an end?
2. Does the researcher include the cultural context in which the story takes place?
3. Is the researcher's story faithful to actual historical happenings it describes?
4. Does the researcher include the embodied nature of the protagonist in his or her description? (This includes physical features such as age, health, disabilities, and any other physical characteristics that might influence the protagonist's worldview.)
5. Does the researcher describe the interactions between this particular protagonist in this particular setting? (Such description is necessary because different people will respond to the same event in different ways.)
6. Are significant others included in the protagonist's story?
7. Does the researcher include sufficient depth?
8. Does the researcher make the events described seem plausible and understandable?
9. Does the research address how and why a particular outcome came about?
10. Does the explanation provided by the researcher satisfy the subjective needs of the reader of the report to understand how the occurrence *could* have come about?
11. Is the research account persuasive?
12. Is the research account aesthetically pleasing?

Obviously, the answers to these questions are highly subjective, in keeping with the nature of narrative inquiry.

Interested readers of narrative research might attach importance to the previous questions to greater or lesser degrees. Blumenfeld-Jones (1995), E. M. Bruner (1986), and Grumet (1988) have all described qualities most likely to affect a reader's response to a narrative study. According to Bruner, truth is the desired outcome of argument, while *lifelikeness* is the desired outcome of narrative. Grumet said, "*Fidelity* rather than truth is the measure of" autobiographical inquiry (p. 66). Both lifelikeness and fidelity contribute to the *believability* of a narrative study, a reasonable portrayal of the specific story that resonates with the audience's experiences. Blumenfeld-Jones proposed, "To assign believability, audiences must experience a congruence with their own experiences of similar, parallel, or analogous situations. They do not have to derive the same meaning as the [researcher's] original meaning" (p. 31). In other words, believability and fidelity are not necessarily damaged by readers' differing interpretations, but the story told in narrative research must seem plausible to readers.

For a reader of narrative research to experience resonance with the story that is told, the reader must either recognize his or her own story in the story being told in the research or conclude that the situation depicted resonates with its own context. Even if a reader does not feel the first type of resonance, a narrative research report still achieves fidelity if the reader experiences the second kind of resonance. This is lifelikeness (for a thorough discussion of fidelity and believability, see Blumenfeld-Jones, 1995).

EXPERT READERS   In designing and carrying out any study, I am always heavily influenced by the evolving criteria for evaluating narrative research developed by experts in the field. Because narrative is one type of qualitative research, it must meet the criteria for qualitative research in general, but it must also meet specific criteria of its own. One repeated criticism of narrative research is that evaluative criteria related solely to the structure and compelling nature of stories are not all that is needed to assess the quality of a narrative study (see, e.g., Phillips, 1994). Riessman (1993) discussed the pragmatic use of narrative studies, or "the extent to which a particular study becomes the basis for others' work" (p. 68). She offers four recommendations for enhancing the pragmatic use of narrative studies: (a) describing how interpretations were attained, (b) making the researcher's processes visible, (c) specifying how each level of transformation of experience was accomplished, and (d) making data—like tapes and transcripts—available to other researchers upon request. I believe a narrative study that meets these four standards and addresses the criteria for effective storytelling will stand up to rigorous evaluation while still allowing for individual readings and understandings of a particular study.

APPLICATIONS TO COUNSELING

Although narrative is not the most commonly practiced type of inquiry within the fields of counseling and counselor education, there are a number of reasons that narrative research is particularly appropriate for counselors who are also researchers. Psychology and psychotherapy are rooted in narrative theory. Narrative research employs many of the skills learned by counselors: building rapport, sensitive listening, eliciting peoples' stories, gradually building understanding of phenomena, and corroborating stories with other aspects of responders' lives.

The types of stories that respondents often tell in narrative research interviews frequently involve issues of interest to counselors and for which individuals seek counseling. Narratives collected by counselors may include the stories of counselors' experiences, of clients' experiences, and of relationships between counselors and clients. Finally, and most importantly, there are numerous ethical issues to which counseling researchers must attend before undertaking a narrative study.

Stories Told in Counseling

Narrative inquiry is an appropriate methodology for counseling researchers because it involves listening to people speak in their own words about what has been significant in their lives over an extended period of time. Indeed, "psychotherapists encounter narratives of personal experience every day and use them to change lives by retelling and constructing new and more fulfilling ones" (Riessman, 1993, p. 2). In the clinical experience, the client comes to the process with a story to tell. Part of the client's treatment consists of transforming the broken and incomplete initial story into a full and rounded one (Horrocks, 2001). Through dialogue, the client and therapist collaborate to transform the story. Because of its interpretive nature, narrative research is also similar in many ways to the counseling relationship. The researcher must look beyond the words spoken by participants to interpret the underlying, implicit meanings behind what they say, just as the counselor must do in therapy. Participants in narrative inquiry, as in counseling, tell stories to construct identity, to make sense of past events, and to cope with painful experiences. I will share examples of how respondents in narrative studies I have conducted told stories for each of these reasons.

CONSTRUCTING IDENTITY   "Personal stories are not merely a way of telling someone (or oneself) about one's life; they are the means by which identities may be fashioned" (Rosenwald &

Ochberg, 1992, p. 1). Because counselors are particularly interested in identity formation, narrative inquiry is a prime method through which counseling researchers may study this phenomenon. In my dissertation study of female teacher educators, each participant had clearly constructed identities through the stories they told about the different phases of their lives. For example, one participant had progressed rapidly through high school and college, began teaching before she turned 20, and continued to achieve professional milestones at earlier ages than her peers. Throughout her life, she had identified herself as a young, driven, super-achiever. However, she also described how she was viewed as a competent professional in the university workplace, but was seen as "the baby of the family who wouldn't eat her vegetables" any time she returned to her family home to visit her parents. A second participant, whose unconventional teaching methods had not been appreciated in her early days as a high school teacher, identified herself during that period of her life as a bad teacher. Many years later, after receiving a doctoral degree and beginning a successful career as a teacher educator, her identity had changed to education expert, creative teacher, and free spirit. In my interviews with gay and lesbian elementary teachers, one man described in detail how he ensured that his sexual orientation did not play any role in his identity at school. Without any specific prompting, all of these interviewees described how they assumed different identities in different settings and different stages of their lives.

MAKING SENSE OF PAST EVENTS   According to Riessman (1993), "A primary way individuals make sense of experience is by casting it in narrative form" (p. 4). Through storytelling, "narrators create plots from disordered experience" (p. 4) and give unity and coherence to their reality. Individuals are especially likely to tell stories about turning points in their lives or about times where they have experienced "a breach between ideal and real, self and society" (p. 3). I found this to be true in my dissertation study. Although I prompted the women I studied to tell me their life stories, those stories within their life narratives to which they gave the most attention included critical decision points (such as leaving public school teaching or pursuing doctoral study) and unexpected events or breaches (such as divorces or being fired from a teaching position). Often, such turning points and breaches are connected and heavily influenced identity. I myself began a doctoral program immediately after a divorce (a major turning point), and that breach in my life was one of the primary experiences that influenced my topic of dissertation study.

COPING WITH PAINFUL EXPERIENCES   Counselors are keenly aware that storytelling is a particularly useful device for coping with painful and traumatic experiences. However, some stories are extremely difficult to tell or to listen to, and social norms prohibit the telling of other stories. In these cases, storytellers often silence themselves (Riessman, 1993). I have discovered this in every narrative study I have conducted and with almost every participant. In my first study on adoption, the birth mother I interviewed told an excruciating story about giving up twin baby girls at birth, a story she rarely shared with anyone. One of the participants in my dissertation described her experiences with an eating disorder, while another recounted an extramarital affair. My study of four homosexual elementary teachers and the large, grant-funded study of child abuse in an urban school district focused on topics considered taboo by many people, and these interviews had to be approached with extreme sensitivity. Often, participants were reluctant to speak in detail, but the need for both of these studies was great, I believe, precisely because the voices of the participants were so frequently silenced—both by society and by the storytellers themselves. Finally, the most recent narratives I have collected have been from survivors of Hurricane Katrina, myself included. This event was so catastrophic that telling and listening to stories about the storm was painful, but in this instance, I could also "bear witness" to a life-changing event, an important role of a narrative researcher (Riessman, 1993, p. 4). When research participants tell stories such as these, counseling researchers are uniquely equipped to listen, interpret, and bear witness.

Ethical Considerations for Counselors

The sensitive nature of narrative inquiry results in specific ramifications for counseling researchers. Ethical concerns about using narratives in research multiply in a therapeutic setting. Cautions for narrative researchers who are also counselors include the following:

- The counselor/researcher should negotiate *process consent* with the client/participant—a mutually negotiated process that is ongoing throughout the course of the research instead of a pre-research informed consent signature.
- The counselor/researcher must assume the responsibility to protect individuals—and the third parties who figure in their narratives—from undue exploitation in the process of telling their stories.
- The counselor/researcher must make responsible decisions concerning review of the research report by the client.
- The counselor/researcher should fully explain to the client/respondent that the narrative will be re-narrated by the researcher in the course of analysis.
- Counselors/researchers need to select clients not only with respect to their suitability for the research envisioned but also with regard to the likely effect on their well-being and on the therapeutic alliance.

While narrative research seems like a natural fit for counseling, counseling researchers must always consider the well-being of the client above any research interest.

ADVANTAGES AND DRAWBACKS OF NARRATIVE INQUIRY

The same attributes that are viewed as weaknesses by critics of narrative research are often embraced as strengths by narrative researchers, or, as Phillips (1994) states, "what for one group are terms of abuse, are terms of endearment for others" (p. 13). The perception of an issue as an advantage or a drawback depends almost entirely on one's perspective, and perspectives toward narrative research fall along a continuum. Most of these issues have already been mentioned in this chapter, but there are four that I would like to further explore: the researcher's passion for the research topic, the ambiguity of narrative inquiry, the closeness of the relationship between researcher and participants, and the lack of models for conducting narrative analysis.

Passion in Narrative Studies

In describing examples of my own narrative studies, I have discussed my passion for particular topics. My teacher, Yvonna Lincoln, impressed upon me that passion is the foundation for compelling narrative inquiry, and she and I are not alone in this belief. However, while Clandinin and Connelly (2000) urged narrative researchers to "fall in love" with their topics of study, they also caution researchers to be aware of the times that they need to slip into "cool observation" (p. 81). Emihovich (1995) asserted that the social sciences have always been "about distancing passion, of pursuing knowledge without being involved, of holding imagination at bay. The academy is suspicious of the language of the heart because it implies the restoration of feeling in the absence of reason" (p. 40). She believes, however, "that emotion and reason can be linked through narratives" (p. 40), and I share her conviction. I also believe that narrative researchers see the ability to pursue topics of investigation that arouse their passion, encourage their involvement with participants, and release their imaginations as advantages. The drawback, then, lies in how their work might be perceived by other members of the academy. Emihovich asked, "If social scientists choose not to distance passion, what implications does this choice have for their being recognized as scientists?" (p. 41). This is a question narrative researchers must consider—but one for which I hope they will find substantive, positive, thoughtful responses.

Ambiguity in Narrative Studies

Polkinghorne (1995) argued that the "multiple uses [of narrative inquiry] have caused some ambiguity to be associated with the term and have sometimes led to a lack of clarity and precision in its use" (p. 5). This is an issue I have discussed throughout this chapter in terms of philosophical stances and interpretive practices of narrative. Very simply, those researchers who are tolerant of ambiguity will be more comfortable with narrative research than those who are not. However, Zeller (1995) suggested that, even in narrative inquiry, researchers often write in ways that mask the subjectivity and ambiguity involved in the research process. Narrative researchers, then, must give careful attention to how comfortable they are not only with ambiguity, but also with revealing that ambiguity in the final research report.

Relationships in Narrative Studies

Participating in narrative studies and the close bonds formed during the research relationship can have advantages for both researchers and respondents. Creswell (2005) stated, "Stories reported in qualitative narrative research enrich the lives of both the researcher and the participant" (p. 473), and I would add that the lives of readers are enriched as well. He continued, "When people tell stories to researchers, they feel listened to" (p. 473). Clandinin and Connelly (2000) highlighted the close bond between researchers and respondents as a benefit to both parties, while critics of narrative research argue that such closeness compromises the objectivity of a study. While this particular criticism is not one to which narrative inquirers give credence—because they do not attempt to produce objective accounts of "reality"—there are dangers involved in the research relationship to which they must attend. One is that the researcher always gains more from a research study than the participants. Because narrative studies often include participants who are particularly vulnerable or marginalized, researchers should look for ways to add value to their participation in a study. Another is the issue of voyeurism. Narrative researchers should strive to ensure that they are not exploiting the personal details of respondents' lives for their own academic gain.

Models of Narrative Studies

As I have mentioned repeatedly, a continuing criticism of narrative research has been the lack of attention to specific processes for analysis. Additionally, no definitive models for writing narrative studies exist. To the narrative researcher, this can be both an advantage and a drawback. I share Casey's (1995/1996) sentiment when she states that she does not wish to "curb the exhilarating experimentation that characterizes the current enthusiasm for narrative research" (p. 211). The openness of narrative initially attracted me to it, and the continual experimentation in the field keeps me increasingly interested. As a doctoral student, being aware of the lack of models for conducting and writing narrative research induced both exhilaration and fear. As a more seasoned researcher who still has a lot to learn, I approach the creative opportunities offered by narrative with more confidence, and I am motivated by the challenge. To reiterate, I urge narrative researchers to answer the criticism of lack of attention to analysis with thorough explications of their own analytic processes, to resist one-size-fits-all models, to hone their literary as well as their academic skills as writers, and to continue to pursue new formats for writing about their work.

Summary

In this chapter you were introduced to the qualitative methodological approach known as narrative research. The history, philosophy, and rationale for the use of narrative research design was presented at the beginning of the chapter. This was followed by a detailed description of participant selection procedures, data-collection, data analysis, and verification procedures. In order to be true to the narrative approach, the concepts presented were reinforced with examples from my (Bedford's) personal experiences or experiences in narrative research. Finally, implications pertaining specifically to counseling research were provided. Hopefully you can now see how narrative research can be an effective and practical means to study phenomena that pertain to counselors, clients, and the field of counselor education.

Review and Discussion Questions

1. Consider your beliefs about the concepts of self, truth, and experience. How will these impact you as a researcher?
2. As you approach research from a narrative perspective, consider how the same story might be told in multiple ways other than through language?
3. What cultural influences might be important to consider as you begin your journey in narrative research. How will you learn more about different cultures?
4. Why is it important to consider autobiographical connections to a research topic?
5. What is an appropriate sample size for narrative research and what are the procedures for sample selection?
6. What does it mean to be an activist researcher?
7. Think about the various methods of data collection in narrative research. Which procedures (e.g., interviews, observations, examination of documents, or a combination of these) would best fit your personality style and why?
8. What techniques or approaches would best foster collaboration with respondents?
9. Think about the vulnerability that results as respondents share stories of experience with one another. How would you attend to this vulnerability as a researcher? What would be some issues that might come up for you in this process?
10. What are some of the methods available for transcribing the stories collected, and how will you keep track of and describe the processes for transcribing?
11. Think about the process needed to document which details to include and which to leave out in a research report. Discuss your reactions to this process.
12. As a narrative researcher, how will you ensure that you are continually putting the well-being of respondents above your own self-interests as a researcher?

CHAPTER 12

Systematic Program Evaluation:
The Foundation of Program Quality

M. Harry Daniels, *University of Florida*

OBJECTIVES
After reading this chapter, you will:

- Be able to describe how program evaluation is linked to the ethical practice of counseling.

- Be able to identify and define key terms that pertain to program evaluation.

- Be able to identify and describe examples of utilitarian and intuitionist/pluralist counseling program evaluation models.

- Be able to identify five characteristics that are used to define and differentiate among counseling program evaluation models.

- Be able to describe systematic program evaluation, and explain how it related to counseling program evaluation.

- Be able to provide an example of how systematic program evaluation can be used to improve the delivery of counseling services to clientele.

OVERVIEW

Counselors have an ethical responsibility to provide effective, high-quality counseling programs and services to the clientele they serve (American Counseling Association, 2005). While this expectation seems logical and straightforward, fulfilling this ethical obligation is probably more complex than it may appear, largely because of all that it entails. Specifically, if counselors are to satisfy this ethical obligation, they must be adept at performing three separate, yet interrelated tasks, each of which requires a unique cognitive orientation and skill set.

The three tasks are program planning, program implementation, and program evaluation. *Program planning* emphasizes the creativity and vision of the counselor. Program planning allows the counselors to set the design of their programs. In doing so, it provides counselors with the opportunity to identify the purposes, goals, objectives, and activities of their programs.

In contrast, *program implementation* pertains to managing the details of program delivery. The tasks of implementing a program involve ensuring that the materials needed to deliver a program are available for use at the time they are needed.

Unlike program planning or implementation, *program evaluation* involves making value judgments about the results of the program as well as its delivery. To achieve this purpose, counselors must be prepared to adopt a role as a critical reviewer and analyst of the program as a whole, its delivery, and its outcomes. From this perspective, counselors can use the results of program evaluations to modify the design and the delivery of the program.

Although program planning, program implementation, and program evaluation are equally important, the focus of this chapter is program evaluation. Program evaluation pertains to making value judgments about the totality of counseling programs, including their processes and outcomes. According to Fitzpatrick, Sanders, and Worthen (2004), process evaluations focus on the delivery of a program, or provide a description of the delivery itself, including the problems and successes that were encountered. In contrast, outcome evaluations are concerned with determining and describing intended and unintended changes that occurred in program participants. (Fitzpatrick et al., 2004). Although process and outcome evaluations assess different dimensions of counseling programs, when considered together they provide evidence of the content validity of the programs (Gysbers & Henderson, 2000). Thus, when asked to demonstrate the validity of their programs, or their work with a particular group of clients, counselors need only point to the results of the evaluations of their programs.

As noted earlier, program evaluation is an integral component of ethical counseling. This means that program evaluation is part and parcel of counseling practice rather than being a stand-alone activity that counselors undertake to document program effectiveness (or lack thereof). Program evaluation is an essential part of the assessment process that informs counseling practice (Erford, McKechnie, & Moore-Thomas, 2004). According to Erford et al., the assessment process contains six steps that are completed sequentially. The beginning point of the process, step 1, is found in the language that defines the mission of the institution or counseling program. In step 2 of the process, the institutional mission is translated into programmatic goals. That is, equipped with knowledge about the institutional mission, counselors are in a position to design, develop, and implement programs that address particular institutional goals and objectives. Once the programs they have are in place, it is important to consider the effectiveness, utility, outcomes, and value of the programs that have been developed and implemented. In step 3, counselors identify the questions about program effectiveness and select one or more strategies for collecting data. Next, in step 4, the data are gathered that will be used to answer the questions that were generated, collected, compiled, analyzed, and interpreted in step 3. Next, with the results of the evaluation in hand, counselors are well positioned to make judgments in step 5 about the value and worth of the program as a whole, or any of its specific elements. Finally, the decisions made in step 5 can be used in step 6 to improve the design and delivery of the program or to discontinue the program altogether.

Once all of the steps of the assessment loop have been completed, and once the intended changes have been made to existing programs, counselors are positioned to reapply the steps of the assessment process to a second administration of the program. It is in this way that the assessment process provides a hint of the importance of systematic program evaluation.

KEY TERMS AND DEFINITIONS

The prospect of evaluating one's programs can seem daunting for many counselors, although it need not be. Nonetheless, counselors have been reluctant to evaluate their programs (Erford et al., 2004; Gysbers, 2004; Hadley & Mitchell, 1995; Hosie, 1994). Some have argued that the primary reason counselors are reluctant to evaluate their programs is a general lack of understanding of program evaluation, its methods and procedures, and how they differ from those employed by researchers. An additional problem involves the lack of familiarity with the terminology of program evaluation. These issues are addressed in the following paragraphs.

The origins of program evaluation and research come from the same traditions of social science research, especially the importance of evidence-based decision making (Fitzpatrick et al., 2004). Despite this common foundation, a number of important differences between program evaluation and research have been described in the literature. There is insufficient room in this chapter to provide a detailed description of all of those differences; instead, I will focus on three of the most important differences: (a) purpose, (b) control, and (c) generalizability of results.

According to Fitzpatrick et al. (2004), "the primary purpose of program evaluation is determining merit and worth because it emphasizes the valuing component of evaluation . . ." (pp. 13–14). Program evaluations seek to describe a program so that judgments about the value of its processes and outcomes are possible. In short, evaluations provide the basis for making judgments about the value of programs. By contrast, the primary purpose of research is to identify new knowledge for a discipline or field of study. Thus, researchers are primarily concerned about reaching conclusions that lead to the creation of new knowledge, whereas program evaluators are focused on describing the elements, outcomes, and value of programs.

A second critical difference between program evaluation and research has to do with the locus of control of the investigation. In the case of research, the control of the investigation rests solely with the primary investigator (i.e., the individual responsible for designing and conducting the experiment). When compared with research, the control of a program evaluation is dispersed among a larger audience of stakeholders. Because many different groups may have a stake in the results of a particular counseling program, they will have an interest in the outcome of the evaluation.

Another essential difference between research and program evaluation is linked to the degree to which the results can be applied to a wider audience. In the case of research, it is important for the researcher to demonstrate that the results of an experiment can be extended (generalized) to a larger audience. By paying careful attention to the internal and external validity considerations of the experiment, the researcher is able to make such claims. Program evaluators, by way of contrast, are interested only in describing the effects of a particular program. The generalizability of the results of the evaluation is not important. From this perspective, the primary criteria used for determining the satisfactoriness of a program evaluation are adequacy (i.e., do the results provide an accurate description of the program?), utility (i.e., do the results provide users with practical information that can be easily used?), feasibility (i.e., are the results and recommendations realistic and doable?), and propriety (i.e., was the evaluation conducted in an ethically appropriate manner?) (Fitzpatrick et al., 2004).

Because program evaluation differs so markedly from research, a special lexicon of terms that is associated with program evaluation has evolved. Some of the key terms, along with their definitions, include the following.

- *Context evaluations* involve assessing the needs of the clientele who will be served by a counseling program, determining if programs that can address these needs are already in place, and deciding if there are sufficient institutional resources to offer the program.
- *Evaluation* is the systematic collection of evidence that will allow for the appraisal of the quality of a counseling program and assist in making decisions that will change counseling service delivery for the better.
- *Evaluation model* refers to the alternative strategies that counselors can use to evaluate their programs. Evaluation models can be differentiated on a variety of factors, including the

(a) primary purpose of the evaluation, (b) criteria for making value judgments, (c) consensual assumptions of the model, (d) anticipated outcomes of the evaluation, and (e) methods used to conduct the evaluation.

- *Evidence* refers to the quantitative, qualitative, or behavioral data that are used to make judgments or decisions about the value and outcomes of counseling programs.
- *Input evaluation* refers to the environmental assessment of available resources in the work environment, including personnel, space, and time considerations.
- *Process evaluation* (also referred to as *formative evaluation*) refers to finding answers to questions that pertain to the implementation of a program and opportunities to make revisions to the implementation plan. Process evaluations can also be used to monitor the progress and outcomes of planned activities and interventions.
- *Product evaluation* (also referred to as *summative* or *outcome evaluation*) is used to identify the extent to which the goals and objectives of a program have been met and to make decisions about program continuation, improvement, or discontinuation. Product evaluations seek to answer two questions: (a) Are there changes in the target audience that can be related to the goals and objectives of the program? (b) More importantly, can the observed changes be attributed to the program?
- *Stakeholder* refers to anyone who is involved with, invested in, or may benefit from a counseling program (Erford & Moore-Thomas, 2003). A list of stakeholders varies according to circumstance and the clientele being served. For example, for school counselors the list of stakeholders may include students; parents; teachers; administrators; community members; the school counselor and other counseling professionals; employers; and recruiters from colleges, technical schools, and the military. For a counselor working in a community mental health center, the list of stakeholders might include those who use the services provided by the center; their families; funding bodies; accrediting bodies; agency administrators and the board of directors; and other community-based agencies such as the police, the department of juvenile justice, and the court system.
- *Systematic evaluation* refers to the regular, ongoing, comprehensive method by which a counselor conducts evaluations of all counseling programs and student outcomes.

PROGRAM EVALUATION MODELS

A variety of different evaluation models are presented in the evaluation literature. In most instances, the evaluation models can be categorized into one of five clusters of models, namely, objectives-oriented models, management-oriented models, consumer-oriented models, expertise-oriented models, and participant models (Fitzpatrick et al., 2004). The models can be differentiated on a variety of factors, including the (a) major purpose of the evaluation, (b) criteria for judging evaluations, (c) consensual assumptions of the model, (d) anticipated outcomes of the evaluation, and (e) methods used to conduct the evaluation (Fitzpatrick et al., 2004). Further, according to House (1983), the cluster of models, as well as the individual models themselves, can be organized along a continuum that extends from utilitarian models on one end to intuitionist/pluralist on the other.

Utilitarian Models

Utilitarian models depend on identifiable objectives, operational definition of key concepts, and numeric data (Loesch, 2001). The objectives-oriented, management-oriented, and consumer-oriented models are examples of the utilitarian perspective.

OBJECTIVES-ORIENTED MODEL   The primary purpose of the *objectives-oriented model* in counseling program evaluation (CPE) is to determine the extent to which program objectives have been achieved. The goal of the evaluation is to identify discrepancies between the stated objectives and observed outcomes. The use of this model assumes that it is possible to identify measurable objectives that all stakeholders agree are important and that there are objective instruments that can be used to collect data that are both reliable and valid.

The Provus discrepancy model is an example of an objectives-oriented model. According to Fitzpatrick et al. (2004), the primary purpose of the Provus discrepancy model is to decide whether to improve, maintain, or discontinue a program, or some element of it. In addition to emphasizing the importance of agreed-upon program definition, the Provus model also considers installation as an important part of the overall evaluation. The model passes through four developmental stages: (a) identification and assessment of program definition, (b) program installation and assessment, (c) assessment of discrepancies between anticipated and observed results, and (d) decisions about whether program goals were met.

The major advantage of the Provus model is that it is easy to use. Because of its focus on outcomes, the results are easily understood and readily accepted by stakeholders. In contrast, an important limitation of the Provus model is its overemphasis on an outcomes orientation (Fitzpatrick et al., 2004). A second limitation is its emphasis on identifiable and agreed-upon objectives. In a diverse society like our own, it is becoming increasingly difficult to achieve consensus on standards and goals. The Provus model forces evaluators to identify objectives, and in so doing, the voices of some stakeholders may not be heard.

MANAGEMENT-ORIENTED MODELS   *Management-oriented models* are designed to provide useful information that can be used by decision makers. This assists them with making rational decisions about programs and also to evaluate all of the phases and elements of counseling programs, including program development, program planning, program delivery and management, and program outcomes (Fitzpatrick et al., 2004). Because of their comprehensive focus, their sensitivity to the informational needs of decision makers, and their systematic approach to decision making, management-oriented models have been widely used by CPE administrators.

Stufflebeam's (1971) CIPP evaluation model is an example of a management-oriented model, one that has been widely used in CPE (Fitzpatrick et al., 2004). CIPP is an acronym for **c**ontext, **i**nput, **p**rocess, and **p**roduct evaluations. The purpose of the CIPP model is to provide managers with a framework they can use to consider each of the CIPP elements.

Context evaluation is associated with planning decisions. Typically, context evaluations involve assessing the needs of the clientele who will be served by a counseling program. This includes determining if programs are already in place to meet the needs of clientele and deciding if there are sufficient institutional resources to offer the program.

Input evaluation involves environmental assessments of available resources, including personnel, space, and time considerations. Decisions about the best alternative strategies for implementing programs are also included in this category.

Process evaluations are used to provide answers to questions concerning the implementation of the program. Is it going well? Are there threats to the success of the program? Does the implementation plan need to be revised in order to guarantee success? Once a program is in place, process evaluations can be used to monitor its progress and outcomes. Used in this manner, process evaluations provide stakeholders with information about the program.

Product evaluations are used to make decisions about program continuation, refinement, or elimination. The purpose is to identify the extent to which the goals and objectives of the program have been met. The goal is to provide a complete description of programmatic outcomes. This outcome may be positive or negative, intended or unintended.

The CIPP has a particular appeal to those who perform CPEs because of its comprehensive and systematic approach to evaluation and its emphasis on programmatic efficiency. Notwithstanding these obvious strengths, the model has its limitations. Specifically, it is a very general model that is ill-suited to address the particulars of a program. In addition, its underlying assumption about the orderliness and predictability of decision making is inconsistent with the complexities of program delivery and CPE.

CONSUMER-ORIENTED MODEL   The primary purpose of the *consumer-oriented model* is to provide information about programs to potential consumers (Fitzpatrick et al., 2004). The audience for the results of consumer-oriented CPE might include other counselors, prospective clients, program administrators, or external stakeholders. The goal of the consumer-oriented model is to provide consumers with a complete picture of all of the effects of a program. In doing so, it is assumed that the evaluator will be able to minimize bias.

Scriven's (1967, 1973) goal-free model is a widely used example of consumer-oriented evaluation. Scriven's purpose is to provide consumers with a complete and unbiased view of a product or program, a goal that is achieved through the use of checklists and product (program) testing that yields reliable data. The primary advantage of Scriven's goal-free model is found in its egalitarian orientation, that is, its position of giving equal weight to all of the responses to a program, including unanticipated ones. A major limitation of Scriven's model is that it places the consumer as the final arbiter about the value of a product (program). While such a position has some intuitive appeal, some may question whether consumers are always in the best position to make such determinations. For example, if a school counselor is conducting a career planning seminar for all of the sophomore students in a particular school, some may doubt that the students in the program know enough about career planning to render a valid opinion about the effectiveness of the program the counselor delivered. Similarly, if a mental health counselor is heading up a program that is designed to teach emotional self-management skills to adjudicated youth, some would question whether the program participants were in a good position to assess the value and merits of the program.

Intuitionist/Pluralist Models

Having completed this review of utilitarian evaluation models, we can now turn our attention to models in the intuitionist/pluralist group. Included in this cluster of evaluation models are the expertise-oriented approaches (e.g., art criticism, judicial and adversary, and accreditation) and participant-oriented approaches (e.g., responsive evaluation and illuminative).

The primary difference between the two clusters of evaluation models centers around the question of who is to be the primary beneficiary of the results of the evaluation. Whereas the utilitarian models focused on the importance of using the results to make decisions about the value and worth of programs for consumers and stakeholders, the intuitionist/pluralist model assumes that the results will be most beneficial for those individuals who are responsible for implementing the program. Another difference between the groups is found in the nature of the criteria that are used to evaluate programs. Utilitarian models rely heavily on empirical evidence to make judgments about the value of a program. In contrast, intuitionist/pluralist models rely primarily on judgments of experts as the basis for determining whether a program meets the accepted standards of the profession.

EXPERTISE-ORIENTED MODEL   The *expertise-oriented model* is one example of the intuitionist/pluralist perspective, and two examples of the expertise-oriented model are Kelly's (1976) judicial and adversary model and the accreditation model (Council for the Accreditation of Counseling and Related Educational Programs [CACREP], 2009). The purpose of these models is to provide professional judgments about the quality of a program as compared with a set of agreed-upon criteria. Typically, decisions about program quality are made by experts who possess expertise in the discipline and experience in making such judgments. The audiences to whom these reports are directed include program administrators and professional peers and the general public, especially interested stakeholders.

Judicial and Adversary Model   The foundation of the judicial and adversary model is the notion that judgments about program quality should be based on human judgment and testimony. A parallel assumption is that the testimony is based on evidence that was systematically gathered and interpreted in an appropriate context (Kelly, 1976).

Quasi-legal procedures are employed in the judicial and adversary model to present information about the program. The application of this model consists of four steps: (a) issue generation,

(b) issue selection, (c) preparation of arguments, and (d) the clarification forum. Once an issue has been identified, the competing sides of the designated issue present evidence that supports their position and refutes all counter-positions to a panel of stakeholders who are charged with evaluating the evidence and making the decision about the program. In some instances, a single individual will be responsible for making the decision about the program.

This model is frequently used during times when there are limited resources and programs have to compete for available resources. Counselors who work in agencies or schools that have adopted a zero-based budgeting model will find the judicial and adversary evaluation model of great benefit. In essence, the zero-based budgeting model is an application of that model, where program providers must make the case for the continuation of their programs. The use of the judicial and adversary model is appropriate in such a setting because it allows for inputs from competing perspectives. It is important to remember that judicial and adversary evaluation uses quasi-legal methods. This means that the application of the model is not governed by a proscribed set of guidelines or rules. Thus, decisions about program continuation, enhancement, or elimination may be based on factors other than the evidence that was presented.

Accreditation Evaluation Model   The accreditation evaluation model is the oldest of the evaluation models. The roots of the accreditation movement have been linked to the effort to standardize medical school training in the last half of the 19th century (Fitzpatrick et al., 2004). The fundamental theme of the accreditation movement is that professions have a vested interest in identifying standards of instruction and practice that should be required of everyone affiliated with that profession. Prospective members gain entry into a profession by completing a required set of courses, satisfying a specified set of learning experiences, and demonstrating proficiency in skills that are deemed to be essential to professional practice. Programs that are interested in establishing and promoting these professional standards join together to form accrediting bodies, which in turn formalize the training standards for the profession. Programs that wish to be considered for inclusion in an accrediting body are required to undergo periodic program evaluations for the purpose of determining whether the program is in compliance with the proscribed standards.

A variety of methods are used to complete an accreditation evaluation, but the process itself follows a clear sequence. Initially, those associated with the program complete a self-study in which program practices are compared with established standards. When completed, the self-study is sent to an accrediting body (or an identified evaluator) for review. At the same time, the program identifies a panel of experts who will be invited to verify the findings of the self-study. After the team visits, this panel provides a written summary of their findings to the administrator of the program. The results of the evaluation are also made available to all who hold membership in the accrediting body.

The expert model has several advantages, including the breadth of coverage that can be provided, its ease of implementation, and its reliance on human judgment. These advantages also point to limitations of the model. Specifically, the potential for the introduction of personal bias into the process is undeniable. Further, because each evaluation is unique, opportunities to verify accreditation decisions are restricted.

PARTICIPANT-ORIENTED APPROACH   As noted previously, the primary purpose of program evaluation is to provide data that can be used by decision makers to make value judgments about the processes and outcomes of a program. Although decision makers may be the intended audience of an evaluation, there is another audience—the participants of the program—with a vested interest in the evaluation of the program. In response to this observed need, a new orientation to program evaluation emerged. One method focused on the firsthand observations of individuals who had experience with the goals, activities, and direction of the program. This new method of evaluation is referred to as a *participant-oriented approach* to evaluation.

Implicit in the participant-oriented models is an ongoing interaction (transaction) between the evaluator and the stakeholder audience. The purpose of this transactive relationship is to obtain descriptive accounts of the program from all who participated in it. Because there are multiple participants, each with a personal experience, different realities are depicted. The critical task for the evaluator is to recognize and use the social plurality of responses (Stake, 1990) that are obtained from any and all stakeholders. Conclusions about the effects of the program are based on the evaluator's synthesis of the multiple perspectives of the stakeholders.

Stake's responsive evaluation model (1981, 1990) is one of the most widely used participant-oriented evaluation models. Conducting a responsive evaluation involves completing the following three steps: (a) initial planning and focusing, (b) conducting observations, and (c) organizing and reporting results. Although the process of evaluation appears to be straightforward, it is important to recognize that the focus of the evaluation may remain fluid, depending on the findings of the evaluation itself. As noted by Fitzpatrick et al. (2004), "The purpose, framework, and focus of responsive evaluation emerge from interactions with constituents, and those interactions and observations result in progressive focusing on issues" (p. 136).

The primary advantage of the responsive evaluation approach is its consideration of the inputs from all stakeholders. Attending to the multiple inputs provides a more complete description of the complexities of a program. Interestingly, the availability of a wealth of data from the stakeholder audience points to a limitation of the model. Specifically, if there is too much input from stakeholders, some important information may be overlooked, or not given sufficient weight.

COLLECTING EVALUATION INFORMATION

As illustrated earlier, there are a number of evaluation models that counselors may use to evaluate their programs. It is also the case that there are a variety of procedures or methods evaluators can use to collect evaluation information. A selected number of the most frequently used strategies are described in this section. For purposes of organization, the methods can be placed into behavioral, group, or individual approaches (Loesch, 2001). *Behavioral strategies* involve using behavioral indicators to track a program's success (or lack thereof). *Group approaches* include the use of surveys, the focus group interview, and the key informant. *Individual approaches* that will be highly useful include the use of performance assessments and portfolio assessment.

Behavioral Indicators

It is common practice for counselors to solicit input from stakeholder audiences regarding the quality and effectiveness of counseling programs. Yet, while it is important to follow this time-honored practice, it is important to limit the number of requests that are made. One way to achieve this goal is to rely on changes in key behavioral indicators to evaluate the effectiveness of a program. A *behavioral indicator* is a specific behavior an individual (program participant) exhibits that may be observed and counted. For example, if a school counselor wants to evaluate the effectiveness of a program that was designed to improve school attendance of underachieving students, the attendance record that the school keeps for each student would provide an excellent behavioral indicator of the success of the program. If a counselor working in a community mental health agency wanted to evaluate the effectiveness of a program that was designed to reduce the use of alcohol among underage adolescents, the arrest records that are kept by the local law enforcement or juvenile justice departments could be a key behavioral indicator of a program's effectiveness.

The primary advantage of using a behavioral indicator is that it is easy to use because the database of interest is always being maintained. The counselor only needs to go through appropriate ethical and legal channels to gain access to it. Another important advantage of this strategy is that the data obtained are usually highly reliable and valid, which means that evaluators can have confidence in the results of the evaluation.

The primary disadvantage of the method is that behavioral indicators may be of limited value when evaluating programs that focus on complex issues. For example, if a counselor wants to evaluate the effectiveness of a psycho-educational program that was designed to promote cultural inclusiveness among adolescents, it might be difficult to identify a behavioral indicator that would serve as an earmark for cultural inclusivity. In the absence of behavioral indicators, evaluators must rely on other strategies to collect evaluation information.

Opinion Survey

The *opinion survey* is the most widely used group approach for obtaining program evaluation data (Loesch, 2001). It is the easiest way to obtain data from large groups of stakeholders. Counselors use opinion surveys to acquire data about the effectiveness of specific aspects of a program. Examples might include program objectives, activities, and outcomes. Alternatively, an opinion survey might be constructed to assess needs, goals, and priorities of the program as a whole.

The key to the use of opinion surveys is the technical adequacy of the instrument that is used to collect data. The development of a survey instrument that will provide valid and reliable data involves the completion of the following steps:

1. Identification of specific topics and issues.
2. Generation and pilot testing of survey items.
3. Determination of the sample.
4. Administration of the survey.
5. Data analysis.
6. Interpretation and dissemination of results. (Fitzpatrick et al., 2004)

A variety of response formats are possible, but the usual procedure is to tailor the response format to the needs of the evaluator. Similarly, data analysis can vary from simple to complex, depending on the expressed purposes of the evaluation.

Focus Group Interviews

The *focus group interview* is an increasingly popular approach for counselors to collect evaluation information. Focus groups were first used by marketing specialists who wanted to know how prospective consumers would respond to specific products. Now, focus groups are widely used in almost every segment of society because they provide a convenient way to discover stakeholders' thoughts and feelings about a particular topic. For counselors, the topic of a focus group might be the significance of a proposed counseling program. Because focus group interviews provide a structured means for collecting information, they also can be used to identify problems that may emerge in the implementation of a program and to provide suggestions about how to improve the operation of a program.

Focus groups can range in size, but the recommended number of participants is "eight to twelve individuals who are relatively homogeneous, but unknown to each other" (Fitzpatrick et al., 2004, p. 351). There is a group moderator, who is responsible for guiding the group's discussion of a finite set of questions that are specific to the topic. The purpose of a focus group is to tap into participants' feelings about the topic. Thus, group members are encouraged to express their affective responses about the topic as opposed to their reasons for feeling as they do.

The primary advantage for using focus groups is that they provide a quick, easy, and low-cost means for gathering feedback and reactions about a topic. An added advantage is that they provide a venue in which participants can build on the comments of others in the group, thereby generating a more comprehensive and complete response. The downside of using the focus group technique is linked to the richness of the information that is obtained. Because the information is rich in texture and often complex, analyzing the data can be time-consuming.

Key Informant Evaluation

Counselors may also elect to use the *key informant* evaluation model to collect information about the quality and effectiveness of their programs. The purpose of the key informant model is to collect information from individuals—including community and school leaders, other professionals, or residents—who have firsthand knowledge about the setting in which the program is being delivered. The basic assumption of the key informant evaluation model is that these community members, because of their unique standing in, and understanding of, the community, can provide insights into the community's response to a program and offer recommendations for improvements.

Key informant interviews are in-depth interviews with people who know what is going on in the community. The chief advantage of using the key informant interview is that it provides respondents with the opportunity to express their candid observations or opinions.

The usual method for collecting key information is through an interview process. Using the key informant interview method involves the following steps:

1. Determine what information is needed.
2. Develop questions that will allow for the collection of needed data.
3. Identify and select key informants.
4. Conduct the interviews.
5. Compile, organize, and interpret the data.

There are a variety of advantages in using the key informant interview procedure. In addition to being quick and easy to use, the procedure can be implemented with little associated cost. Further, the individuals who participate in the interview process may be of assistance in establishing the legitimacy of the program itself. The primary disadvantage of the procedure is that the sampling procedure introduces the possibility of obtaining biased results. Similarly, because the key informants are drawn from a restricted range of a community (or school), the results are not generalizable.

Performance and Portfolio Assessment

Performance and portfolio assessments are individual evaluation strategies that are commonly used in counselor education programs. Thus, readers may already have some familiarity with each of these strategies, but not the terminology. The meaning of *performance evaluation* is very straightforward: an individual is evaluated on his or her ability to display a defined behavior in a particular context. For example, every student who has taken an introductory counseling skills course is expected to be able to use open-ended and closed-ended questions within the context of a counseling session. Students can either demonstrate this skill in a counseling session, or they cannot. The instructor uses performance evaluation strategies when assessing students' taped performances. Similarly, if a counselor is conducting a group that is designed to enhance participants' career self-efficacy, an evaluation of the program may involve observing how participants act on their own behalf in situations where they have the opportunity to do so.

Portfolio assessment techniques are linked to the evaluation of a portfolio that has been developed by an individual. A *portfolio* is a compilation of a variety of types of evidence that demonstrates students' ability to perform certain instructional, learning, or behavioral tasks. For example, a counselor who is working with displaced homemakers who are seeking admission to an educational program may ask the women to develop a portfolio that illustrates their readiness for admission to an educational program that is appropriate to their circumstance. In this instance, evidence of readiness in the portfolio may include a personal goal statement, a current résumé, excerpts from a narrative that provides a description of the woman's journey, and letters of testimony and support from friends and relatives.

As is the case with the other collection strategies, performance evaluation and portfolio assessment have advantages and disadvantages. One advantage is that they provide an opportunity to evaluate observable behaviors, meaning that evaluators can have confidence that the data they are observing are reliable and valid. They also provide clients with the opportunity to own their presentation of themselves. This particular strength also points to a limitation of the strategies. Specifically, because both techniques are highly individualized, the data included in the portfolios may be unreliable, raising questions about their validity (Loesch, 2001).

SYSTEMATIC PROGRAM EVALUATION

The primary focus of this chapter has been to provide descriptions of a variety of program evaluation models and methods that counselors can use to consider the value and worth of the programs they deliver. The focus has been on how a particular evaluation model can be used to evaluate a specific program, or some element of it. While the evaluation of individual program elements is important in its own right, counselors must also be cognizant of the fact that the landscape of program evaluation is changing. Specifically, it is becoming more complex and demanding. Increasingly, stakeholders will expect counselors to provide comprehensive, systematic, and continuous evidence of program effectiveness. In addition, counselors will need to demonstrate that they use the results of program evaluations to improve program quality. These new expectations mean that counselors will have to think about program evaluation from a broader, systemic perspective. When program evaluation is considered from this perspective, it becomes an integral element of the comprehensive counseling program itself. Counselors must position themselves so that they can respond to these new expectations.

Considered from a systematic perspective, program evaluation provides the basis for making decisions that will guide the delivery of the overall program, including its specific elements. As decision makers about their programs, counselors will assume multiple roles at different points in the decision-making process (Howard, 2001). According to Howard, making quality decisions involves a series of specific and mandatory actions, each of which requires a particular mindset or orientation. A primary mindset is that of "user." As a "user," counselors are interested in making decisions about, or influencing the direction of, their programs. But in order to achieve this purpose, counselors must first identify the critical concepts or issues they want to measure and then select or develop measures that provide useful and pertinent information. Once these "user" decisions have been made, the counselor adopts the role of the "supplier" or "gatherer" of information. In this role, the counselor acts to collect information from consumers and stakeholders, code it, and then store it for later use. Counselors then assume the role of "producer." In this capacity, counselors are responsible for working with the stored information to produce reports that can be used to make decisions. In the role of "producer," counselors may reorganize, analyze, and integrate the data that have been gathered for the purpose of reporting outcomes. With these reports in hand, counselors can once again adopt the role of "user" and use the results to make decisions about the value and worth of the program or to modify it. In either instance, the decision by the user marks the starting point for a second application of the decision-making cycle. The cyclical application of this multistep, systematic process provides counselors with the means to document their accountability.

A useful application of this systematic approach to program evaluation is found in Astramovich and Coker's (2007) Accountability Bridge Model for Counselors (ABM-C). According to Astramovich and Coker, ABM-C "organizes counseling evaluation into two reoccurring cycles that represent the continual refinement of service based on outcomes, stakeholder feedback and the needs of the population served" (p. 166). The two cycles are *counseling program evaluation,* which focuses on the delivery and outcomes of the services that are provided; and *counseling context evaluation,* which considers the impact of counseling services on users and stakeholders. Each of the cycles is defined by a sequence of steps that complete the cycle. The components of context evaluation cycle include (a) feedback from stakeholders, (b) needs assessment, (c) strategic planning, and (d) service objectives. For the program evaluation cycle the sequence of steps involves (a) program planning, (b) program implementation, (c) program monitoring, and (d) outcomes assessment. Considered in tandem, an accountability bridge that provides for the dissemination of the findings of any evaluation to the stakeholder audience links the two cycles.

Either of these systematic program evaluation approaches provides counselors with a structure for evaluating their programs in a regular, ongoing, and comprehensive manner. Yet, in applying either of these approaches, counselors need to be prepared to make choices about which of the evaluation models that have been discussed in this chapter should be used to undertake a particular evaluation study. If counselors are to implement a systematic approach to program evaluation, it will be important to understand it is not a good idea to rely on a single evaluation model to conduct all evaluations (Fitzpatrick et al., 2004). Instead, counselors need to become familiar with the different purposes, characteristics, uses, benefits, and limitations of a variety of models.

Fitzpatrick et al. (2004) recommend that counselors adopt an eclectic approach to program evaluation. As they point out, the choice of an evaluation model is not factually based; rather, it is determined by the context in which the evaluation will be conducted and the questions that the evaluator expects to answer. Different contexts and questions call for the use of different evaluation models. Adopting an eclectic approach provides counselors with the opportunity to choose the appropriate evaluation model to use so that their programs will benefit.

EXAMPLE OF SYSTEMATIC PROGRAM EVALUATION

The following program evaluation example is provided to illustrate how counselors can apply the principles and methods of systematic program evaluation to improve the effectiveness of a counseling program. The example pertains directly to the experience of a group of school counselors who worked together in a large, comprehensive high school, but it is assumed that the steps of the process of systematic program evaluation that are illustrated in the example are also applicable in other counseling programs. The six steps of the assessment loop that were described earlier in this chapter are used to guide the reader through the example. In addition, key concepts that have been defined in the chapter are presented in italics.

Step 1: Institutional Mission

The school district had a comprehensive *mission statement* that focused on providing resources and programs that would enhance students' development in three areas: academic performance, career planning and development, and personal/social relationships. It is important to note that the local school board adopted the mission statement after holding *focus group* meetings for interested *stakeholders* at various locations throughout the community. The importance of this fact is that it meant that the mission statement was widely supported by the community as a whole. Because of the socioeconomic composition of the community, participants in the focus group meetings expressed a special interest in ensuring that all students found a suitable career-related placement after the completion of their high school experience.

Step 2: Program Design, Development, and Implementation

Noting that the language of the district's mission statement stressed the importance of postsecondary school placement for all students, the counselors *designed a strategy to* achieve this goal. The goal of the strategy was to ensure that every student had the opportunity to meet with his or her counselor at least two times per year, once each semester. There were two purposes for the meetings: (a) to monitor students' progress toward graduation and (b) to assist with their plans for after graduation. In terms of *implementing* this strategy, it was important to create a fair distribution of the workload, meaning that all counselors had approximately the same number of students with whom they would work. In this instance, grouping students together on the basis of their last name and then assigning groups of students to counselors achieved an equitable distribution of students to counselors. With this strategy in place, all counselors became actively involved in meeting with their students.

It is important to note that the counselors had made a good-faith effort to respond to the expectations of community stakeholders. The strategy for program delivery that they designed was specifically linked to the expressed concerns of the community and the personnel resources available to the program. Once it was in place, the program and the counselors who designed it were positioned to receive feedback from *stakeholders*. This included those who would be using the services of the program (students) as well as individuals from the community (parents of students). Both sets of comments about the program represent a form of *consumer feedback* data that can be collected through the *value-free evaluation model* (Scriven, 1967, 1973).

Step 3: Program Evaluation

Stakeholders' evaluations of the program were mixed. Some students (and their parents) were pleased to receive individual attention about these important career-planning matters from one of the counselors. Other students were dissatisfied with the program because they were unable to find a time to meet with their counselor. Still other students were unwilling to use the program because it meant that they would have to go to the counseling office to do so, and the stigma of such an event was too much to risk. The counselors were disenchanted with the program because there was not enough time to meet with all of their students. In addition, a *key informant* in the community (the building principal) was providing them with feedback about complaints about the program that were being directed to him. The number and frequency of calls that the principal received provided an important *behavioral indicator* of parental approval of the program. Given the available feedback, the counselors recognized that it would be important to question whether their strategy for delivering career counseling to students was working.

Step 4: Collecting Data

Noting that the evaluation data were acquired primarily through *informal procedures,* the counselors decided to adopt a more *formal strategy* for collecting evaluation data. Specifically, the counselors decided to monitor those among the student body who were using their services, and for what reasons, for an entire semester. An instrument and procedure for collecting the needed time-and-services information was constructed and implemented. Analysis of the data at the end of the first semester indicated that the counselors were spending approximately 70% of their time working individually with senior students on career-related matters. An additional 25% of the counselors' time was spent helping sophomore students adapt to the demands of high school. The remaining proportion of counselors' time was spent with students in the junior class who were getting a head start on postgraduation planning. In terms of the evaluation models presented in this chapter, the counselors employed an aspect of the *CIPP evaluation model* (Stufflebeam, 1971) for the purpose of making and *objective assessment* of the *context* of the school setting.

Step 5: Judging the Worth of the Program

After examining the results of the time-and-services distribution study, the counselors were able to identify several factors that contributed to the negative evaluations of the existing career counseling program. Three of the more important discoveries were that (a) there was insufficient time in a single semester to hold individual appointments with all senior students; (b) waiting until the senior year to work with students concerning their postgraduation plans contributed to the sense of crisis that many students (and their parents) felt, which resulted in angry calls to the building principal; (c) adopting a preventive, developmental strategy for attending to career needs of students may be a more effective strategy for initiating the career-planning process.

Step 6: Program Improvement

Armed with the results of the time-and-services study, the counselors met with the principal and *proposed an alternative procedure for providing career planning services to all students.* The cornerstone of the plan was a career-planning class that would be required of all students and completed during the second semester of their junior year. The organization of the course would focus on ensuring that students were (a) aware of their standing with regard to graduation requirements, (b) conscious of their strengths and weaknesses as students and prospective employees, and (c) knowledgeable about the steps that they needed to complete in order to pursue their postgraduation goals. With these organizational goals in place, the counselors developed or selected instructional activities and materials that were appropriate for the course and proceeded to implement it.

Consistent with the principles of systematic program evaluation, the counselors continued to evaluate the effectiveness of the new model. Because the model had not been previously tried, the counselors were interested in conducting both *formative and summative evaluations* of the program. In terms of the *formative evaluation,* they were interested in obtaining student opinions about the effectiveness of the activities and materials that they had developed or selected, as well as their opinions about the course itself. In terms of *summative evaluations,* the counselors focused on the *product dimension* of the CIPP evaluation model (Stufflebeam, 1971). Specifically, the counselors considered a variety of *behavioral indicators,* including objective accounts of a reduction in the number of career-planning crisis sessions during the following year, increased parental satisfaction about their children's interactions with the counseling center, and a decrease in the number and frequency of phone calls from angry parents to the principal. After its initial implementation, the CIPP model provided a framework for conducting an annual evaluation of the processes and outcomes of the program, and the results were used to make modifications in the program.

Summary

Counselors are committed to providing effective, high-quality counseling programs and services to the clientele they serve. This chapter provided descriptions of a variety of strategies that counselors can (and do) use to assess and make judgments about the quality and effectiveness of their programs. In essence, program evaluation is focused on a single question: "How does one determine if a counseling program is effective?" And, as illustrated, finding an answer to the question of effectiveness gives rise to other important questions:

- Who gets to decide if a program is effective?
- What methods will be used to make a statement about program effectiveness?
- What criteria or evidence will be used to determine whether a program is effective?
- Who is responsible for collecting the evidence?

- Who is responsible for reporting the results of the evaluation, and to whom will the results be reported?
- How will the results be used?

These are questions that guide program evaluation for all counselors, and they are questions that will serve as guides for you as you enter into your professional career. Program evaluation requires an inquiring mind, in addition to a commitment to provide quality programs to the people you will serve. This chapter provided an introduction to this topic, and, it is hoped, pointed out its importance. After you obtain your initial counseling position, you will be expected to evaluate your programs on a regular basis. In doing so, you will add to the foundation of knowledge provided in this chapter.

Review and Discussion Questions

1. What are the similarities and differences between the utilitarian and the intuitionist/pluralist models of program evaluation?
2. Consider the example of systematic program evaluation. If you were conducting the evaluation what would you do differently? What was learned from the process as it was conducted?
3. What are the steps involved in conducting systematic program evaluation?
4. Why do you think it would be important for you to use a systemic lens when conducting program evaluation activities?

5. Consider the accreditation model of program evaluation. If you were in charge of evaluating your counselor-preparation program, how would you go about the process? What aspects of the evaluation do you think might be the most difficult?
6. Considering all of the models of program evaluation presented, which ones fit more closely with your personality style? Which ones are more different? What rationale do you have for your choices?

CHAPTER 13

Mixed Methods Designs

April Heiselt, *Mississippi State University*
Carl J. Sheperis, *Walden University*

OBJECTIVES
After reading this chapter, you will:

▪ Be able to describe the purpose of mixed methods research.

▪ Be able to provide terms used in mixed method designs.

▪ Be able to describe the types of methodology employed in mixed methods research.

▪ Be able to identify the criteria for completing a mixed methods research project.

▪ Be able to identify the types of research questions involved in using mixed methods designs.

▪ Be able to discuss the types of samples appropriate in mixed methods.

▪ Be able to explain various approaches to collecting mixed methods (i.e., quantitative and qualitative) data.

▪ Be able to explain various approaches to analyzing mixed methods (i.e., quantitative and qualitative) data.

OVERVIEW

Many counseling researchers declare themselves to be either quantitative or qualitative in their approach. As you read through the various designs specific to quantitative and qualitative research, you no doubt became aware of the benefits and limitations to each. Perhaps you even wondered, "why not combine the two?" Mixed methods research designs do just that. In this chapter, we discuss the foundational principles of mixed methods research and provide you with the criteria for completion of a mixed methods study. Further, we introduce you to the procedures for defining sample sizes, collecting data, and completing analyses.

PRINCIPLES OF MIXED METHODS DESIGNS

Up to this point in your reading you have learned about quantitative and qualitative methodologies employed in counseling research. We would guess that as a student, it is difficult for you to determine the benefits of one methodology over another. The good news is that you don't have to decide. If you have access to both qualitative and quantitative data you have an opportunity to use *mixed methods research*. Of course, as with using either quantitative or qualitative methods independently, there are challenges and benefits to using mixed methods. Some of these challenges include the additional time required to obtain and analyze data, as well as the research skills needed to conduct both quantitative and qualitative research (Onwuegbuzie & Johnson, 2004; Teddlie & Tashakkori, 2003).

While conducting mixed methods research can be a difficult undertaking, the benefits of a mixed methods design far outweigh its challenges. In using both qualitative and quantitative research, you have the opportunity to expand your understanding of a phenomenon using different data sources. The use of mixed methods designs can shed light on research that would remain a mystery if only one research methodology were employed.

An example that highlights how using both qualitative and quantitative research can be beneficial is reflected in a study conducted by researchers from Northwestern University (Viadero, 2005). Using an embedded mixed methods design (see Types of Mixed Methods Designs later in this chapter) Gibson-Davis and Duncan (2005) studied families who took part in an anti-poverty program that provided wage supplements, insurance benefits, and childcare subsidies to families. The researchers distributed the Child and Family Survey, which highlights family practices and child well-being to the participants (Gibson-Davis & Duncan, 2005). After analyzing the survey data, researchers found a significant difference between the girls and boys that were studied.

Boys whose families participated in the anti-poverty program performed better in school than the boys whose families did not participate. On the other hand, girls fared about the same regardless of whether or not their families participated in the anti-poverty program.

The explanation to this disparity came when findings were shared by the researchers who had interviewed the children's parents. It was discovered that local street gangs were tempting boys to join by offering them expensive shoes and other items. The mothers of the boys took the money from the anti-poverty program and purchased shoes for their sons, but as their daughters were not tempted by the gang members, they did not receive new shoes or additional luxuries, thus explaining the gender differences in the research.

Without the use of both quantitative and qualitative research, the researchers would not have made the link between the shoes and the boys' performance in school, which shed light on the gender disparities in the study. In this case, using mixed methods provided the researchers with answers to their seemingly unexplainable findings.

Not only do mixed methods designs help clarify and assist in answering difficult questions; they also allow researchers to use two types of data to verify findings (Sechrest & Sidana, 1995), more deeply develop their theoretical frameworks, and produce a richer dataset (Jick, 1979; Madey, 1982).

BACKGROUND ON MIXED METHODS RESEARCH

Mixed methods research has existed since the early 20th century, although it may have been difficult to identify as it has taken on a variety of names from its inception until the present time. Early researchers identified the use of qualitative fieldwork with quantitative data (Young, 1939). These studies serve as the foundation for what we know today as mixed methods research.

The multi-trait/multi-method approach initiated by Campbell and Fiske (1959) employed multiple quantitative methods in their psychological experiments of personality traits. This research was the first to include several quantitative methods within a single study, creating opportunities for other researchers to discuss multiple research techniques. However, the Campbell and Fiske research was only quantitative in nature, which provided room for future researchers to combine qualitative and quantitative methods.

Several years later, Sieber (1973) integrated qualitative fieldwork and quantitative surveys within a single study. Sieber argued that this type of combined research provided "enormous opportunities for mutual advantage in each of three major phases—design, data collection, and analysis" (p. 1337).

In 1979, Jick brought the term *triangulation* into use as he believed using different methods could "uncover some unique variance which otherwise may have been neglected by a single method" (p. 603). To illustrate the use of triangulation, Jick conducted a study on the effects of a company merger on departmental employees. He collected survey data, conducted semi-structured interviews, made participant observations, and examined archival information (Cizek, 1999). His objective was to take the qualitative and quantitative data and verify his results in an attempt to reduce the potential bias that can occur when using only one method of data collection.

As the years continued, other researchers followed, with each providing a new name with which to define mixed method research. These names included such things as *integrated* or *combined* methods (Stecker, McLeroy, Goomdan, Bird, & McCormick, 1992); *methodological triangulation* (Morse, 1991); *combined research* (Creswell, 1994); and *mixed methodology* (Tashakkori & Teddlie, 1998).

Because the amount of research being conducted using mixed methods designs, and with the printing of the *Handbook of Mixed Methods in Social and Behavioral Research* (2003), the term *mixed methods research* has become a name by which this research is now most frequently identified (Creswell & Plano Clark, 2007).

Frameworks for conducting mixed methods research have been created by several of the health and social and behavioral science fields, including education (Johnson & Onwuegbuzie, 2004), sociology (Hunter & Brewer, 2003), counseling psychology (Haverkamp, Morrow, & Ponterotto, 2005), and management and organization research (Currall & Towler, 2003).

Throughout the history of the counseling field, a vast majority of research has been quantitative, yet qualitative research is continuing to become more prevalent (Kottler & Shepard, 2004). Moreover, Berrios and Lucca (2006) found, in their five-year study of four professional counseling journals, that over one-sixth of printed research articles now focus on qualitative research and those numbers continue to increase.

Kottler and Shepard (2004) noted how the overlap of quantitative and qualitative methods mirrors the manner in which counselors both work with and think about their clients. For example, qualitative research emphasizes how counselors interact with clients, whereas quantitative research speaks to how counselors conceptualize client problems. As such, mixed methods designs provide an ideal framework for counseling research.

Often, counseling researchers ground themselves in either quantitative or qualitative methodology and focus their work in their chosen area. As can be seen from the information in the previous chapters, there is a great deal to learn about each format of research. Counseling researchers who employ mixed methods have to be well-versed in both quantitative and qualitative approaches. The best way to begin your integration of approaches is to understand the terminology associated with mixed methods.

DEFINITION OF TERMS

To assist you in understanding the terms used in this chapter, we provide the following definitions. As you will see, some of the terms are common to all types of research.

- *Hypothesis*:   a declarative statement of the relationship between two or more variables (Mason & Bramble, 1989).
- *Methodology*:   the application of particular procedures toward acquiring the answers to a wide variety of research questions.

- *Mixed Methods Research Design*: a type of research design where the researcher employs both quantitative and qualitative research methods to collect and analyze data, and report research findings in a single study (Creswell, 1999; Creswell & Plano Clark, 2007).
- *Population*: an entire unit or group; includes all units of interest in the study (i.e., all students, all clients, all employees).
- *Purposeful Sample*: a group of individuals who have experience with the phenomenon under study.
- *Qualitative Research*: an open approach to the study of social phenomena; some aspects include: emergent design, being grounded in the lived experiences of individuals, and drawing on multiple methods. Data are in narrative form.
- *Quantitative Research*: research that employs the use of predetermined instruments in order to measure and observe; some aspects include: experiments, and the collection of survey data via predetermined instruments. Data are in numerical form.
- *Research Design*: an outlined plan for data collection and analysis; the purpose of the study determines the design that will be used.
- *Research Question*: questions that the researcher seeks to answer.
- *Sample*: a subset of the larger population.
- *Triangulation*: the use of multiple methods to ensure that the data collected are trustworthy and accurate (Creswell, 1998; Eisner, 1991; Lincoln & Guba, 1985). Denzin (1978) identified within-methods triangulation, referring to the use of multiple quantitative or qualitative approaches from between-methods triangulation, which involves the use of both qualitative and quantitative approaches.

RESEARCH QUESTIONS

One of your first steps in conducting research is to identify the questions at hand. In a mixed methods design, identifying the research questions has the added benefit of assisting you in determining how quantitative and qualitative methods will be used in the study. To make your study a true mixed methods design, both qualitative and quantitative research questions must be included (Creswell, 1999).

Qualitative Research Questions

As you already know, the word "qualitative" implies an emphasis on *quality*. Accordingly, quality needs to be addressed when considering the meaning and processes of the phenomenon being studied. This includes the types of research questions that are created.

Qualitative research includes broad, open-ended questions that answer the *how* or *what* about a particular phenomenon. Rather than compartmentalizing research in one direction, qualitative research is an emerging design that allows the study to take shape as information is gathered and does not constrict where information might lead (Lincoln & Guba, 1985; Marshall & Rossman, 1999). The emergent nature of qualitative research also allows you to interpret meanings within their context. This being the case, research strategies cannot be finalized before beginning the data collection process (Patton, 1990). However, this does not mean that qualitative research strategies are nonexistent. Qualitative research proposals can identify primary questions to be explored as well as plans for data collection strategies.

Qualitative inquiry takes many forms and qualitative research questions should be related to the research design employed in the study (Creswell, 2005). As you know from the qualitative section of this text, research questions in a phenomenological study would be different from those in a study using grounded theory. For further distinctions related to types of qualitative inquiry, see the chapters in this text on grounded theory, narrative, and phenomenology.

When creating qualitative research questions, consider the following:

- Use "how" or "what" to begin your question. This illustrates the open-ended nature of qualitative research and provides study participants with a broad base from which to approach your questions.
- Use language that conveys the emerging design of qualitative research (e.g., the researcher *discovers*, *explores*, or *describes* a phenomenon) (Creswell, 2005). For example, "In this study, we will explore the attitudes of parents of children with disabilities."
- Ask only one or two central research questions. More than this can become too difficult to address in a single study.
- If desired, write subquestions to support your main research questions. Miles and Huberman (1984) suggested you use no more than a dozen research questions in all.
- Link your research questions to the questions to be asked in the study's interviews and focus groups.
- Relate the research question to the methodology employed. For example, questions in an ethnographic study will be different from those in a study using grounded theory.

Examples of Qualitative Research Questions:

- How does college counseling impact the coping mechanisms of college freshmen?
- What impact do peer educators have on high school students?

Quantitative Research Questions

Quantitative studies emphasize measurement and variables, not processes (Denzin & Lincoln, 2003). In quantitative research, questions are directional because they state either a relationship between two or more independent and dependent variables or a comparison between two or more groups of dependent variables (Creswell, 1994).

Unlike broad qualitative research questions, quantitative researchers determine specific research questions or hypotheses. A *hypothesis* is a statement of the relationship between two or more variables (Mason & Bramble, 1989). Creswell (1994) identified four forms in which to write hypotheses: "literary null, literary alternative, operational null, and operational alternative" (p. 74). Creswell posited that hypotheses written in the *literary form* represent variables in the abstract, while hypotheses in the *operational form* represent specific information about the variables in the study. Of course, the *null hypothesis* is a written statement that predicts that there is no difference, or no relationship, between groups related to a particular variable. Examples of all four types of hypotheses are included below.

Examples of Quantitative Hypotheses:

- *Literary null hypothesis*: There is no relationship between student support services and the academic persistence of first-generation college students.
- *Literary alternative hypothesis*: The more first-generation college students use student support services, the more they will persist academically.
- *Operational null hypothesis*: There is no relationship between the number of hours first-generation students use the academic advising center and their persistence at college after their freshman year.
- *Operational alternative hypothesis*: The more that first-generation college students use the academic advising center, the more they will persist at college after their freshman year.

Quantitative research questions also reflect the relationship between variables, but place this information in the form of a question (Krathwohl, 1988). There are descriptive and multivariate questions that can be created in quantitative research. *Descriptive questions* are written for each independent and dependent variable and any significant *mediating variables* in the study. A mediating or intervening variable is one that mediates the effect of the independent variable on the dependent variable (Creswell, 2005). These questions are followed by the *multivariate questions* that compare or relate variables. Questions involving mediating variables follow the multivariate questions.

When creating quantitative research questions, consider the following:

- Write either research questions, or hypotheses—not both. Mixing research questions and hypotheses can be excessive and may not provide additional information to the study.
- Measure and write about the independent and dependent variables separately. This will allow you to more easily recognize cause-and-effect relationships (Creswell, 1999).
- Link your questions and hypotheses to the theory you are using in your study.

In order to illustrate the nature of quantitative research questions, consider a study done by Eaves, Emens, and Sheperis (in press). In their study, the authors were interested in determining the best method of training counselors in the development of clinical skills. Specifically, they wanted to determine the efficacy of training counselors in the Data-based Problem-Solver Model. For their study, the research question was: "What are the effects of training on client outcomes?" In this study, the researchers divided counselors-in-training into two groups and examined the reduction in client symptomology (pre and post measures) across treatment and control groups. The authors used multivariate procedures to statistically analyze their data. As you can guess from the question and procedures employed, this was a purely quantitative study.

Mixed Methods Research Questions

If you are going to employ mixed methods, then your research questions must address both the quantitative and qualitative aspects of your study. It is important to note that in a mixed methods design, the order of the questions determines the priority of qualitative or quantitative methods. For example, if you were to use a qualitative research question first, this would indicate that you place more weight on the qualitative answers to research questions.

As you move into the world of mixed methods research, you will note that the development of research questions is not as straightforward as those in a purely quantitative study. That is to say that the research questions you develop for a mixed methods approach depend on the type of mixed method used in the design (see Types of Mixed Methods Designs later in this chapter).

One of the most basic decisions in mixed methods research is whether you will employ a single phase or multiple phase approach. When using a *single-phase approach* (see Triangulation Design) both qualitative and quantitative questions can be identified as one set of questions that does not rely on the other. For example, Hertlein and Lambert-Shute (2007) examined the factors that influenced students' decisions to enroll in marriage and family therapy graduate training programs. In their study, the authors employed a single-phase approach via the Internet. For the quantitative aspect, the authors surveyed students currently enrolled in MFT programs about factors relevant to their selection process and used descriptive statistics to analyze the data. For the qualitative aspect of their study, Hertlein and Lambert-Shute included a set of open-ended questions aimed at clarifying the results of the survey data.

In a *two-phase approach*, the second part of the approach elaborates on the first—see Explanatory or Exploratory Designs. For example, Carl Sheperis, one of the authors of this chapter, in conjunction with one of his doctoral students (Amy Davis), is conducting an ongoing mixed methods study on counselor readiness to treat Autism (ASD). In the first phase of this study, the researchers are surveying professional counselors to identify their level of counseling involvement with children diagnosed with ASD; their level of training for treating ASD; and their overall knowledge of issues related to ASD. The researchers are asking participants who have had experience working with children diagnosed with ASD to consider participating in phase two of the study. In phase two, the researchers are conducting in-depth interviews with counselors to identify the themes of their lived-experiences in working with children with ASD.

Because the process of identifying unknown themes can be somewhat nebulous, it is often difficult to specify questions for two-phase studies beforehand. After the study is completed the researcher can provide questions from both phases. Regardless of whether you choose a one- or two-phase approach to mixed methods research, you should consider the following when creating mixed methods questions:

- Relate your questions to the type of design you are using within your mixed methods research.
- Ensure that your questions are specific and measurable relative to the type of design employed.

CONSIDERATIONS WHEN MAKING DECISIONS ABOUT A MIXED METHODS DESIGN

Understanding your research questions is a truly important task. However, there are initial considerations prior to determining the type of mixed methods design you will employ. Creswell (1999) suggested the following strategies of inquiry in a mixed methods design:

1. ***Determine the order in which you will implement the qualitative and quantitative aspects of your study.*** How will you collect the quantitative and qualitative data in your study? Will you collect it concurrently or in sequence? As you make your determination about how to implement the qualitative and quantitative data in the study, you illustrate the intent of the study. For example, if collecting qualitative data first, the focus of the study is on providing depth to the study and identifying some of the larger concepts of the phenomenon. These concepts are to be expanded upon during the second phase of data collection when quantitative data are obtained from large numbers of people verifying the qualitative data.

2. ***Determine the weight that will be given to the quantitative and qualitative data.*** This is particularly important in the data collection and analysis phase of the study. Here, you must determine the extent to which each type of data will be incorporated into the study. Does the research topic call for questions that provide a *depth approach* (qualitative) followed by a *breadth approach* (quantitative), or the other way around? Will the data be analyzed concurrently? When making these decisions the researcher must consider his or her own interests, the interests of the potential readers of the study, and the study's purpose.

3. ***Determine how the two types of data will be mixed/combined.*** The researcher must determine how these two types of data will be combined to illustrate concepts found in the study. Creswell (1999) provides an example: "Mixing at the stage of data analysis and interpretation might involve transforming qualitative themes or codes into quantitative numbers and comparing that information with quantitative numbers and comparing that information with quantitative results" (p. 212). When will the data be combined? Which data will help inform the other?

4. ***Determine the theory that will guide your design.*** The theory chosen for your design will guide you through the study. Mixed methods researchers can make their theory explicit and use it to guide them in the way the study is conducted. Examples of theories used in mixed methods research include ethnographic, grounded theory, and phenomenological.

Answering these questions at the outset of the study will provide you with a greater sense of direction as you make decisions about a mixed methods design.

TYPES OF MIXED METHOD DESIGNS

Tashakkori and Teddlie (2003) found nearly 40 types of mixed methods designs in their review of literature for the *Handbook of Mixed Methods in Social and Behavioral Research*. These 40 designs span fields of research from health to education. While each design is unique to that particular discipline, Creswell and Plano Clark (2007) studied, summarized, and consolidated this information into four specific mixed methods designs. Each of these four designs has additional subdesigns associated with them that, because of space restrictions, are not discussed in this chapter (for a full description of the subdesigns, see Creswell & Plano Clark, 2007). Prior to implementing your research study you will want to carefully read and understand each design type in order to determine which fits best with your research questions and purpose of study.

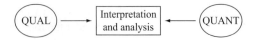

FIGURE 13.1 Triangulation Design

Triangulation Design

Triangulation is the most common of the four design types (Creswell & Plano Clark, 2007). The intent of this design is to "simultaneously collect both quantitative and qualitative data, merge the data, and use the results to understand a research problem" (Creswell, 2005, p. 514). This design takes the weaknesses of quantitative research (large numbers of participants, generalization) and complements them with the strengths of qualitative research (small number of participants, emerging design).

This is a one-phase design (see Figure 13.1), meaning that the researcher will implement the quantitative and qualitative aspects of the study concurrently. This indicates that both types of research carry equal weight. An example of this type of research was conducted by Hitchcock, Sarkar, Nastasi, Burkholder, Varjas, and Jayasena (2006). In their study, the researchers examined the cultural factors that impact psychological constructs measured by assessment instruments. Their goal was to develop a valid mental health assessment tool for adolescents in Sri Lanka. In order to develop this assessment tool, the authors used a combination of ethnographic research techniques (a type of qualitative research) and factor analytic approaches (a quantitative approach used in instrument development). The authors collected their qualitative data via interviews and focus groups while collecting their quantitative data via rating scales. The authors then used the information (themes) from the qualitative data to triangulate with the quantitative data as a form of validation.

Weaknesses of the Triangulation Design:

- Most challenging of the four types of designs because of the amount of researcher effort necessary.
- Large amount of time needed to implement design because you must concurrently gather qualitative and quantitative data.
- Differing findings between qualitative and quantitative research may require additional research and data collection to clarify disparities.

Strengths of Triangulation Design:

- Ideal design for research teams as the data collection can be divided.
- Efficient in that both types of research are collected concurrently.
- Combines the weaknesses of one type of data (quantitative) with the strengths of another type (qualitative).

Embedded Design

When you think of embedded design, think of a good movie. In a good movie there is often a leading actor who is the star of the show. Not to be outdone, the leading actor is supported by a cast of actors that make the lead actor's job a bit easier. Similarly, embedded design places one type of data in the "lead" role with the other type of data acting as a "supporting" actor. Accordingly, this design is used when researchers need to answer questions from a different perspective and their research has primarily focused on one type of data. This type of design is particularly useful when the researcher seeks to embed, or insert, a qualitative component within a quantitative design (Creswell & Plano Clark, 2007). Quantitative components may also be embedded in a qualitative design, but this rarely occurs.

With embedded design, the researcher begins by collecting one type of data, embedding it within a methodology framed by the other data type. Data are analyzed and interpreted using the primary form of data and then by using the other type of data to support the first analysis (see Figure 13.2).

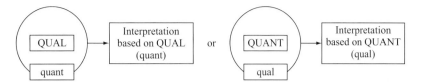

FIGURE 13.2 Embedded Design

The anti-poverty study by researchers at Northwestern University, provided at the beginning of this chapter, is an example of embedded design.

Weaknesses of the Embedded Design:

- Difficult to integrate the results when two methods are used to answer different research questions.
- Very few examples exist of integrating quantitative data with qualitative data.

Strengths of the Embedded Design:

- Provides you with an opportunity to follow-up on early results.
- You focus on one type of design, reducing your research time and effort.
- More manageable because one method requires less data than another.

Explanatory Design

This is a two-phase mixed methods design in which qualitative data help explain initial quantitative results. This design can be ideal for researchers who are looking for additional qualitative data to explain quantitative results.

As a researcher, you begin an explanatory design by collecting quantitative data and then collecting qualitative data to assist in explaining the quantitative results. Quantitative data provide the initial picture of the research problem, and the additional qualitative analysis explains the larger picture of the research. Unfortunately, this type of design is not widely employed in counseling research. Ivankova, Creswell, and Stick (2006) developed a guide for researchers interested in sequential explanatory design. In their article, the researchers provided an illustrative study of students' persistence in the Distance Learning Doctoral Program in Educational Leadership in Higher Education at the University of Nebraska-Lincoln. While this study does not include counseling-related issues, counseling training programs are increasingly using online formats for course delivery. Thus, this example can be informative for those interested in distance learning for counselor preparation.

In their study, Ivankova, Creswell, and Stick (2006) were interested in identifying the factors that related to doctoral students' persistence in their online educational program. They began the process by surveying 278 current and former students. From these data, the researchers then purposefully selected four individuals for participation in a qualitative case study. In the quantitative phase, the researchers discovered internal and external variables that related to persistence and then developed questions based on these variables for the qualitative case studies.

While the nature of sequential explanatory mixed methods design may appear to be straightforward, its implementation is complex. For those of you who are interested in conducting this type of research, we suggest that you thoroughly review the article by Ivankova, Creswell, and Stick (2006) to understand the transition from theory to practice (see Figure 13.3).

Weaknesses of the Explanatory Design:

- Requires you to have skills in quantitative and qualitative data collection. Thus, this type of design is labor intensive.
- Sometimes difficult to determine aspects of the study for qualitative follow-up.

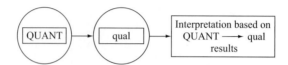

FIGURE 13.3 Explanatory Design

- As a researcher, you must determine whether study participants should be used in both phases of the research or go back to the original population and obtain a new sample for the qualitative portion of the study.
- Institutional Review Board approval can be difficult to obtain because you cannot identify the number of qualitative participants needed until the quantitative portion of the study has been conducted (Creswell & Plano Clark, 2007).

Strengths of the Explanatory Design:

- Easy for the reader to understand and identify. Each part of the process (i.e., the quantitative and then the qualitative) is highlighted in the research.
- You do not have to integrate two types of data.
- Methods conducted separately, research team is unnecessary.

Exploratory Design

Similar to the explanatory design, the exploratory design is a two-phase design where qualitative results are obtained first, followed by the quantitative in order to inform the qualitative data. Creswell and Plano Clark (2007) stated that this design is used when there are no measurements or instruments available to guide the study, when the variables are unknown, and when the study has no guiding framework or theory in use.

This design begins qualitatively and explores a phenomenon in rich detail; it allows the researcher to develop and test instruments, identify variables, generalize results to different groups, or test an emerging theory (Creswell, 1999; Morgan, 1998; Morse, 1991). In order to address issues of research bias in a qualitative study, researchers seek to disconfirm their hypotheses and initial interpretations of data. Seeking to disconfirm, rather than confirm, provides more legitimacy to the results through a reduction of bias.

As a researcher, you would begin by using qualitative methods to answer your research questions. Sussman, Williams, Leverence, Gloyd, and Crabtree (2006) used an exploratory design in their study of primary care clinicians' preventative counseling decisions. The purpose of their research was to identify factors that influence clinicians' decisions to include preventive counseling in brief primary care encounters.

Sussman et al. (2006) began their study with individual, in-depth interviews of 22 clinicians of various rank to determine the factors influencing delivery of preventative counseling. The participants were to reflect on the demands in the brief primary care encounter as a case study.

The research team read and analyzed the transcripts and identified emerging themes. The interview protocol was modified based upon the themes and to test ongoing interpretations. Data collection continued until the team developed a theoretical framework.

Following this, the research team conducted focus groups with 10 clinicians who were not interviewed previously. The research team included these clinicians in order to refine and disconfirm their preliminary interpretations while obtaining new data for analysis. Next, the team analyzed the focus group data and, based on the data from the interviews and focus groups, created a survey questionnaire. The survey focused on frequencies of agreement with the factors identified in the qualitative aspect of the study. The survey was pilot tested and mailed to study participants.

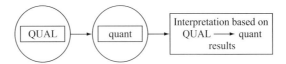

FIGURE 13.4 Exploratory Design

The quantitative data were returned and analyzed with multivariate regression tests to determine the association between predictor variables in the study. A factor analysis was also conducted.

The research obtained from the Sussman et al. (2006) research team was in-depth and provided additional insight into the phenomenon that one method could not provide alone (see Figure 13.4).

Weaknesses of Exploratory Design:

- Requires more time to implement; you need to take this into consideration (especially for a thesis or dissertation).
- Difficult to specify procedures of quantitative phase when applying for internal review board approval.

Strengths of Exploratory Design:

- Design is easily applied to multiphase and single studies.
- Emphasizes qualitative component, includes quantitative component as additional strength to the study.

SAMPLING

Now that we have covered some of the basic designs in mixed methods, it is important to discuss how we determine the participants for our research. Sampling is used in everyday aspects of your life, but you may not identify it as such. For example, have you ever been in a supermarket and asked to try the latest brand of orange juice? Or, have you ever test driven different vehicles in hopes of finding one to purchase? Often, if we are happy with the car or the juice we make a generalization that it is good. We then relate that information to the larger group, in this case a larger group of juices or particular brand of automobile, without trying all varieties. This is sampling (Adams & Schvaneveldt, 1991).

Samples can be random, convenient, stratified, or clustered, to name a few types. When a sample is determined correctly it provides "an unbiased, practical, and valid method of describing various aspects of the entire population" (Adams & Schaveneveldt, 1991, p. 179). Although sampling is addressed in other chapters in this text, it is important to discuss the unique nature of sampling when considering a mixed methods design.

Purposeful Sampling

Purposeful samples are those that you specifically choose and that contain a certain element that will highlight and inform a particular aspect of the study. Accordingly, when you use a purposeful sample, the sample is not random and may become subject to researcher bias (Bailey, 1978; Som, 1973).

FINDING A SAMPLE SIZE THAT IS "JUST RIGHT"   In the children's story *Goldilocks and the Three Bears*, Goldilocks is on a quest to find the perfect breakfast. She found one that was "just right" but only after she sampled a few others. So what is the ideal sample size to ensure that the study will provide enough information without drowning you in mounds of data? The answer is that it depends; finding the ideal sample size depends on the *method of data collection* in use.

Quantitative Sampling

More rigorous sampling methods are employed when using quantitative research. The sample needs to be large enough to perform the statistical procedures you use to make inferences about study findings. You need to be able to have some degree of confidence that the findings are valid and reliable. To find an adequate sample size in quantitative research, you can use sample size formulas available in statistics textbooks, or if using survey data, sampling error formulas are available to assist you in identifying an appropriate sample size for the study.

When considering your quantitative sample, keep the following in mind:

1. *Sampling error.*   The larger the difference between the sample size and the population, the bigger the sampling error (in terms of the sample being an accurate representation of the entire population).
2. *Method of data collection.*   Some collection methods are very expensive, such as multiple participant interviews; other methods are less expensive such as mailed questionnaires.
3. *Degree of precision desired in final results.*   If you wish to compare one group to another on the same issue you must have a sufficiently large sample to assure that the groups are represented in large enough numbers to make your findings accurate.

Qualitative Sampling

The selection of a qualitative sample depends on the purpose of the study and the information that will be most useful. Some qualitative studies focus on in-depth detail and employ a smaller number of participants but go into deep detail with each. Other studies require more breadth, including larger numbers of participants (though not to the extent of quantitative research samples), in order to examine a phenomenon in more detail.

One caveat in qualitative research: the larger the number of participants, the less depth and detail that can go into the data collection with each. There is no exact number of individuals that makes a qualitative study trustworthy. Patton (1990) stated: "Qualitative inquiry typically focuses in depth on a relatively small sample, even single cases ($n = 1$), selected purposefully" (p. 169). Instead of identifying the ideal number of qualitative participants, the number is based on the approach used in the study. Accordingly, there will be different numbers of participants chosen in a case study as compared with the number of participants in a grounded theory or phenomenological study (Creswell, 1998).

Summary

At this point in your journey toward understanding research and its role in professional counseling, you have learned about quantitative and qualitative research, and the combination of the two; and mixed methods research designs. As you can surmise from this chapter, mixed methods designs result in a more comprehensive understanding of research data but require you to be skilled in both quantitative and qualitative procedures. As a result, mixed methods studies are often employed by more senior researchers or by doctoral students under the close supervision of a dissertation director.

Should you choose to implement mixed methods in your counseling research, some of the primary decisions you will make will be about the appropriate model and the emphasis on quantitative or qualitative methods. In this chapter, we provided you with a general overview that will help guide you in those decisions. However, as is the case with any research effort, you will have to fully explore the world of mixed methods if you choose to use this approach. For more information on mixed methods research, here are some resources for you to consult.

Review and Discussion Questions

1. What are some of the advantages and disadvantages associated with using mixed methods designs in counseling research?
2. How do mixed methods approaches combine quantitative and qualitative methodologies?
3. Assume you are going to conduct a mixed methods study on the effectiveness of cognitive behavioral therapy on reducing anxiety, what would your research questions be? How would you select a sample? What data collection procedures would you use?
4. Take some time to search your library databases for mixed methods studies. How do these compare to other articles that you have read?
5. Compare and contrast the four approaches to mixed methods research? Does any one appear to be more comprehensive than the others? Why?
6. What factors should you consider in determining whether to conduct a single or multiple phase study?

Helpful Resources

Clark, V. L., Creswell, J. W., Green, D. O., & Shope, R. J. (2008). Mixing quantitative and qualitative approaches: An introduction to emergent mixed methods research. In S. N. Hesse-Biber & P. Leavy (Eds.), *Handbook of emergent methods* (pp. 363–387). New York: Guilford Press.

Creswell, J. W. (1999). Mixed-method research: Introduction and application. In G. J. Cizek (Ed.), *Handbook of educational policy* (pp. 455–472). San Diego: Academic Press.

Creswell, J. W., Plano Clark, V., Gutmann, M., & Hanson, W. (2003). Advances in mixed method design. In A. Tashakkori & C. Teddlie (Eds.), *Handbook of mixed methods in* the *social and behavioral sciences*. Thousand Oaks, CA: Sage.

Tashakkori, A., & Teddlie, C. (2003*). Mixed methodology: Combining qualitative and quantitative approaches*. Thousand Oaks, CA: Sage.

CHAPTER 14

Data Management and Using SPSS Software

Anastasia D. Elder, *Mississippi State University*
Vanessa Esparza, *Mississippi State University*

OBJECTIVES

After reading this chapter, you will:

- Be able to understand the benefits of using a statistical computer software package like SPSS.
- Be able to create a code book for data.
- Be able to set up a data file on SPSS.
- Be able to enter data on SPSS.
- Be able to perform preliminary analyses in SPSS.
- Be able to understand the following key terms:
  - SPSS
  - Code book
  - Data view
  - Variable view
  - Data entry

OVERVIEW

The goal of this chapter is to provide you with guidance in managing data and in using a computer-based statistical software package for analyzing data. Much of what we discuss in this chapter is honed from years of teaching novice student-researchers about good research practices for maintaining data records and about their initial utilization of computer software in analyzing research. In this chapter, the data management techniques will be discussed in reference to Statistical Package for the Social Sciences (SPSS) for Windows. SPSS is a statistical software package widely used in behavioral sciences including education, psychology, and counseling.

Simply put, SPSS is a statistical tool for any researcher, novice or seasoned professional, with the goal of understanding and making meaning from a pile of "stuff" that they have collected. It is a computer-based software package that allows you to maintain a dataset of your collected research and which includes powerful processing capabilities to produce a wide range of statistical analyses in an effort to provide answers to your research questions.

VALUE LABEL

The computer and statistical analysis software serve as valuable tools in analyzing research. While several statistical analysis programs exist, one often employed by counseling researchers is SPSS. Because we cannot review the procedures of all available software programs, we hope that an introduction to SPSS will offer some understanding for your data analysis using any program. In this chapter, we will provide guidance for you to set up a data file for the first time. We will provide steps for setting up a data file, steps for data entry on SPSS for Windows, and steps for running descriptive statistics on SPSS. It is not intended to be a primer for your understanding of statistics or to describe how to run many statistical analyses on SPSS. Instead, it is intended to fill in the gap between the collection of data and the "running" or analyzing of data. Often, this information is not systematically spelled out in research texts, statistics texts, or in how-to manuals for using statistical software packages. Nonetheless, the material covered in this chapter is important in setting up and analyzing your data smoothly. In addition, this chapter will help you to familiarize yourself with basic skills and concepts for using SPSS for Windows in analyzing your own data file and interpreting your results. Much of what you will see here is appropriate for recent iterations of SPSS and likely any future version. Overall, this chapter is organized around questions that a student-researcher may have, including: Why SPSS? I have data, now what? How do I get data into SPSS? How do I go about using SPSS to answer my research questions?

WHY SPSS?

SPSS is a statistical software package that simplifies data analysis. It is frequently used in the behavioral sciences, including the fields of education, psychology, and counseling. Many statistics courses use SPSS in instruction for learning statistical procedures. Many researchers turn to the SPSS program as opposed to spreadsheet programs (which SPSS shares appearance with) because SPSS is a better tool for statistics: it is specifically designed for performing statistical analyses, it provides statistical information needed in research reports, it can perform advanced statistics, and it is menu driven to perform these analyses, unlike the popular spreadsheet programs.

For the purposes of this text, SPSS is a tool that can help you transform research data you have collected into meaningful and useful information. Instead of applying time-consuming statistical formulas with paper and pencil, SPSS allows you to input your data, set some conditions, and apply menu-driven commands to generate statistical tests. In this way, you, as a researcher, can focus your energy on asking questions and drawing conclusions about the information you have gathered instead of performing multiple calculations and computations on numerous observations. Note, this does not mean you have no need for learning and understanding statistics: you will still need to have that skill. SPSS is a powerful tool to "crunch" numbers, but it will not magically decide which statistics to run. That is your job.

Analyzing data is not just about calculation of numbers; it is about finding answers to research questions you have asked, attributing meaning to the numbers based on your research design and chosen statistics, and finally, about drawing conclusions about human behavior. Ultimately, the data analysis phase of research is an exciting culmination during which you are able to answer your own research questions. If you are conducting an actual research project, it is likely that you have experienced all aspects of the research—conceptualizing the study, planning the methods, and collecting the data—and now you get to see the results of all your hard work!

In your research, you will more than likely collect quantitative data; data that have a numerical value, or that can be transformed to have a numerical value; and data that correspond to individual participants' responses on various variables (Kerr, Hall, & Kozub, 2002). For example, if you are interested in social anxiety among college freshmen you might collect students' responses to items that ask for their: (1) age, (2) gender, (3) personal interests, (4) locations they perceive as conducive to relaxation, (5) places they perceive as provoking anxiety, and (6) emotions they feel while participating in five typical college social situations. These are all different characteristics of an individual that will vary from person to person. Each of the variables in this example are quantifiable in that you can assign numbers to them (e.g., 1 = male and 2 = female). When you quantify a variable, you can then use some type of statistical analyses to answer your research questions.

For example, if you were to lay out all the data you collected for 100 participants on each of the variables, you would quickly realize how difficult a task it would be to make sense of all the information. Statistics and statistical software packages, like SPSS, enable one to organize and summarize the data and hence foster the discovery of patterns in the gathered information. In this manner, the 100 individual pieces of information become manageable. SPSS serves as a practical tool that you can use to process the data and reduce them to a more functional form (Kerr, Hall, & Kozub, 2002).

You may just be starting out on your research journey, so keep in mind that with SPSS you can keep it simple and perform basic descriptive types of analyses (e.g., frequencies, means, etc.) or perform more advanced inferential statistical techniques (multiple regression, analysis of covariance), depending on your research purposes and the type of information that you have collected. At first, you may just be interested in the overall picture of your data. For example, you may be asking yourself, "What patterns came up in my data? What do the overall scores in my sample look like? Did some cases stand out more than others?" On the other hand, the researcher can use SPSS to answer more specific questions, such as, "Was there a difference among treatments? Did age (or some variable) make a difference?" Regardless of the type of question you have, SPSS can be used to explore data and get answers to specific research questions.

I HAVE DATA, NOW WHAT?

Four Steps to Complete Before You Go Near the Computer and SPSS

At this point, you have collected your data and are eager to begin your analysis process. Before jumping onto the computer, there are four helpful steps that will foster your research and data analyses. The suggestions that follow aid in good research practice and build on the methods and requirements of statistical analyses in general and SPSS specifically. To paraphrase a popular advertisement: entering data over again, because the first time was rushed and not thought out, *3 hours*; having to dig through original data because you did not keep good records, *30 minutes of irritation*; cannot remember what you called a variable in your dataset, *migraine-inducing*; avoiding typical mistakes by following the next steps for good research practice, *priceless*.

Step One: Connect Data to Each Individual Participant

For accurate analyses, it is important that all information is lined up and attached to the particular individual from which it came. It is not enough to know that you collected data on 12 males and 15 females and that 5 of each of those received psychodynamic therapy, 5 behavioral, and 5 cognitive. Instead, SPSS must know, for example, that a single participant was female, is 19, had psychodynamic therapy, scored 12 on your social anxiety scale pretest; is highly extroverted, and so on. That is, you must enter the exact information for each individual participant on each variable. In effect, you must respect that you are collecting this information on individuals and thus relate that information to SPSS via the computer. Building on this understanding, the following practices allow for smooth data entry and analysis using SPSS.

Step Two: Give Each Participant a Unique Number (i.e., Assign Subject Numbers)

If you collect questionnaires or have information tied to an individual participant, it is good research practice to assign a unique subject number to each person. A good starting point is usually the number "1." The number can be written directly on the questionnaire, so that the subject number then replaces the participant's name in the dataset. Separately, you should keep a list of subject numbers and names, but with no data. Then you can delete names from your dataset in accordance with ethical guidelines for human subjects. See the discussion in Chapter 17, Ethical Consideration in the Practice of Research.

Using a number to identify research participants is a good idea for several reasons. First, it is always important because it separates identity of individuals from their data and thus fosters confidentiality of data, which may often be sensitive. Also, by working with subject numbers and not names, you guard against potential experimenter effects or biases,which can occur when an experimenter knowingly or unknowingly lets his or her opinions, feelings, or prejudices have a positive or negative effect on the process of collecting or investigating data. As an ethical researcher, you want to avoid influencing the data in any way that is not intended as part of the study so that the results found from the research can be unbiased and thus considered generalizable to the population of interest and not specific to just this one study. Finally, by assigning a number to each individual you have a way to look up data later. That is, if you enter data without a subject number and if you later find an error, it is impossible to look up that person's data (since the name was likely removed to accommodate the ethical guidelines for working with human subjects!).

Some researchers may choose to embed other information in the subject number (classroom, group, etc.) and may assign numbers in the hundreds to represent the group (e.g., treatment group is in the 200's and control group is in the 100's) and then may use 101,102 . . . 199 and 201, 202 . . . 299. Please note that the most participants you can have per group in this scheme is 99; if you have more than 99 participants, then you can start your numbering with 1001.

Step Three: Create a Codebook

A codebook is a sort of personal dictionary of your research variables that helps in translating the data you collected into variables for the computer. Creating a codebook may seem a bit time-consuming when you are eager to get started on your data analysis, but it is extremely helpful. Basically, codes are the numbers you enter in an SPSS data file (computers like to work with numbers), and the way to tell SPSS what the numbers mean. Think of this as a process by which categories become numbers (e.g., strongly agree = 5) and variables—or a question from a survey—have nicknames (e.g., The item "I feel very comfortable speaking in public to a group" becomes COMFORT).

A codebook is the way for you to keep track of what names and labels you assign to all your variables and values in a separate document, to aid in your memory. It is very easy to forget what nickname is what and whether you assigned "male" a "0" or a "1." Thus, creating and maintaining this document can prevent potential problems and headaches in the future. This enables the researcher to work between the statistical program and back again to the original collected information (e.g., questionnaire or psychological test) without taxing one's fragile memory.

If your dataset is small (15 variables or less), you can make the codebook for your research data directly on a blank questionnaire. If your data contain many variables (and most will), your codebook should be created in a separate document. In addition, this information can be kept in SPSS under variable view (more on this later). Especially for new researchers, it is good practice to create the codebook. Even for seasoned researchers, creating a codebook is helpful because often their datasets are large with many variables and transformations of those variables that become too numerous to keep in one's head for any length of time. Furthermore, it is good to have access to this information when you are not near the computer. See Figure 14.1 for a portion of a codebook.

Step Four: Name the Variables Carefully

The trick in naming variables is to make them precise, descriptive, and user friendly when typed into the computer. Naming the variable with a label that is related to the concept is good for many variables (e.g., "age" for age of participant; "subjno" for subject number; "gender" for sex of participant, etc.). However, when obtaining responses to many items on a questionnaire that are interrelated, it may be easiest to name the variable after the question number (e.g., Q1, Q2, etc.). This makes it

---

Section I. Background Information

Variable Name:	subjno
Description:	identification number
Coding:	
Variable Name:	gender
Description:	gender
Coding:	0 = female; 1 = male
Variable Name:	age
Description:	age in years
Coding:	numeric variable
Variable Name:	race
Description:	ethnic background
Coding:	1 = Amer. Indian or Alaskan Native
	2 = African–American
	3 = Hispanic
	4 = Asian or Pacific Islander
	5 = White/Caucasian
	6 = Other
Variable Name:	treatment
Description:	type of treatment received for 4 weeks
Coding:	1 = counseling-psychodynamic
	2 = cognitive
	3 = behavioral
Variable Name:	preanxq1
Description:	My anxiety inhibits me from talking to a classmate
Coding q1–q11	1 = strongly disagree
	2 = disagree
	3 = agree
	4 = strongly agree
Variable Name:	preanxq2
	I feel comfortable trying new things
Variable Name:	postanxq1
	(after treatment) My anxiety inhibits me from talking to a classmate

---

FIGURE 14.1 Sample Codebook

easier to locate and choose a particular variable when running SPSS analysis. (And the codebook next to you helps you remember to what exactly Q1 refers.) It is easier to remember and/or locate items from an SPSS analysis dialogue box named Q1, Q5, Q7, and Q8 than to remember and/or locate items, self-efficacy; self-concept; self-esteem in those same circumstances. Furthermore, if you later need to revise the variable, then naming the revised variable becomes less of a linguistic task: Q1r, Q2rev becomes easy to create, locate, and mark on your codebook.

Furthermore, at this point it is helpful to create a variable for group affiliation if your research design required it. For example, if you subjected participants to one of three different types of counseling—psychodynamic, cognitive, and behavioral—then you should have a variable that reflects that group assignment. You might call it "treatment" and name the levels the three types—psychodynamic, cognitive, and behavioral. Having a separate variable fosters analyses comparing the groups. Some students mistakenly either forget this variable, or create two different datasets. However, in order for the statistical analysis (on SPSS or any other software) to compare groups, there needs to be a variable defining the groups, and this variable needs to be in the same dataset as other variables you will be using.

HOW DO I GET DATA INTO SPSS?

I Am FINALLY Ready for the Computer!

Now that you have collected your data and completed the steps that require no software, it is time to get settled in front of your desktop and start SPSS. This will take some comfort with maneuvering the computer mouse, as well as a basic understanding of manipulating menu-driven software.

Beginning the Program

To begin with, you can start SPSS in one of two ways. If your computer screen has the "SPSS" icon, then you can simply double-click the icon and this will start SPSS. If not, you can begin by going to the bottom left-hand corner of your screen and single clicking "Start." Next, you will point your cursor over the "Programs" or "All Programs" text. This will bring up a narrow row of different options. Select "SPSS for Windows" by pointing the arrow over the text, but do not click the text. When you scroll your cursor over "SPSS for Windows" a new list of options will appear. Single-click on "SPSS for Windows." Depending on which version of SPSS you are using, the text may read "SPSS 14.0 for Windows" or "SPSS 13.0," and so on.

Once you have started SPSS, two screens will simultaneously appear. The first will ask you, "What would you like to do?" For most of you this will be your first time entering data, or your first time entering this data file, so you will single-click the radio button beside "Type in data" and then single-click "OK." If you have previously entered your data and are coming back to it, you will single click the radio button beside "Open an existing data source" and then single-click "OK." Scroll up or down until you find your dataset. When you spot the name of the data file that you wish to work with, single-click the title to highlight the data and then single-click "OK." This window will disappear and you will have full view of a grid-like screen (see Figure 14.2).

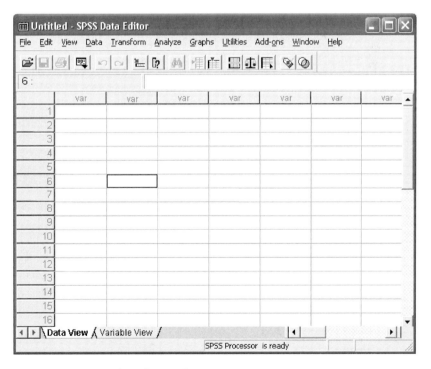

FIGURE 14.2 Screenshot of Data View

Using the Data Editor

This grid-like screen presenting a spreadsheet is known as the SPSS data editor (see Figure 14.2). You will notice that at the top of the screen you have your menu bar which includes the following options: File, Edit, View, Data, Transform, Analyze, Graphs, Utilities, Add-ons, Window, and Help. These options are known as your menu commands. Each menu command will help you with the unique tasks that you encounter as you work with data in SPSS. A brief overview of each menu command is provided in Table 14.1.

Below the menu bar there are icons. These icons serve as shortcuts to some of the options found in the menu commands. Instead of having to use the menu commands, you can simply single-click the icon. If you are unsure of the action of the icon, hold your cursor over the picture and text will appear. This text will remind you of the action. For example, if you forgot what single-clicking the binoculars icon will do, scroll your cursor over the picture and a text box will appear that reads "Find" reminding you that single-clicking this icon will find a saved file or folder.

Another special feature of your spreadsheet is found at the bottom left-hand corner of your screen. You will notice two tabs. One tab is labeled "Data View," which is the view you are in at the moment, and the other tab is labeled "Variable View." "Data View" (Figure 14.2) is the view which shows you the data you enter and is the view from which you can run statistical analyses. "Variable View" (Figure 14.3) is the view in which you can assign notations to variables. Please make note of these tabs! Many students become frustrated with SPSS because they do not understand why their information is not being entered correctly and it is simply because they are not on the right screen.

TABLE 14.1   An Overview of SPSS Menu Commands

File	Useful for tasks that involve opening, creating, saving, and printing data files.
Edit	Allows you to edit your data file with functions such as copy, cut, paste, insert variables, or insert cases. These editing functions can be applied within your data editor screen or in combination with other files and programs. In addition, the edit menu allows you to undo a mistake or redo your last actions within your SPSS editor screen by simply single-clicking the option.
View	Allows you to change your view from "data view" to "variable view." You can also select to view the "value labels" of your data input by selecting "value labels," which will change the view from the codes you inputted in variable view to the actual values they represent.
Data	This command is practical for tasks that involve defining, sorting, and weighing cases in your data input. Also useful in merging or aggregating files.
Transform	This command is commonly used to compute anything from basic arithmetic to highly specified statistical formulas. Under this command you will also find the option to rank your data cases.
Analyze	This is more than likely the command you will use most often with SPSS. All data analysis begins by selecting this command.
Graphs	Can be used to create graphs such as bar charts, pie graphs, and histograms.
Utilities	You will probably not be using this command as a beginner. This command helps in tasks that require highly complex statistical procedures.
Add-ons	Yields options of other statistical programs for procedures that are not offered within SPSS.
Window	Allows you to minimize your SPSS window screen.
Help	An option to select if you feel lost or need some guidance about statistical procedures that you can apply when using SPSS.

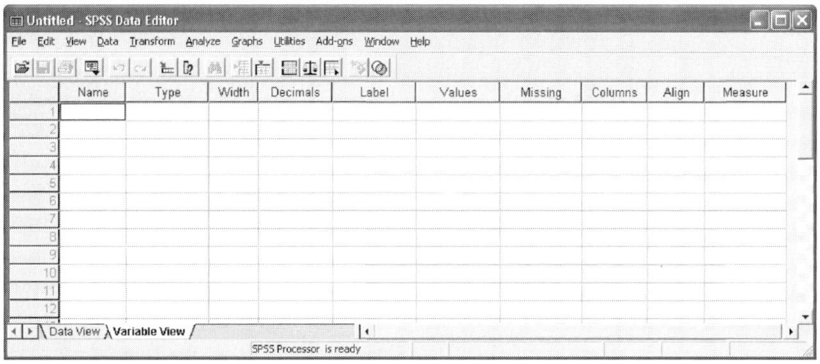

FIGURE 14.3 Screenshot of Variable View

In order to assure yourself that you are working with the right screen, all you need to do is check that the tab of the spreadsheet screen you wish to be working with is in bold. It will be to your benefit to become familiar with these options and where they are located. (Keep in mind that although this may seem like a lot of information to take in right away, the more that you use SPSS the more these characteristics of the program will become second nature to you.)

Next, it is important to notice that running horizontally across the top of the data editor screen you will see "VAR" in the spreadsheet cells (this is while you are in "Data View"; see Figure 14.2). "VAR" is short for variables. The names of the variables from the data that you input will be located in these cells and will replace "VAR." Also, running vertically down the spreadsheet you will note numbers in cells that start with number "1" and progressively increase as they go down your screen. These cells represent a running count of the number of subjects in your dataset. So, each row represents each participant, a column represents each variable, and a cell represents a single piece of information, that is, the response of a single participant on a single variable. It is very important to understand this for entering data on SPSS.

Defining Your Variables

Now, you are ready to begin defining your data. For starters, single-click the "Variable View" tab. This will bring you to your new screen (see Figure 14.3). "Variable View" allows you to input your variables and define their value. You will note that across the top of your grid the columns are already labeled. The tags include: Name, Type, Width, Decimals, Label, Values, Missing, Columns, Align, and Measure. For the purpose of this introduction to SPSS, it is good to be aware of all the tags, but Name, Decimals, Label, and Values will be discussed in more depth than the others. Note that these tags are the computer method of creating a codebook, so you should match the information you assign in these tags to that in the written codebook you have already started. Once you become adept at SPSS and have a relatively small dataset you may skip the codebook step and work directly with these tags. If your data are particularly dense with lots of variables, it may be still helpful to have both codebook and tags available to you.

NAME   This tag allows you to title your variables. To get started, single-click in the first cell under "Name" and type in the name of your first variable. The name should match what you assigned to the variable in the codebook. In our sample codebook the first variable is "subjno" (see Figure 14.1) so the first variable you will enter under "Name" will be "subjno" (see Figure 14.4). Continue to type in one variable per cell down this column. Be sure to enter only one variable per cell. To transition to the next cell you can: (1) use the curser keys or (2) point your mouse to the next cell and single-click. Depending on the version of SPSS that you are using, the default setting will only

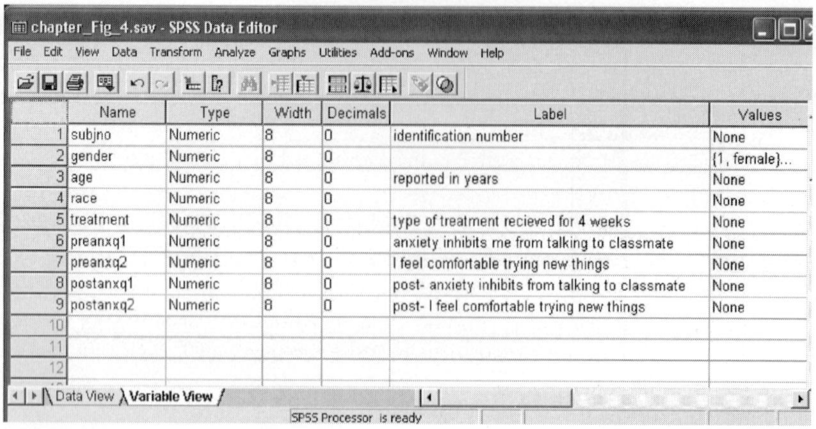

FIGURE 14.4 Creating Variable Names in SPSS

allow a limited number of letters (about 10) to show in the variable cell. Adjust the name of your variable to fit this width. Reminder: SPSS is not case sensitive. In other words, "AGE" will read the same as "age" and "Age."

DECIMALS   For each variable you will need to set the decimal place. The SPSS default setting is 2 decimal places (e.g., 1.00). However, you can change this by single-clicking the cell of the decimal place you wish to change. Next, two blue arrows will appear in the right corner of the cell. Adjust up or down accordingly. When you are entering discontinuous values—values that are whole numbers or categorical such as gender—it is probably best to set your decimal place to 0. When you are working with continuous values—values that are not just whole numbers but also include decimals such as G.P.A.—then you may want to increase the decimal placement. In this way, when you are looking at the "Data View" screen you can be reminded of the scale of measurement of the variable.

LABEL   This tag becomes handy when you would like a reminder of the variable. For example, if you are entering scores on an anxiety scale and SPPS only allows you to enter "prescore" under "Name," you can enter a description, such as "score on anxiety measure before treatment" under "Label." This will serve as a short description that helps to remind you of what "prescore" stands for when you run your data analysis (see Figure 14.4). This is especially helpful when you are working with a large number of variables. Furthermore, if the name of the variable is somewhat cryptic (e.g., Q1preanx), the label allows you to more fully describe it (e.g., question 1 on pretest anxiety assessment). However, even when you are only defining a few variables it can still serve as a helpful cue and a good habit to practice. In both SPSS analysis window commands and output tables, it is possible to print the variable labels and not just the variable name.

VALUES   Not all the data that you enter into SPSS are originally of a numerical value. SPSS allows you to define the value of your variables so that you can assign numbers to different levels or conditions of a variable. The "Value" option is used when you are coding the levels of your variable (e.g., therapy: 1 = psychodynamic, 2 = cognitive, 3 = behavioral). The value itself is the code that you assign to each level. These are nominal variables and thus the "value" that you assign will not change the actual meaning of the variable. In other words, the fact that you assign the value of "1" to psychodynamic and "2" to cognitive does not mean that the cognitive treatment "has more value" than the psychodynamic treatment. It will simply make it possible for SPSS to read the levels of your variable.

Entering Data

At this point you are ready to enter your collected data into SPSS. Let us start with an example. Suppose that you have collected information from 65 counseling clients who have received treatment for their social anxiety over the course of eight weeks. You are interested in comparing the effectiveness of three different treatments that were administered. You have collected data on: gender, age, type of treatment, pretest score on social anxiety scale, mid-treatment score on social anxiety scale, and posttest score on social anxiety.

In order to start the process of inputting this data you will begin by defining your first variable. In this example, the first variable is subject number (subjno). *Single-click* the first cell under "Name" to select the cell and type in your first variable just as you named in it your codebook (subjno). For an illustration of this process, see Figure 14.4. Next, highlight the cell under "Decimals" and set your decimal place to 0 by single-clicking the arrow down until the 0 appears. No additional information is necessary here. Remember the subject number is an identification number for your participants and each number should be different for every case.

Your second variable is gender, a nominal variable in which numerical values are assigned to the levels or characteristics of the variable. First, type in your variable name (gender). Next, set your decimal place to 0, and then single-click under "Values." A small grey box will appear in the right-side corner of the cell; single-click the small grey box. The "Value label" box will appear (see Figure 14.5). First, single-click the narrow white box beside "Value," and assign a numerical value, such as the number 1; single-click in the next white box next to "Label," and type in the label, such as female. Once you have entered both your value and your label, single-click "Add." The information that you entered will appear in the large white box and you can go on to create a value and label for the next item. I chose 1 for "female" and 2 for "male." Once you have done this, single-click "OK." This should match the information you have created in your codebook—same variable names and labels and assigned values, and so on.

This is the same process you will complete *each time* for your other nominal variables. Note that for nominal variables we are assigning numbers to characteristics, but there is no actual quantitative distinction between those characteristics. That is, if 1 = female and 2 = male, the numbers just stand for the two types of gender, nothing more. You cannot perform any calculations on these numbers in any meaningful manner. For variables that already have a numerical value, such as age,

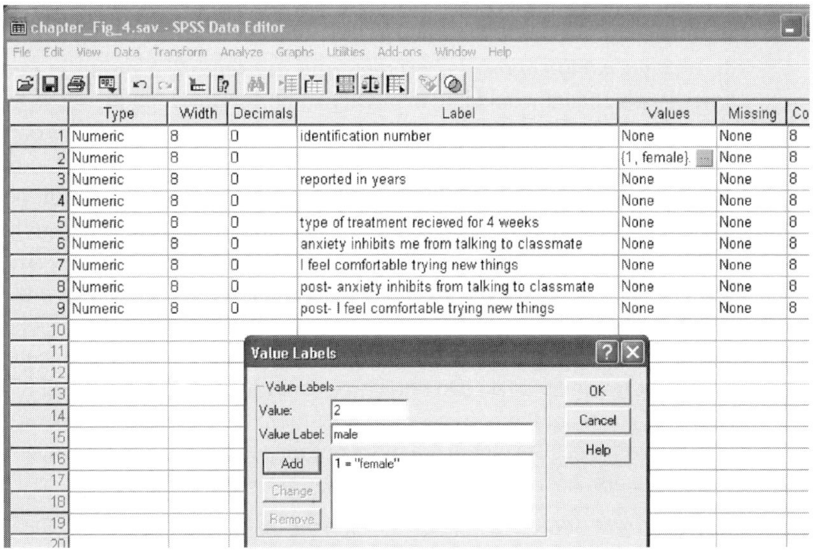

FIGURE 14.5 Displaying Value Label

there is no need to change the value because it is already a quantitative value; just enter it as it is (e.g., 38) with no label.

Wow, I bet you want to take a breather after all of that! The good news is that once you have defined your variables you are ready to enter your data! You can do this by single-clicking the "Data View" tab located at the bottom left-hand corner of your screen. Across the top of your screen where it previously read "VAR," you should now see the names of the variables you defined from your data file. Enter data (i.e., values for each variable) by case or individual. This means that each individual will be represented by a single row, and that you will enter data going across a row.

A single piece of information goes into each cell. You should have the raw or paper data with you. In addition, the codebook is helpful at this point. Go ahead and enter the information for the first participant. You probably needed to look back at the codebook often to check on variable names and labels. It gets quicker with time. Before continuing with the rest of the data entry, please read the following section, which offers advice to make data entry proceed smoothly.

Tips on Data Entry

1. *Enter your data going across.* It is important to enter data into SPSS by individual/case, not by variable. You should be going across a row to enter data on SPSS (you may use the arrow keys on your keyboard to move around the database). As researchers, our questions to be answered by statistics usually involve figuring out relations among variables or differences between groups. Either way, it is important that data be identifiable by individual or linked accurately to the right individual so that you can perform meaningful statistical analysis. By entering your data going across a row, you minimize your chances of getting off track and accidentally assigning one person's information to someone else. This means entering data one individual participant or questionnaire at a time.

2. *Use the original order and form of your data.* Enter the variables in SPSS in the same order that they appear on the original form. Again, this results in less room for error (putting in the wrong value). If you do prefer to have your variables in a different order, you can always rearrange the order of it in SPSS later. It is best to keep the task of entering numbers as "error-proof" and mindless as possible by entering the variables in the order in which they appear in the questionnaire. Also, use the codebook you created. Again, the aim is to make data entry process as free from errors as possible by not challenging your attention too much. By having written resources in front of you and going in order of the original questionnaire or data sheet, you, as the researcher, are concentrating exclusively on accurately putting values into the SPSS data file. Remember: mindless as possible so it is error free. (Look on the bright side: when else does research and/or statistics demand mindlessness?)

3. *Wait on modifications to variables and use the SPSS program to make later.* There might be times in which you would like to modify some variables. Perhaps how you originally entered a particular variable is not appropriate for how you would like to analyze your data. It is recommended that you use the powerful processing capability of SPSS to perform any modifications. It can perform these modifications more quickly, efficiently, and accurately than if you performed them yourself. The power of statistical packages like SPSS is to let it do the things it can, that is, things computers like to do: reassigning numbers, combining groups, calculating means, adding up numbers, and so on. Leaving such tasks to the software is easier on you, the researcher, and results in less room for error.

As mentioned earlier, a quick note here: if you collect data like AGE and your participants supply such information by simply reporting a number (e.g., 30), enter it that way (see variable in codebook in Figure 14.1). Do not worry about making groupings on it yet (e.g., 18–24; 25–31; etc.). Again, if you want them, SPSS can make them for you with less error. Also, many times continuous data are better because there are more options on the type of statistics to run. Again, do not alter any variables yet—keep data entry mindless.

4. *Save your data.* It is important and makes good sense to save your work frequently when using SPSS. While you are working in SPSS you are constantly making changes to your data file and running different analyses. It is to your benefit to keep the work you have produced on file and as current as possible. You can save your Data Editor input even before you begin to enter your data. Scroll to your menu bar and single-click File > Save as . . . a Save Data As window will appear. Select the location in which you wish to save your work by single-clicking the arrow bar next to "save in." A drop-down menu will appear. As with other files, you have the option of saving to external hardware (USB memory stick, disc, etc.) or directly to your computer hard drive. Be sure to select the appropriate location to store your data, because often a default setting on the computer may not be the one you want. Many times students believe they have "lost" their data when, in fact, they mistakenly saved it to the default setting instead of where they intended. Once you have selected your location, it will appear in the "save in" box.

Next, be certain to give your work a title that you will easily recognize in the future and single-click "OK." Datasets in SPSS are saved as .sav files. This allows the computer and program to recognize the type of file it is (just like .pdf is an Adobe Acrobat file). So do not use a period (.) in the name of your file and do not take out the .sav suffix—SPSS will not recognize it as a data file and you will have problems opening the file in SPSS again in the future.

Once you have named and saved your file once, you should continue to periodically save your work. It takes just a second to update the status of what you have saved. Simply go to File > Save (you have previously titled your work), or single-click the Save icon that is symbolized by a diskette on your icon bar. Also, save your work in more than one location. Disks (as you might already know) are not fool proof. You can lose your disk, or it can crash at the most inopportune time. If you are working at a student computer lab, it would be a good idea to e-mail your data file to yourself and/or to save your data file on another reliable external drive. In addition, do not discard the original (raw/paper) data just because you have them saved on a disk or have them on your computer. A good rule of thumb is to keep your original data for five years in a safe, private place. In the future, you may need to access these data.

5. _Double-check your data._   The last step in effective data entry is not inputting the last number; instead, good data entry requires that you take some time to double-check your data entry. Two methods for checking data are described. It is recommended that both are done; they work jointly with each other, not as either-or alternatives to each other. First by eye, recheck to see if what is entered on the computer is what is on paper. It might be best to go "backwards" here, that is, read what is on the screen to see if it matches what is on paper, since originally to enter the data you went from the paper first. Do this with approximately 20% of cases. Also, look for the "extra" case, that is, an empty row of data in the dataset; this tends to happen especially at the end. It may look like a series of missing data cells (ones with periods [.] in them). You can tell because SPSS will have a number highlighted/assigned to that row on the far left, yet you will not have any data points in the subject number variable or any values entered in that row.

In addition to rechecking as described above, another way to check your data entry is to run some simple descriptive analyses (see below) on all your variables to see if the mean, minimum and maximum values, and the total number of cases (N) make sense. The question you need to ask yourself is: Do they match what is possible for that variable? This is a quick way to find mistakes. For example, if "55" showed up as the maximum score for an item that was on a Likert scale of 1 to 5, you know that you made a mistake. You then can peruse the column of that variable in your data to find the "55" and once you find the subject number you can return to the "raw" or original (paper) data/questionnaire and fill in the correct value. At that point you would likely want to check the other items surrounding the one with the mistake on it; there may very well be other errors with the data entry of that participant. In addition, the N listed for any variable should match the number of participants for which you have entered data on that variable. This way of checking the data—running descriptives—is good to do as supplementary to the first suggestion, not instead of the first suggestion.

6. _A note on missing data points._   Although as researchers we strive to have complete data, sometimes data are missing. Usually, by collecting pilot data, writing clear items, and checking equipment prior to data collection, we can avoid the problem of missing data. However, incidences of people forgetting to fill out an item are bound to happen. Sometimes we are concerned with issues of why data are missing and trying to understand more about patterns of missing data (e.g., in large-scale analysis of survey data). If that is the case, additional references should be sought for how to best perform missing data analysis.

SPSS offers a way to label missing data in which you can assign certain codes (numbers) to represent missing information. This can be done in the variable view section in which you are defining your variables. Defining missing data in this way would offer you a way to do missing data analysis. Often, we may not be that concerned with the missing information. If the occurrences are infrequent, you may want to leave the cell blank for that item. This will result in SPSS leaving a period in the cell [.] and referring to it as system missing in any output (e.g., the N for that variable may read 49, though you know you have 50 participants). Note, however, that SPSS System missing means that SPSS still regards that value as valid and treats it as it would a number or code filled in for a variable.

HOW DO I GO ABOUT USING SPSS TO ANSWER MY RESEARCH QUESTIONS?

Simple Analyses with SPSS and Obtaining Descriptive Statistics

Your database sheet should now contain the accurate information that you entered. At this point, you have just spent many hours "mindlessly" entering data: you have successfully put all the variables and all your participants' information into an SPSS data file in the manner suggested in this chapter. In addition, you have double-checked the data and saved your data file as a .sav file on your computer or portable device. Phew! Give yourself a pat on the back: you have set up the file in a user-friendly manner and are ready to begin the exciting part of getting SPSS to perform analysis in an effort to answer your research questions. In this section, we explain how to perform modification to variables (mentioned in the previous section), and running descriptive statistics and frequencies as a way to describe your data.

Modifying Variables

Recall in the previous section that it was recommended that you wait to make changes to variables until all your data are entered and that you use the capabilities of the software program to perform such changes. One such helpful menu-driven tool found within SPSS is the "Recode" option. "Recode" will help you to create a new variable by dividing up an already-existing variable, such as "age." This can be done by going through a few quick steps. SPSS allows you to create new categories or groups based on a range of numbers that are found within a variable that is already part of your data set. This is known as recoding variables into different variables. For instance, in the case of the variable "age," instead of having one variable that includes a range of ages from 1 to 99 you could create a new "age" variable that divides up the ages into categories. Thus, the new variable you created and named yourself will include new groups that already exist. For example, you could create an adolescence category that includes ages 13–17, a young adult category that includes ages 18–24, and so on. The groups that are created are completely dependent upon your specifications. For detailed instructions on recoding your data, refer to George and Mallery (2006).

Another helpful tool found in SPSS is the "Compute" option. The "Compute" option allows the researcher to implement arithmetic operations quickly and efficiently without a calculator: for example, let us say you were interested in tallying up scores on a number of variables in your dataset. Before you start counting up numbers or reaching for your calculator, just use SPSS! However, SPSS can do much more than just add up scores. It can also be used for more complicated arithmetic operations. For more detailed information on how to implement this option and how it can make data analysis less complicated for you, check out George and Mallery (2006).

Descriptive Statistics

If your main goal is simply to describe your data, then once your dataset has been entered and checked for errors regarding the input you are ready to run descriptive statistics. Furthermore, any time you are explaining the findings in your study or that of another study, you will need to run descriptive statistics. Once you have collected a sample of scores, you will want to report the central tendencies and variances of those scores in addition to the more detailed analyses you may later generate. The type of descriptive statistics that you report will depend on the type of data you collected. You will need to take into account the measurement scales of the dependent variables and the types of distribution your sample of scores create. Having considered these points in making your decisions, you are prepared to simply run descriptive statistics.

Single-click "Analyze" and a drop-down box will appear. Select "Descriptive Statistics" > "Frequencies." Select your variables and single-click the arrow icon. This will place the variable(s) you select in the variable(s) box. In order to display frequency tables make sure the "Display Frequency Tables" box is selected. If you do not want to display frequency tables then leave the box unselected. Next, open statistics. This will bring up a new menu box. From this new menu box you will have the option of selecting a variety of descriptive statistics functions. These options include percentile values, measures of central tendency, dispersion, and distribution. From this point select measures that are related to the characteristics of your data.

For example, the measures of central tendency will describe the average value of each variable (mean), the value that separates the lower half of the distribution from the upper half of the distribution (median), and the value that was most frequently given (mode). From this menu select the three measures of central tendency: (a) mean, (b) median, and (c) mode. Once you have selected these options single-click "Continue." You will see the original "Frequencies" menu box and single-click "OK." You should now have a graphical presentation that summarizes your data file and reports of central tendency.

If you would like to create a chart of your descriptive data, select "Analyze" > "Descriptive Statistics" > "Frequencies." Once in the "Frequencies" menu box, single-click "Charts." Select your chart type and click "Continue." Note: bar charts apply to nominal and ordinal variables, where as histograms apply to interval and ratio values.

Other descriptive options include: (a) range, (b) standard deviation, and (c) variance. These are measures of variability. These statistical tests are important because measures of central tendency do not describe the variation among data values. In other words, running tests of variability will allow you to see how your values are dispersed. To run these measures single-click "Analyze" > "Descriptive Statistics" > "Descriptives." Select your variable(s) and single-click the arrow icon. Once you have selected the variable(s) you want to analyze single-click "Options." In the options box you are given several statistical operations to choose from: (a) range, (b) standard deviation, and (c) variance. Click "Continue" > "OK."

In general, run Descriptives in SPSS for interval and ratio variables. This will give you mean, standard deviation, minimum, maximum, and number of cases for each variable. Remember, this can be an important way to check data input (see earlier section on double-checking your data) and can tell you if something is off. Also, run Frequencies for nominal or ordinal variables, because it will report frequencies by level. Again, this can provide a check on your data entry (match N to total cases). Simply stated, descriptive statistics allow you to display your data and summarize the responses of your participants. Descriptive statistics can be run alone or in combination with other statistical procedures such as the t-test to make the analysis more meaningful. When reporting the significance of your findings you will need to use descriptive statistics to make meaning of the conclusions from your analysis.

Summary

This chapter was intended to provide you with useful information to aid in your data management and statistical analysis for your research. It reviewed steps for preparing the data for data entry; helpful hints for entering your data; details on maneuvering in SPSS; and some information on running preliminary descriptive analyses. It was written to provide advice to new student-researchers who are just becoming familiar with the research process and statistical analyses. Good luck, and have fun with your first research project! We think you will find the process exciting and stimulating as you move from a pile of paper data to an SPSS data file to SPSS output that ultimately enables you to answer your research questions.

Review and Discussion Questions

1. Why is SPSS useful to researchers?
2. What are the steps a researcher should take to ensure good data management before even getting on the computer?
3. What information does the researcher enter into the "Data View" screen? What is the purpose of the "Variable View" screen?
4. Why do the authors recommend that data entry be as "mindless" as possible?
5. Name and briefly describe two methods for checking data.
6. Consider one pitfall that you want to be wary of when you set up your data file.

CHAPTER 15

Basic Statistical Concepts and Descriptive Statistics

Sang Min Lee, *Korea University*

OBJECTIVES
After reading this chapter, you will:

- Be able to understand the basic principles of statistical analysis.
- Be able to understand the differences between various scales of measurement.
- Be able to understand the concepts of reliability and validity.
- Be able to understand the basic descriptive statistics.
- Be able to understand variability.
- Be able to understand measures of central tendency.
- Be able to understand standard scores and their distributions.

OVERVIEW

Counselors and mental health professionals who do not have knowledge of basic statistical concepts and descriptive statistics may experience difficulty in analyzing counseling data; interpreting cognitive, aptitude, and achievement testing results; and reviewing scholarly research articles. Understanding basic statistical procedures is vital for counselors and mental health professionals to administer psychological assessments, analyze testing data, interpret psychological testing results, and explain results to their clients. This chapter introduces the readers to basic statistical concepts and descriptive statistics used when conducting program evaluation, psychological assessment, and grant proposal writing.

Basic statistical concepts are all around us. In fact, it would be difficult to go through a full week without using basic statistics. Without statistics, we could not plan our budgets, pay our taxes, enjoy games to their fullest, and evaluate classroom performance. The most basic form of statistics is those that describe and summarize our observations, which are known as descriptive statistics. Descriptive statistics are typically distinguished from inferential statistics. While descriptive statistics are simply describing data or what the data show, inferential statistics attempt to reach conclusions that extend beyond the immediate data alone to a larger population. In other words, descriptive statistics describe what is going on in sample data and inferential statistics are used to make inferences from the sample data to the population. Inferential statistics were discussed in earlier chapters. This chapter focuses on basic statistical concepts and descriptive statistics. As you read, you will likely find that you already know more than you think about descriptive statistics.

MEASUREMENT

In statistics, the level of measurement of a variable is a classification proposed to describe the nature of information contained within numbers assigned to objects and, therefore, within the variable. The four levels were first proposed by Stanley Smith Stevens in his 1946 article "On the theory of scales of measurement." Different statistical procedures on variables are possible, depending on the level at which a variable is measured. The four levels of measurement proposed by Stevens (1946) are:

- Nominal
- Ordinal
- Interval
- Ratio

When conducting research, the researcher needs to identify these levels of measurement for the research variables. Depending on which scale is used, different descriptive statistics should also be used. A summary of the levels of measurement and their properties is given Table 15.1.

NOMINAL SCALE   A nominal scale consists of numbers assigned to groups or categories. No inherent quantitative value of the information is conveyed and no ordering of the numbers is implied. Nominal scales are therefore qualitative rather than quantitative. Some examples are gender (female, male), race (African American, Asian American, Hispanic, Native American, White American), religion (Buddhist, Christian, Hindu, Jewish, Muslim), or concentration in a counseling

TABLE 15.1   Summary of Four Scales of Measurement

	Examples	Key Characteristics	Mathematical Operations	Appropriate Statistics
Nominal	Gender Ethnicity Marital Status Religion	Identity	None	Chi Square (χ^2) Percent of Total Mode
Ordinal	Top 10 ratings for music The rank order of anything	Identity Magnitude	Ranking	Median Inter-quartile range
Interval	Temperature IQ Curved grades	Identity Magnitude Equal interval	Addition Subtraction	Mean Standard Deviation Correlation & Regression ANOVA Factor analysis
Ratio	Age Weight Annual income	Identity Magnitude Equal interval True zero	Addition Subtraction Multiplication Division	All of possible statistics

(handwritten note in left margin: Categories / not #s)

program (college counseling, community/agency counseling, marriage and family counseling, school counseling). The numbers assigned to each condition of the variable serve as names or labels. However, the assigned numbers are completely arbitrary and have no true numerical value. For example, you may assign a "1" to females and a "2" to males, but this does not mean that a female is half of a male or somehow less than a male. The only statistical analysis permitted on the nominal scale is counting of frequencies in each category.

u know order but not how much is btw 2 #'s (may not be =)

ORDINAL SCALE   Ordinal scale divides observations into categories and provides measurement by order and rank. Ordinal scale permits the measurement of degrees of difference, but not the specific amount of difference. Measurements within ordinal scales are ordered in the sense that higher numbers represent higher values. However, the intervals between the numbers are not necessarily equal. For example, tornado or hurricane speed might be measured as high, medium, or low, but we would not say that the difference between high and medium wind speed is equal to (or any arithmetic transformation of) the difference between a medium and low tornado or hurricane speed. The "distance" between a rank of "1 (high)" and "2 (medium)" is not necessarily the same as the "distance" between ranks of "2 (medium)" and "3 (low)." That is, the distances between points on an ordinal scale are not meaningful. Ordinal scales are very common in counseling research. Any questions that ask the respondent to rate something are using ordinal scales. The statistics permitted on the ordinal scale are the mode and median, not the mean. The range and percentile ranking can also be calculated, but not the standard deviation.

Likert scales, which range from strongly agree to strongly disagree and rate people's attitudes, are commonly used in counseling research. It would be reasonable for a counselor to conclude that a client who answers "1 (strongly agree)" to the statement, "My counselor understands me well," has a more favorable attitude toward his or her counselor than a student who indicates a "5 (strongly disagree)." While some counseling researchers classify Likert scales as ordinal, others consider them to be roughly interval or approximately equal interval scales. Counseling researchers who classify Likert scales as ordinal have pointed out that the distance between scale points is unequal. Counseling researchers who classify Likert scales as roughly interval consider the distance between scale points to be "approximately equal intervals." As a counseling researcher, I believe there is no one "correct" answer. This is up to the researchers. As a researcher and data analyst, you need to decide.

INTERVAL SCALE   Interval scale takes the notion of ranking items in order one step further, since the distance between scale points are equal. Many of the standardized tests in the counseling profession use interval scales. An IQ (Intelligence Quotient) score from a standardized test of intelligence is a good example of an interval scale score. Given the equal distance between scale points, the meaning of the difference between a score of 100 and a score of 101 would represent the same difference in IQ as would a difference between a score of 130 and a score of 131. Interval scales do not have a true zero point; therefore, it is not possible to make statements about how many times higher one score is than another. For example, no one thinks of a person as having zero intelligence (even though we may be tempted to make that evaluation frequently). Realistically, if someone scored a zero on an IQ test, it would indicate that the test was invalid rather than an absence of intelligence. Similarly, for standardized scales of personality or other psychological attributes—a zero point is an arbitrary point on a scale and does not indicate the absence of a quality or characteristic. Therefore, it would not be valid to say that a person with an IQ score of 150 is twice as intelligent as a person with a score of 75. The interval scale of measurement only permits use of the following statistical procedures:

No true zero

- Mean and Standard Deviation
- Correlation and Regression
- Analysis of Variance (ANOVA)
- Factor Analysis

RATIO SCALE   Ratio scale is like the interval scale except that it has a true zero point. If the researcher asks participants their ages, the difference between any two years would always be the same, and "zero" signifies the absence of age or birth. Hence, a 50-year-old person is indeed twice as old as a 25-year-old one. In the counseling field, a children's play therapist might count how many times a client misbehaved during a one-hour counseling session. If the client exhibited misbehavior 10 times in the first counseling session but only 2 times during the second counseling session, the play therapist could report that the client was 5 times less likely to misbehave during the second session than the first one. The true zero point allows researchers to know how many times greater or lesser one case is than another. Because of its true zero point, the ratio scale allows us to apply all of the possible statistical procedures in data analysis. Because the ratio scale permits most statistical procedures, it is generally preferred by researchers.

Reliability and Validity

Most counselors have probably experienced the following question: "What type of data do I need to collect to understand this particular client better?" It is crucial to be free of bias and distortion on any type of data collection procedure (e.g., survey, questionnaire, interview, personality scale). Reliability and validity are two concepts that are important for defining and measuring bias and distortion. Therefore, before using psychological tests (e.g., IQ tests, personality assessments) it is important to know the test's validity and reliability information as part of the counseling process. Just as we would not use a weight scale to measure height, we would not want to use psychological assessments that were not truly measuring what they are supposed to measure. In addition, if you measured your weight twice in a row with the same bathroom scale and the scale gave different weights each subsequent time, you would need to suspect the scale's reliability. If the test methods are flawed, obviously, the data we analyze will also be unreliable and invalid. In this section, we will focus on measurement reliability and validity issues that counselors need to know when using psychological assessment.

RELIABILITY   Reliability refers to the extent to which assessments are consistent. A reliable measurement is free from error, is accurate, and provides consistent results. Obviously, all tests contain some types of error. This is especially true for educational and psychological tests in the counseling field. In measuring length with a ruler, for example, there may be systematic error associated with where the zero point is printed on the ruler and random error associated with your eye's ability to read the marking and extrapolate between the markings. One goal in the field of measurement and evaluation is to keep these errors down to levels that are appropriate for the purposes of the test. Reliability focuses only on the degree of errors that are nonsystematic; these are called random errors. *Random error* refers to error that is the result of pure chance. Random errors of measurement may inflate or depress the score in an unpredictable way. Random error can be due to a number of chance factors, such as respondents' carelessness and scoring errors. The reliability is the degree to which the scores are the result of systematic rather than chance factors. When random error is minimal, scores can be expected to be more consistent from administration to administration. There are several approaches commonly used to estimate the reliability of a set of test scores for a group of respondents: test-retest reliability, parallel form reliability, split-half reliability, and internal consistency reliability are the most common. The next section reviews these four different approaches to assessing a measurement's reliability. A summary of the four different approaches to obtaining reliability coefficients is given Table 15.2.

TEST-RETEST RELIABILITY   One way to estimate the reliability of a test is to administer the same test on two occasions and to correlate the paired scores. The closer the two results are, the greater the test-retest reliability of the test. The correlation coefficient between such two sets of responses is called a test-retest reliability coefficient. For example, a group of clients take a test to assess their anxiety level: each client is tested twice—the two tests are given, say, two weeks apart. The correlation

TABLE 15.2   Summary of Four Reliability Indices

	Description
Test-Retest Reliability	Reliability coefficient is obtained by administering the same test twice and correlating the scores.
Parallel Form Reliability	Reliability coefficient is obtained by administering similar, but not identical, tests and correlating the scores.
Split-Half Reliability	Reliability score is obtained by dividing a test into halves, correlating the scores on each half.
Internal Consistency	Reliability score is obtained by correlating the individual items of a test to each other.

coefficient between the two sets of scores is a reasonable measure of the test-retest reliability of this test. Ideally, both scores coincide for each respondent and, hence, the correlation coefficient is 1.0. In reality, this is almost never the case; the scores produced by a respondent would vary if the test were carried out several times. Normally, correlation values higher than .80 are considered as satisfactory or good.

A test-retest coefficient assumes that the characteristic being measured by the test is stable over time. Because of this assumption, it is not appropriate for measuring traits that fluctuate over time, such as emotions. The appropriate length of the interval depends on the stability of the variables, which causally determine that which is measured. A year might be too long for an opinion item but appropriate for a physiological measure. In counseling-related measurement, a typical interval is several weeks. Sometimes, this reliability procedure is not recommended in counseling practice because of its limitations. If the time interval is short, people may be overly consistent because they remember some of the questions and their responses, which is known as *memory effect*. On the other hand, if time between testing is too long, differential learning and maturation may be a problem. Also, respondents could learn to answer the same questions in the first test and this affects their responses in the next test.

PARALLEL FORMS RELIABILITY   Parallel forms reliability, which is also referred to as the alternative, or equivalent-form reliability, produces a reliability coefficient based on the administration of two forms of the same test (Form A and Form B) to one group of people. The parallel forms are typically matched in terms of content and difficulty. The correlation of scores on pairs of parallel forms for the same respondents provides the parallel forms reliability coefficient. A high parallel forms reliability coefficient indicates that the different forms of the test are very similar, which means that it makes virtually no difference which version of the test a person takes. On the other hand, a low parallel forms reliability coefficient suggests that the different forms are probably not comparable; they may be measuring different things and therefore cannot be used interchangeably.

The parallel form reliability of a test helps to overcome the memory effect discussed previously in relation to the brief time intervals in test-retest procedures. *Practice effect* is still a concern with this form of reliability procedure in that respondents have taken one version of the test and then take a similar form at a later date. However, an advantage to this reliability procedure is that it controls for test sensitization and yields a coefficient that reflects two aspects of test reliability: variation from one time to another as well as variation from one form of the test to another. Despite these advantages, this is the most demanding, expensive, and difficult procedure for determining the reliability of a test. In addition, even with the best test and item specifications, each test would contain slightly different content and, as with test-retest reliability, maturation and learning may confound the results.

SPLIT-HALF RELIABILITY   Split-half reliability is based on the correlation between halves of the measure. That is, split-half reliability coefficient is obtained by dividing a test into halves, correlating the scores on each half, and then correcting for length (longer tests tend to be more reliable).

The split can be based on odd- versus even-numbered items, randomly selecting items, or manually balancing content and difficulty. The most common procedure is to correlate the scores on the odd-numbered items of the test with the scores on the even-numbered items. If each respondent maintains a very similar response on the two sections (odd items versus even numbered items), the reliability coefficient would be high.

A concern with the split-half procedure revolves around the shortening of a test. Generally speaking, longer tests are more reliable than shorter tests. If everything else is equal, more items produce more variation in test scores, which increases reliability. In the split-half reliability procedure, we take a 100-item long test, and split it into two 50-item tests, which decreases its reliability. If we want to retain the reliability of a 100-item test, we would need to use a 200-item test. For this reason, an adjustment to the split-half reliability is recommended. The Spearman-Brown Formula can be employed when estimating the reliability using the split half method.

$$R = \frac{2 \times (r)}{(1 + r)}$$ **(Equation 15.1)**

R = Total test reliability; r = correlation between dividing two tests

For example, the correlation between odd and even halves of a test is 0.75. Putting this into the formula, the estimated reliability of the entire test would be

$$.86 = \frac{2 \times (.75)}{(1 + .75)}$$

Another concern with the split-half procedure is that the reliability estimate will vary as a function of how the test was split. Some splits may give a much higher correlation than other splits. It is also not appropriate on tests in which speed is a factor. Therefore, other procedures are recommended for these types of tests, known as *speeded tests*. Despite these disadvantages, this reliability procedure has an advantage in terms of getting a measure of reliability from a single administration of one form of a test.

INTERNAL CONSISTENCY   Internal consistency focuses on the degree to which the individual items are correlated with each other. The test that has a high degree of internal consistency reliability has items that are homogeneous, measure a single construct, and correlate highly with each other. Internal consistency reliability could be computed using the *Kuder-Richardson Formula 20 (KR-20)* or *Cronbach's alpha*. The KR-20 is a measure of *homogeneity* which functions under the assumption that all items on a test measure the same thing or are of the same difficulty level. As discussed above (split-half reliability), there are several ways to split a test, all yielding different reliability coefficients. The KR-20 solves this problem by computing an average between all the possible split-halves and yielding an overall reliability estimate. In addition, this type of split-half procedure is also a less expensive, although less direct way of taking into account different samples of test items (for example, evaluating whether all items on a test are measuring the same construct). However, KR-20 formula should not be used if the test has items that are scored other than just zero or one.

Cronbach's alpha (symbolized as α) is the most popular and widely used reliability procedure to check internal consistency of tests in the counseling field. While KR-20 can be applied to dichotomously scored data only, Cronbach's alpha can be used for both binary-type and large-scale data. Cronbach's alpha ranges from $\alpha = .00$ (indicating that the test is entirely in error) to $\alpha = +1.00$ (indicating that the measure has no error). Generally speaking, the higher the alpha is, the more reliable the test is. It is a common misconception that if the Cronbach's alpha is low, it must be a bad

[handwritten margin note: to measure if test measures single construct (quests. are related).]

test. The test may measure several constructs rather than one, and if so, the Cronbach's alpha may be deflated. For example, it is expected that the scores of GRE-Verbal, GRE-Quantitative, and GRE-Analytical may not be highly correlated because they evaluate different types of knowledge. On the other hand, when a high overall Cronbach's alpha is obtained, many researchers assume a single construct and do not further investigate whether the test carries subscales. However, consistency and dimensionality of a test must be assessed separately. Even though a test is internally consistent, it does not necessarily mean it entails only one construct.

VALIDITY   Validity has been defined broadly as the extent to which a test measures the construct or variables which it purports to measure. Validity is also defined as the applicability, meaningfulness, and usefulness of the specific inferences made from scores. A test might be reliable without being valid. For example, if the researchers take daily measures of head weight to determine the participants' intelligence, the researchers would find the weight of each participant's head is going to remain approximately the same. The researchers would then conclude that this is a very reliable measure in the sense that it shows a substantial test-retest correlation. Can the researcher really conclude that this test is a valid measure of intelligence? Surely not! Although the test is reliable, it is not necessarily valid because it does not measure what it was designed to measure. In addition to reliability, therefore, the counselors should understand the concepts of test validity. Although psychometric texts list many types of validity, three types of evidence are traditionally examined to support the validity of a measurement: content, construct, and criterion. A summary of the three different approaches is given Table 15.3.

CONTENT VALIDITY   Content validity refers to the extent to which the measurement adequately samples the content domain. This validity is particularly appropriate to ability and achievement tests. For example, a math ability test that contained basic math concepts such as adding, subtracting, multiplying, and dividing numbers would lack content validity because there are other types of content domains (e.g., algebra, geometry, calculus, etc.) that measure math ability.

Content validity also refers to the extent to which a test-taker's responses to a given test reflect that test-taker's knowledge of the content area that is of interest. For example, a student who has English as a second language takes a history exam in English. This exam may unintentionally be more reflective of the student's language skills than knowledge of history. The researcher would conclude that the student has not mastered the content knowledge covered by this exam when in actuality that student does not understand the questions. The researcher has misinterpreted the evidence thus rendering the interpretation invalid. Content validity is commonly determined by an expert or expert panel who can judge the representativeness of the items on a test.

CONSTRUCT VALIDITY   Construct validity refers to the extent to which the test is an accurate measure of a particular construct or variable. Unlike physical variables such as weight and height, most variables used in the counseling field are intangible and cannot be directly observed. For example, we believe in the existence of personality because we believe that people can react differently to a particular event, and we believe that these different patterns of reaction are due to an

TABLE 15.3   Summary of Three Major Approaches to Validity

	Description
Content	The extent to which the measurement adequately samples the content domain.
Construct	The extent to which the test is an accurate measure of a particular construct or variable.
Criterion	The extent to which a test is related to some external criterion of the construct being measured.

underlying attribute we call personality. Since we cannot measure an individual's personality directly, determining construct validity is a complicated and indirect process.

One way of assessing construct validity is to demonstrate the evidence of both convergent and discriminant validity. *Convergent validity* refers to the degree to which scores on a test correlate highly and positively with scores on other tests that are designed to assess the same construct or trait. For example, if scores on a specific form of a depression test are similar to people's scores on other depression tests, then convergent validity is high. *Discriminant validity* refers to the degree to which scores on a test do not correlate highly with scores from other tests that are not designed to assess the same construct or trait. For example, if discriminant validity is high, scores on a test designed to assess depression should not be highly correlated with scores from tests designed to assess self-esteem. In other words, correlations between theoretically similar tests should be "high" while correlations between theoretically dissimilar tests should be "low."

One way of assessing convergent and discriminant validity is through a *multi-method—multi-trait matrix* (MTMM, developed by Campbell and Fiske (1959). The MTMM is simply a matrix or table of correlations arranged to facilitate the interpretation of the assessment of construct validity. The MTMM assumes that you measure each of several traits (e.g., depression, anxiety, and exhaustion) by each of several methods (e.g., self report survey, direct observation, and personal interview). Correlation of measures of the same trait but with different methods (i.e., convergent validity) should be higher than correlations of measures of different traits by the same or different methods (i.e., discriminant validity).

Another way of assessing construct validity may be through factor analysis. Factor analysis is a statistical procedure for analyzing the interrelationships among a set of variables to uncover the underlying dimensions or constructs that explain the relationships among observed variables. Through the factor analysis procedure, items that measure the same construct will be grouped together. These constructs are then named according to their characteristics, allowing a researcher to break down information.

CRITERION VALIDITY   Criterion validity refers to the extent to which a test is related to some external criterion of the construct being measured. That is, criterion validity is a test that predicts an outcome based on information from other measurements. These other measurements are often represented as criteria. For example, let us say we are conducting a research study on validity for a new college entrance test. If we find there is a high positive correlation between student college entrance exam scores and their success in obtaining a college degree (the higher the test scores, the more degree attainment), we would say there is high criterion validity between the test scores and the criterion variable (college degree attainment). Essentially, the test scores students received can be used to predict their success to obtain a college degree.

There are two types of criterion validity: *concurrent validity,* which yields scores at the time of administration; and *predictive validity,* which yields scores at a later time from administration. In concurrent validity, the test scores and criterion measures are obtained at roughly the same time. For example, if the intelligence test scores are compared with the students' most recent school grades, we would be assessing the concurrent validity of the intelligent test scores. In predictive validity, the test scores are kept on record and compared with a criterion measure obtained sometime in the future. For example, a high school math test has predictive validity if it can predict some aspect of college performance (e.g., college GPA, degree completion).

COMPARING RELIABILITY AND VALIDITY   Since reliability and validity are interconnected in their use in research design, measurement, and instrumentation, they are both useful, and it is difficult to designate one as more important to the other. However, the literature consistently and strongly suggests that in terms of the selection of an instrument, validity is more important than reliability because without validity, a test has no interpretable meaning. In fact, a test may be reliable without being valid, while a test cannot be valid without being reliable. Explicitly stated, a test may be reliable, that is to test a construct repeatedly and consistently over time, but may not measure the construct it is actually designed to measure; for a test to be valid, however, it must measure the construct it purports to measure consistently over time.

Usually, the researcher would like a test that has both high validity and reliability. Up to a point, it is possible to get more of both simply by being thoughtful. But sometimes, more validity requires less reliability, and vice versa. In these cases, reliability and validity seem to be in conflict. Therefore, the researcher needs to know that reliability and validity have various levels of importance under diverse conditions. For the purposes of predicting future behavior, scores, success, and performance, as well as for diagnostic purposes, validity is generally more important. For the purposes of estimating consistency and stability of the scale, reliability becomes the primary area of concern and reliability seems to be more important.

Descriptive Statistics

Descriptive statistics are used to describe the basic features of the data in a study, including what the data are or what they show. Descriptive statistics help us to simplify large amounts of data by providing a summary that may enable comparisons across people or other units. Particularly in the counseling field, one of our goals is to understand human behavior. To achieve this, we need to be able to describe the human behavior. Descriptive statistics often function as a bridge between measurement and understanding. Raw data are unwieldy and often uninterpretable. Trying to understand raw data can be somewhat chaotic. Statistics can be a means of finding order and meaning in this apparent chaos of numbers. Usually the raw data can be reduced to one or two descriptive summaries such as the mean and standard deviation, or illustrated visually through various graphical procedures such as histograms, frequency distributions, and scatter plots. In this section, you will learn how to find some order or meaning in the data through descriptive statistics.

THE FREQUENCY DISTRIBUTION   The distribution is a summary of the frequency of individual values or ranges of values for a variable. The most common way to describe a single variable is through a frequency distribution. This is a way of displaying the chaos of numbers in an organized manner. For instance, suppose you try to look at years of experience of counselors in your counseling agency. Table 15.4 shows the years of experience frequency distribution for counselors.

TABLE 15.4   Frequency Distribution of Counselors' Years of Experience

Years of experience (X)	Frequency (*f*)	Percentage	Cumulative Percentage
13	1	10.0%	100.0%
12	0	0.0%	90.0%
11	0	0.0%	90.0%
10	0	0.0%	90.0%
9	1	10.0%	90.0%
8	0	0.0%	80.0%
7	0	0.0%	80.0%
6	1	10.0%	80.0%
5	0	0.0%	70.0%
4	4	40.0%	70.0%
3	2	20.0%	30.0%
2	0	0.0%	10.0%
1	1	10.0%	10.0%
	N = 10	100.0%	

The first column in the table contains all the different values of the raw data (referred to as the values of "X"); in our example, X is the variable *years of experience* and the first column lists all the years of experience of the counselors (or the participants), starting from the highest value. The second column contains the frequency or number of participants of each year. For instance, one participant has 1 year of experience as a counselor and 4 counselors have 4 years of experience as counselors. The third column in the frequency table contains the percentage of participants at each year, which is computed by dividing the number of participants of a given year by the total number of participants (N) and then multiplying by 100. For example, 2 counselors have 3 years of experience, so the percentage is equal to:

$$\text{percentage of group who have 3 years of experience} = \frac{2}{10} \times 100 = 20\%$$

Therefore, 20% of the counselors in this group have 3 years of experience as counselors.

The fourth column gives a cumulative frequency. This shows the total number of participants who fall at the given year or below. For example, we can see that 8 participants have 6 years of experience or less. We can also use this cumulative frequency to create a cumulative percentage by taking the percentage of participants that fall at each year or below. Here, we see from the cumulative frequency column that 8 counselors have 6 years of experience or less:

$$\text{cumulative percentage for 6 years of experience or less} = \frac{8}{10} \times 100 = 80\%$$

Therefore, 80% of the counselors have 6 years of experience or less.

In a distribution of only 13 years of experience, it is not too difficult to arrange the years of experience in this manner; however, it would be hard to display all years if the range of years were more varied. In that case, you could group the values into intervals. Note that the intervals must be equal in size, as shown in Table 15.5.

GRAPHING FREQUENCIES   Another way to look at frequencies is graphically. The three most common methods of graphing a distribution are histogram (bar graph) and the frequency (or percentage) polygon. The *histogram* uses bars to indicate the frequencies for each value of *x* (which are placed along the horizontal *x-axis*). The height of the bars indicates the frequencies (which are on the vertical *y-axis*). The bars on the histogram are continuous and are a visual reminder of the increasing quantity of the variable. Figure 15.1 presents an example of a histogram for frequencies of counselors' years of experience. Histograms can be used to represent percentages instead of, or in addition to, frequency. When the vertical *y-axis* is expressed in percentage, rather than frequency units, the figure becomes a percentage histogram as shown Figure 15.1.

TABLE 15.5   Frequency Distribution of Counselors' Years of Experience

Years of experience (x)	Frequency (f)	Percentage	Cumulative Percentage
13–15	1	10.0%	100.0%
10–12	0	0.0%	90.0%
7–9	1	10.0%	90.0%
4–6	5	50.0%	80.0%
1–3	3	30.0%	30.0%
	N = 10	100.0%	

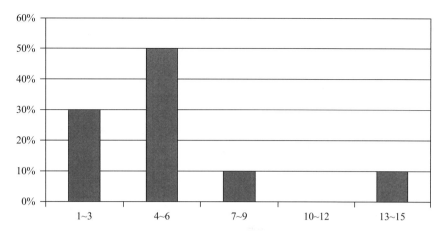

FIGURE 15.1 Frequency Histogram of Counselors' Years of Experience in Table 15.5

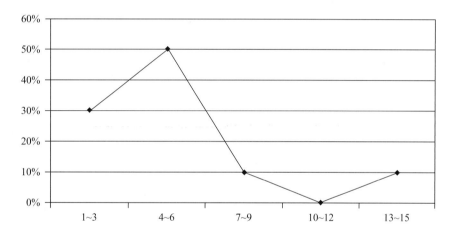

FIGURE 15.2 Frequency Polygon for Counselors' Years of Experience

Another type of graph that is appropriate for quantitative data is a *frequency polygon*. Figure 15.2 presents an example of a frequency polygon that plots the years of experience data from Table 15.5. Here the years of experience are plotted on the *x-axis,* and the frequency is on the *y-axis.* An interval having zero frequency is added below the interval containing the lowest value, and a second interval with zero frequency is added above the interval containing the highest value. With polygons, a point is located above the midpoint of each interval to denote the frequency of cases in each interval. Frequency polygons are especially useful for continuous data (such as age or height). Also, when comparing two or more distributions within the same figure, polygons are typically more effective than histograms. When the two distributions have different numbers of observations, percentages rather than frequencies are needed to make comparisons clear.

TYPES OF DISTRIBUTIONS   For quantitative variables, the pattern of scores in the distribution can be determined by visually examining the frequency polygon. In large datasets, if there is a pattern at all, it generally fits one of three possible patterns: symmetrical, skewed, multimodal. We commonly call a *symmetrical distribution* a normal distribution or normal curve (you may also see the term "bell curve"). You could think of many situations that fall within a normal distribution. If you look at any test results in a school, you can easily see a normal distribution. Check the heights of adults

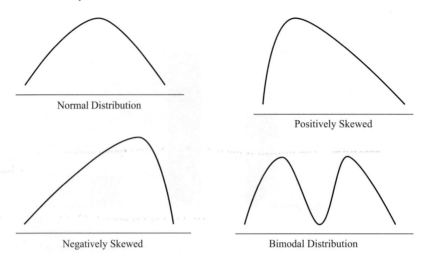

FIGURE 15.3 Different Types of Distribution

or children; you could see a normal distribution as well. The curve is constant and is always bell-shaped. In any one situation, the values within it vary. The mean is not always the same number; the overall shape may be more broadly spread or more compressed, depending on the situation being represented.

However, sometimes a variable does not fall within a normal distribution. Its distribution might be *skewed*. If the peak lies to the left midpoint, we call the distribution *positively skewed*. If the peak lies to the right midpoint, the distribution is *negatively skewed*. Figure 15.3 presents different types of distributions. For example, look at the values in Table 15.4. The extreme value "13" is located in the tail of the distribution (in this case in the positive end). Therefore, we can say that the distribution is positively skewed.

MEASURES OF CENTRAL TENDENCY   There are several common methods to estimate measures of central tendency. The measures of central tendency are intended to describe the most average or "typical" score in the distribution. The three most common measures are the mean, the median, and the mode. Each of these three can serve as an index to represent a group as a whole.

MEAN   The mean is probably the most commonly used method of describing central tendency. This is the arithmetic average of all scores. To compute the mean, all you do is add up all the values and divide by the number of values as shown in the formula below:

$$\bar{X} = \frac{\sum X}{N} (\text{sample})$$ **(Equation 15.2)**

Where $\bar{X}$ = the sample mean,

$$\text{or } \mu = \frac{\sum X}{N} (\text{population})$$ **(Equation 15.3)**

Where:

μ = the population mean.

N = the number of observations.

The $\bar{X}$ (read as "X bar") is the symbol for the sample mean and the μ (read as "Mew") is for the population mean. The Greek letter sigma (Σ) is known as the summation sign and X denotes each individual observation. For instance, the sample mean or average years of experience as counselors in Table 15.4 is determined by summing all the scores and dividing by the number of counselors ($N = 10$). Consider the values:

$$1, 3, 3, 4, 4, 4, 4, 6, 9, 13$$

The sum of these 10 values is 51, so the mean is 51/10 = 5.1.

MEDIAN The median is the value found at the exact middle of the distribution. One way to compute the median is to list all scores in numerical order, and then locate the score in the center of the sample. For example, consider the 9 scores below;

$$16, 17, 19, 19, 20, 23, 25, 27, 29$$

You can find that the value 20 separates the distribution exactly in half. Thus, the median of this distribution is 20. You could compute the median mathematically with an odd number of values by using the equation:

$$Md = \frac{N + 1}{2}$$

(Equation 15.4)

Where:

N = number of cases

In this case, $N = 9$, therefore, $\frac{9 + 1}{2} = 5$. Thus, the fifth score in the ordered list is the median, which is the value 20.

Let's consider another example. List all 10 values in Table 15.4. In this example, we have a distribution with an even number of scores.

$$1, 3, 3, 4, 4, 4, 4, 6, 9, 13$$

Given this distribution of values, the point below which 50% of the cases fall is halfway between 4 and 4. To find the midpoint between two numbers, add them together and divide by 2; thus, the median of this distribution is equal to (4 + 4) ÷ 2 = 4. We listed 10 values in rank order, and then found the point below which one-half of the scores lie. You also could use a mathematical equation to compute the median with an even number of cases.

$$Md = \text{half way between } \frac{N}{2} \text{ and } \frac{N + 2}{2}$$

(Equation 15.5)

Where:

N = number of cases

Look at another example.

$$16, 17, 19, 19, 20, 21, 23, 25, 27, 29$$

When you list these values in rank order, you could find that the value 20 and 21 represent the halfway point. In this case, $N = 10$, therefore, the median would be halfway between $\frac{10}{2}$ and $\frac{10 + 2}{2}$.

Thus, the median would be between the fifth and sixth value, which is between 20 and 21. $Md = (20 + 21) \div 2 = 20.5$. The median is 20.5.

MEAN VERSUS MEDIAN   The mean and median are both measures of central tendency. The mean and the median can be both meaningful for symmetric distributions. In general, the mean will be higher than the median for positively skewed distributions and lower than the median for negatively skewed distributions. In addition, the mean is more affected by extreme scores than the median (see Figure 15.4). Thus, the mean is not a good measure of central tendency for extremely skewed distributions.

MODE   The mode is the easiest measure to understand since it is determined by inspection rather than by computation. It simply reports the most frequent score in the variable. On a frequency polygon, the mode is the score at the peak of the distribution. For example, we can determine the modal years of our 10 counselors in Table 15.4 by looking at the second column (f) and finding the largest value of f; in this instance, 4. Therefore, the modal year for the group is 4 years of counseling experience. Sometimes there is more than one mode in a distribution. For example, if you hire three more counselors with 9 years of experience each, then we would have two modes: 4 years and 9 years. The distribution would be bimodal. A distribution also could have no mode when no value appears more than once.

The mode is a useful descriptive statistic when studying nominal (categorical) variables such as gender and race, where the mean and median are not useful descriptive measures. However, the mode is not often a useful indicator of central tendency in a distribution. Because of its instability, changes in the frequencies of one or two values can change the mode.

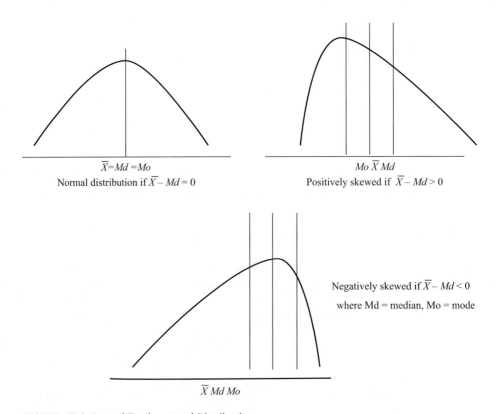

$\overline{X} = Md = Mo$
Normal distribution if $\overline{X} - Md = 0$

$Mo\ \overline{X}\ Md$
Positively skewed if $\overline{X} - Md > 0$

Negatively skewed if $\overline{X} - Md < 0$
where Md = median, Mo = mode

$\overline{X}\ Md\ Mo$

FIGURE 15.4 Central Tendency and Distributions

VARIABILITY   Variability refers to the extent to which the scores in a distribution differ from each other; that is, how "spread out" a group of scores is. Basically, variability refers to the distance between each score and the group mean (mathematically $X - \bar{X}$). If a distribution is lacking in variability, we may say that it is *homogenous* (note that the opposite would be *heterogeneous*). There are three frequently used measures of variability: the range, variance, and standard deviation. We will look at each of these in more detail.

RANGE   The range is the simplest measure of variability to calculate, and one you have probably encountered many times in your life. The range is given simply by taking the highest score in the distribution minus the lowest score. Let us look at our counselors' example. The highest score was 13 and the lowest score was 1, so $13 - 1 = 12$. The range is 12. Let us suppose there is one dataset with the highest number 29 and the lowest number 12. In this example, the range is: $29 - 12 = 17$. You could have a million scores and all you are going to do is take the lowest one and subtract it from the highest one. You throw away all the information from all the other scores. This is the major disadvantage of the range. The range does not include all of the observations. The range gives you a very quick kind of measure of variability, but it obviously excludes a lot of information.

VARIANCE   Variability can also be defined in terms of how close the scores in the distribution are to the mean. An important measure of variability is variance. Variance is the average of the squared deviations from the mean. The formula for the variance of a population is given below:

$$\text{Variance for a population} = \sigma^2 = \frac{\sum (X_i - \mu)^2}{N} \qquad \textbf{(Equation 15.6)}$$

Where:

σ^2 is the variance, μ is the mean, and N is the number of cases.

The formula for the variance of a sample of scores, called "*s*-squared," is given below:

$$\text{Variance for a sample of scores} = s^2 = \frac{\sum (X_i - X)^2}{N - 1} \qquad \textbf{(Equation 15.7)}$$

Where:

s^2 is the estimate of the variance and $\bar{X}$ is the sample mean.

Since, in practice, the variance is usually computed in a sample, this formula is most often used. If you look at the formula you will notice that the heart of the variance is the deviation of the score from its mean $(X - \bar{X})$. The deviation of the scores generates variance. If the deviations are small then the scores are close to the mean. If the deviations are large then the scores are spread out. However, the problem with deviations is that they add up to 0. Therefore, we need to square them. When we square them, the negative deviation scores turn into positive numbers. So, the squaring of scores accomplishes the same function as using the absolute value. To compute the variance the following steps are used:

- Find the mean.
- Find the difference between each observation and the mean.
- Square these differences.
- Sum the squared differences.
- Since the data are a sample, divide the number (from step 4) by the number of observations minus one, i.e., n−1 (where n is equal to the number of observations in the dataset).

Let us again use the example of counselors in Table 15.4. Following the above steps, the variance is calculated as follows (see Table 15.6):

The total years = 51 and sample size = 10, therefore, the mean = 51/10 = 5.1 years. When you add up all deviation scores they should be equal to zero ($\sum(X-\bar{X}) = 0$). The total of squared

TABLE 15.6 Variance Calculation Method

Years of experience (X)	Deviation ($X-\bar{X}$)	Squared Deviation ($X-\bar{X}$)^2
13	13 − 5.1 = 7.9	62.41
9	9 − 5.1 = 3.9	15.21
6	6 − 5.1 = .9	.81
4	4 − 5.1 = −1.1	1.21
4	4 − 5.1 = −1.1	1.21
4	4 − 5.1 = −1.1	1.21
4	4 − 5.1 = −1.1	1.21
3	3 − 5.1 = −2.1	4.41
3	3 − 5.1 = −2.1	4.41
1	1 − 5.1 = −4.1	16.81
N = 10	Total = 0	Total = 108.9

TABLE 15.7 Example of Variance Calculation Method

Job Satisfaction (X)	Deviation ($X-\bar{X}$)	Squared Deviation ($X-\bar{X}$)^2
45	45 − 34 = 11	121
43	43 − 34 = 9	81
43	43 − 34 = 9	81
39	39 − 34 = 5	25
37	37 − 34 = 3	9
34	34 − 34 = 0	0
34	34 − 34 = 0	0
29	29 − 34 = −5	25
20	20 − 34 = −14	196
16	16 − 34 = −18	324
N = 10	Total = 0	Total = 862

deviation scores is 108.9. Thus, the variance for this data set is: $s^2 = 108.9/(10-1) = 12.1$. Let us look at another example. Suppose that the 10 counselors took an instrument to measure how much they were satisfied with their jobs. The scores are given as below:

$$34, 20, 49, 43, 37, 15, 39, 29, 43, 34$$

You can compute the variation by following the above steps (see Table 15.7). The mean of the data set is 34. The total of squared deviation scores is 862. Thus, the variance for this dataset is: $s^2 = 862/(10-1) = 95.8$

As you see in the above examples, the variance is not expressed in the same units as the observations. The variance is hard to understand because the deviations from the mean are squared, making it too large for logical explanation. These problems can be solved by working with the square root of the variance, which is called the standard deviation.

STANDARD DEVIATION The variance and the standard deviation are essentially the same idea. They provide the same information in that one can always be obtained from the other. The standard deviation is the square root of the variance as shown below and it is always expressed in the same units as the raw data.

$$\text{standard deviation} = S = \sqrt{s^2} \qquad \textbf{(Equation 15.8)}$$

$$\text{or} = \sqrt{\frac{\sum (X_i - \overline{X})^2}{N - 1}} \qquad \textbf{(Equation 15.9)}$$

For instance, the variance of the first example was 12.1. The standard deviation is the square root of 12.1 which is equal to 3.48 years (expressed in same units as the raw data). The standard deviation tells us the "average" difference between individual scores and the group mean. Therefore, on average, the scores in the data set were 3.48 points away from the mean. For the second example, the variance was 95.8, thus the standard deviation is 9.79. It tells us that the scores were typically, 9.79 points away from the mean. Generally we can interpret the standard deviation as indicating that many of the scores were "within one standard deviation from the mean." For the first example, we can interpret that counselors had a mean experience of 5.1 years and a standard deviation of 3.48 years, many of the counselors had between approximately 1.62 and 8.58 years of experience as counselors. For the second example, we can conclude that many of the counselors scored between approximately 24.21 and 43.79 points in their job satisfaction measure.

Standard Normal Distribution and Standard Scores

Z SCORES If the mean and standard deviation are known, the individual scores can be pictured relative to the entire set of scores in the distribution through standardization. Standard normal distribution is the normal distribution with a mean of 0 and a standard deviation of 1. Therefore, you could make all normal distributions the same units of size: σ with the mean μ as center. When you standardize a raw score to a Z-score, it provides you information about how far a person is from the mean, in the metric of standard deviation units. A score that is one standard deviation above the mean has a Z-score of 1. A score that is one standard deviation below the mean has a Z-score of -1. A score that is at the mean would have a Z-score of 0. The formula for the standard score is as below:

$$z = \frac{X - \mu}{\sigma} \qquad \textbf{(Equation 15.10)}$$

Where:

X is a raw score to be standardized

σ is the standard deviation of the population

μ is the mean of the population

Calculating z requires the population mean and the population standard deviation, not the sample mean or sample standard deviation. However, it would be very difficult to measure the true standard deviation or mean of a population. For example, it would be hard to fully measure the job satisfaction of a counselor population. In this case, the standard deviation may be estimated using a random sample. Let us look at an example using data from Tables 15.4 and 15.6. The mean of years of experience was 5.1 and the standard deviation was 3.48. For a counselor who had 6 years of experience,

$$z = \frac{6 - 5.1}{3.48} = .26$$

To find the proportion of the score that falls in a standard normal distribution, you could use the normal curve shown in Figure 15.5, which we will discuss later in greater detail. In this example, the Z-score would be between 0 and 1, which means slightly above the mean. Using the values from Tables 15.4 and 15.6, the Z-score for a counselor with 1 year of experience is equal to

$$z = \frac{1 - 5.1}{3.48} = -1.18$$

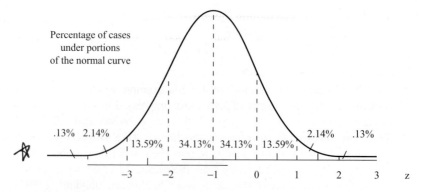

FIGURE 15.5 Standard Normal Distribution and Z-scores

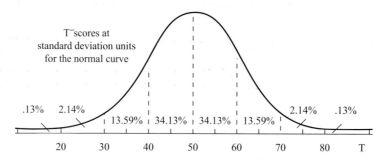

FIGURE 15.6 Standard Normal Distribution and T-scores

The counselor's Z-score would be between −1 and −2, which is below the mean.

There are some advantages to using standard Z-scores. First, we can use standard scores to find *percentile scores:* the proportion of people with scores less than or equal to a particular score. Centile scores are intuitive ways of summarizing a person's location in a larger set of scores. Second, standard scores provide a way to standardize or equate different metrics. Each score comes from a distribution with the same mean (0) and the same standard deviation (1). However, there are also some disadvantages. First, the same person can have different Z-scores when assessed in different samples because a person's score is expressed relative to the group. Second, if the absolute score is meaningful, it will be obscured by transforming it to a relative metric.

T-SCORES T-scores are standardized scores which are used widely to report performance on standardized tests and inventories. A score of 50 represents the mean. A difference of 10 from the mean indicates a difference of one standard deviation. The distribution of scores are displayed in Figure 15.6. To convert Z-scores to T-scores, you can use the formula below:

$$T = 50 + 10z \qquad \textbf{(Equation 15.11)}$$

We looked at two examples to convert raw scores to Z-scores. The first example had a Z-score of .26 for a counselor with 6 years of experience. Using the above formula, the T-score is T = 50 + 10(.26) = 52.6. For the counselor with 1 year of experience, the Z-score was −1.18. The T-score would be T = 50 + 10(−1.18) = 38.2.

TABLE 15.8 **Calculating Stanines**

Result Ranking	4%	7%	12%	17%	20%	17%	12%	7%	4%
Stanine	1	2	3	4	5	6	7	8	9

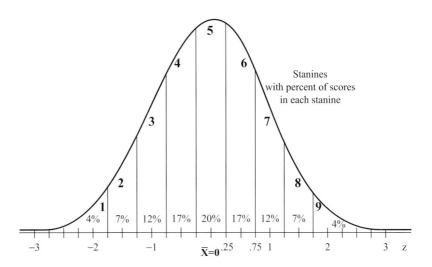

FIGURE 15.7 Standard Normal Distribution and Stanines

STANINE (STANDARD NINE)   Stanine is a method of scaling test scores on a nine-point standard scale with a mean of 5 and a standard deviation of 2. To scale raw scores to stanine scores, first we need to rank the results from lowest to highest, then give the lowest 4% a stanine of 1, the next 7%, 2, and onward until we complete the distribution. See Table 15.8 for an example of Stanines on a normal curve.

Relating stanines to the normal curve, each stanine score represents a wide band of raw scores and percentile ranks. A normal distribution is divided into nine intervals, each of which has a width of one half of a standard deviation excluding the first and last intervals. The mean lies in the center of the fifth interval. Stanine scores are useful in comparing a student's performance across different content areas (see Figure 15.7). Typically, stanine scores are interpreted as above average (9, 8, 7), average (6, 5, 4), and below average (3, 2, 1). For example, a 6 in Mathematics and an 8 in Reading generally indicate a meaningful difference in a student's learning for the two respective content areas.

Summary

Basic statistical concepts are necessary and valuable elements of research. Counselors must understand both basic concepts and the role of descriptive statistics in data analysis and interpretation. Statistics are useful in evaluation of program data, conducting psychological testing, and helping counselors become critical consumers of published research. It is imperative that counselors understand how variables are scaled and measured, the role of reliability and validity, and how to interpret what the data show. A basic knowledge of these concepts will be invaluable to counselors as scientist-practitioners of this profession.

Review and Discussion Questions

1. List the variables you want to use for your research and name the scale of measurement for each one.

2. You read the test manual and found that this test has high Cronbach's alpha coefficient but low test-retest reliability coefficient. What does that mean?

3. Compare the content, construct, and criterion validity. Which validity is the most important?

4. As a school counselor, you want to develop a new instrument to measure students' self-esteem. Name a criterion you might use to build criterion validity.

5. Discuss the types of tests in which predictive validity is generally considered to be the most relevant.

6. Discuss the primary advantage of factor analysis as a validation technique.

7. Name a population and a variable that you think might have a positive skew.

8. Suppose a teacher gave a test score report to a school counselor and said, "The average was 67.89." What additional information should the school counselor ask for?

9. What is meant by the term "variability"?

10. Wendi got a score of 75 on a test having a mean of 60 and a standard deviation of 15. What is the alternative way to describe this test result?

CHAPTER 16

Developing a Research Report

Craig S. Cashwell, *University of North Carolina at Greensboro*
Kerrie N. Kardatzke, *University of North Carolina at Greensboro*

OBJECTIVES
After reading this chapter, you will:

- Be able to describe the purpose of the research report.
- Be able to describe the types of research reports and distinguish nuances within each type of report.
- Be able to discuss the discrete sections of the research report.
- Be able to identify the relevant content that fits within each section of the research report.
- Be able to identify common mistakes made in research report development.
- Be able to describe the journal review process.

OVERVIEW

Having considered how to begin the research process, review the literature, and establish the methods for the study, it is now important for you to learn how to develop a research report. If a research project is poorly designed and has serious methodological flaws, the quality of the write-up is irrelevant. That is, a good write-up cannot salvage a study of poor quality. On the other hand, a well-designed and implemented study that is reported ineffectually loses credibility. It is unfortunate when the useful results of a well-designed study are obscured by a bewildering report. Thus, our focus in this chapter is to build on the previous chapters and to help you develop a well-written report of your research findings.

PURPOSE OF A RESEARCH REPORT

The research report is the permanent record of counseling research. As such, the report becomes the document that archives the research for other scientist-practitioners. Although report quality typically has some management (e.g., from journal editors or conference juries), there are many journals and conferences that have limited oversight and, as a result, poorly written reports (and poorly designed studies) are disseminated frequently. When these results are consumed by counselors and students like yourselves who are just learning the research process, the potential result is a poorly informed counseling practitioner operating under faulty assumptions. Thus, the ultimate responsibility for solid research design and effective report writing falls on the researcher. As you have learned throughout this text, it will be your responsibility to determine if the research and resulting reports are of a quality nature.

Our primary focus in this chapter is on the development of a manuscript to be submitted for peer review. At the same time, we also will briefly discuss other types of research reports, including dissertations and theses, conference papers, and reports for policy makers. Also covered in this chapter will be details related to research report format and practical guidelines for developing a research report.

TYPES OF RESEARCH REPORTS

Research reports can take different forms, depending on at what point a counseling researcher is in her or his career, and the audience for which the topic is best suited. Although there are various types of research reports, three common types are *journal articles, dissertations* or *theses,* and *dissertation* or *thesis proposals.*

Journal Article

The most common and widely accessed avenue for publishing research reports is through refereed journals. Most professional organizations and subdivisions of those organizations publish periodical journals, specific to their discipline and particular area of interest. For instance, the American Counseling Association (ACA) and its subdivisions currently have 11 journals. Each journal has an editorial staff and a large number of professionals in the field who serve as peer reviewers of submitted manuscripts. The review process will be discussed more thoroughly later in the chapter, but here we will simply note that the peer-review process is designed to uphold the standards, integrity, and quality of published research.

Dissertation/Thesis

Some master's students and all doctoral students are required to complete a research project culminating in a thesis or dissertation as a final requirement before graduating. Each institution has its own policies and guidelines for this project, but certain elements are fairly common. Most theses and dissertations consist of four or five chapters, depending on whether the introduction and review of literature are included in different chapters. These chapters correspond to the main sections of the research report that will be discussed later in this chapter.

Dissertation/Thesis Proposal

Before proceeding with the study, graduate students typically write a research proposal that includes the first three chapters of the dissertation or thesis (introduction, literature review, and methodology). If you have a thesis or dissertation requirement for your degree, your proposal will likely be presented to the faculty or a pre-selected group of individuals (i.e., the student's doctoral committee) in order to get feedback and approval to move forward with the study. Often, students conduct a pilot study and report the results of the pilot study as part of the proposal process.

FORMAT OF THE RESEARCH REPORT

The format and organization of a research report can vary, depending on the type of research design and who the intended audience is. Typically, however, you should expect to find the following basic components in a research report: *title page, abstract, introduction, review of literature, methods, results, discussion or conclusions, and references.*

Title Page

The title of a research project is an important detail. Research is only useful to future researchers and practitioners if it can be accessed. Consider how many times you have browsed through tables of contents, reference lists, or search engine results to find titles that seem to fit your purpose. Abstracting and information databases also use titles to index and organize articles, so that they can be appropriately accessed. Therefore, the best titles are informative, catchy, and should provide important details such as the independent and dependent variables, the population of the study, the design, and clues to the outcome of the study. In order to squeeze all of this information into the 10–12 words recommended by the *Publication Manual of the American Psychological Association* (APA, 2001), it is important for you to avoid nonessential or redundant words, such as "A Study of " or "The Results of." For example, "A Study of Facilitative Skills" is a poor title because it is not descriptive of the study. A better title might be "Facilitative Skills Among Master's-level Counseling Interns."

Abstract

The abstract is intended to give readers a brief, but thorough, summary of the article. Aside from the title, the abstract is the most frequently read part of a research report. Readers often use the abstract to determine whether they will read the rest of the article and, like the title, abstracts are used by information databases to catalogue and index articles so they can be appropriately retrieved. The abstract should be succinct, well-organized, and should accurately represent the content of the article. It may help you to think of the abstract as an outline of the report in paragraph form. In fact, most sections of the research report should be represented in the abstract: the introduction (purpose of the study, research questions or hypotheses), methods (participants, type of study, research design), results (what is the outcome?), and conclusion (what is the impact of the study?). The abstract should not, however, include any additional information that is not in the report itself. The abstract also should be self-contained. In other words, readers should not have to seek out additional information in order to understand the abstract. Abbreviations and acronyms should be defined or avoided altogether. Although the APA style manual (APA, 2001) suggests that abstracts should not be more than 120 words, individual journals at times specify lengths that differ from this standard. The following is an example of a brief descriptive abstract:

> A random sample of 505 American Counseling Association (ACA) members completed a questionnaire that evaluated respondents' ratings of the importance of 9 competencies developed at the Summit on Spirituality (G. Miller, 1999; "Summit Results," 1995) meetings to effectively address spiritual and religious issues in counseling practice. Results suggest that, in general, ACA members strongly support the importance of the competencies for effective counseling practice.

Introduction

As a writer, you are probably already aware that a clear and well-organized introduction provides the framework for the rest of a paper. The same issue applies to the development of a research report. The introduction can be considered a map that begins with a statement of the problem (imagine a sign that says "You are here!"), guides the reader through the contextual terrain of relevant research, and points the way toward the researcher's strategy for addressing the problem. Although the introduction in most research reports is only a few paragraphs, it contains a great deal of important information. The introduction usually consists of a *statement of the problem,* a *brief overview of related research and theoretical underpinnings,* and a *list of the research questions and hypotheses.*

STATEMENT OF THE PROBLEM Before the researcher can describe the study itself, he or she must first provide a reason for conducting it. The statement of the problem is a description of the current state of knowledge related to the research topic. In sales and marketing, this would be considered the "hook" that catches the reader's attention and stimulates interest in the topic. When you are developing your problem statements, you should provide your readers with answers to the following questions: Why is this issue important? Whom does this issue impact? What is the purpose of this study? What practical outcomes does the researcher hope will emerge from the study?

OVERVIEW OF RELEVANT RESEARCH   Once you have introduced the problem to be addressed, the next step in writing a research report is to begin building a framework for how this particular study will address the problem. This framework is developed by providing an overview of the existing empirical and theoretical research on the topic. Some researchers object to the term *literature review*, because it suggests that a comprehensive summary and integration of all related research will be provided when, in fact, this is rarely the case. Typically, what is expected in an overview of the literature is a brief, but thorough, description of previous research findings, relevant methodological issues in previous research (e.g., clear operationalized definitions of variables, common sampling concerns with the population of interest, limitations of previously used measurement instruments, and important conclusions that inform the researcher's decisions about how to study the issues at hand). The overview of the literature may contain any research that addresses one or more of the variables being studied or the theoretical basis for the study. All of this background information serves to strengthen the framework the researcher uses to approach the study. It is in this section that you answer questions like: Where are the gaps, or what is missing from the existing research? What is the next logical step in addressing this problem?

The statement of the problem and the overview of the relevant literature should be so clearly written and logically organized that the reader can follow your rationale for the current study. At this point, the reader should be able to guess what the research questions and hypotheses are! The length of the literature review varies, depending on the type of report. For example, dissertations are often much longer and more in-depth than journal articles because of page constraints set by individual journals.

RESEARCH QUESTIONS AND HYPOTHESES   After developing a solid framework and rationale for the study, your next step is to state the research questions and/or hypotheses, which drive the rest of the study. The research questions are what help to focus the rest of the report, by centering on the purpose of the study. The questions should be specific, clearly worded, and a logical extension of the introduction and rationale. Clear, operationalized definitions for each variable should be provided, if they have not already been stated. Examples of operational definitions of variables are provided below:

- Depression as measured by the Beck Depression inventory.
- Physical energy level as measured by a 7-point likert-type scale (0 = very low energy to 7 = very high energy).

Methods

While clarity is essential for all sections of a well-written research report, the methods section, in particular, should be clear and detailed enough for readers to have the pertinent information to critique the validity of the study and to replicate it. The methods section can be likened to a "how-to manual" that walks the reader through each step of the research study. The four main areas in the methods section are *participants, instruments, research design,* and *procedures.*

PARTICIPANTS   In this subsection, you should answer the following questions: Who are the participants of this study? How were they selected? How many participants make up the sample? Are there different groups of participants (an experimental and control group, or other types of groups being compared), and if so, how many participants are in each group? What are the demographics of the sample, such as age, gender, ethnicity, region of residence, or other relevant characteristics? Although the participants subsection is usually rather brief and to the point, it is important that the information about participants is thorough and accurate, in order to avoid faulty interpretation of the results.

INSTRUMENTS OR MEASURES   By this point in the research report, readers should have a good idea about what you are planning to measure (it was stated in the research questions), but they have not been told *how* the variables will be measured. A useful way of organizing this section is to address each construct or variable and dedicate a minimum of one paragraph to describing the instrument used to measure it. The instrument description should include, at minimum, the full name of the instrument, authors of the instrument, appropriate citations, previous evidence of reliability and validity for the measure, information about the sample on which it was normed, number of items, and type of items (e.g., Likert scale).

RESEARCH DESIGN   At this point, you should let the reader know research design is being used. In other words, how are you organizing the variables in the study in order to answer the research questions? Is the design correlational, ex-post facto, causal-comparative, experimental, or quasi-experimental in nature? In one simple sentence about the research design, the writer can communicate a wealth of information about the study to the reader.

PROCEDURES   Finally, the procedures section provides the reader with a detailed, step-by-step guide to how the study was conducted. In this section, you should describe precisely what was done, and when, where, and how each step was completed. This includes how the participants were contacted (e.g., telephone, mailed survey, electronic survey, face-to-face, direct or indirect; through a parent, employer, teacher, or school administrator); how informed consent and parental permission (if applicable) were addressed; how the instruments were administered and in what order; instructions that were given to the participants; how experimental conditions were manipulated. If data were collected in multiple ways or at multiple times, a chart or graph may be helpful in illustrating the research process. In addition, you should disclose any information that might impact the participant responses or investment in the study (e.g., what incentives, if any, were offered to the participants). When possible, copies of the informed consent, instructions given to participants, and the actual instrumentation should be included in the appendices of the document.

RESULTS   Finally, what everyone has been waiting for—the results! This is the section in which the actual findings of the study are presented. What statistical tests were run and what were the results of these analyses? You should provide the reader with a summary of the statistical results, along with the statistical significance, effect size, and power. It should be easy for the reader to connect the findings with the stated research questions and to determine whether the findings support or refute your hypotheses. In the results section, the findings are reported in a factual manner, as conclusions will be drawn in the discussion section.

DISCUSSION   In this section, you have the opportunity to draw conclusions about the results of the study (i.e., What do the results mean?), and connect the findings to the body of existing research described in the introduction. In addition, you should address the following questions: What limitations of the study impact the conclusions that can be drawn (e.g., reliability, internal or external validity concerns, low power, low effect size, small sample size, other sampling concerns)? What ethical concerns impact the interpretation of results? What are some implications of these results for practitioners? What now? That is, what are some directions for future research?

QUALITATIVE RESEARCH REPORTS

There are some important characteristics of qualitative research reports that distinguish these reports from their quantitative counterparts. Qualitative research is unique in its philosophy, purpose, and methods. It is only fitting that the written product of qualitative research reflect this uniqueness. Some of these differences are evident in the importance of language (both the researcher's and the participant's), the acknowledgment of bias, and the intended audience.

Because the purpose of qualitative research is to understand personal experiences, the language that people use to describe those experiences is critical. Although qualitative researchers attempt to discover patterns and themes in participant accounts, excerpts of participant statements are often reported verbatim in the research report. If you conduct a qualitative research project, you should not attempt to condense your data into numbers or statistics, but should allow the reader access to the emotion and personal quality of the participants' voices.

In addition to the participants' voices, your voice also is more accessible to the reader. Qualitative researchers are more interactive, subjective, and participatory than quantitative researchers, and this is evident in the tone and style of writing. Often, qualitative researchers write in the first person and inform the reader of any personal investments he or she has in the research topic. This allows you to take a more active role in promoting social change.

If you are thinking to yourself, "Hmm, that sounds like researcher bias to me," you are right! Qualitative researchers openly acknowledge and accept the presence of bias in their writing. Consistent with the constructivist philosophy of qualitative research, they recognize that their personal construction of meaning will affect the way they understand and interpret participants' experiences.

Given the qualitative research goals of critiquing and changing problematic social structures, the target audience is often broader than that of quantitative research. In addition to academicians, fellow researchers, and practitioners, the products of qualitative research are often aimed at policy makers, the local community, and the general public. In fact, participants of qualitative studies may be the most powerful audience, by participating in a discourse that adjusts their perspective of the social order.

In order to achieve consistency in philosophy, purpose, methods, and presentation, qualitative research writing must reflect the underlying values of constructivism and critical theory. We have described some of the unique elements of qualitative research reports, including the importance of language, the acknowledgment of bias, and the intended audience.

BUILDING SKILLS FOR EFFECTIVE RESEARCH REPORT WRITING

In addition to understanding the typical sections of the research report, and what content is included within each section, there are a number of general guidelines offered here to support research report development. These include three major sections entitled *Developing as a Writer*, *Preparing in Advance*, and *Writing Guidelines*.

Developing as a Writer

There is an often-used adage, relevant to developing research reports, that goes something like this:

> Question: *How do you get to Carnegie Hall?*
> Answer: *Practice, practice, practice.*

Unfortunately, some researchers, particularly early in their careers, can become overly focused on the final outcome of their research report; that is, whether the report is accepted for publication. The skill of developing research reports is, like any other skill, one that is developed over time and through predictable processes. To hone your report-writing skills over time, it is important to *practice with opportunities for feedback, anticipate opportunities to re-write,* and *avoid writer's block.*

PRACTICE WITH FEEDBACK   Often, beginning researchers erroneously think that the initial review of a research report comes from the juried review process. In fact, most researchers routinely ask colleagues and peers to review their work prior to submitting to a journal for review. It will be important for you to develop collaborative relationships with colleagues and friends who will provide candid feedback on your report. In many cases, this need not be someone with expertise in the content area. It is common for report writers to lose perspective on their writing and, often, reviewers without content expertise can be useful. At times, "content experts" have their own biases that may influence their review. Reviewers with expertise in research report writing, but not necessarily expertise in the content area being discussed, may be particularly helpful. At the same time, informal reviewers with content expertise may be able to add useful insights about targeting the report to a particular audience, and whether a report might be appropriate for the selected outlet.

ANTICIPATE OPPORTUNITIES TO RE-WRITE   Once the report has undergone an informal collegial review and you determine it is appropriate, it is submitted for a peer-review process that will be described more fully later in this chapter. Many beginning researchers do not realize that some journals have acceptance rates as low as 8–12% of submissions. Journals with such a rigorous review process often provide detailed feedback to the author(s) to support both the improvement of the report and the report-writing skills of the author(s). Unfortunately, some reviewers write these reviews more to demonstrate their own expertise than to support the professional development of the author(s). If done well, though, the feedback is provided in a way that is encouraging and developmental in nature, regardless of the quality of the report. Carefully reviewing this feedback and implementing changes that are appropriate can provide tremendous learning opportunities.

Journals with more rigorous review processes rarely accept research reports without requiring revisions. As such, even if a manuscript receives a favorable review, opportunities for revision and improvement often are available. Most editors do not assume that all suggested revisions will necessarily be implemented. As a report writer, it is useful to go through the reviews and carefully consider which suggestions will be implemented and which will not. These decisions should be delineated in detail in a letter to the editor accompanying revisions to the report, along with a rationale for those suggestions that were not implemented.

AVOIDING WRITERS BLOCK   All writers of any genre, including research scientists, have at some point faced the challenge of staring at a blinking cursor on a blank computer screen. The process of developing a research report is a time-consuming and daunting task and, as such, it can be difficult to start the process and the ubiquitous *writer's block* may occur. A general guideline, at the risk of sounding like an advertisement for a popular shoe brand, is *Just Do It*. That is, just write. Beginning report writers, in particular, tend to get caught in the trap of assuming the first draft is "the" draft. It is much easier, however, to edit and revise a first draft than it is to develop the first draft. Philosophically, the lead author on this chapter does not even consider the first draft a draft, choosing instead to think of it simply as putting ideas onto the computer screen. It is only after this occurs that the true writing takes place, as these ideas are shaped, edited, and refined into a workable draft. Also, by getting the ideas onto paper, you can begin to solicit the support of others who can provide an informal review, as indicated above, to help you refine your work.

Prepare in Advance

In addition to recognizing the importance of practice with feedback for skill development, preparing in advance will help you in the development of each research report that you write. Specifically, it is important to *know your audience in advance, understand the guidelines for authors for your chosen outlet,* and *be familiar with publication guidelines for your profession.*

KNOW YOUR AUDIENCE IN ADVANCE   Starting well before the research report is begun, it is important to consider a target audience and a potential outlet for the research report. In this manner, it is possible to tailor language specifically to the audience of interest.

PUBLICATION GUIDELINES   Most journals adhere to specific publication styles. In the counseling profession, this is most often based on the *Publication Manual of the American Psychological Association* (APA, 2001). Prior to developing a research report, it is important to be familiar with these publication guidelines. Although there is personal variance in opinions as to the ideal writing style, this variance occurs within the constraints of the publication in which the writing will appear.

GUIDELINES FOR AUTHORS   In addition to the publication style used (e.g., APA), there are often additional guidelines provided within journals. Once you have identified a potential outlet for your report, it is important to review the *Guidelines for Authors* for that particular publication. Although strict adherence to these guidelines will not salvage a study with unsound methodology, failure to follow these guidelines could preclude publication or, at the least, make for more extensive revisions in subsequent drafts. Particular guidelines, such as maximum page length and other formatting requirements, should be closely adhered to in report preparation.

Writing Guidelines

Once you have developed the mindset that report writing is a skill developed over time with practice and feedback, and done the preparatory work necessary to know your targeted outlet and the guidelines for publication, there are additional general guidelines that can strengthen the actual writing of the report. Although some additional recommendations will be provided later in the book as examples of how to avoid common mistakes, we focus here on three writing guidelines: *Build a bridge to your study, interpret and recommend within existing data,* and *be transparent in your writing.*

BUILD A BRIDGE   At the point in the report at which you begin discussing the methodology of your study, the reader should be left with no questions as to why this study was conducted and why it is important. This *bridge* occurs through an organized overview of the literature in which you build a clear argument for the study. The key question that has to be answered is, Why *this* study *now*? That is, given what researchers have already examined, how does this study provide a logical extension of the current knowledge base? This review culminates in a parsimonious statement that clearly delineates the purpose of the study. An example of a bridge is provided below. Please note that the example is fictitious, constructed as a hypothetical for illustrative purposes only:

> Although previous researchers have considered the effect of spiritual practice on depression level (Cashwell & Young, 2008), researchers have not considered how mindfulness and emotional expression may interact to affect depressive symptomology. Therefore, the purpose of this study is to examine the effects (main and interactive) of spirituality, mindfulness, and emotional expressiveness on depression level among a diverse sample of young adults.

INTERPRET AND RECOMMEND WITHIN THE EXISTING DATA   In the discussion section of the research report, the author(s) commonly interpret the results of the study to make meaning of these results and provide recommendations both for counseling practice and for future research. These interpretations and recommendations are important aspects of the research report. It is imperative, however, that these interpretations and recommendations be consistent with the findings of this study and previous research on the topic. Although this may sound like common sense, making interpretations and recommendations that extend beyond the available data is a common problem in report writing.

BE TRANSPARENT   All too often, scholars either fail to report limitations of their study, reframe limitations in a way to implicitly suggest they are not *really* limitations, or otherwise minimize these limitations. All research projects have methodological limitations that exist either a priori or that evolve over the course of the study. These limitations should be spelled out explicitly, as should cautions on how interpretations of findings might be influenced by these limitations.

COMMON MISTAKES IN RESEARCH REPORTS

There are a number of common mistakes that routinely plague research reports. These can be categorized as *general writing problems, problems in the review of existing literature, problems in reporting methodology,* and *problems in writing discussion sections.*

General Writing Problems

Many common mistakes are made in the overall writing style and tone of the research report. Commonly, these include *failure to follow author guidelines, failure to follow publication style guidelines, use of discriminatory language, transition and heading problems,* and *a weak abstract.*

FAILURE TO FOLLOW AUTHOR GUIDELINES   Virtually all journals publish author guidelines. Typically these are available in back issues and via the Internet. Common guidelines include maximum page length and restricting the use of tables and figures, both related to publication costs. Routinely, however, journal editors receive manuscripts well in excess of the length restriction and with unnecessary tables and figures. Regardless of the quality of the research study, failure to follow author guidelines may reduce the likelihood of acceptance for publication.

FAILURE TO FOLLOW RELEVANT PUBLICATION MANUALS   One detail that typically is chronicled in author guidelines is what publication style should be followed; most commonly for counselors, this is APA-style (APA, 2001). Minor style problems typically do not substantially hinder the review process as these are easily remedied during the copyediting process, but major style problems in the writing may negatively impact the review process (Miller, 2006).

DISCRIMINATORY LANGUAGE   Another common problem exists when research report authors include language, often inadvertently, that is discriminatory in nature. For example, the term *homosexual* is now considered pejorative, and most style manuals suggest using *gay men and lesbians* instead. Although the problems with such language are apparent, discriminatory language is probably most often used without negative intent. Further, these types of problems could be easily corrected through the copyediting process. Such language may be particularly problematic, however, if a reviewer has a strong reaction to the discriminatory language that may create a negative bias in the review process.

TRANSITION AND HEADING PROBLEMS   A writing problem common to research reports is inattention to the overall flow of the report. Often, individual sections are written without sufficient attention to transitions. As a result, individual sentences and paragraphs may be well written, but the report as a whole does not flow well. This can be corrected by attending to introductory sentences and phrases, and in using closing sentences and phrases in a section to segue into the next section. The appropriate application of headings also helps the reader transition to new sections. As an example of this, you might review the three levels of headings used in this section of this chapter.

WEAK ABSTRACT   Many authors fail to see the importance of the abstract and, consequently, spend little time on its development. The abstract should follow the author guidelines, particularly for length, and briefly describe the study. It is important to keep in mind, particularly in the era of online databases, that the abstract will often be the only text available for a reader to make a decision about whether he or she wants to download the full text of the article. Whether it be hard copy or online full-text articles, readers should not be "surprised" to find that the abstract does not accurately or fully describe the study.

Common Problems in the Literature Review

Problems also may emerge in the review of the literature. Common problems in this section of the report include *failing to build a logical argument for the study* and *bias in reviewing existing literature.*

FAILURE TO BUILD A LOGICAL ARGUMENT FOR THE STUDY   As noted above, the introduction and review of the literature is a critical section of the research report. As the reader transitions to the methodology section of the report, he or she should clearly understand the answer to the question, "Why *this* study *now?*" To answer these questions, it is incumbent on the report writer to build an argument, grounded in existing empirical and theoretical literature, as to why this study was conducted. As may be apparent, this is important not only in report writing but in the original conceptualization of the study. What is imperative, though, is that this argument be clearly and explicitly delineated for the reader. Failure to do so leaves the reader, who may not be a content expert in the area of inquiry, without a context for the study. This argument also is important as a context for the discussion section of the report, providing a foundation on which to discuss the results of the study and make recommendations for practitioners and future research.

BIAS IN REVIEWING EXISTING RESEARCH   Another issue related to the review of the literature involves a bias around reviewing the existing theoretical and empirical literature. In many, if not most, areas that have received substantial inquiry in the social sciences, there are studies with seemingly contradictory findings. In some unfortunate instances, report writers will only review those studies that support the argument they hope to make with their findings. Another way in which this bias may be introduced is by exaggerating limitations of studies with findings contradictory to the bias of the author(s), and minimizing or ignoring limitations of studies with findings consistent with this bias. It is the responsibility of the report writer to provide a balanced and fair review of existing literature, including an objective account of methodological limitations in previous research.

Common Problems in Methodology Sections

Because the methods section of the report provides the blueprint of how the study was carried out, it is an essential aspect of the research report. Common problems in reporting methodology include *insufficient detail* and *failure to provide evidence of validity and reliability.*

INSUFFICIENT DETAIL IN METHODOLOGY   Replication and extension of existing research are hallmarks of the social sciences. The goal, then, of the methods section of the report is to provide sufficient detail to allow replication. A reader should know exactly what he or she would need to do to replicate the study. Sufficient detail should be provided about participants, instrumentation, and procedures so that the study can be easily replicated by others if they so desire. If page limitations preclude inclusion of all information necessary to allow replication, this should be noted explicitly in the report, along with contact information that allows a reader to obtain additional information.

FAILURE TO PROVIDE EVIDENCE OF INSTRUMENTATION VALIDITY AND RELIABILITY   A common mistake made in research reports is to provide inadequate evidence of instrumentation validity and reliability. This mistake usually takes one of two forms. In the first, writers fail to provide any evidence of validity and reliability. A second common mistake occurs when writers provide evidence of instrument validity and reliability *only* from previous research. Research instruments are not valid and reliable per se, but rather are valid and reliable only for a specific sample. Because of this, it is necessary to report psychometric information for the sample of *each* study. Failing to do so may lead to results and conclusions that are based on psychometrically unsound and, at times, virtually useless information.

Common Problems in Results Section

The results section of the report, in which the answers to the research questions are first delineated, is the heart of the written report. Common problems within the results section include issues related to *statistical versus clinical significance,* and *providing discussion within the results section.*

STATISTICAL VERSUS CLINICAL SIGNIFICANCE   Historically, researchers established an a priori alpha level, usually .05, and conducted statistical analyses accordingly, willing to allow a 5% chance that the findings could be due to chance. One problem that exists with this approach is that statistical significance is not the same as clinical significance. For example, significance tests are influenced by sample size, and it is possible to have an F-statistic or Pearson r be statistically significant with little practical utility, that is, not be clinically significant. For example, in the hypothetical study referenced earlier in this chapter, it is possible that the authors could collect data on a very large sample and find that spirituality accounts for 5% of the variance in depression level. Given a sufficiently large sample size, this might be statistically significant. In reality, however, this finding has little practical utility because such a small amount of the variance in depression has been accounted for by the independent variable of spirituality.

Increasingly, researchers have turned to reporting effect size as an alternative to significance testing. Although a thorough discussion of reporting effect sizes is beyond the scope of this chapter, readers are encouraged to review Thompson (2006a, 2006b) for additional information about effect sizes.

PROVIDING DISCUSSION WITHIN THE RESULTS SECTION   Another common problem occurs when the report writer offers discussion content, including interpretations and implications of findings, within the results section. In other words, it is inconsistent with APA style guidelines to intermingle the results and discussion sections. One exception to this occurs in limited instances when the published *Guidelines for Authors* indicates that there should be a *Results and Discussion* section, in which case the editor is expressing a preference that the two be included together. In general, though, unless guidelines request this, it is necessary to include all interpretations and implications of findings in the discussion section rather than the results section.

Common Problems in Discussion Sections

A number of common problems also exist within discussion sections of research reports. Problems frequently noted in these sections include *failing to delineate limitations to the study, going beyond the data, failing to note implications for practitioners,* and *recommendations for future research.*

FAILURE TO DELINEATE LIMITATIONS TO THE STUDY   As previously mentioned, it is imperative that the report writer be transparent and candid about methodological limitations of the study. A frank discussion of the methodological limitations will inform future research as well as provide a context for the results of the study. When a report writer fails to report limitations to the study, this provides a disservice to the profession. Future researchers may not be fully aware of potential problems of a study, and practitioners may be making clinical decisions based on research findings that are flawed. When a report writer fails to discuss limitations of the study, it is left to the reviewer to determine whether (1) the study is flawless (which is not realistic), (2) the writer intentionally chooses not to discuss limitations, or (3) as is most often the case, the report writer is unsophisticated in the importance of discussing limitations. In any event, the failure to candidly discuss limitations is seen as highly problematic by reviewers. A caveat should be included here, however. In some instances, in an effort to be transparent, report writers *overstate* the magnitude of the methodological limitations and, as a result, findings that might simply need cautious and tentative interpretations are dismissed by the report writer.

GOING BEYOND THE DATA   Although it is expected that the report writer will provide interpretations of the results of the study and recommendations for counseling practice and research, it is important that these findings be consistent with the findings of the current study and previous research findings. At times, report writers will make the mistake of offering interpretations or recommendations that go beyond the data or, even more problematic, that are inconsistent with existing data. This is usually due to researcher bias, but it is indicative of limited rigor in the report and is a common "fatal flaw" in the report that precludes publication.

FAILURE TO DISCUSS IMPLICATIONS AND RECOMMENDATIONS   The opposite of going beyond the data may also occur when the report writer fails to discuss implications for counseling practitioners and recommendations for future research. At the point in time that a report writer is writing a discussion section, he or she has conducted a thorough review of the literature, conceptualized the study within the context of existing knowledge, developed specific methodology for completing the study, collected and analyzed data, and written the results section. As a result of these endeavors, the report writer has developed a level of knowledge and expertise in the content area that places her or him in a unique position to offer perspectives on the implications of results for counseling practitioners and recommendations for follow-up research. If the results are considered the "what" of the study, the implications for practitioners might be considered the "so what" of the study, and recommendations for future research the "now what" of the study. For example, a hypothetical "so what" might be:

> Because emotional expressiveness, mindfulness, and spirituality all contributed significantly to the prediction of depression, counselors are encouraged to assess each of these client attributes. In particular, because emotional restriction accounted for the most variance in depression, assessing the client's capacity to experience and express emotions seems salient.

Relatedly, a hypothetical "now what" might be:

> The current study suggests that emotional expressiveness, mindfulness, and spirituality all contribute to depression. Because the current study uses correlational methods, however, additional research is needed to determine if programs to help clients express emotions, live more mindfully, and develop their spiritual lives changes levels of depressive symptomology.

These implications and recommendations should be clearly connected to existing knowledge gained from the current study and previous research. Failing to include implications and recommendations limits the impact of the research report.

Manuscript Review Process

The purpose of this section is to delineate the manuscript review process. Although, as noted earlier, there are other types of research reports, there is great variance among how these types of reports are reviewed and the report writer must be familiar with the idiosyncrasies of each process. Manuscript reviews are typically more uniform, although variance certainly exists, and it is this review process that is the focus of this section.

Once the manuscript is complete, it is submitted to a journal editor, typically a senior scholar in the area. In more recent years, journals are increasingly going to electronic submission of manuscripts because it is more time- and cost-effective; it is incumbent on the report writer to ascertain the appropriate submissions format. A good rule of thumb for report writers is to note when the manuscript was submitted, but then to forget about the manuscript for a period of approximately three months while the paper is under peer review. Although peer review occasionally occurs more quickly than this, three months is a typical response time and, in some instances, it may take the editor even longer to provide a response. Although authors should avoid overly frequent contact with the journal editor, it is appropriate to make inquiry about the status of the manuscript after three months.

Typically, when the editor receives the manuscript, he or she determines whether the manuscript will be distributed for peer review. An editor usually opts not to send the manuscript out for review and informs the report writer of this decision only in cases where the content is inappropriate for that particular journal or where the quality of the work is extremely poor. At the same time, reports that are marginally well written or studies that are poorly designed often receive peer reviews. This is because the purpose of the review is to provide feedback on this particular report *and* to support the development of the report writer(s) through developmental feedback. That is, it is the responsibility of the peer-review process to provide feedback to the writer about the scientific merit of the study, the quality of the written report, and the degree to which the report informs future work (Kaplan, 2005).

Manuscripts that are submitted for peer review are usually sent out to between two and four reviewers, typically members of the editorial board. For most journals, the review process is blind, meaning that the reviewers do not know the identity of the writer, and vice versa. Other journals, however, use a more transparent review process where reviewer and author names are known. The reviewers read and study the report, and provide a detailed review to the editor, including feedback on the merits of the study and the quality of the written report. The norm is certainly that the reviews are fair and objective, and that feedback is provided in a tone and manner that is supportive and developmental in nature. As one might expect, however, there are exceptions to this that occur when reviewer values and biases impact the review, or when the reviewer is unnecessarily caustic or sarcastic in tone. Although difficult to tolerate, a negative tone by a reviewer should not be taken personally.

The editor compiles the reviews and, in many cases, also reviews the manuscript. Following this, he or she generates an *action letter*, detailing the adjudication of the manuscript and recommended changes. The most common decisions are *Accept As Is* (though this rarely occurs and is usually more indicative of a weak review process than a flawless initial report), *Accept Pending Minor Revisions, Revise and Resubmit*, and *Reject*. If revisions are requested, a timeframe in which these should be received is provided. If a manuscript is rejected, it may be resubmitted to another journal, although ethically it may be under review by only one journal at a time. Whether the manuscript is resubmitted to the same journal or a different journal, the writer should consider carefully the comments of the editor and reviewers and thoughtfully revise the manuscript before resubmitting. This does not mean, however, that all recommended changes should be made. When submitting a revised manuscript to the same journal, the report writer should provide a detailed account to the editor of the changes that were made *and* a rationale for any recommendations that were not followed.

Many reports go through multiple revisions and reviews, a process that in and of itself can take many months to over a year. Add to this the length of time that it takes to write the report after data collection is completed, and the publication lag (time from acceptance to publication) that can be in some cases over a year. This presents a potential problem when the data are particularly time sensitive. On the other hand, such a thorough review process is necessary to provide quality control over the research that is being disseminated and to ensure that each written report is as well written as possible.

Summary

The purpose of this chapter has been to help you gain knowledge to develop a well-written report of your research findings. Perhaps most important in this chapter, though, is the point that writing research reports is a skill and, like other skills, it is refined by experience, practice, feedback, and more practice. Even the most experienced and well-published researchers have many stories of challenging review processes and projects that ended up in file cabinets rather than published in journals.

Building these skills, however, is an invaluable process. Through the communication of quality research studies through well-written reports, the counseling profession will continue its long history of the practitioner-scientist approach to counseling and counselor education.

Review and Discussion Questions

1. How do scholars share their research findings with others?
2. Through what steps does a research project go as it is considered for publication in a scholarly journal?
3. What are the major sections of a research report, and what content is included in each section?
4. What challenges do you personally anticipate that you would likely need to guard against in developing a research report?
5. How is writing a research report different from writing the papers that you write for a graduate course?

Helpful Resources

American Counseling Association website: **http://www
.counseling.org**

American Psychological Association (2001). *Publication manual of the American Psychological Association* (5th ed.). Washington, DC: American Psychological Association.

Heppner, P. P., Kivlighan, D. M., & Wampold, B. E. (2007). *Research design in counseling* (3rd ed.). Belmont, CA: Wadsworth.

Leedy, P. D., & Ormrod, J. E. (2005). *Practical research: Planning and design* (8th ed.). Upper Saddle River, NJ: Pearson Prentice Hall.

Rudestam, K. E., & Newton, R. R. (2001). *Surviving your dissertation: A comprehensive guide to content and process.* Thousand Oaks, CA: Sage Publications.

CHAPTER 17

Ethical Consideration in the Practice of Research

Kelly L. Wester, *University of North Carolina at Greensboro*

OBJECTIVES

After reading this chapter, you will:

▪ Be able to understand and define *research ethics* and *research integrity*.

▪ Be able to apply the principles of responsible research conduct to the counseling field.

▪ Be able to describe problems in past research studies that led to the development of current ethical standards related to the use of human participants.

▪ Be able to explain the various ethical considerations in conducting a research study, from development of a research idea through publication of results.

▪ Be able to identify the three central components of the Belmont Report and how each applies to research within the field of counseling.

OVERVIEW

This chapter is designed to provide an overview of the important ethical considerations that must be made when completing research involving human subjects in counseling.

As a counselor, you have been working with Debbie, a 26-year-old Caucasian female who presented with Major Depressive Disorder, self-injurious behavior, and substance abuse. Debbie has suffered many losses throughout her life that have led to her presenting concerns, and thus, she voluntarily entered counseling six months ago. It appears, at the six-month mark, that many of Debbie's presenting concerns have diminished; however, you are unsure to what extent her symptoms have improved.

This is a typical experience that many counselors will face throughout their counseling careers. One way to be sure of your clients' progress in counseling, and to determine if the methods you are using are effective, is to engage in the process of research (e.g., using surveys, questionnaires, or interviews to empirically track the changes of clients). For example, to quantify the progress Debbie has made you could have her complete symptom questionnaires (e.g., Beck Depression Inventory; Deliberate Self-Harm Inventory) at intake, at 3 months, and at 6 months.

This would allow you to assure yourself and your client that it is appropriate to terminate, or to examine the progress that has been made and to explore the next steps that need to be taken.

Evaluating your progress with clients and examining your effectiveness is a practical means of engaging in evidence-based practice; yet before conducting research there are many ethical considerations that need to be given attention in order to ensure proper client care. Ethical considerations in research (e.g., assessing Debbie's progress using questionnaires) are rarely discussed in clinical practice, trainings, or the counseling literature. Yet, the Council for Accreditation of Counseling and Related Educational Programs (2001, 2009) indicated that research is a core area that must be taught within counselor preparation programs. A component of this is ethical practice while conducting research. Thus, research ethics will be the primary focus of the current chapter. Throughout this chapter, the terms "human participant" and "client" will be used synonymously.

Research ethics and integrity have not been widely discussed in relation to counseling professionals in general. Yet counselors, in all positions, are ethically responsible when it comes to conducting and applying research. Before beginning to discuss the responsibilities you will have with regard to research, definitions are provided.

RESEARCH ETHICS, INTEGRITY, AND RESPONSIBLE CONDUCT OF RESEARCH

In your everyday personal and professional lives, you will make moral decisions as situations arise. Professionally, these decisions could be determining which clients you are trained to work with, when to break a client's confidentiality, what to do when a client gives you a gift, or the appropriate methods to use in treating a particular client. Suggestions on how one should approach these decisions are provided by our principal professional organization, the American Counseling Association (ACA, 2005). Furthermore, other organizations provide their own ethical codes for members (e.g., Association of Counselor Educators and Supervisors, National Board for Certified Counselors, American School Counselors Association, etc.).

Ethical codes related specifically to research are included in the ACA ethical guidelines (see section G, ACA, 2005). Examples of ethical decision making related to research practice include informed consent, ensuring the best treatment for your client, and ensuring client anonymity in research data and future publications or presentations. Thus, research ethics are not designed to provide specific answers to ethical dilemmas, but to guide one's judgments and decision-making processes.

Research ethics is defined as the "study or science of right and wrong—of what one ought to do when confronted with conflicting values or obligations" (Steneck, 2003, p. 240). ACA specifically states that "Counselors [should] plan, design, conduct, and report research in a manner that is consistent with pertinent ethical principles, federal and state laws, host institutional regulations, and scientific standards governing research with human research participants" (ACA, 2005, G.1.a).

When you adhere to the ethical codes of your professional organization, you are considered to be engaging in research integrity. *Research integrity* is defined as "a commitment to intellectual honesty and personal responsibility" (Institute of Medicine, 2002) and "adherence to rules, regulations, guidelines, and commonly accepted professional codes or norms" (Office of Research Integrity [ORI], 2003). Therefore, as long as you adhere to the ACA's and your employment organization's (e.g., university, agency, school) research ethical codes, you would be acting with integrity in your research.

If, as a counselor, you follow the ACA ethical codes and maintain research integrity, you are considered to be engaging in the *responsible conduct of research* (RCR). Responsible conduct of research is defined as "conducting research in a manner that fulfills the professional responsibilities of a researcher, as defined by his or her professional organization [e.g., ACA], the institutions for which they work [e.g., university, school district, state agency, community agency], and when relevant, the government and public" (Steneck, 2006, p. 55). While ACA provides us with guidelines to ensure that we are ethically responsible in the area of research, the Office of Research Integrity

[ORI] provides us with nine core areas to consider if we are to engage in responsible conduct of research (see Table 17.1). These nine areas include:

1. Data acquisition, management, sharing, and ownership;
2. Mentor/trainee relationships;
3. Publication practices and responsible authorship;
4. Peer review;
5. Collaborative science;
6. Human subjects;
7. Research involving animals;
8. Research misconduct; and
9. Conflict of interest and commitment.

When engaging in the process of research, one should combine the nine ORI areas with the ACA (or other professional organization) ethical codes to ensure research integrity and the responsible conduct of research (see Table 17.1).

TABLE 17.1 The Office of Research Integrity's Nine Core Areas of Responsible Conduct of Research

Responsible Conduct of Research Core Area	Description	American Counseling Association's Code of Ethics for Research (2005)
1. Data acquisition, management, sharing, and ownership	Accepted practices for acquiring and maintaining research data. Proper methods for record keeping and electronic data collection and storage in scientific research. Includes defining what constitutes data; keeping data notebooks or electronic files; data privacy and confidentiality; data selection, retention, sharing, ownership, and analysis; data as legal documents and intellectual property, including copyright laws.	G.1.e Principal Researcher Responsibility G.1.g Multicultural/Diversity Considerations in Research G.2.e Confidentiality of Information G.2.j Disposal of Research Documents and Records G.4.d Identity of Participants G.4.e Replication Studies
2. Mentor/trainee relationships	The responsibilities of mentors and trainees in predoctoral and postdoctoral research programs. Includes the role of a mentor, responsibilities of a mentor, conflicts between mentor and trainee, collaboration and competition, selection of a mentor, and abusing the mentor/trainee relationship.	G.5.e Agreement of Contributions G.5.f Student Research
3. Publication practices and responsible authorship	The purpose and importance of scientific publication, and the responsibilities of the authors. Includes topics such as collaborative work and assigning appropriate credit, acknowledgments, appropriate citations, repetitive publications, fragmentary publication, sufficient description of methods, corrections and retractions, conventions for deciding upon authors, author responsibilities, and the pressure to publish.	G.4.a Accurate Results G.4.b Obligation to Report Unfavorable Results G.4.c Reporting Errors G.5.a Recognizing Contributions G.5.b Plagiarism G.5.c Review/Republication of Data or Ideas G.5.d Contributors G.5.e Agreement of Contributions G.5.f Student Research G.5.g Duplicate Submission

(continued)

TABLE 17.1   The Office of Research Integrity's Nine Core Areas of Responsible Conduct of Research *(continued)*

Responsible Conduct of Research Core Area	Description	American Counseling Association's Code of Ethics for Research (2005)
4. Peer review	The purpose of peer review in determining merit for research funding and publications. Includes topics such as the definition of peer review, impartiality, how peer review works, editorial boards and ad hoc reviewers, responsibilities of the reviewers, privileged information and confidentiality.	G.5.h Professional Review
5. Collaborative science	Research collaborations and issues that may arise from such collaborations. Includes topics such as setting ground rules early in the collaboration, avoiding authorship disputes, and the sharing of materials and information with internal and external collaborating scientists.	G.2.i Informing Sponsors G.5.e Agreement of Contribution
6. Human subjects	Issues important in conducting research involving human subjects. Includes topics such as the definition of human subjects research, ethical principles for conducting human subjects research, informed consent, confidentiality and privacy of data and patient records, risks and benefits, preparation of a research protocol, institutional review boards, adherence to study protocol, proper conduct of the study, and special protections for targeted populations (e.g., children, minorities, and the elderly).	G.1.a Use of Human Research Participants G.1.b Deviation from Standard of Practice G.1.c Independent Researchers G.1.d Precautions to Avoid Injury G.1.e Principal Researcher Responsibility G.1.f Minimal Interference G.1.g Multicultural/Diversity Considerations in Research G.2.a Informed Consent in Research G.2.b Deception G.2.c Student/Supervisee Participation G.2.d Client Participation G.2.e Confidentiality of Information G.2.f Persons Not Capable of Giving Informed Consent G.2.g Commitments to Participants G.2.h Explanations After Data Collection G.2.j Disposal of Research Documents and Records G.3.a Nonprofessional Relationships G.3.b Relationships with Research Participants G.3.c Sexual Harassment and Research Participants G.3.d Potentially Beneficial Interactions
7. Research involving animals	Issues important to conducting research involving animals. Includes topics such as definition of research involving animals, ethical principles for conducting research on animals, federal regulations governing animal research, institutional animal care and use committees, and treatment of animals.	NA

TABLE 17.1** The Office of Research Integrity's Nine Core Areas of Responsible Conduct of Research (*continued*)

| 8. **Research misconduct** | The meaning of research misconduct and the regulations, policies, and guidelines that govern research misconduct in PHS-funded institutions. Includes topics such as fabrication, falsification, and plagiarism; error vs. intentional misconduct; institutional misconduct policies; identifying misconduct; procedures for reporting misconduct; protection of whistle-blowers; and outcomes of investigations, including institutional and federal actions. | G.4.a Accurate Results
G.5.b Plagiarism
G.5.g Duplicate Submission |
| 9. **Conflict of interest and commitment** | The definition of conflicts of interest and how to handle conflicts of interest. Types of conflicts encountered by researchers and institutions. Includes topics such as conflicts associated with collaborators, publication, financial conflicts, obligations to other constituencies, and other types of conflicts. | G.2.i Informing Sponsors
G.3.d Potentially Beneficial Interactions |

IMPACT OF IRRESPONSIBLE CONDUCT OF RESEARCH

It is imperative that as a counselor, regardless of position, you become familiar with and adhere to your profession's ethical codes on research because of the implications that irresponsible conduct could have for your profession and your clients. There are various implications of unethical research practices (Steneck, 2006). One of the most serious is that engaging in unethical research (from designing a study, to data collection, to misrepresenting published research) can lead to client or human participant harm. An extreme example is the fatal impact research had on two human participants. Recently, research projects in the medical community resulted in the deaths of two patients (Curry, 2001; Stolberg, 1999). It was believed that these deaths could have been avoided if the researchers had read the existing literature on appropriate treatment, and if they had voiced a conflict of interest in the research study (Steneck, 2006). While deaths as a result of research have not been reported in the counseling literature, client harm does occur (e.g., Brown & Espina, 2000; Kocet & Freeman, 2005; Sanders & Freeman, 2003).

For example, imagine that a counselor is conducting research to compare which method of treating clients with depression is more effective (e.g., therapy as usual or psychopharmacology). While conducting this research, the counselor separates her clients into two groups: Group 1 receives counseling and medications; Group 2 receives only counseling. She learns that some clients in her therapy-only group exhibit severe depression that merits antidepressant medicine. However, in order to complete the study, she continues collecting data for another month. Therefore, by refusing to provide the therapy-only group with the option to take medicine these clients will experience continued disruption of their lives (see ACA ethical code G.1.f) or more extreme, a suicide attempt by a research subject.

While research ethics are not frequently discussed in relation to clinical practice, irresponsible research practices have taken place in the counseling field. The ACA ethics committee provides information regarding the reports and queries received related to possible ethical violations. Almost every year for the past 10 years, approximately 1% of the informal inquiries made have been related to research and publication (e.g., Brown & Espina, 2000; Kocet &

Freeman, 2005; Sanders & Freeman, 2003). Unfortunately, the ethics committee has never provided great detail about these inquiries or determined where the questionable research behaviors lie.

A study by Davis, Wester, and King (2008) specifically examined irresponsible conduct of research among a sample of 189 professionals in the counseling field. This sample included counselor educators at universities (45%), masters/doctoral students (31%), and counseling professionals and supervisors (24%). Each participant was provided with multiple vignettes that described scenarios related to research ethics (e.g., data management, informed consent, using deception with clients). Davis et al. found that between 2 and 24% of the counseling professionals self-reported the likelihood that they would engage in unethical research behavior. Specifically, 24% reported they would be "likely" to inappropriately use deception with clients to persuade them to participate in a study. Furthermore, 2 to 4% indicated they would be "extremely likely" to report inaccurate significant results in order to obtain grant funding or have an article published. Clearly, it is highly likely that unethical behavior related to research exists in our field. For this reason, it is imperative that all counseling professionals learn and become familiar with the ACA's ethical codes and other pertinent ethical codes, *and* engage in research integrity.

One way to become familiar with ethical research practices is to engage in training in ethics. For example, before collecting data, counselor educators submit their proposed study to a committee which reviews the proposed study to ensure that human subjects are protected (see later discussion on Institutional Review Boards).

ROLES AND RESPONSIBILITIES OF RESEARCHERS IN THE COUNSELING PROFESSION

All counselors, including students-in-training, counselor educators, and counseling practitioners, are ethically bound to engage in the responsible conduct of research and follow the ethical guidelines of their profession and the setting in which they work. The responsibilities that counselors have in this process exist regardless of whether they are collecting data to publish or present; or collecting data to inform their counseling practice.

Researcher Responsibilities

Imagine that you are planning to conduct a study that involves gathering data from counseling clients. What responsibilities do you believe you hold for the well-being of these individuals? Is your responsibility dissuaded by the potential of your research to help others if you make important discoveries?

Years of research in the behavioral sciences, including missteps and serious injury to human subjects, have led to the current perspective that you, as a counseling professional who engages in research, bear the overall responsibility for every aspect of the research process. A major facet of the responsible conduct of research is the obligation you have to abide by ethical research practices throughout the entire research process. Specifically, this means that you must consider how human subjects are affected by:

1. The research question(s) you decide to investigate.
2. The design of your study.
3. The methodology you select.
4. The instrumentation you use to collect data.
5. The possible risks to participants by participating in your research.
6. Taking steps to minimize those risks.
7. The actual data collection process.
8. The presentation of informed consent information.
9. The data analysis process.

10. The confidentiality procedures you use to protect information you collect on subjects
11. How you share the results of your research through discussions, workshops, presentations, and publications.
12. Your decisions to uphold participants' rights throughout your study.

Regrettably, such considerations as those listed above are not always made when people design or conduct research involving human subjects. In fact, there have been many studies in the past in which the rights of human participants were egregiously violated. In particular, four studies from the 20th century led to the development of today's ethical standards to protect human rights: (a) the Nazi Medical War Crimes, (b) the Tuskegee Syphilis Study, (c) the Jewish Chronic Disease Hospital Study, and (d) the Willowbrook Study (National Institute of Health [NIH], 2002).

Nazi Medical War Crimes

In World War II, Nazi physicians conducted horrendous medical experiments on thousands of prisoners in concentration camps to investigate how the human body would react to various extremes. These researchers subjected prisoners to forms of torment including injecting humans with gasoline or live viruses, immersing prisoners in ice water or forcing them to ingest poisons. As expected, the majority of these medical experiments resulted in anguish, disease, suffering, and death. When the outside world learned of these studies, members of the scientific community were outraged, which led to high ranking officials in the Nazi party to be tried for crimes against humanity.

Tuskegee Syphilis Study

The Tuskegee Syphilis Study was one of the longest running, and most unscrupulous studies to ever occur within the United States. The study lasted for 40 years beginning in 1932 and ending in 1972. It was an experimental study that included approximately 600 black males, and its goal was to examine the impact of syphilis on humans. Without informed consent, and through active misinformation, medical researchers collected data from over 400 black males who presented with syphilis and compared them to 200 black males without syphilis. The participants were told they would receive free treatment; however, the treatment they obtained had nothing to do with the cure for syphilis. Instead the treatment included medical examinations such as spinal taps. By 1936, it was apparent to the researchers that those participants infected with syphilis had a greater number of and more serious complications than those participants who did not have syphilis. Within 10 years, the researchers had determined that the death rate for subjects with syphilis was double that of the control participants. While no genuine cure existed for syphilis at the start of the study, in the 1940s penicillin was found to be an effective treatment for the disease; nevertheless, the participants of the study were neither informed of the possible treatment nor were they provided with the antibiotic. Regrettably, this study continued for an additional 30 years!

Jewish Chronic Disease Hospital Study

In 1963, at the Jewish Chronic Disease Hospital in New York, a study was conducted to examine whether the human body could reject cancer cells, and if the inability to fight off cancer was related to debilitation in the body (e.g., other medical diseases). Therefore, medical researchers asked patients if they would participate in the study, yet the researchers did not inform the subjects that they would be injected with live cancer cells, nor did they provide written documentation about the nature of the study to potential subjects. Remarkably, when questioned after the fact, the researchers indicated they did not believe that written documentation was necessary as it was commonplace to engage individuals in medical procedures without signed consent forms. Furthermore, the researchers admitted they did not inform patients about injecting them with cancer cells because they believed it would frighten the patients!

Willowbrook Study

The Willowbrook State School was originally developed for children who were "mentally defective." A study at Willowbrook examined the effects that the hepatitis virus had on children within a controlled environment. From 1963 to 1966 the school informed parents that limited space was available in the school, and that if they wanted to admit their child they would have to consent to have the child injected with the hepatitis virus. The school rationalized to the parents that the children would eventually become infected anyway since the conditions of the school were crowded and unclean. This study raised questions as to the adequacy of informed consent and the freedom of human participants since (a) even if parents decided to admit their child, they were not asked to provide consent; (b) the school did in fact, have other openings; however, the staff limited admissions to those children whose parents would consent to having their child injected with the virus; and (c) the parents were provided inadequate informed consent as they were not told of the child's risk for later developing chronic liver disease.

While the studies discussed above include examples of appalling treatment of human subjects by researchers, these are only four illustrations of the many times unethical research practices have been carried out. As horrendous as the behaviors of researchers in these and other studies were, these unfortunate cases led to the development of ethical codes designed to protect the rights of human subjects.

Belmont Report Principles and Their Relation to Counseling Research Ethics

Specifically, the Belmont Report arose in part because of the legal implications resulting from the Tuskegee Syphilis Study. The Belmont Report was created by the National Commission for the Protection of Human Subjects of Biomedical and Behavioral Research in 1979, and is considered to be the "cornerstone document of ethical principles and Federal regulations for the protection of research participants based on respect for persons, beneficence, and justice" (NIH, 2002, p. 10). These three ethical principles discussed in the Belmont Report are the foundation of most ethical codes surrounding the research of human subjects. These three principles are described below.

RESPECT FOR PERSONS This principle includes two standards; first, the autonomy of individuals and second, protection for those with diminished capacity. The first standard suggests that individuals should be treated as autonomous agents (NIH, 2002), meaning that human participants' opinions, thoughts, and choices should be heard and respected by, and never obstructed by, a researcher. Examples of obstructing a participant's choice would include failing to provide all information to a client regarding your study, or leading a client to believe that research "is just a part of counseling" when it does not have to be. Suggesting to a client that she would not be able to continue in counseling unless she became a participant, or informing a student that participation or nonparticipation may impact his or her academic grade in a course are all obstructions to a research subject's choice (see ACA, 2005, G.2.c *Student/Supervisee Participation* and G.2.d *Client Participation*). In short, as the researcher, you must provide full disclosure regarding your study with no consequences for nonparticipation. This will ensure that you do not hinder a potential subject's ability to decide to participate in your study. In other words, you are providing "informed consent."

Specifically, the ACA code states that all human participants should be provided with informed consent regarding the purpose of the study; procedures the participant will be put through; details on new experimental procedures; and benefits, risks and limitations (see ACA, 2005, G.2.a *Informed Consent in Research*).

When providing informed consent, it is important that you ensure that the person is competent to understand the information given. Thus, additional protections for people with diminished autonomy are required (e.g., mental health disabilities, developmental disabilities, language barriers, dementia, and children). When the ability to comprehend is limited for any reason, you must take extra precautions to ensure the participant's safety. For example, if you wished to include a 7-year-old in a study you were conducting, a legal guardian should be consulted to provide the initial consent and determine if the child is capable of engaging in or would benefit from the study. Following the legal guardian's consent, the child should still have the opportunity to provide his or her own consent to agree to or refuse participation.

Revisiting the case of Debbie, who was introduced at the beginning of this chapter, during the intake you should have provided informed consent indicating that data may be collected throughout counseling via interviews or assessments, to evaluate her progress in counseling and determine the methods or techniques that might best facilitate her growth. However, if informed consent was not provided to her during intake or shortly after, and you later decide you would like to engage in research or evaluate her progress, you can still provide her with informed consent regarding what the assessments are for, what clinical determinations you will make with them, and what you are going to do with outcomes. Important questions might be:

- Will you put her assessments in her client file?
- Will you keep her name anonymous?
- Will you put her information and data collected in a larger database that houses other clients from your counseling practice?
- What if she refuses to participate?
- What would be the benefits of participating?

These questions and others might arise as elements of informed consent to discuss with Debbie.

Are there occasions when you could give too much informed consent? In short, yes. There are times when you might believe that by giving a client very detailed information relevant to research or assessment would negatively impact the client's ability to participate. This might include telling a client that by completing the Minnesota Multiphasic Personality Inventory (MMPI) you will have greater clarity as to his or her potential for suicide. If a client knew this she might misrepresent herself on the assessment. Therefore, if, in your professional opinion, research or evaluation are absolutely necessary but you believe that informing Debbie of the true purpose of the assessment would cause her to underreport or overreport symptoms, then the use of deception is a possibility. The ACA ethical code (G.2.b *Deception)* states that counselors should not use deception unless alternative procedures are not possible, and the research is essential and does not cause harm. Thus, if these circumstances existed then you could use deception with Debbie and inform her that the assessments are for another purpose. However, once Debbie has completed the assessments, you would need to inform her of the true purpose of the study and the assessments, thus removing the deception. Keep in mind that this deception could impact the relationship you have with your client and should only be used when absolutely necessary.

BENEFICENCE   The principle of beneficence is defined as "the quality or state of being beneficent [doing or producing good]" (Merriam-Webster Online Dictionary, 2005). Thus, in relation to participants in a research study, the Belmont Report indicates that it is the researcher's responsibility to ensure that the benefits of a study outweigh any risks.

According to the ACA Code of Ethics (2005), you as the researcher are ultimately responsible for designing, planning, conducting, and reporting research in a manner that meets the guidelines of your professional organization, federal guidelines (e.g., ORI), state laws, and/or organizational regulations (e.g., agency, school, or university). Subsequently, when thinking about a study you might conduct, you should consider the clients' rights and the costs and benefits of serving in your study. If, for example, you hoped to evaluate the use of a "new" procedure with a client, then consultation with colleagues should occur, along with ongoing reexamination of the impact your treatment may have on the individuals involved (see ACA, 2005, G.2.b). Constant examination of the impact will help you determine if the new procedure or treatment is too risky or detrimental to the research participant and will ensure his or her well-being and safety (see ACA, 2005, G.1.d *Precautions to Avoid Injury).*

Practically speaking, how do you decide if you are abiding by the principle of beneficence or doing good? A well-known evidence-based treatment for depression is Cognitive-Behavioral Theory (CBT; e.g., Miranda et al., 2006); however, imagine that you wanted to investigate the efficacy of dance/movement therapy with a particular client because you are curious to determine if it might be more effective in decreasing depressive symptoms. Before implementing dance movement therapy with Debbie, and evaluating the impact on her depressive symptoms and other presenting concerns, it would be important that you discuss the procedures with a colleague or examined research on dance movement therapy and depression. In addition to consultation, it is important that you select instruments, surveys, or assessments that will determine the impact of your treatment not only on Debbie's depressive symptoms, but also on her self-injurious behaviors, substance abuse, and other areas in her life. This will assist your examination of the new treatment method (i.e., dance/movement therapy) to understand if it is in fact beneficial to Debbie or causes her more harm than good.

As ACA (2005) indicates, it is imperative that your research study, including methods, procedures, and outcomes, has minimal interference on a client's life (see G.1.f). Thus, the research study or the new treatment method should not increase Debbie's symptoms, cause disruptions in her life (e.g., interfering with her work schedule or impeding her relationships). If there are known disruptions that will be caused by being a participant in your research study, then Debbie should be notified of this during informed consent so she can make an educated decision.

The challenge in acting with beneficence is that there is no "right way" to determine if the benefits outweigh the risks for a participant. The majority of the time beneficence is a judgment call for the researcher. Of course, the researcher should ensure that he or she is not intentionally causing injury to the participant (e.g., not treating syphilis with penicillin when it was known to be an effective medicine).

In most research situations, however, it is not so easy to determine when benefits outweigh risks. For instance, imagine you are interested in researching the best method for assisting a couple in recovering from an extramarital affair. You might ask some couples to disclose and discuss affairs with one another, while with other couples you ask them not to disclose an affair to their partner. Your ultimate goal would be to determine what is more healing to the relationship. Both of these methods contain risks, including hurting the partner's feelings, keeping secrets, or damaging the relationship, but both contain benefits as well, including healing the relationship and being open and honest. While some counselors may believe in the latter part (i.e., open and honest relationship), it is a judgment call as to what will cause the participant more harm in the study (or in counseling); thus, understanding the risks and benefits ahead of time is a great benefit. Engaging in ethical research practice is sometimes a matter of professional judgment. If questions still exist in your mind regarding an evaluation or research study, always consult with peers or with an Institutional Review Board.

JUSTICE The principle of justice deals with fairness related to the question of who bears the burden of risks and who should receive the benefits in research? Risks such as participant safety, interference with life, population and sample selection, as well as ensuring that participants receive what they were promised (e.g., benefits, specific treatment, outcomes) are all elements of the justice principle.

A breach of justice occurs when research participants are deprived of a benefit for no rational reason. For example, research participants may have been promised $50.00 for participating in the study. If for some reason some do not receive their payment, injustice has occurred. Another example would be if clients who are placed on a waiting list as the control group are assured they will receive treatment at the end of the research period; however, for various reasons they do not receive treatment and the study ends. Within the ACA code of ethics, section G.2.g *Commitment to Participants* speaks to the justice principle by stating that "counselors take reasonable measures to honor all commitments to research participants" (ACA, 2005, p. 17).

Another form of injustice relates to who receives the benefits of the findings. Historically, patients in medical and mental wards bore the burden of serving as research participants, yet they often did not receive the benefits of the findings. Instead, clients who came for outpatient counseling and medical treatment through community agencies and private practices would receive the newest treatments based on research findings. Thus, those that participate in your research studies should be given the opportunity to receive benefits.

The principle of justice also refers to the selection process for the sample you will study. For example, if you will examine effective treatment when working with depression in clients, is there a particular reason you would select Debbie, a 26-year-old Caucasian female, and not Marcia, a 44-year-old African American, pregnant female, or Matthew, a 12-year-old Native American male? While there may be good reasons for excluding the latter two, it is important to determine the reasons for the exclusion. It is important to ask if exclusionary criteria are inappropriate for your research question or study (e.g., your study is examining effective methods in working with young adult females in minimizing depression, not males or older women). Are your instruments inappropriate for the latter two populations or is it simply easier to access Debbie because she is a client sitting in your office while the latter two populations do not frequent your agency?

The National Institute of Health (NIH; 2002) speaks to the selection of human subjects and indicates that selection should be equitable. Thus, no population should be overburdened to participate in research without benefits, nor should a population be excluded without good reason. In the past, some individuals have been unwilling participants (e.g., prisoners in concentration camps in Nazi Medical War Crimes), while others were selected solely due to ease or convenience (e.g., undergraduate student population). Women and minorities are also groups that have often been underrepresented in past research. Thus, NIH (2001) developed a policy on including women and minorities in research, indicating that a clear rationale must exist if these groups are excluded.

Institutional Review Boards

To assist with ensuring respect, beneficence, and justice of human participants, the Institutional Review Board (IRB) was created. IRBs exist at all universities, as well as at other state and federal organizations (e.g., school districts, hospitals, and some community agencies). IRBs are typically made up of a minimum of five individuals from various disciplines (e.g., counseling, theology, business) who examine your research study prior to your conducting it (Leedy & Ormrod, 2005). Their task is to weigh the risks versus benefits and determine how the client will be directly impacted; also, to examine what protections you have in place for possible risks, the procedures participants will endure, and the method in which you are providing informed consent.

However, there are agencies that may not have an IRB (e.g., private practice). In these instances it is solely up to the researcher to take on the task of the IRB. The ACA ethical code addresses the independent researcher by stating that those researchers without the benefit an IRB "should consult with researchers who are familiar with the IRB procedures to provide appropriate safeguards" (2005, p. 17, G.1.c). Researchers familiar with the IRB procedures can be found at almost any university.

Additional Researcher Responsibilities

This chapter has focused largely on client rights as human research participants. However, there are additional ethical considerations on which researchers must reflect in the process of a study or evaluation. These include the researcher's relationships with study participants, collaboration with sponsors or other agencies, confidentiality of data and data management, and the ethical reporting of research results.

RELATIONSHIP WITH RESEARCH PARTICIPANTS   Similar to the ACA ethical code on relationship with clients, comparable standards exist when working with research participants. Specifically, nonprofessional relationships (e.g., friendships, family members, sexual or intimate relationships, going out to lunch or dinner) should be avoided between researcher and participant (G.3.a; G.3.b). Needless to say, researchers should not sexually harass research participants (G.3.c). The ACA ethical code goes further, stating that when a nonprofessional interaction between researcher and participant is unavoidable or could be beneficial, the researcher should document a rationale for the interaction prior to engaging in the nonprofessional interaction (2005, G.3.d).

COLLABORATION WITH SPONSORS   At various times, researchers need assistance from sponsors, including grant agencies who provide funding to support research, organizations who allow the researcher entrance to collect data, or administrators who provide resources or access to areas of an organization or client populations. Both the ACA and ORI speak to the importance of keeping sponsors informed about data collection procedures, changes in methodology (e.g., instruments, research questions, methods of data collection), and results of the study.

The ACA ethical code (2005, G.2.i) states that counselors should inform sponsors and organizations of research procedures and outcomes and ensure that appropriate individuals have information regarding the study.

CONFIDENTIALITY AND DATA MANAGEMENT   An important aspect of respecting participant rights is to ensure confidentiality in the use of data after they have been collected. This includes removing all identifying information (e.g., participant names, counseling dates, or other various identifying points of information) from raw data (e.g., paper instruments or assessments, audiotapes of interviews) and electronic databases. If identifying information is kept, it should be protected by locking paper instruments in a secure file, or by removing names from paper copies of assessments. Electronic databases can be pass-coded so that only those with authority can gain access. Furthermore, all identifying information in an electronic database can be deleted—especially if this information is not needed as part of the study. The ACA ethical codes request that researchers determine up front how they will dispose of research documents (2005, G.2.j). This includes destroying all instruments used to collect data by shredding paper copies of instruments, erasing and cutting apart audio or videotapes, or deleting electronic files.

REPORTING RESULTS   Reporting results of your study is important not only to the counseling profession but to other counseling professionals and clients who seek treatment. Providing your results to others is what eventually leads to evidence-based practices that clients are expected to receive. However, numerous ethical concerns are related to reporting results (see ACA, 2005, section G.4 and G.5). These include making sure that published results are accurate; making sure to report not only those results that are significant (i.e., your treatment method worked) but also those that are not significant (i.e., your treatment method did not work); and avoiding plagiarism or reproducing others ideas without proper citation.

Summary

Because of the potential benefit to our clients, students, and the general public, it is essential that counselors engage in quality research. However, there are ethical considerations beyond those relevant to general clinical practice that counselors and researchers must consider when including human participants in research. While there is no clear-cut answer to many ethical dilemmas, the central principles to follow include: respect for research participants; acting with beneficence, and with justice; respecting research participants' autonomy, rights, and confidentiality; engaging in informed collaboration with colleagues and sponsors; and reporting results accurately.

Assessing and reassessing risks and benefits to human research participants to make certain that risks never outweigh benefits is an ongoing obligation of counselors who are conducting research. Similarly, ensuring that participants are not unduly subjected to research studies without benefit is a major responsibility of researchers. The more effort devoted up front to considering potential ethical issues and risks to participants the better off both human subjects and counselor researchers will be.

Review and Discussion Questions

1. In comparing the ethics of conducting research for medical practitioners with those faced by counselors, what challenges exist in both fields? What ethical predicaments might you expect to arise specific to counseling research?
2. Considering the case of Debbie, if you were to use assessment as part of research related to progress in counseling, what would you do to assure respect for Debbie as a person and client, to show beneficence, and to act with justice?
3. What arguments can be made for and against using human subjects in research? Do these arguments change if the human participant is a student of a professor conducting research, if the participant is a client of a counselor, or the participant is a stranger to the researcher?

Helpful Resources

American Counseling Association. (2005). *ACA code of ethics 2005*. Retrieved online, January 19, 2006, at *http://www .counseling.org/Resources/CodeOfEthics/TP/Home/ CT2.aspx*

Ethics in Mental Health Research. (n.d.). *Ethics in mental health research*. Retrieved online, June 22, 2005, at *http://www.emhr.net/index.htm*

Houser, R. (1998). *Counseling and educational research: Evaluation and application*. Thousand Oaks, CA: Sage.

Leedy, P. D., & Ormrod, J. E. (2005). *Practical research: Planning and designing*. Upper Saddle River, NJ: Pearson.

Office of Research Integrity. (2000). *PHS policy on instruction in the responsible conduct of research (RCR)-suspended*. Retrieved online, January 27, 2006, at *http://ori.hhs.gov/ policies/RCR_ Policy.shtml*

Steneck, N. (n.d.). *ORI introduction to the responsible conduct of research*. Office of Research Integrity. Retrieved online, January 7, 2005, at *http://ori.dhhs.gov/documents/ rcrintro.pdf*

Wester, K. L. (2005). *Conducting research responsibly: Cases for counseling professionals. Handbook and DVD*. Author & NBCC.

CHAPTER 18

Multicultural Issues in Research

Catherine Y. Chang, *Georgia State University*
Danica G. Hays, *Old Dominion University*
Geneva Gray, *Argosy University*

OBJECTIVES
After reading this chapter, you will:

- Be able to discuss the challenges of defining culture in the research process.
- Be able to distinguish the etic and emic approaches in research.
- Be able to understand the complexities of interpreting cultural differences in research findings.
- Be able to present the benefits and challenges of using various research designs in multicultural research.
- Be able to delineate the process of establishing empirically supported treatments and culturally sensitive treatments for diverse populations.
- Be able to understand the characteristics of an effective multicultural researcher.
- Be able to be aware of essential components of a research training environment.
- Be able to outline current trends in multicultural research.

OVERVIEW

In this chapter, we discuss the importance of addressing multicultural issues in research. Although multicultural issues in counseling in general (i.e., assessment, training, direct treatment, and supervision) have received increased attention over the past 30 years, there is still a dearth of researchers conducting sound research that is culturally sensitive and culturally relevant. There has been some focus on multicultural issues in research within the past decade in counseling-related journals, with increased attention to the role of culture in counseling training and practice. In this chapter, we will discuss the importance of and the rationale for conducting multicultural research; issues in conducting multicultural research, including methodological issues, current trends in addressing multicultural issues in research, and guidelines for infusing multicultural issues in research. It is our hope that this introduction to multicultural issues in research will help you, as counselors-in-training, to become better at critical evaluation of research results and their implications for multicultural populations. For those of you who become counseling researchers, this chapter will serve as a guide for your work with multicultural samples.

DEFINING MULTICULTURAL RESEARCH

Before discussing the importance of, and rationale for, conducting multicultural research, we believe that we need to first define what we mean by multicultural research. Oftentimes, when individuals discuss multicultural research, what they are referring to is either cross-cultural research (i.e., studies that compare and contrast one cultural group with another cultural group) or cultural research (i.e., studies that examine within group differences). Multicultural research can also include any research that is culturally sensitive and culturally relevant, and that takes into consideration the growing diversity in the United States. For the purpose of this chapter, we will be using *multicultural research* in the broadest sense to include cross-cultural, cultural, and culturally sensitive research.

Why should counselors be concerned with addressing multicultural issues in research or concerned with conducting multicultural research at all? This question is no different than asking why counselors conduct research. Research involves the pursuit of knowledge—it involves gathering information to answer questions. Following the scientist-practitioner model, it is important for counselors to understand and conduct research in order to inform their direct practice. Hadley and Mitchell (1995) outlined several benefits of counselors as active seekers of knowledge: (a) research informs effective interventions; (b) clinical experience informs relevant research; (c) conducting research keeps the counselor up-to-date in the field; (d) conducting research allows the counselor to immediately implement findings from the research; and (e) conducting research can lead to networking with others in the field. Although Hadley and Mitchell were discussing research in general, all the previously cited benefits are relevant for multicultural research. To this list we would add that conducting cross-cultural research and cultural research has these additional benefits: (a) validates and increases knowledge of a growing diverse population; (b) increases our ability to understand how various constructs are conceptualized in different cultures (i.e., how wellness is understood from the perspective of various cultural groups); (c) promotes cultural awareness, cultural competence, and social justice; and (d) increases the external validity of a study (i.e., generalizability).

In addition to the benefits of conducting multicultural research, we assert that researchers can no longer conduct sound research without addressing multicultural issues given the growing diversity within the United States, the globalization of testing and research, and the recent publications of the 2005 ACA Code of Ethics (ACA, 2005) and the Guidelines on Multicultural Education, Training, Research, Practice, and Organizational Change for Psychologists published by the American Psychological Association (APA, 2003). For example, in 2000, over 70% of the U.S. population was non-Hispanic whites. That number will decrease to 40% by 2100, while black, Hispanic-origin, and Asian and Pacific Islander populations will increase steadily (U. S. Census Bureau, 2000; U. S. Department of Commerce, 1996). Hambleton and de Jong (2003) noted that "international exchanges of tests have become more common . . . and interest in cross-cultural psychology and international comparative studies of achievement has grown" (pp. 127–128). According to the ACA Code of Ethics (2005), "counselors minimize bias and respect diversity in designing and implementing research programs" (p. 16) and "counselors are sensitive to incorporating research procedures that take into account cultural considerations" (p. 17). Additionally, the National Institutes of Health (NIH) requires all federally funded research to include ethnic minority individuals. This growing diversity within the United States and the globalization of testing and research bring with them issues that must be considered. Because you are learning to implement the science and practice of counseling, it is important for you to be able to understand these multicultural issues as you learn to evaluate research outcomes.

ISSUES IN CONDUCTING MULTICULTURAL RESEARCH

While there is a strong impetus for increased multicultural research, counseling researchers have several methodological considerations when planning, conducting, interpreting, and applying research in the counseling profession. Before investigating issues related to various research designs and interventions, there are general considerations that pertain both to research on diverse populations (e.g., a specific racial group such as Native Americans) and to "diversifying" samples (i.e., ensuring that a sample is heterogeneous enough to enhance generalizability). Some of the considerations include: (a) defining and identifying the parameters of a cultural group; (b) using an etic or emic approach in multicultural research; and (c) evaluating whether cultural differences are "real" in findings. Before we address these issues, it is important for you to understand the significance of cultural issues in research.

Defining Culture

Counseling professionals in planning, conducting, and interpreting research often struggle with how to define culture. If you have taken a course in multicultural counseling, you are already aware that many definitions for culture exist. For our purposes, culture within the counseling profession can be defined as the totality of the human experience for social contexts. This experience is mediated by biological, psychological, historical, and political events. Culture includes behaviors, attitudes, feelings, and cognitions related to our identities living within the world. It organizes how groups as a whole, individuals within a particular group, and individuals as a human race behave, think, and feel. The extent to which a group membership is labeled as *cultural* depends on how broadly you define culture. For example, a broad definition might include variables such as race, ethnicity, gender, sexual orientation, educational status, language, and geographical origin. A more narrow definition might label culture as race and ethnicity only (Hays, McLeod, & Erford, in press).

A narrow or focused perspective of multiculturalism includes only racial and ethnic minorities for fear that defining multiculturalism too broadly may cause counselors to avoid or ignore focusing on racial and ethnic concerns, such as racism. Typically, a more broad definition of culture is used in counseling today as it reflects the intersecting identities of clients and the complexities of their daily experiences. Attending to race, ethnicity, language, class or socioeconomic status, sexual identity, gender, religious or spiritual identity, ability status, and age acknowledges that all people have numerous cultural identities that interact with each other and may become more or less salient across time and situation. A broad definition of culture also helps to avoid stereotyping by acknowledging within-group differences, and allows researchers to examine how various aspects of their cultural identities may impact research findings or applications.

However, the definition of culture typically gets represented in research as racial/ethnic diversity (i.e., African/Black, Asian/Pacific Islander, Caucasian/European, Hispanic/Latino, and Native American). These labels have been criticized for ignoring heterogeneity within a racial/ethnic group as well as excluding other racial/ethnic groups and individuals with multiple racial/ethnic identities (Hall, 2001).

While there has been increased attention to expanding the definition of multicultural to include other aspects of diversity such as gender, sexual orientation, and spiritual identity, a majority of multicultural research still focuses on race/ethnicity (Arredondo, Toporek, Brown, Jones, Locke, Sanchez, & Stadler, 1996; Delgado-Romero, Galván, Maschino, & Rowland, 2005; Hall, 2001). The lack of consensus of the definition of culture might explain why Delgado-Romero et al. (2005) found for a 10-year period (1990–1999) that many studies did not report cultural information. When studies did report samples' cultural makeup, race and ethnicity variables were presented in broad categorical manner, omitting information about biracial or multiracial identities.

In addition to debate over what constitutes culture, there is a belief that attending to cultural variables in research may perpetuate stereotyping, as some counselors may inaccurately apply findings to clients (Stuart, 2004). Some counseling researchers fear that in an effort to be culturally sensitive, one may interpret findings for a particular cultural group to be applicable to one's clients who belong to that group, without examining how the sample or definitions of culture for that sample may be limited, or by ignoring the individual characteristics (e.g., immigration history, acculturation level, ethnic identity) of one's clients. For example, consider a study with findings that demonstrate racial identity status (i.e., one's sense of belonging to a particular racial group) predicts counseling satisfaction for racial/ethnic minorities. While results may indicate that higher racial identity statuses (greater identification with one's racial background) predict use of counseling services, counselors cannot apply these findings to all racial/ethnic minorities because of the presence of between- and within-group variation in racial identity attitudes and the limited sampling methods. That is, findings relevant for one racial group cannot be generalized to another racial group due to experiences unique to each racial group (i.e., between-group variation). Additionally, each individual for each racial group experiences racial identity development in an idiosyncratic manner (i.e., within-group variation); therefore, findings are not necessarily applicable to clinical practice with that racial group. Another issue involves sampling bias. A majority of studies with cultural groups (racial/ethnic groups in most cases) use convenient samples, which limits generalizability. Another issue with conducting multicultural research is that individuals' cultural makeup is always changing and becoming increasingly complex, as culture is viewed as a dynamic process that involves an individual's worldview, practices, and psychological and physical characteristics.

Whether counseling researchers are interested in research applicable to a specific group or applying findings to a larger, culturally diverse sample, it is important to articulate a clear definition of culture for a particular study so that you, as a consumer of research, can interpret the results and apply them to your client populations in a culturally appropriate manner. Researchers have not reached consensus on what constitutes culture and thus a cultural group, making it difficult to conduct and apply research in a systematic manner. One way that researchers have attempted to resolve the difficulty in defining culture in research is by taking an etic or emic approach to the research process.

Etic and Emic Approaches in Research

Deciding whom to include or exclude in a sample is a genuine dilemma for researchers as they increase representation of diversity in studies to maximize generalizability, which are known as *etic approaches*. Researchers may decide to focus on more narrow definitions of diversity for the purpose of increasing scholarship about specific cultural groups, thus taking an *emic approach*. Those who support etic approaches in research believe that universal aspects of human behavior are enough that findings may be applied generally in clinical interventions. For example, using an etic approach, Constantine (2002) discussed predictors of counseling satisfaction using a racially and ethnically diverse sample, with an intention to understand rating across several racial and ethnic groups. In another example of the etic approach to research, Vinson and Neimeyer (2000) examined the relationship between racial identity development and multicultural counseling competences among a racially diverse sample.

An emic approach would attend more to cultural variations with an emphasis on culturally specific interventions (Hall, 2001). For example, Yeh, Inman, Kim, and Okubo (2006) highlighted coping strategies specific to Asian American family members of the September 11 attacks. Hays, Chang, and Havice (in press) explored the relationship between white racial identity status, and white privilege awareness is another example of the emic approach to research. Thus, an etic approach would encourage a more diverse sample across several cultural groups (i.e., addressing cultural similarities and differences among several groups) while an emic approach would be more exclusive for a deeper understanding of a specific aspect of a group (i.e., examining individuals' cultural differences within a group).

With the attention on evidence-based counseling practice, counseling researchers conducting multicultural research are often faced with the challenge of focusing on either within-group (emic) or between-group (etic) variation. That is, do we, as researchers, focus on making comparisons between cultural groups such as between Asian Americans and European Americans, or examine within-group differences for a cultural group such as African American males and African American females? Those who support focusing on between-group differences in research may be motivated to show that specific cultural groups have specific needs and considerations. As a result, they may contend such research findings may be applied in a more generalizable manner to that cultural group.

There is also some bias toward examining cultural groups as a whole because of sample size requirements in studies involving statistical analyses. For example, research that looks at with-in group differences will have to have adequate sample size for each group in order to conduct advanced statistics. Because most researchers use convenience samples, finding enough participants for each cultural group may be difficult. However, those who support examining within-group variation believe that selecting a sample with the intention of looking at differences between two independent cultural groups, such as in the case of racial-comparative studies, may be overused and may perpetuate stereotypes for a group (Ponterotto, 1988). Examples of racial-comparative studies include studies that explore the help-seeking behaviors of whites versus persons of color and the achievement gap between whites and blacks.

There are limitations for using an emic approach in research. To accurately demonstrate conclusions within groups, a great amount of time and effort is often involved in collecting large amounts of data (Delgado-Romero et al., 2005). Thus, counseling researchers may be limited in their abilities to examine idiosyncratic differences among individuals for a particular cultural group. This limitation can lead to misrepresentation of groups because researchers cannot accurately examine heterogeneity within a cultural group, which compromises generalizability and insight into dynamics within a group. Examples of these dynamics include gender differences and the influence of socioeconomic status. While there is always a trade-off between generalizability across cultural groups and degree of understanding of individuals within these groups, a compromise may be to combine these approaches in a way that is appropriate to the research question(s). As you can see, the issues inherent in multicultural research are complex. While it may be difficult to understand some of these issues, it is important for you, as a developing scientist-practitioner, to have an awareness of them. The next step is to develop a knowledge base of cultural implications in research and then to enhance your skills in the application of multicultural research outcomes with your client population.

Are There Really Cultural Differences?

How do you begin to develop a knowledge base of culturally relevant implications of counseling research? Determining whether results portray cultural differences is a difficult task, even for researchers, as results may be limited by the type and size of a sample, the use of instruments or interventions, and the methods of analyses. Additionally, findings that reflect cultural differences may not be cultural differences but bias within the counseling researcher. For example, cultural bias may lead to more severe diagnosis of clients of oppressed statuses (e.g., racial/ethnic minorities, females). Depending on how researchers determine and represent diversity within a sample, cultural differences can be reflected as within-group or between-group cultural differences, or both.

Thus, researchers will differ in what aspects of culture they focus on in research designs. Further, findings that demonstrate differences between groups cannot be readily identified as cultural differences. This is particularly true if interventions or tools in the research design are not culturally relevant, as some interventions or assessment tools may be unfamiliar to a portion of the sample, and results may be misleading. Also, differences between cultural groups may actually be due to other variables that were not directly studied, such as acculturation, socioeconomic status, or characteristics of a setting or environment (Quintana, Troyano, & Taylor, 2001). Finally, the type of results presented depends on which variables researchers focused on in the study, as well as which types of analyses were conducted. It is difficult to compare results across various research designs (i.e., quantitative, qualitative, single-case), even if similar research questions are asked.

While you may have been hoping for an easy method for developing your cultural research knowledge base, you can see that it will take a concerted effort and quality analytical skills. For example, consider research examining the role of culture and the prevalence of depression using various designs and analyses. In quantitative studies, some researchers may examine relationships between two variables, such as race and depression. Other researchers may use more complex statistical analyses to examine how the intersection among race, socioeconomic status, education level, and treatment history predict depression.

Alternatively, those conducting qualitative research may interview individuals of various cultural groups who have been diagnosed with depression to discuss the degree to which they believe that the diagnosis is accurate as well as what factors they perceive may be related to depression. Another qualitative study may examine a specific cultural group, such, as Latinos, to explore within-group differences of socioeconomic class and gender in prevalence of depression. In a time-series design, researchers may examine how a structured sequence of intervention components affects depression over time for a small number of Asian clients.

While each of these designs potentially provides helpful information about culture and depression, it may be difficult for you to combine these results to make inferences about these variables to determine if cultural differences exist. Practically speaking, you will have to use your knowledge of multicultural research to evaluate each of the studies for their relevance to your particular client and then make decisions about methods for implementing the results in your counseling practice.

Considerations for Counseling Researchers

There are several questions that you may want to reflect upon with respect to the above issues. As you review available research or even engage in research, consider the following:

- Which aspects of participants' culture are used as indicators of diversity within a sample?
- How are cultural data (e.g., demographic information) collected in this study? Do participants self-identify their cultural identities or select from existing categories?
- Do research questions and results explore intersecting identities?
- How might findings be helpful for working with various clients? How might findings stereotype clients who are similar to those in a sample?
- To what degree does the research design adhere to an etic approach? Emic approach?
- What are the potential benefits of using an etic approach? Emic approach?
- What are the potential challenges of using an etic approach? Emic approach?
- How might cultural differences in findings be related to the ways by which data were collected and analyzed?
- How might any cultural variations present in the findings be a result of other factors?

RESEARCH DESIGNS WITH MULTICULTURAL POPULATIONS

Research designs with multicultural populations typically are categorized as quantitative and qualitative approaches. As you evaluate research studies in an effort to increase your awareness, knowledge, and skills with multicultural clients, it is important for you to understand the various types of counseling research conducted. There are several benefits and challenges associated with these approaches when addressing culture in counseling research.

Quantitative Research

Quantitative research refers to scientific inquiry with the goal of either describing a certain phenomenon or making inferences based on a certain phenomena. Quantitative research typically requires large sample sizes and quantification of constructs, thus allowing for statistical control and generalizability across various populations (see chapters 5, 6, 7, and 8 for a broader description of quantitative research). With the use of culturally relevant interventions and sampling procedures, quantitative approaches may allow for theory-building across different cultures using large samples and carefully controlled conditions. Quantitative research allows for large data collection opportunities using survey and experimental methods. When data are collected on well-defined psychological characteristics, valuable information on cultural variables may be obtained.

However, there are many challenges in multicultural research using quantitative research methods. Many of the constructs associated with counseling are complex and poorly defined in research. While there are clear benefits to quantitative research—including isolation and control of variables for generalizability—these benefits may come at the cost of insufficiently exploring a construct in an in-depth manner. Quantitative research has been criticized for often minimally focusing on within-group differences, because large samples are typically needed to reach statistical significance in various quantitative designs. It is often difficult to obtain large samples for a cultural group because the population may be inaccessible or increased time and efforts are necessary. Thus, what tends to occur in quantitative approaches is that easily accessible populations (e.g., student populations) are used, which typically are not representative of diverse cultural groups (Ponterotto, Costa, & Werner-Lin, 2002). Further, many of the interventions and assessment tools used in various quantitative designs may not be culturally relevant and thus may produce misleading findings.

Qualitative Research

Qualitative research refers to inductive inquiry whereby a researcher enters a naturalistic setting to understand the phenomena of interest and provide rich descriptions in order to give voice to multiple perspectives (see chapters 9, 10, and 11 for a broader description of qualitative research). These methods may present similar skills (e.g., openness, taking a questioning stance, empowering the participants, flexibility, and rapport building) used in multicultural counseling and thus may be a suitable approach for addressing culture in counseling research. Morrow, Rakhsha, and Castañeda (2001) identified several benefits for the use of qualitative research in addressing culture in counseling. First, qualitative research allows for a deeper understanding of how context influences clients' mental health and experiences in counseling. A focus on context includes addressing how experiences of oppression and power affect mental health status, utility of counseling services, and the counseling relationship. Second, qualitative research provides a forum for topics that have been minimally addressed or where there are mixed findings among quantitative studies. As researchers explore these topics, voices are acknowledged that may not typically be heard in a thorough and accurate manner. Additionally, complex cultural constructs may be conceptualized through the use of qualitative methods. Third, this type of research focuses on participants' meanings that get attributed to a particular phenomenon being studied. In examining different meanings, any cultural lens that participants use to describe or make meaning are acknowledged and better understood.

Finally, the role of researcher is highlighted, as qualitative research methods call for active self-reflection to minimize the biases a researcher may have that could influence the way data are collected and interpreted. Some examples of active self-reflection, or bracketing, include using multiple researchers, keeping a reflexive journal, and using negative case analysis (see chapters 9, 10, and 11). Through active self-reflection emerging ideas can be challenged by a research team. Researchers can then note differing attitudes and subsequently consider different data collection and analysis techniques to disconfirm themes. Thus, bracketing is especially important for multicultural research. Oftentimes, biases of those conducting research originate from worldviews and attitudes derived from cultural experiences. Biases can originate from unanswered questions about a researcher's cultural background, or they may impact the research process itself. Examples of the relationship between cultural identity and research interests might include white counseling researchers investigating topics related to whiteness or white privilege, or those with strong religious identities assuming religious variables are important to study. A case where the researcher's worldviews and attitudes influence the research process is when a majority culture takes a more directive approach to interviewing. As a practicing counselor, it will be very important for you to evaluate the potential researcher bias that may have influenced outcomes before deciding to incorporate the research into your practice.

While qualitative research approaches possess many advantages in multicultural research, they have been criticized as a subjective process with smaller sample sizes in which results have limited generalizability. This may pose a challenge for etic approaches because it can be difficult to discuss between-group differences with smaller samples. Further, without proper validity checks in place, researchers may bias the way data are collected and analyzed in that the research process is carried out in an ethnocentric manner. Thus, as a counselor, you are again challenged to evaluate qualitative studies in relation to your particular client and to make an informed choice about which aspects of the research will enhance your awareness, knowledge, and skills.

CURRENT TRENDS

The importance of and interest in addressing multicultural issues in research is growing. As you consider multicultural issues in research, there are a couple of additional concerns that need to be highlighted. These include test adaptation problems and the debate between empirically supported therapy (EST) and culturally sensitive therapy (CST).

Test Adaptation

If you have taken a course in assessment, you may be aware that a major concern related to research with multicultural populations involves the availability of relevant assessment inventories. To truly conduct cross-cultural research and cultural research, assessment instruments must be available in the participants' primary language. Research that involves individuals whose primary language is not English is needed to increase the knowledge base of the counseling profession and to determine external validity (generalizability) of such research. This is especially important given the growing number of immigrants in the United States, many of whom do not speak English as their primary language. In 2007, the number of immigrants reached a high of 37.9 million or roughly one in eight people in the United States (Camaroto, 2008). While the foreign-born population from Europe has been decreasing as a percentage of the U.S. population, the percentage of foreign-born people from Asia and Latin America has been increasing. To address this concern, it is imperative that we have assessment inventories available in the participant's language of choice. Because many instruments do not have multiple language formats, this process will involve *test adaptation*.

Instruments often need to be adapted from a *source-language* (the original language of the instrument) to a *target-language* (language other than the original language). For example, if a researcher is interested in investigating the wellness of Hispanic Americans compared with Caucasian Americans and using a wellness measure developed in English, then English would be the source language and Spanish the target language. The purpose of adapting such instruments, whether it is a psychological test or any other kind of test, is to permit research among members of different cultures. The goal of test adaptation is to have two versions of an instrument. Both versions will elicit equal probabilities of a specified response from individuals with equal amounts of that trait or ability assessed by the test item, regardless of the language of the test. Basically, the adapted instrument will be equivalent to the source instrument and understood by the target audience (Chang & Myers, 2003; Hambleton & Bollwark, 1991).

Test adaptation has been identified as the most challenging aspect of cross-cultural research (Brislin, Lonner, & Thorndike, 1973). Since that time, literature related to test adaptation and assessment standards that incorporate test adaptation issues have increased substantially (see *Standards for Educational and Psychological Testing*, American Educational Research Association, 1999; *Standards for Multicultural Assessment*, Association for Assessment in Counseling, 2003). Additionally, the International Test Commission (ITC, http://intestcom.org/itc_projects.htm) has developed guidelines for adapting educational and psychological tests and has conducted studies to develop strategies for increasing the validity of cross-cultural test adaptations (see Hambleton, 2001; Hambleton & Patsula, 1998).

It is important for you to recognize that oftentimes in multicultural research there is an assumption that the variable of interest exists in both cultures, and that sufficient differences exist for that variable to warrant further investigation (Hambleton & Bollwark, 1991). For example, if a researcher is interested in exploring wellness across cultures, the researcher is assuming that the construct of wellness exists in both cultures and that there are between-group differences in wellness between the two groups. In order to truly conduct cross-cultural research and cultural research, assessment instruments must be available in the participants' primary language. Having participants complete the instruments in their primary language increases fairness and the validity of the study. Numerous adaptation issues exist not only due to language and cultural differences but to dialect and subcultural differences within cultures. There are both advantages and challenges to test adaptation. By adapting an instrument, the researcher is able to utilize the already existing data of the instrument to compare with newly acquired data, thus allowing for cross-cultural studies on both the national and international levels. Test adaptation can conserve time and expenses as well. It can also lead to increased fairness in assessment by allowing individuals to be assessed in the language of their choice and providing a sense of security if using an established and respected test. Of course, the primary disadvantage of test adaptation is the risk of imposing conclusions based on concepts that exist in one culture but may not exist in the other. There are no guarantees that a concept in the source culture exists in the target culture. Additionally, if certain constructs measured in the original version are not found in the target population or if the construct is manifested in a different manner, the resulting scores can be misleading (Chang, Hays, & Tatar, 2005). For more discussion related to practical guidelines for test adaptation, see Van de Vijver and Hambleton (1996).

EST Versus CST

As a developing scientist-practitioner, a key question you may have about research across cultures involves the efficacy and effectiveness of counseling interventions. There are two approaches (i.e., EST and CST) that will help you to structure interventions and that will inform your decisions about which are most suitable for clients. EST, or *empirically supported therapies*, are treatments that have been proven to be more effective than a placebo or another treatment (Chambless & Hollon, 1998). EST are further divided into *Well-Established Treatments* and *Probably Efficacious Treatments*. To be classified as a Well-Established Treatment, two independent researchers must demonstrate that the treatment is more effective than the pill or psychological placebo or another treatment, or equivalent to an already established treatment. The investigation must include either two between-group experimental designs or 10 or more single-case design experiments. The criteria for Probably Efficacious Treatments include two experiments showing the treatment is more effective than a waiting-list control group, or one or more experiments that meet the criteria for the Well-Established Treatment, or four or more single-case design experiments that meet the criteria for the Well-Established Treatment (Atkinson, Bui, & Mori, 2001; Hall, 2001). An example of an EST that you probably already know is the efficacy of cognitive therapy with depression.

Since the EST approach is primarily concerned with establishing the efficacy of a treatment, this approach is more concerned with average response of the participants and adheres to strict quantitative methodologies. Several authors have criticized the criteria of the EST for ignoring important variables. Criticism of the EST criteria include: (a) the EST criteria are founded on a disorder-driven medical model and thus may not be applicable to therapists whose focus is on promoting personal growth; (b) due to the randomized clinical trials requirement, EST are overrepresented by cognitive and behavioral treatments, which are more amenable to experimental research design while other treatment modalities are underrepresented; and (c) the counseling profession's propensity for only publishing significant results of large group designs has been criticized. In addition to criticisms related to the criteria of the EST, the EST have been criticized for neglecting individual variables (e.g., client characteristics, counselor variables, relationship variables, cultural characteristics) that may affect the outcome of the treatment, and for providing inadequate empirical support that they are effective with ethnic minorities (Atkinson, Bui, & Mori, 2001; Hall, 2001). For example, cultural factors are considered when diagnosing and counseling minority clients, yet the criteria of EST do not recognize the important role that culture plays in determining what constitutes abnormal and normal behavior.

While the EST approach emphasizes the importance of treatment as the active agent in therapy to the point of ignoring the importance of other variables, CST, or *culturally sensitive therapies,* take into consideration the sociocultural context of the individual involved in the treatment. The CST approach calls for psychotherapy treatment and research with ethnic minorities to incorporate cultural and sociopolitical context. Examples of CST include: psychotherapy approach with African Americans that includes exploration of one's racial identity development; psychotherapy with Asian Americans that includes investigation of the role of stigma and shame as well as Asian Americans' conceptualization of distress and healing; focusing on family structure when working with Hispanic Americans.

The CST approach is based on strong ethical (e.g., ACA Code of Ethics) and conceptual foundations (e.g., Multicultural Counseling Competencies) and may be more amenable to qualitative methodologies. An important distinction between EST and CST is that EST researchers are primarily European Americans and CST researchers are primarily ethnic minorities (Hall, 2001). Hall argued that in order for research with ethnic minorities to advance, there needs to be collaboration between EST researchers and CST researchers. He astutely argued that EST that do not consider the cultural context of the individual will be irrelevant for ethnic minority clients and CST are not likely to become mainstream without strong empirical (quantitative) basis. For example, standardizing a treatment for phobias is limited by the degree to which cultural variation (e.g., racial/ethnic diversity) is ignored in sample selection; by the content and construct bias of screening items of assessments; and by the interpretation of findings. Alternatively, a qualitative finding outlining the expression of phobic responses for a specific cultural group will make a broader impact on the understanding of phobias for that particular culture if additional research methodologies (particularly large-scale quantitative designs) are used in conjunction with qualitative methodology.

GUIDELINES FOR INFUSING MULTICULTURAL ISSUES IN RESEARCH

Increasing Sensitivity of Researchers

Multicultural competence is described by many authors as the ability to understand, identify, and relate to the uniqueness of each client with regard to their individual cultural perspective. Multicultural competence also involves constant awareness of the demographic changes in the structure of society in order to effectively meet the needs of a diverse population (Arredondo et al., 1996). Stuart (2004) suggested 12 practical methods that will help you to achieve multicultural competence. Based on his suggestions for increasing multicultural competence, we have outlined several methods for increasing the multicultural sensitivity of researchers. Multiculturally competent researchers must: (a) obtain a skill for exploring each individual cultural perspective; (b) be aware of their own cultural biases and be able to articulate, explore, and challenge the validity of their worldview; (c) always remain aware of cultural differences but without making them the major focus; and (d) be considerate of participants' ethnic, racial, and cultural views when developing methodology. It is important to note that these suggestions involve appropriate behaviors of the researcher; however, multicultural competence is also related to creating a research environment that is conducive to respecting diversity.

In conducting research with vulnerable populations, it is important for the researcher to conduct that research in an environment that is safe and encouraging of the participant. For example, in a study examining the barriers to accessing community resources in intimate partner violence (IPV) survivors, it was important for the researcher to interview these IPV survivors in an open setting of their choice, where they felt safe and empowered to make that decision (McLeod, Hays, & Chang, 2008).

Research Training Environment

The research training environment (RTE) has been supported as contributing to changes in research attitudes, self-efficacy, and productivity (Gelso & Lent, 2000). We believe that in order to change the culture of research to focus on multiculturalism we must begin in the education process.

For example, in the 2009 CACREP standards (CACREP, 2009) for doctoral programs, there is a section called *Research and Scholarship,* which points to the importance of training students to be effective researchers. In counselor education, we grow researchers and understand that faculty must be sensitive to the needs of multicultural research methods. Kahn and Gelso (1997) asserted that there are nine ingredients within two higher-order factors (i.e., interpersonal factors and instructional factors) that contribute to the RTE. We believe that these nine ingredients, when adapted and expanded, can provide essential guidelines for faculty in helping to infuse multicultural issues in research.

Interpersonal Factor

1. Faculty modeling of appropriate scientific behavior. Faculty members can model the importance of addressing multicultural issues in research for their students and future researchers by conducting culturally relevant and culturally sensitive research and integrating that information into their classrooms.

2. Positive reinforcement of scientific activity. Given the strong interpersonal orientation of most individuals who enter the helping profession, faculty members will want to positively reinforce their students who are engaging in multicultural research and as an extension, administrators will want to positively reinforce faculty members who engage in multicultural research.

3. Early involvement of students in [multicultural] research in a nonthreatening manner. Faculty members will want to encourage and invite graduate students to participate in their multicultural research at various levels, depending on the skills level and comfort level of the student.

4. Emphasis on the social nature of scientific inquiry. Again, given the strong interpersonal orientation of most individuals who enter the helping professions, it is essential for students to recognize the interpersonal nature of research. Having a positive relationship with a faculty member who conducts multicultural research can potentially increase research attitudes and efficacy for the student, thus encouraging the student to conduct his or her own multicultural research in the future. Faculty members can increase the social nature of scientific inquiry by establishing research teams that include students from diverse backgrounds.

Instructional Factor

5. Teaching that all research studies are limited and flawed. Students must understand the limitations of research and that research studies often lead to more questions. This is especially important when discussing multicultural research.

6. Instructing that there are varied research approaches. It is essential that students understand that there are different research methodologies and that each methodology has its advantages and challenges when conducting multicultural research. There may be some methodologies that are more appropriate when considering cross-cultural and cultural research.

7. Teaching students to look inward for research ideas. Research can be a very personal experience and researchers who look inward for research questions are more likely to be passionate about their research. This is especially true for multicultural research given that a majority of researchers who conduct multicultural research are studying issues that are relevant in their lives.

8. Teaching the connection between research and practice. It is important for students to understand that sound multicultural research informs practice and that practice leads to informed scientific inquiry. Faculty members can model this by integrating new and relevant studies into their teaching.

9. Teaching relevant statistics and logical research design. Students must understand the basics of statistics and have the skills to develop logical research designs that are multiculturally sensitive and multiculturally relevant. This is not only so that they can conduct sound research, but so they can be informed consumers of multicultural research.

Additional Suggestions

In addition to increasing the cultural sensitivity of the researcher and establishing an RTE that fosters addressing multicultural issues in research, we suggest the following for infusing multicultural issues in research:

- Researchers actively seek out a diverse sample rather than relying on convenience samples that tend to be predominantly white college students. This means conducting research that includes historically underrepresented groups.
- Researchers expand research designs to include topics that address multicultural issues in clients' lives.
- Researchers utilize empirically validated (for all racial/ethnic groups) inventories. This includes focusing some attention on test adaptation.
- Researchers advocate for more funding for research that focuses on racial and ethnic minorities.
- Researchers begin considering more qualitative methodologies that are oftentimes better suited to study multicultural issues in research.
- Challenge white researchers to become more actively involved in multicultural research.
- Validate EST with specific minority groups.
- Participate in research that includes both EST and CST.

Summary

With the growing diversity of the United States and globalization of testing and research, it is clear that all counselors and researchers must consider multicultural issues in counseling. Multicultural research is defined as research that includes cross-cultural research, cultural research, and research that is culturally sensitive and culturally relevant. There are several methodological issues related to addressing multicultural issues in research, including defining the sample, the challenge between the etic and the emic approach, and determining whether differences found in the research are based on cultural differences or other characteristics. Additionally, in considering multicultural research, the researcher needs to weigh the advantages and challenges associated with both quantitative and qualitative methodologies. Within multicultural research there are two major trends that need to be considered: test adaptation and the debate between EST and CST. We suggest that in order to conduct multicultural research, test adaptation issues must be addressed and more tests need to be adapted to use across cultures. Additional suggestions for infusing multicultural issues in research include increasing the sensitivity of the researcher and creating an RTE that is culturally sensitive.

Review and Discussion Questions

1. What are the benefits of conducting "multicultural" research?
2. Discuss why the authors believe that all research must address multicultural issues in research in order to be relevant.
3. Describe how the definition of culture affects data collection methods.
4. What are the benefits and challenges to using an etic approach in multicultural research? Emic approach?
5. What is test adaptation and why is it an essential aspect of cross-cultural and cultural research?
6. Discuss the differences between the EST and the CST approach.
7. What are some of the criticisms of the EST approach?
8. Discuss ways to increase the cultural sensitivity of the researcher.
9. Discuss the interpersonal and instructional factors related to RTE. Which factors are most salient for you as a student researcher and which ones have you already experienced or wish to experience?

Helpful Resources

American Educational Research Association (AERA)
http://www.aera.net/

Association for Assessment in Counseling and Education
http://www.aac.ncat.edu/
International Test Commission (ITC)
http://www.intestcom.org

APPENDIX A

PREAMBLE AND RESEARCH SECTION OF THE AMERICAN COUNSELING ASSOCIATION CODE OF ETHICS 2005

ACA CODE OF ETHICS PREAMBLE

The American Counseling Association is an educational, scientific, and professional organization whose members work in a variety of settings and serve in multiple capacities. ACA members are dedicated to the enhancement of human development throughout the life span. Association members recognize diversity and embrace a cross-cultural approach in support of the worth, dignity, potential, and uniqueness of people within their social and cultural contexts.

Professional values are an important way of living out an ethical commitment. Values inform principles. Inherently held values that guide our behaviors or exceed prescribed behaviors are deeply ingrained in the counselor and developed out of personal dedication, rather than the mandatory requirement of an external organization.

ACA CODE OF ETHICS PURPOSE

The *ACA Code of Ethics* serves five main purposes:

1. The *Code* enables the association to clarify to current and future members, and to those served by members, the nature of the ethical responsibilities held in common by its members.
2. The *Code* helps support the mission of the association.
3. The *Code* establishes principles that define ethical behavior and best practices of association members.
4. The *Code* serves as an ethical guide designed to assist members in constructing a professional course of action that best serves those utilizing counseling services and best promotes the values of the counseling profession.
5. The *Code* serves as the basis for processing of ethical complaints and inquiries initiated against members of the association.

THE *ACA CODE OF ETHICS* CONTAINS EIGHT MAIN SECTIONS THAT ADDRESS THE FOLLOWING AREAS:

Section A: The Counseling Relationship

Section B: Confidentiality, Privileged Communication, and Privacy

Section C: Professional Responsibility

Section D: Relationship with Other Professionals

Section E: Evaluation, Assessment, and Interpretation

Section F: Supervision, Training, and Teaching

Section G: Research and Publication

Section H: Resolving Ethical Issues

Each section of the *ACA Code of Ethics* begins with an Introduction. The introductions to each section discuss what counselors should aspire to with regard to ethical behavior and responsibility. The Introduction helps set the tone for that particular section and provides a starting point that invites reflection on the ethical mandates contained in each part of the *ACA Code of Ethics*.

When counselors are faced with ethical dilemmas that are difficult to resolve, they are expected to engage in a carefully considered, ethical decision-making process. Reasonable differences of opinion can and do exist among counselors with respect to the ways in which values, ethical principles, and ethical standards would be applied when they conflict. While there is no specific ethical decision-making model that is most effective, counselors are expected to be familiar with a credible model of decision making that can bear public scrutiny and its application.

Through a chosen ethical decision-making process and evaluation of the context of the situation, counselors are empowered to make decisions that help expand the capacity of people to grow and develop.

Section G

Research and Publication

Introduction

Counselors who conduct research are encouraged to contribute to the knowledge base of the profession and promote a clearer understanding of the conditions that lead to a healthy and more just society. Counselors support efforts of researchers by participating fully and willingly whenever possible. Counselors minimize bias and respect diversity in designing and implementing research.

G.1. RESEARCH RESPONSIBILITIES

G.1.a. Use of Human Research Participants.   Counselors plan, design, conduct, and report research in a manner that is consistent with pertinent ethical principles, federal and state laws, host institutional regulations, and scientific standards governing research with human research participants.

G.1.b. Deviation from Standard Practice.   Counselors seek consultation and observe stringent safeguards to protect the rights of research participants when a research problem suggests a deviation from standard or acceptable practices.

G.1.c. Independent Researchers.   When independent researchers do not have access to an Institutional Review Board (IRB), they should consult with researchers who are familiar with IRB procedures to provide appropriate safeguards.

G.1.d. Precautions to Avoid Injury.   Counselors who conduct research with human participants are responsible for the welfare of participants throughout the research process and should take reasonable precautions to avoid causing injurious psychological, emotional, physical, or social effects to participants.

G.1.e. Principal Researcher Responsibility.   The ultimate responsibility for ethical research practice lies with the principal researcher. All others involved in the research activities share ethical obligations and responsibility for their own actions.

G.1.f. Minimal Interference.   Counselors take reasonable precautions to avoid causing disruptions in the lives of research participants that could be caused by their involvement in research.

G.1.g. Multicultural/Diversity Considerations in Research.   When appropriate to research goals, counselors are sensitive to incorporating research procedures that take into account cultural considerations. They seek consultation when appropriate.

G.2. RIGHTS OF RESEARCH PARTICIPANTS (SEE A.2., A.7)

G.2.a. Informed Consent in Research.   Individuals have the right to consent to become research participants. In seeking consent, counselors use language that

1. accurately explains the purpose and procedures to be followed,
2. identifies any procedures that are experimental or relatively untried,
3. describes any attendant discomforts and risks,
4. describes any benefits or changes in individuals or organizations that might be reasonably expected,
5. discloses appropriate alternative procedures that would be advantageous for participants,
6. offers to answer any inquiries concerning the procedures,
7. describes any limitations on confidentiality,
8. describes the format and potential target audiences for the dissemination of research findings, and
9. instructs participants that they are free to withdraw their consent and to discontinue participation in the project at any time without penalty.

G.2.b. Deception.   Counselors do not conduct research involving deception unless alternative procedures are not feasible and the prospective value of the research justifies the deception. If such deception has the potential to cause physical or emotional harm to research participants, the research is not conducted, regardless of prospective value. When the methodological requirements of a study necessitate concealment or deception, the investigator explains the reasons for this action as soon as possible during the debriefing.

G.2.c. Student/Supervisee Participation.   Researchers who involve students or supervisees in research make clear to them that the decision regarding whether or not to participate in research activities does not affect one's academic standing or supervisory relationship. Students or supervisees who choose not to participate in educational research are provided with an appropriate alternative to fulfill their academic or clinical requirements.

G.2.d. Client Participation.   Counselors conducting research involving clients make clear in the informed consent process that clients are free to choose whether or not to participate in research activities. Counselors take necessary precautions to protect clients from adverse consequences of declining or withdrawing from participation.

G.2.e. Confidentiality of Information.   Information obtained about research participants during the course of an investigation is confidential. When the possibility exists that others may obtain access to such information, ethical research practice requires that the possibility, together with the plans for protecting confidentiality, be explained to participants as a part of the procedure for obtaining informed consent.

G.2.f. Persons Not Capable of Giving Informed Consent.   When a person is not capable of giving informed consent, counselors provide an appropriate explanation to, obtain agreement for participation from, and obtain the appropriate consent of a legally authorized person.

G.2.g. Commitments to Participants.   Counselors take reasonable measures to honor all commitments to research participants. (See A.2.c.)

G.2.h. Explanations After Data Collection.   After data are collected, counselors provide participants with full clarification of the nature of the study to remove any misconceptions participants might have regarding the research. Where scientific or human values justify delaying or withholding information, counselors take reasonable measures to avoid causing harm.

G.2.i. Informing Sponsors.   Counselors inform sponsors, institutions, and publication channels regarding research procedures and outcomes. Counselors ensure that appropriate bodies and authorities are given pertinent information and acknowledgment.

G.2.j. Disposal of Research Documents and Records.   Within a reasonable period of time following the completion of a research project or study, counselors take steps to destroy records or documents (audio, video, digital, and written) containing confidential data or information that identifies research participants. When records are of an artistic nature, researchers obtain participant consent with regard to handling of such records or documents. (See B.4.a., B.4.g.)

G.3. RELATIONSHIPS WITH RESEARCH PARTICIPANTS (WHEN RESEARCH INVOLVES INTENSIVE OR EXTENDED INTERACTIONS)

G.3.a. Nonprofessional Relationships.   Nonprofessional relationships with research participants should be avoided.

G.3.b. Relationships with Research Participants.   Sexual or romantic counselor–research participant interactions or relationships with current research participants are prohibited.

G.3.c. Sexual Harassment and Research Participants.   Researchers do not condone or subject research participants to sexual harassment.

G.3.d. Potentially Beneficial Interactions.   When a nonprofessional interaction between the researcher and the research participant may be potentially beneficial, the researcher must document, prior to the interaction (when feasible), the rationale for such an interaction, the potential benefit, and anticipated consequences for the research participant. Such interactions should be initiated with appropriate consent of the research participant. Where unintentional harm occurs to the research participant due to the nonprofessional interaction, the researcher must show evidence of an attempt to remedy such harm.

G.4. REPORTING RESULTS

G.4.a. Accurate Results.   Counselors plan, conduct, and report research accurately. They provide thorough discussions of the limitations of their data and alternative hypotheses. Counselors do not engage in misleading or fraudulent research, distort data, misrepresent data, or deliberately bias their results. They explicitly mention all variables and conditions known to the investigator that may have affected the outcome of a study or the interpretation of data. They describe the extent to which results are applicable for diverse populations.

G.4.b. Obligation to Report Unfavorable Results.   Counselors report the results of any research of professional value. Results that reflect unfavorably on institutions, programs, services, prevailing opinions, or vested interests are not withheld.

G.4.c. Reporting Errors.   If counselors discover significant errors in their published research, they take reasonable steps to correct such errors in a correction erratum, or through other appropriate publication means.

G.4.d. Identity of Participants.   Counselors who supply data, aid in the research of another person, report research results, or make original data available take due care to disguise the identity of respective participants in the absence of specific authorization from the participants to do otherwise. In situations where participants self-identify their involvement in research studies, researchers take active steps to ensure that data are adapted/changed to protect the identity and welfare of all parties and that discussion of results does not cause harm to participants.

G.4.e. Replication Studies.   Counselors are obligated to make available sufficient original research data to qualified professionals who may wish to replicate the study.

G.5. PUBLICATION

G.5.a. Recognizing Contributions.   When conducting and reporting research, counselors are familiar with and give recognition to previous work on the topic, observe copyright laws, and give full credit to those to whom credit is due.

G.5.b. Plagiarism.   Counselors do not plagiarize; that is, they do not present another person's work as their own work.

G.5.c. Review/Republication of Data or Ideas.   Counselors fully acknowledge and make editorial reviewers aware of prior publication of ideas or data where such ideas or data are submitted for review or publication.

G.5.d. Contributors.   Counselors give credit through joint authorship, acknowledgment, footnote statements, or other appropriate means to those who have contributed significantly to research or concept development in accordance with such contributions. The principal contributor is listed first, and minor technical or professional contributions are acknowledged in notes or introductory statements.

G.5.e. Agreement of Contributors.   Counselors who conduct joint research with colleagues or students/supervisees establish agreements in advance regarding allocation of tasks, publication credit, and types of acknowledgment that will be received.

G.5.f. Student Research.   For articles that are substantially based on students' course papers, projects, dissertations or theses, and on which students have been the primary contributors, they are listed as principal authors.

G.5.g. Duplicate Submission.   Counselors submit manuscripts for consideration to only one journal at a time. Manuscripts that are published in whole or in substantial part in another journal or published work are not submitted for publication without acknowledgment and permission from the previous publication.

G.5.h. Professional Review.   Counselors who review material submitted for publication, research, or other scholarly purposes respect the confidentiality and proprietary rights of those who submitted it. Counselors use care to make publication decisions based on valid and defensible standards. Counselors review article submissions in a timely manner and based on their scope and competency in research methodologies. Counselors who serve as reviewers at the request of editors or publishers make every effort to only review materials that are within their scope of competency and use care to avoid personal biases.

APPENDIX B

Sample Research Paper

Running head: ASSESSING RACIAL IDENTITY IN JUVENILE OFFENDERS

Assessing Racial Identity in Juvenile Offenders:

Development of the BARIS

Carl J. Sheperis

Department of Counseling & Educational Psychology

Walden University

M. Harry Daniels

Department of Counselor Education

University of Florida

Abstract

This study investigated the factorial structure of the Black Adolescent Racial Identity Scale (BARIS). The scale was administered to 327 black adolescent male offenders and non-offenders.

Development of the BARIS

Racial identity development is a complex construct relating to how and when individuals come to understand themselves as racial/ethnic beings. Information derived from measures of it can be useful in all aspects of the counseling processes, from supervision to identifying salient issues in treatment. However, there have been inherent problems with the psychometric properties of existing instruments (Helms, 1989; Ponterotto, 1989). Additionally, the focus of current instruments has been on adult populations (Carter, 1991, 1995; Harris, 1995; Helms, 1989; Parham, 1989; Parham & Helms, 1985a; Ponterotto, 1989).

Although identity development is a process that occurs across the life span, it is particularly important during adolescence. According to Spencer (as cited in Harris, 1992), children begin to develop an awareness of self and others in the first two years of life. By the time a child reaches the age of five, there is an understanding of ethno-racial groups, although there may not be understanding of the permanence of belonging to these groups. By the time children reach adolescence, they are attempting to develop a sense of individuality while resisting pressures to belong to a group and to conform to expectations set forth by parents, peers, teachers, their ethno-racial group, and others. Thus, although an adolescent's personality traits contribute to the manner in which his or her identity is formed, there are other factors that contribute as well; self-esteem, social context, race, ethnicity, and gender all play roles in identity formation.

Characteristics of Juvenile Offenders

According to the 1998 Uniform Crime Report, black youth are overrepresented within the juvenile of-fender population (Federal Bureau of Investigation, 1999). In fact, black youth accounted for 26% of all juvenile arrests even though they only make up 15% of the juvenile population. Self-report studies regarding delinquency, such as the National Youth Survey, have documented a history of disproportional delinquent activities by black youth (Elliot, 1994; Hawkins, Laub, Lauritsen, & Cothern, 2000; Huizinga, Loeber, & Thornberry, 1994; Snyder & Sickmund, 1999). While delinquency involvement by race has been mostly consistent over the past 30 years (LaFree, 1995), violent crime rates increased substantially for black youth in the late 1980s and early 1990s (Snyder & Sickmund, 1999). Therefore, it makes good sense to address the issues that black youth face first. The focus should be not only on the individuals as juve-nile offenders, but also as males in a race where 1 in 4 spends time in jail and where 1 in 21 males will be murdered in their lifetime (Miller, 1994). It also makes sense to consider the history of oppression that has faced this population and the effects that this history can have on identity development (Vontress, 1996).

Many factors have been identified that contribute to juvenile delinquency. For example, frequently adolescents in the juvenile justice system have come from seriously dysfunctional family back-grounds (Loeber et al., 1993; Pope & Feyerherm, 1995; Scholte, 1992; Snyder, 1997; Tolan, Guerra, & Kendall, 1995). Evidence of addiction and alcoholism also is prevalent in the families of juvenile offenders. Concomitantly, families involved in the juvenile system are overwhelmingly in the poverty-level category (Hawkins, 1999; Reiss & Roth, 1993).

Although researchers have identified several factors that contribute to delinquency, the increasing juvenile crime and recidivism rates across the United States suggest that an important con-sideration may be being overlooked. It is possible that a pragmatic transition from identifying factors to utilizing them in prevention and treatment has not occurred. For example, while salient factors con-tributing to delinquency include drug and alcohol abuse, uncontrolled aggression, family and mental health problems, and poverty, which are typically addressed in counseling programs utilized by juve-nile offender treatment facilities, juvenile offender recidivism continues to increase. In fact, according to Snyder (1998), the recidivism rate for juvenile offenders is 90% within a 12-month period.

ASSESSING RACIAL IDENTITY IN JUVENILE OFFENDERS 4

Recently, some researchers have begun to speculate that factors associated with race may be a missing consideration (Juvenile Justice Accountability Board, 1999; Pope & Feyerherm, 1995; Snyder, 1997). At present, the population of incarcerated juvenile offenders in the United States is 56% black/African American (Pope & Feyerherm, 1995; Snyder, 1997). The percentage of (all) minority juvenile offenders is an alarming over-representation (Pope & Feyerherm, 1995; Snyder, 1997). This rate becomes even more frightfully disproportional as youths progress through the various levels of restrictiveness within the juvenile justice system (Juvenile Justice Accountability Board, 1999; Snyder, 1997). However, there is no adequate research base to explain the over-representation of minorities (Hawkins, 1993, 1999).

Understanding the true impact of racial identity on juvenile offenders and their respective rehabilitation efforts requires the use of a valid and reliable assessment instrument. Several instruments have been developed to test racial identity development in general populations (e.g., Carter, 1991, 1995, 1996; Helms, 1990; Ibrahim, Ohnishi, & Sing Sandhu, 1997; Mays, 1986; Parham, 1989; Parham & Helms, 1985a, 1985b; Plummer, 1995; Ponterotto, 1989; Poston, 1990; Richardson & Helms, 1994; White, Oliviera, Strube, & Meertens, 1995). However, most of these instruments have not been designed to address racial identity development in adolescents (i.e., they are intended for use with adult populations). Furthermore, the instruments specifically have not been tested on the juvenile offender population (Bierman et al., 1992; Coie & Jacobs, 1993; DiLalla, Mitchell, Arthur, & Pagliocca, 1988; Hooper & Evans, 1984). Assessment of racial identity development among black adolescent male (BAM) juvenile offenders necessitates the availability of an instrument specifically appropriate to them. Thus, the purpose of this study was to develop a valid and reliable instrument to assess racial identity development among BAM juvenile offenders. The Black Adolescent Racial Identity Scale (BARIS) was developed to assess the racial identity statuses of BAM juvenile offenders.

The development of a scale to measure racial identity in the BAM juvenile offender population provides an opportunity to control for some of the methodological problems inherent in other studies, but also helps identify notable issues for the counseling process. The development of a specific scale for BAM juvenile offenders provides useful information in the areas of counselor training, juvenile justice program development, counseling research, and counseling practice. The development of this instrument ultimately benefits the juvenile offenders who participate in culturally specific therapy and rehabilitation programs resulting from the identification of culturally relevant issues.

Review of the Literature

Over the last 30 years, many models of racial-identity development have emerged. However, few of these models have undergone validation studies (Carter, 1991; Cross, Parham, & Helms, 1991; Helms, 1993; Helms & Carter, 1990; Parham, 1989; Ponterotto, 1989; Vontress, 1996). In 1971, Thomas began to investigate the development of racial identity among black/Afro-Americans (as cited in Carter, 1995). In his original model of Negromachy, he hypothesized that Afro-Americans, a term consistent with that time in American history, had developed a need to seek approval from whites in all activities. In turn, this need created a means by which Afro-Americans could measure their level of success or failure as human beings. Because of this external source of personal validation, the person's belief system led to repressed rage, compliance, subservience, and a high sensitivity to racial issues (Carter, 1995).

Cross (1977), whose model of racial identity development is cited most often in the counseling literature, developed a five-stage developmental process that consists of (a) Pre-encounter, (b) Encounter, (c) Immersion–Emersion, (d) Internalization, and (e) Internalization–Commitment. This model, termed Nigrescence, was designed to explain the process by which African Americans came to value their blackness and their culture.

According to Helms (1994b), racial identity development is a process experienced by all individuals regardless of race, culture, gender, or social status. Much like the Cross and Thomas models, Helms identified levels of racial identity that develop in statuses. Helms (1994a) defined statuses as "the dynamic cognitive, emotional, and behavioral processes that govern a person's interpretation of racial information in her or his interpersonal environments" (p. 184). According to Helms, racial identity instruments identify schemata that are behavioral manifestations of the statuses. Rather than having to complete lower levels of development (much like Erikson's model of psychosocial development), Helms postulated that individuals might demonstrate behaviors and attitudes of several statuses at the same time but that the individuals will have a dominant status. Helms' model includes five statuses: Conformity (Pre-encounter), Dissonance, Immersion/Emersion, Internalization, and Integrative Awareness.

In addition to the importance of identifying models of racial identity development in this study, it is also important to define accurately the social forces that impact an individual's development. These social forces have a direct impact on an individual's racial identity development (Helms, 1994b). Historical hostility is a theme suggested by Vontress and based on the theory of the collective unconscious espoused by Jung (Vontress & Epp, 1997). According to the theory of collective unconscious, human beings are affected by their personal histories as well as the history of the human race (Berger, 1988; Carver & Scheier, 1992; Liebert & Spiegler, 1990; Stone & Church, 1984). Archetypes, or the psychological traces of previous generations, have a direct impact on a human being's development from birth to death. Within this framework, it is plausible that individuals are impacted by potent experiences such as racism and oppression that may have occurred in past. Vontress (1997) claims that historical hostility differs from common day-to-day anger, hostility, rage, and other episodic negative events. Much like an archetype, historical hostility remains part of the collective "cultural" unconscious, and the message is automatically passed from generation to generation. This message lies dormant within each individual until it is made conscious by a powerful emotional experience. If Vontress were correct, then accurate identification of issues related to historical hostility would be very important in the treatment of juvenile offenders.

Racial identity theory may be refined through the development of this instrument. Considering the long history of psychology as a discipline, racial identity research is relatively infantile (although new information is being gathered daily). If theory development is to continue to progress, then there must be valid and psychometrically sound measures of important constructs.

Initial Development of the Black Adolescent Racial Identity Scale

Development of the BARIS was based on sound theoretical and psychometric theory. The first step was to identify the areas to be assessed. In their review of the racial identity development literature, Resnicow and Ross (1997) identified three themes for racial ethnic identification (REI), including (a) beliefs about being black; (b) attitudes toward whites; and (c) recognition and perceptions of racism on the social, institutional, and individual levels. These themes were used as a conceptual framework for creation of an item pool for the BARIS.

Items in the BARIS question pool were generated through review of existing instruments and a review of the related literature. All were based on the dynamics of racial identity development espoused in the Cross (1991) five-status model of Nigrescence. The stages of Nigrescence were put into measurable form by Helms and Parham (1993). Many other racial identity development researchers followed Helms' and Parham's lead and developed other instruments based on this five-status model. However, racial identity development researchers have yet to present an instrument having widely accepted psychometric credibility. Researchers investigating the validity of current instruments have not found support for a five-factor model, but rather have found a consistent set of three factors in racial identity development research: Assimilation, Self-Segregation, and Universal Acceptance.

Assimilation is characterized by adaptation of white lifestyles and development of a belief system that values the "white" culture while denigrating elements of the Afrocentric culture. This status includes behaviors such as listening to "white" music, attending predominantly "white" social functions, and a desire to have more Caucasian-like physical features.

Self-Segregation is characterized by a change from assimilation into the dominant (white) culture to immersion in Afrocentric belief systems. Individuals with dominance in this status of identity development have developed an awareness of black history, have come to value themselves as racial beings, and have developed a sense of distrust and anger toward the majority (white) culture.

Movement toward multicultural competence characterizes the third status, Universal Acceptance. Individuals whose attitudes are dominant in this status are more likely to be open-minded toward experiences with people from other cultures. These individuals also are more tolerant of differences and place greater value on people from all types of backgrounds. As individuals develop dominance in this status, they become more likely to have a multicultural circle of friends and ability to interact with individuals from all cultures and races.

The questions in the BARIS are related to these three factors. As is the case with other research into racial identity statuses, individuals may possess qualities in all three statuses while also demonstrating dominance in a particular status. By using items that addressed developmental issues in each of the three statuses, we reasoned that a clearer picture of the individual's racial identity attitudes could be determined and, subsequently, specific counseling interventions that take these issues into consideration could be devised.

ASSESSING RACIAL IDENTITY IN JUVENILE OFFENDERS 8

Using these criteria, an item pool consisting of 70 items was generated by the first author. Each of the items was intended to uncover the components of an individual's inner self at the time of assessment. Change is an inevitable condition in the human process; thus, it is important to view the assessment of racial identity attitudes as an overall snapshot of a moment in an individual's life. Although the model presented to depict racial identity development addresses only the processes within the inner and outer selves, it should be noted that environment factors play an important role in the development of racial identity development. For example, environmental factors such as school setting, family values, friendship circles, and the media can effect an individual's racial identity development.

Each of the 70 items in the BARIS item pool was developed with consideration of possible reading difficulties among the juvenile offender population. Therefore, a sixth-grade reading level was chosen as the maximum acceptable level to allow adequate comprehension of the items. Each item was reviewed by an independent, certified reading specialist and determined to be below the sixth-grade reading level; most of the items in the pool fell at or below the fourth-grade reading level.

A four-point Likert scale was selected as the most appropriate response format, including the following response choices: agree, sort of agree, sort of disagree, and disagree. Because racial identity development is based on statuses rather than stage-wise progression, BARIS responses were scored with regard to overall factor scores to indicate specific factor dominance. More simply stated, an individual's racial identity attitudes can be identified by the strength of his or her scores in each factor.

Three independent reviewers with expertise in the areas of multicultural and racial identity development (e.g., had publications related to the topic area, made professional presentations related to the topic area, or held membership in professional organizations related to the topic area) were recruited to evaluate the content validity, consistency, format, and clarity of the BARIS. One of the reviewers was a professor of counselor education who taught courses in multicultural counseling. The second reviewer was a school guidance counselor who had conducted workshops on multicultural and racial identity issues. The third reviewer was a doctoral student in a CACREP accredited graduate program in counselor education who was conducting dissertation research on racial identity issues at the time of the review. All reviewers were Association for Multicultural Counseling and Development (AMCD) members.

Copies of the BARIS, the demographic form, the scoring sheet, and an explanation of the Tri-Status model were mailed to the reviewers, along with directions for completing the review. Reviewers were specifically asked to evaluate the BARIS and its related forms for adequate sampling of the issues related to each of the statuses within the Tri-Status model of racial identity development, clarity of presentation, redundancy, and content validity, and to provide detailed feedback on each of these areas.

In general, the reviewers determined that the BARIS adequately sampled the domain of issues related to racial identity development and that the structure of the instrument had adequate content validity. Eight of the items in the initial pool were determined by the reviewers to be redundant and thus were removed from the initial version of the BARIS. The reviewers did not suggest changes in regard to the clarity or format of the items.

Data Collection

Participants were recruited for the initial study from both rural and urban school districts in Mississippi. These school districts were selected on the basis of access and willingness to participate. Each of the school districts' populations was primarily black. The total population of black students in all three school districts was 3,500. In general, Mississippi public schools serve students from a lower economic base. Two of these school districts were located in the Mississippi delta area. This section of the country receives the most federal aid annually.

Several information-gathering meetings were held with each school district in an effort to increase participation. Descriptions of the research project and consent forms were sent home to every black male student between the ages of 12 and 18 who attended school in one of these districts at the time of the study. A total of 1,735 information packets and consent forms were distributed.

The return rate for consent forms for the initial project was 22% (n = 379). All students who turned in consent forms also assented to participating in the research project. However, 52 BARIS instruments were deemed unusable due to missing data points. Thus, the resulting sample for the initial study was 327 BAMs.

The population for this study consisted of 327 black, adolescent males (BAMs), from Mississippi ranging in age from 11 to 18, who were attending school or actively involved in a juvenile justice program. Participation in this study was voluntary.

ASSESSING RACIAL IDENTITY IN JUVENILE OFFENDERS 10

According to Sudman (1976), at least 100 subjects from each major subgroup, as well as an additional 20 to 50 subjects for each minor subgroup, were needed for effective survey research. In this study there were two major subgroups (juvenile offenders and non-offenders) and at least five minor subject groups. Thus, the resulting sample should have contained no less than 300 subjects. Another consideration in the decision about sample size was the type of statistical analyses to be performed on the data. In this case, a factor analysis with orthogonal, Varimax rotation was used to identify the initial factor structure of the BARIS. When conducting a factor analysis, the general guideline is to have a minimum of five participants per item (Crocker & Algina, 1986). In this case, the initial version of the BARIS contained 59 items, thus resulting in the need for 295 participants in order to satisfy the minimum requirements for factor analysis. This sample thus met Crocker and Algina's criterion for sample size.

Procedures

Individual counselors from schools and agencies agreeing to participate in the research administered the BARIS in group situations. These assistants were instructed to read the instrument aloud to the group in order to compensate for any physical disability and/or inability to read. They also were trained to avoid bias in presentation by reading each item in a controlled, neutral tone and with a consistent pace. The assistants were directed to report any problems regarding the administration or completion of the BARIS. They also were instructed to avoid discussion of individual items. Upon completion of the respective administrations, the assistants visually scanned instruments to check for responding errors. Participants were asked to complete any items omitted, if they so desired at that time. All information collected was held as confidential as was legally possible. Only the assistants and the researcher saw the questionnaires. Individually identifying information for each respondent was not obtained.

At the time of the initial study, participants also were asked to complete an evaluation form. The participants were asked to report any items that were difficult to answer, any words that they did not understand, their understanding of instructions on how to complete the instrument, their impression of it, and any additional comments they had. The results of the feedback were overwhelmingly positive. Individual participants believed that this was a worthwhile project and that it was beneficial to them. There were no adjustments made to the BARIS as a result of information from the feedback form.

Results

Items on each completed BARIS were screened for scoring errors, missing values, or out-of-range items. The missing values on each instrument were examined and it was determined that no discernable pattern, other than participant error, accounted for the data errors. However, any instrument with missing data points was excluded from the data analyses. A total of 52 scales thus were determined to be unusable, which resulted in a total sample of 327 participants. The final item to participant ratio was 5:1, which met the criterion for minimum sample size recommended by Crocker and Algina (1986). It should be noted that a sample was selected prior to this initial study, the results from which had to be discarded (n = 375) because one school district failed to follow the procedures and training instructions provided. Therefore, their data were deemed unusable.

A principal components analysis (PCA) was used to determine the factor structure of the instrument. Eighteen factors with eigenvalues greater than 1.0 were found for the initial rotation. Upon examination of the Scree Plot, it was determined that a distinct "elbow" occurred between the third and fourth factors, thus suggesting that a three-factor solution was appropriate (Cattell, 1966).

The respective factor loadings of the items on these three factors were then examined. Items that loaded at .40 or above on two or more components were eliminated (Hair, Anderson, Tatham, & Black, 1998). According to a formula provided by Stevens (1996), a sample size of 327 requires a factor loading of at least .30 for the item to be valid. However, since other instruments developed within the field of racial identity development research have failed to provide adequate psychometric properties, a more conservative factor loading of .50 was established to retain items on the BARIS.

In order to determine the applicability of an orthogonal rotation, inter-factor correlations were examined. None of the inter-correlations were found to be statistically significant which suggests that all three factors are independent. Thus a three-factor solution was maintained. This solution accounted for 36% of the total variance.

Using the criteria described above, 37 items were eliminated from the final form of the BARIS, which resulted in a 22-item scale, including nine items related to assimilation, six items related to Self-Segregation, and seven items related to Universal Acceptance. Although three factors emerged in the analysis, it is important to note that the order of the factors with regard to strength of presence on the Screen Plot was Dominant Affiliation, Universal Acceptance, and Self-Segregation.

Scoring

The initial item pool for the BARIS was based on the Tri-status model of racial identity development and therefore scoring of the BARIS was directly related to each of the three statuses. Because each of the statuses is permeable and they may overlap, it is important to recognize status dominance and salient characteristics of a score within each status area. Thus, a separate score for each status area is produced. The resulting scores are compared in an effort to identify status dominance. Since the BARIS identifies issues within each status area and not an overall level of racial identity development, a total score is not valid in this case. Identification of salient issues can also be done through review of the characteristics of each status and individual item responses.

In order to score the BARIS, individual item responses (raw scores) were recorded on the score sheet in the box with the corresponding question number (e.g., the score from question three on the BARIS was entered in the Assimilation column next to question three). After entering all raw scores from the BARIS, the entries for each column on the score sheet were totaled and then divided by the total number of items in that column in order to create equity in possible scores (e.g., column one was divided by 18, column two was divided by 27, and column three was divided by 21.) The resulting scores provided evidence of the individual respondent's status dominance and relative standing on the remaining statuses within the Tri-status model.

After completion of the initial study, the scoring method was revised to account for changes in the BARIS. Revisions were made based on item and factor analyses. Specifically, the initial version of the BARIS was reduced from 59 to 22 items. Thus, those items that were eliminated from the BARIS were also eliminated from the revised score sheet. Items were eliminated based on factor loadings and communalities. Although the rationale for scoring remained the same, the procedure changed to reflect the number of items in each column (e.g., column one was divided by nine, column two was divided by seven, and column three was divided by six). Also, the initial PCA produced four significant, negative factor loadings on the Assimilation factor. Thus items 3, 9, 12, and 13 were reverse scored on the 22-item BARIS.

Demographic Data Analysis

In order to examine the nature of the demographic characteristics, the resulting 22-items of the BARIS were extracted from the original sample of 327 and analyzed. The sample for this study consisted mostly of individuals between 11 and 14 years of age (n = 176, 53.8%). A majority of participants identified themselves as black (n = 224, 68.5%), a trend consistent with recent survey data on black Americans (Parham & Williams, 1993). Most of the participants identified themselves as middle class (n = 227, 69%). However, considering the nature of the population of the areas in which the data were collected, and the SES of families in those areas, it is highly likely that these data are not accurate. Social desirability may have prevented participants from accurately reporting their socioeconomic status. Another demographic characteristic that is likely to be inaccurate is that of history of arrest. Participants were asked to respond to whether they have ever been arrested. The participants were supposed to respond by checking either yes or no. Most respondents were involved in the juvenile justice system, thus indicating they had indeed been arrested. However, only 58 out of 327 participants checked yes for this question (18%). Thus, it is difficult to accurately identify differences between those individuals who had been arrested and those who had not.

Juvenile offender participants in this study had been arrested between one and five times (18%) and the majority of juvenile offender participants were involved in some type of court-initiated alternative services program (15%). It should be noted that respondents were asked to place a check next to the type of program with which they were involved. Several participants marked a number of spaces, indicating several levels of involvement. In these cases, the highest level of involvement marked was used to compute the data analyses.

In order to determine if differences existed on the basis of demographic characteristics of the sample, several statistical analyses were conducted. However, because there was an unequal number of participants in each demographic category (e.g., age, location, number of arrests, and level of involvement) and unequal variances, it was necessary to perform nonparametric tests (Shavelson, 1996). Kruskal-Wallis tests were performed to determine whether differences between BARIS factor scores were statistically significant based on each demographic characteristic. Statistically significant results were detected for every demographic characteristic except age (e.g., racial designation, socioeconomic status, involvement in juvenile justice system, number of arrests, and types of programs).

ASSESSING RACIAL IDENTITY IN JUVENILE OFFENDERS 14

Discussion

It was the purpose of this article to develop and test an instrument that would more adequately assess racial identity in juvenile offenders. An overall assessment tool was developed, tested for rating bias, and administered to African American youths both within the school and juvenile systems. The BARIS is the assessment instrument that was developed and tested in the spirit of yielding more culturally friendly and effective counseling strategies to utilize in one of the most represented races in the juvenile system, the African American population.

It is clear from the results of this study that there are culturally specific methodological concerns that must be accounted for in order to truly assess racial identity and draw information that would adequately contribute to the development of culturally sound counseling strategies or rehabilitation programs. A review of significant findings includes that reading levels, length of questionnaire, SES, arrest history, and overall social desirability may possibly be protagonists to accurate assessment among African American offenders.

Future implications and contributions of this study warrant consideration to be given to the current push for multicultural infusion into counselor preparation programs and the advantage of utilizing these results to impact the ways in which counselors are trained. It also provides counselor preparation programs with a valid and reliable means to gather data from which to direct their suggested interventions with BAM juvenile offenders.

Counselors using the BARIS will have a tool to identify salient issues in a quicker and more efficient manner. The instrument will serve as an aid in creating discussion around difficult and serious issues such as racism and prejudice, thus breaking down some barriers that may be inherent in the current juvenile justice treatment system.

Overall, this study demonstrates specific areas to address in reducing the recidivism of BAM juvenile offenders. It verifies the need for the development of culturally relevant treatment approaches that differ from the previous approaches, which have yielded few successes. Furthermore, it reinforces that by developing psychometrically sound measurement tools counselors can begin to adequately formulate applicable, realistic treatment goals, objectives, and interventions based on the needs of a specific population.

TABLE 1 Factor Loadings for a Varimax, Orthogonal, Three-Factor Solution for the Black Adolescent Racial Identity Scale ($\underline{N}$ = 327)

Item	Factor Loading			Communality
	1	2	3	
3. It is important to take part in black activities.	.209	−.006	**.503**	.296
5. Whites get more chances in life.	.007	**.564**	.006	.327
6. It is good to be around blacks and other races.	**−.594**	.016	.187	.398
7. Whites are more trustworthy than blacks.	.009	**.613**	.003	.386
8. It is easier to get along with black people.	.141	**.516**	−.276	.363
17. People should be proud of their race.	.009	−.172	**.549**	.339
18. Teenagers should only date people from the same race.	**.622**	.002	−.321	.490
22. People from all races have good things about them.	−.140	−.353	**.599**	.504
25. It is good to get along with all kinds of people.	**−.736**	.102	−.007	.557
27. Children should know what it means to be black.	.121	.276	**.526**	.367
29. White counselors are better than black counselors.	**.661**	−.003	.125	.453
30. It is good to do things with people from all types of backgrounds.	**−.569**	.293	.319	.512
32. It is OK to date somebody from another race.	**−.588**	.195	.387	.534
34. White friends are better than black friends.	**.595**	−.005	.101	.367
35. People from all races should get along.	−.101	−.005	**.751**	.576
42. It's OK for whites and blacks to mix.	−.007	−.187	**.569**	.364
43. Black counselors understand kids better than white counselors.	.188	**.601**	−.006	.400
46. It is better to have lighter skin.	**.592**	.235	−.007	.410
47. Whites have nicer hair than blacks.	**.529**	.204	−.116	.334
49. It is important to belong to a black church.	.007	**.594**	−.008	.364
52. It is good to learn about the race and background of others.	−.003	−.120	**.520**	.286
54. It is better to be more like whites.	.265	**.612**	−.195	.483

Note: boldface indicates highest factor loadings

TABLE 2 Racial Designations of Black Adolescent Males
Aged 11–18 on the Three BARIS Factors

Number of arrests	Participants (n = 327)	Mean Rank	X^2
Factor 1			4.10
1	244	169.67	
2	100	149.68	
3	3	217.67	
Factor 2			.44
1	244	165.89	
2	100	160.52	
3	3	138.67	
Factor 3**			16.09
1	244	176.56	
2	100	131.90	
3	3	146.67	

1 = Black, 2 = African American, and 3 = Negro

**p < .01

TABLE 3 **Demographic Data for Participants by Program or School (N = 327)**

	n	%
Age at time of survey (years)		
11–12	93	28
13–14	83	25
15–18	151	46
Racial designation		
Black	224	69
African American	100	31
Negro	3	<1
Biracial	0	
Colored	0	
Other	0	
Socioeconomic data		
Poor	40	12
Middle class	227	70
Well off	60	18
Arrests		
Yes	58	18
No	269	82
Number of arrests		
0	268	82
1–3	42	13
4 or more	17	5
Types of programs		
None	0	0
House arrest	18	6
Teen court	14	4
Alternative services	14	4
Level 6	2	<1
Level 8	6	2
Level 10	1	<1

ASSESSING RACIAL IDENTITY IN JUVENILE OFFENDERS 18

References

Berger, K. S. (1988). *The developing person through the life span*. New York: Worth Publishers, Inc.

Bierman, K. L., Coie, J. D., Dodge, K. A., Greenberg, M. T., Lochman, J. E., & Mcmahon, R. J. (1992). A developmental and clinical model for the prevention of conduct disorder: The fast track program. *Development and Psychopathology, 4*, 509–527.

Carter, R. T. (1991). Racial identity attitudes and psychological functioning. *Journal of Multicultural Counseling and Development, 19,* 105–113.

Carter, R. T. (1995). *The influence of race and racial identity in psychotherapy: Toward a racially inclusive model*. New York: Wiley.

Carter, R. T. (1996). Exploring the complexity of racial identity attitude measures. In G. R. Sodowsky & J. Impara (Eds.), *Multicultural assessment in counseling and clinical psychology*. Lincoln, NE: Buros Institute of Mental Measurement.

Carver, C. S., & Scheier, M. F. (1992). *Perspectives on personality* (2nd ed.). Boston: Allyn and Bacon.

Cattell, R. B. (1966). The screen test for the number of factors. *Multivariate Behavioral Research, 1*, 245–276.

Coie, J. D., & Jacobs, M. R. (1993). The role of social context in the prevention of conduct disorder. *Development and Psychopathology, 5*, 263–275.

Crocker, L., & Algina, J. (1986). *Introduction to classical & modern test theory*. Fort Worth, TX: Harcourt Brace Jovanovich College Publishers.

Cross, W. E., Jr. (1977). The Thomas and Cross models of psychological Nigrescence: A review. *Journal of Black Psychology, 5,* 13–31.

Cross, W. E., Parham, T. A., & Helms, J. E. (1991). Stages of Black identity development: Nigrescence models. In R. L. Jones (Ed.), *Black Psychology* (3rd ed., pp. 319–338). New York: Harper & Row.

DiLalla, L. F., Mitchell, C. M., Arthur, M. W., & Pagliocca, P. M. (1988). Aggression and delinquency: Family and environmental factors. *Journal of Youth and Adolescence, 17*(3), 233–246.

Elliot, D. S. (1994). Serious violent offenders: Onset, developmental course, and termination—The American Society of Criminology 1993 presidential address. *Criminology, 32*(1), 1–21.

Federal Bureau of Investigation. (1999). *Crime in the United States 1998. Uniform crime reports*. Washington, DC: U.S. Department of Justice, Federal Bureau of Investigation.

Hair, J. F., Anderson, R. E., Tatham, R. L., & Black, W. C. (1998). *Multivariate data analysis* (5th ed.). Upper Saddle River, NJ: Prentice Hall.

Harris, D. J. (1992). A cultural model for assessing the growth and development of the African-American female. *Journal of Multicultural Counseling and Development, 20,* 158–167.

Harris, S. M. (1995). Psychosocial development and black male masculinity: Implications for counseling economically disadvantaged African American male adolescents. *Journal of Counseling & Development, 73*(3), 279–287.

Hawkins, D. F. (1993). Crime and ethnicity. In B. Forst (Ed.), *The socio-economics of crime and justice* (pp. 89–120). Armonk, NY: M.E. Sharpe.

Hawkins, D. F. (1999). What can we learn from data disaggregation? The case of homicide and African Americans. In M. D. Smith & M. Zahn (Eds.), *Homicide: A sourcebook of social research* (pp. 195–210). Thousand Oaks, CA: Sage Publications, Inc.

Hawkins, D. F., Laub, J. H., Lauritsen, J. L., & Cothern, L. (2000). *Race, ethnicity, and serious and violent juvenile offending*. Washington, DC: U.S. Department of Justice, Office of Justice Programs, Office of Juvenile Justice and Delinquency Prevention.

Helms, J. E. (1989). Considering some methodological issues in racial identity counseling research. *The Counseling Psychologist, 17,* 227–252.

Helms, J. E. (1990). An overview of Black racial identity theory. In J. E. Helms (Ed.), *Black and white racial identity: Theory, research, and practice* (pp. 9–31). New York: Greenwood Press.

Helms, J. E. (Ed.). (1993). *Black and white racial identity: Theory, research, and practice*. Westport, CT: Praeger Publishers.

Helms, J. E. (1994a). The conceptualization of racial identity and other "racial" constructs. In E. J. Trickett & R. J. Watts et al. (Eds.), *Human diversity: Perspectives on people in context* (pp. 285–311). San Francisco, CA: Jossey-Bass.

Helms, J. E. (1994b). *Helms' racial identity theory*. Paper presented at the Annual Multicultural Winter Roundtable, Teacher's College, Columbia University, New York.

Helms, J. E., & Carter, R. T. (1990). Development of the White Racial Identity Inventory. In J. Helms (Ed.), *Black and white racial identity: Theory, research, and practice* (pp. 67–80). Westport, CT: Greenwood.

Hooper, F. A., & Evans, R. G. (1984). Screening for disruptive behavior of institutionalized juvenile offenders. *Journal of Personality Assessment, 48*(2), 159–161.

Huizinga, D., Loeber, R., & Thornberry, T. P. (1994). *Urban delinquency and substance abuse: Initial findings.* Washington, DC: U.S. Department of Justice, Office of Justice Programs, Office of Juvenile Justice and Delinquency Prevention.

Ibrahim, F., Ohnishi, H., & Sing Sandhu, D. (1997). Asian Americans identity development: A culture specific model for South Asian Americans. *Journal of Multicultural Counseling and Development, 25,* 34–50.

Juvenile Justice Accountability Board. (1999). *Annual report and juvenile justice fact book* (99-001-JJAB). Tallahassee: Florida Legislature.

LaFree, G. (1995). Race and crime trends in the United States, 1946–1990. In D. F. Hawkins (Ed.), *Ethnicity, race, and crime: Perspectives across time and place* (pp. 169–193). Albany, NY: State University of New York Press.

Liebert, R. M., & Spiegler, M. (1990). *Personality: Strategies and issues* (6th ed.). Belmont, CA: Brooks/Cole Publishing Company.

Loeber, R., Wung, P., Keenan, K., Giroux, B., Stouthamer-Loeber, M., Van Kammen, W. B., & Maughan, B. (1993). Developmental pathways in disruptive child behavior. *Development and Psychopathology, 5,* 101–133.

Mays, V. M. (1986). Identity development of Black Americans: The role of history and the importance of ethnicity. *American Journal of Psychotherapy, 40,* 582–593.

Miller, J. G. (1994). From social safety net to dragnet: African American males in the criminal justice system. *Washington and Lee Law Review* (Spring), 479–490.

Parham, T. A. (1989). Cycles of psychological nigrescence. *The Counseling Psychologist, 17*(2), 187–226.

Parham, T. A., & Helms, J. E. (1985a). Relation of racial identity attitudes to self-actualization and affective states of Black students. *Journal of Counseling Psychology, 32,* 431–440.

Parham, T. A., & Helms, J. E. (1985b). Attitudes of racial identity and self-esteem of Black students: An exploratory investigation. *Journal of College Student Personnel, 26,* 143–147.

Parham, T. A., & Williams, P. T. (1993). The relationship of demographic and background factors to racial identity attitudes. *Journal of Black Psychology, 19*(1), 7–24.

ASSESSING RACIAL IDENTITY IN JUVENILE OFFENDERS 21

Plummer, D. L. (1995). Patterns of racial identity development of African American adolescent males and females. *Journal of Black Psychology, 21*(2), 168–180.

Ponterotto, J. G. (1989). Expanding directions for racial identity research. *The Counseling Psychologist, 17*(2), 264–272.

Pope, C. E., & Feyerherm, W. (1995). *Minorities and the juvenile justice system: Research summary* (NCJ 145849). Washington, DC: Office of Juvenile Justice and Delinquency Prevention, U.S. Department of Justice.

Poston, W. S. C. (1990). The biracial identity development model: A needed addition. *Journal of Counseling and Development, 69*, 152–162.

Reiss, A. J., & Roth, J. A. (1993). *Understanding and preventing violence*. Washington, DC: National Academy Press.

Resnicow, K., & Ross-Gaddy, D. (1997). Development of a racial identity questionnaire for African American adults. *Journal of Black Studies, 23*(2), 239–254.

Richardson, T. Q., & Helms, J. E. (1994). The relationship of the racial identity attitudes of Black men to perceptions of "parallel" counseling dyads. *Journal of Counseling & Development, 73*(2), 172–177.

Scholte, E. M. (1992). Prevention and treatment of juvenile problem behavior: A proposal for a socio-ecological approach. *Journal of Abnormal Child Psychology, 20*(3), 247–262.

Shavelson, R. J. (1996). *Statistical reasoning for the behavioral sciences* (3rd ed.). Boston: Allyn and Bacon.

Snyder, H. N. (1997). *Juvenile Justice Bulletin*. The Office of Juvenile Justice and Delinquency Prevention. Retrieved December 1998, from http://www.ojjdp.ncjrs.org/jjbulletin/9812_2/intro.html

Snyder, H. N. (1998). *Juvenile arrests 1997*. Washington, DC: U.S. Department of Justice Programs, Office of Juvenile Justice and Delinquency Prevention.

Snyder, H. N., & Sickmund, M. (1999). *Juvenile offenders and victims: 1999 national report*. Washington, DC: U.S. Department of Justice, Office of Justice Programs, Office of Juvenile Justice and Delinquency Prevention.

Stevens, J. (1996). *Applied multivariate statistics for the behavioral sciences* (3rd ed.). Mahwah, NJ: Lawrence Erlbaum Associates.

Stone, L. J., & Church, J. (1984). *Childhood and adolescence: A psychology of the growing person* (5th ed.). New York: Random House.

ASSESSING RACIAL IDENTITY IN JUVENILE OFFENDERS 22

Sudman, S. (1976). *Applied sampling*. New York: Academic Press.

Tolan, P. H., Guerra, N. G., & Kendall, P. C. (1995). A developmental-ecological perspective on antisocial behavior in children and adolescents: Toward a unified risk and intervention framework. *Journal of Counseling and Clinical Psychology, 63*(4), 579–584.

Vontress, C. E. (1996). A personal retrospective on cross-cultural counseling. *Journal of Multicultural Counseling and Development, 24,* 156–166.

Vontress, C. E., & Epp, L. R. (1997). Historical hostility in the African American client: Implications for counseling. *Journal of Multicultural Counseling and Development, 25,* 170–183.

White, A. M., Olivieira, D. F., Strube, M. J., & Meertens, R. H. (1995). The Themes Concerning Blacks (TCB) projective technique as a measure of racial identity: An exploratory cross-cultural study. *The Journal of Black Psychology, 21*(2), 101–103.

REFERENCES

Adams, G. R., & Schvaneveldt, J. D. (1991). *Understanding research methods* (2nd ed.). White Plains, NY: Longman Publishing.

Alexander, A. F. (2002). *Supervisees' perspectives on childhood memories and receptivity to corrective feedback in group supervision.* Unpublished doctoral dissertation, University of New Orleans.

American Counseling Association. (2005). *ACA code of ethics.* Alexandria, VA: Author.

American Educational Research Association. (1999). *Standards for educational and psychological testing.* Washington, DC: Author.

American Psychological Association. (2003). Guidelines on multicultural education, training, research, practice, and organizational change for psychologists. *American Psychologist, 58,* 377–402.

American Psychological Association. (2001). *Publication manual of the American Psychological Association* (5th ed.). Washington, DC: Author.

Arredondo, P., Toporek, R., Brown, S., Jones, J., Locke, D. C., Sanchez, J., & Stadler, H. (1996). Operationalization of the multicultural counseling competencies. *Journal of Multicultural Counseling and Development, 24,* 42–78.

Ashworth, P. (1999). Bracketing in phenomenology: Renouncing assumptions in hearing about student cheating. *Qualitative Studies in Education, 12*(6), 707–721.

Association for Assessment in Counseling (2003). *Standards for Multicultural Assessment.* Alexandria, VA: Author.

Astramovich, R. L., & Coker, J. K. (2007). Program evaluation: The accountability bridge model for counselors. *Journal of Counseling & Development, 85,* 162–172.

Atkinson, A., & Coffey, P. (1996). *Making sense of qualitative data: Complementary research strategies.* Thousand Oaks, CA: Sage Publications.

Atkinson, B., Heath, A., & Chenail, R. (1991). Qualitative research and the legitimization of knowledge. *Journal of Marital and Family Therapy, 17*(2), 175–180.

Atkinson, D. R., Bui, U., & Mori, S. (2001). Multiculturally sensitive empirically supported treatments—An oxymoron? In J. G. Ponterotto, J. M. Casas, L. A. Suzuki, & C. M. Alexander (Eds.), *Handbook of multicultural counseling* (2nd Ed.) (pp. 542–574). Thousand Oaks, CA: Sage.

Auxier, C. R., Hughes, F. R., & Kline, W. B. (2003). Identity development in counselors-in-training. *Counselor Education and Supervision, 43*(1), 25–39.

Babbie, E. (1992). *The practice of social research* (6th ed.). Belmont, CA: Wadsworth Publishing Company.

Bailey, K. D. (1978). *Methods of social research.* New York: The Free Press.

Balkin, R. S., & Roland, C. B. (2005). Identification of differences in gender for adolescence in crisis residence. *Journal of Mental Health, 14,* 637–646.

Barlow, D. H., & Hersen, M. (1984). *Single case experimental designs: Strategies for studying behavior change* (2nd ed.). New York: Pergamon Press.

Barone, T. (2001). *Touching eternity: The enduring outcomes of teaching.* New York: Teachers College Press.

Bedford, A. W. (in press). Lessons for elementary teacher educators: A conversation with gay and lesbian teachers In I. Killoran & K. Pendleton-Jiminez (Eds.), *Talking about sexual orientation and gender diversity in education.* Olney, MD: Association for Childhood Education International.

Berrios, R., & Lucca, N. (2006). Qualitative methodology in counseling research: Recent contributions and challenges for a new century. *Journal of Counseling and Development, 84,* 174–186.

Best, J. W., & Kahn, J. V. (2006). *Research in education* (10th ed.). Boston: Pearson Education.

Black, T. R. (1999). *Doing quantitative research in the social sciences: An integrated approach to research design, measurement and statistics.* Thousand Oaks, CA: Sage Publications Inc.

Blaikie, N. (2003). *Analyzing quantitative data.* Thousand Oaks, CA: Sage Publications Inc.

Bloom, M., & Fischer, J. (1982). *Evaluating practice: Guidelines for the accountable professional.* Englewood Cliffs, NJ: Prentice Hall.

Bloom, M., Fischer, J., & Orme, J. (2005). *Evaluating practice: Guidelines for the accountable professional* (5th ed.). Boston: Prentice Hall.

Blumenfeld-Jones, D. (1995). Fidelity as a criterion for practicing and evaluating narrative inquiry. In J. A. Hatch & R. Wisniewski (Eds.), *Life history and narrative* (pp. 25–35). London: Falmer Press.

Blumer, H. (1969). *Symbolic interactionism.* Englewood Cliffs, NJ: Prentice Hall.

Blythe, B. J., & Tripodi, T. (1989). *Measurement in direct practice.* Newbury Park, CA: Sage Publications.

Bond, T. (2004). Ethical guidelines for researching counselling and psychotherapy [electronic version]. *Counselling & Psychotherapy Research, 4*(2), 10–19.

Brawer, F. B. (1996, April). *Retention-attrition in the nineties.* (ERIC Document Reproduction Service No. ED393510). Retrieved November 21, 2007, from ERIC database: http://www.eric.ed.gov/contentdelivery/servlet/ERICServlet?accno-ED393510.

Brislin, R. W., Lonner, W. J., & Thorndike, R. M. (1973). *Cross-cultural research methods.* New York: Wiley.

Britzman, D. P. (1992). The terrible problem of knowing thyself: Toward a poststructural account of teacher identity. *Journal of Curriculum Theorizing, 9,* 23–46.

Brosnan, M. J. (1998). The impact of computer anxiety and self-efficacy upon performance. *Journal of Computer Assisted Learning, 14*(3), 223–234.

Brosnan, M. J., & Thorpe, S. J. (2006). An evaluation of two clinically-derived treatments for technophobia. *Computers in Human Behavior, 22*(6), 1080–1095.

Brown, L., & Gilligan, C. (1991). Listening for voice in narratives of relationship. In M. Tappan & M. Packer (Eds.*), Narrative and storytelling: Implications for understanding and moral development* (pp. 43–62). San Francisco: Jossey-Bass.

Brown, S. P., & Espina, M. R. (2000). Report of the ACA ethics committee: 1998–1999. *Journal of Counseling and Development, 78,* 237–241.

Brumfield, K. A. (2006). *African American parents' perceptions of play therapy.* Doctoral dissertation, University of New Orleans, August 2006.

Bruner, J. (1986). *Actual minds, possible worlds.* Cambridge, MA: Harvard University Press.

Buckley, M. R. (1997). Validation: How counselors develop a personal counseling style beyond graduate training. *Dissertation Abstracts International, 58* (02A), 0320 (University Microfilms No. AAG9723984).

Butt, R. L., & Raymond, D. (1989). Studying the nature and development of teachers' knowledge using collaborative autobiography. *International Journal of Educational Research, 13,* 403–419.

Camaroto. S. (2008). *Immigrants in the United States 2007: Profiles of the foreign population.* Retrieved on January 31, 2008, from http://www.ilw.com/articles/2007,1219-camarota.shtm

Campbell, D. T., & Fiske, D. W. (1959). Convergent and discriminate validation by the multitrait-multimethod matrix. *Psychological Bulletin, 56,* 81–105.

Campbell, D. T., & Stanley, I. C. (1966). *Experimental and quasi-experimental designs for research.* Chicago: Rand McNally.

Carr, J. E., & Burkholder, E. O. (1998). Creating single-subject design graphs with Microsoft Excel-super™. *Journal of Applied Behavior Analysis, 3,* 245–251.

Casey, K. (1995/1996). The new narrative research in education. *Review of Research in Education, 21,* 211–253.

Chambless, D. L., & Hollon, S. D. (1998). Defining empirically supported therapies. *Journal of Consulting and Clinical Psychology, 66,* 7–18.

Champe, J. (2004). Experiences in live supervision: Student perceptions across three counseling modalities. *Dissertation Abstracts International, 65*(07A), 0320 (University Microfilms No. AAI3138926).

Chang, C. Y., & Myers, J. E. (2003). Cultural adaptation of the Wellness Evaluation of Lifestyle (WEL): An assessment challenge. *Measurement and Evaluation in Counseling and Development, 35,* 240–251.

Charmaz, K. (2006). *Constructing grounded theory.* Thousand Oaks, CA: Sage.

Chase, S. (1995). Taking narrative seriously: Consequences for method and theory in interview studies. In A. Lieblich & R. Josselson (Eds.), *Narrative study of lives: Vol. 3. Interpreting experience* (pp. 1–26). Thousand Oaks, CA: Sage.

Cherry, A. L. (2000). *A research primer for the helping professions: Methods, statistics and writing.* Belmont, CA: Wadsworth/Thompson Learning.

Cherry, D. K., Messenger, L. C., & Jacoby, A. M. (2000). An examination of training model outcomes in clinical psychology programs. *Professional Psychology: Research and Practice, 21,* 562–568.

Christensen, T. M. (1999). A naturalistic exploration of group supervision with group counselors. *Dissertation Abstracts International, 60*(03A), 0320 (University Microfilms No. AAG9922534).

Christensen, T. M. (2005). Research and writing in counseling. In D. Capuzzi & D. R. Gross (Eds.), *Introduction to the counseling profession* (4th ed.). Needham Heights, MA: Allyn & Bacon.

Christensen, T. M., & Kline, W. B. (2000). A qualitative investigation of the process of group supervision with group counselors. *Journal for Specialists in Group Work, 25*(4), 376–393.

Cizek, G. J. (1999). *Handbook of educational policy.* New York: Academic Press.

Clandinin, D. J., & Connelly, F. M. (2000). *Narrative inquiry: Experience and story in qualitative research.* San Francisco: Jossey-Bass.

Cohen, J. A. (1960). A coefficient of agreement for nominal scales. *Educational and Psychological Measurement, 20,* 37–46.

Cone, J. D., & Foster, S. L. (1993). *Dissertations and theses from start to finish: Psychology and related fields.* Washington, DC: American Psychological Association.

Constantine, M. G. (2002). Predictors of satisfaction with counseling: Racial and ethnic minority clients' attitudes toward counseling and ratings of their counselors' general and multicultural counseling competence. *Journal of Counseling Psychology, 49*(2), 255–263.

Cooper, J. O., Heron, T. E., & Heward, W. L. (2007). *Applied behavior analysis.* Upper Saddle River, NJ: Pearson, Merrill, Prentice Hall.

Corrie, S., & Callanan, M. M. (2001). Therapists' beliefs about research and the scientist-practitioner model in an evidence-based health care climate: A qualitative study. *British Journal of Medical Psychology, 74,* 135–149.

Cortazzi, M. (1993). *Narrative analysis.* London: Falmer Press.

Council for Accreditation of Counseling and Related Educational Program. (2009). *2009 Standards.* Retrieved December 28, 2008, from http:// www .cacrep.org/2009standards.html

Crane, R. D., & McArthur, H. (2002). Meeting the needs of evidence-based practice in family therapy: Developing the scientist-practitioner model. *Journal of Family Therapy, 24,* 113–124.

Creswell, J. W. (1994). *Research design: Qualitative and quantitative approaches.* Thousand Oaks, CA: Sage.

Creswell, J. W. (1998). *Qualitative inquiry and research design: Choosing among the traditions.* Thousand Oaks, CA: Sage.

Creswell, J. W. (1999). Mixed-method research: Introduction and application. In G. J. Cizek (Ed.), *Handbook of educational policy* (pp. 455–472). San Diego: Academic Press.

Creswell, J. W. (2005). *Educational research: Planning, conducting, and evaluating quantitative and qualitative research* (2nd ed.). Upper Saddle River, NJ: Pearson.

Creswell, J. W., & Maiette, R. C. (2002). Narrative research. In D. C. Miller & N. J. Salkind (Eds.), *Handbook of research design and social measurement* (6th ed.) (pp. 147–151). Thousand Oaks, CA: Sage.

Creswell, J. W., & Plano Clark, V. L. (2007). *Designing and conducting mixed methods research.* Thousand Oaks, CA: Sage Publications.

Currall, S., & Towler, A. J. (2003). Research methods in management and organizational research: Toward integration of qualitative and quantitative techniques. In A. Tashakkori & C. Teddlie (Eds.), *Handbook of mixed methods in social and behavioral research* (pp. 513–526). Thousand Oaks, CA: Sage Publications.

Curry, D. (2001). Patient dies in lung study at Johns Hopkins U. *The Chronicle of Higher Education,* June 15, Washington, DC.

Davis, M. S., Wester, K. L., & King, B. (2008). Narcissism, entitlement, and questionable practices of research in counseling: A pilot study. *Journal of Counseling and Development, 86*(2), 200–210.

Delgado-Romero, E. A., Galván, N., Maschino, P., & Rowland, M. (2005). Race and ethnicity in empirical counseling and counseling psychology research: A 10-year review. *The Counseling Psychologist, 33,* 419–448.

Denzin, N. K. (1978). *The research act: A theoretical introduction to sociological methods.* New York: Praeger.

Denzin, N. K., & Lincoln, Y. S. (Eds.). (2000). *Handbook of qualitative research* (2nd ed.). Thousand Oaks, CA: Sage.

Denzin, N. K., & Lincoln, Y. S. (2003). *The landscape of qualitative research: Theories and issues.* Thousand Oaks, CA: Sage Publications.

Dick, B. (2005). *Grounded theory: A thumbnail sketch.* [Online] Retrieved September 12, 2007, from http://www.scu.edu.au/schools/gcm/ar/arp/grounded.html

Dillman, D. (2007). *Mail and internet surveys: The tailored design method* (2nd ed). Hoboken, NJ: John Wiley & Sons, Inc.

Dollard, J. (1935). *Criteria for the life history.* New Haven: Yale University Press.

Dougherty, A. M. (2000). *Psychological consultation and collaboration in school and community settings* (3rd ed.). Belmont, CA: Wadsworth/Thomson.

Durndell, A., & Haag, Z. (2002). Computer self-efficacy, computer anxiety, attitudes towards the Internet and reported experience with the Internet, by gender, in an East European sample. *Computers in Human Behavior, 18*(5), 521–535.

Eaves, S., Emens, R., & Sheperis, C. J. (in press). Counselors in the managed care era: The efficacy of the Data-based Problem Solver Model. *The Journal of Professional Counseling: Theory, Research and Practice.*

Eaves, S. H. (2007). Attachment styles, self-esteem, and perceived peer norms as predictors of sexually risky behaviors among 17–24 year old college students (Doctoral dissertation, Mississippi State University, 2007). Dissertation Abstracts International, 68, 03A.

Eaves, S., Sheperis, C. J., Craft, S., Frasier, R., & Wells, D. (2008). Reviewing the literature. In B. T. Erford (Ed.), *Research and evaluation in counseling.* Lahaska, PA: Lahaska Press.

Edwards, R. (1987). Implementing the scientist-practitioner model: The school psychologist as data-based problem solver. *Professional School Psychology, 2,* 155161.

Egan, G. (1998). *The skilled helper: A problem-management approach to helping* (6th ed.). Pacific Grove, CA: Brooks/Cole.

Eimers, M. T., & Pike, G. R. (1997). Minority and non-minority adjustment to college: Differences or similarities? *Research in Higher Education, 38,* 77–97.

Eisner, E. W. (1991). *The enlightened eye: Qualitative inquiry and the enhancement of educational practice.* New York: Macmillan Publishing Company.

Emihovich, C. (1995). Distancing passion: Narratives in social science. In J. A. Hatch & R. Wisniewski (Eds.), *Life history and narrative* (pp. 37–48). London: Falmer Press.

Erford, B. T., McKechnie, J. A., & Moore-Thomas, C. (2004). Program assessment and evaluation. In B. T. Erford (Ed.), *Professional school counseling: A handbook of theories, programs, and practices.* Austin: CAPS Press.

Erford, B. T., & Moore-Thomas, C. (2003). Program evaluation and outcomes assessment. In J. Wall & G. Walz (Eds.), *Measuring up.* Greensboro, NC: ERIC-CAPS.

Erlandson, D. A., Harris, E. L., Skipper, B. L., & Allen, S. D. (1993). *Doing naturalistic inquiry: A guide to methods.* Newbury Park, CA: Sage.

Fitzpatrick, J. L., Sanders, J. R., & Worthen, B. R. (2004). *Program evaluation: Alternative approaches and practical guidelines.* Boston: Allyn & Bacon.

Foster, L. H., Watson, T. S., Meeks, C., & Young, J. S. (2002). Single-subject research design for school counselors: Becoming an applied researcher. *Professional School Counseling, 6,* 145–154.

Fox, J., Murray, C., & Warm, A. (2003). Conducting research using web-based questionnaires: Practical, methodological and ethical considerations. *International Journal of Social Research Methodology, 6*(2), 167–180.

Fraenkel, J. R., & Wallen, N. E. (2006). *How to design and evaluate research in education* (6th ed.). New York: McGraw Hill.

Furlong, N., Lovelace, E., & Lovelace, K. (2000). *Research methods and statistics: An integrated approach.* Orlando, FL: Harcourt Brace & Company.

Gall, M. D., Gall, J. P., & Borg, W. R. (2006). *Educational research: An introduction* (8th ed.). Boston, MA: Allyn & Bacon.

Galvan, J. L. (1999). Writing literature reviews: A guide for students of the social and behavioral sciences. Los: Pyrczak Publishing.

Gay, L. R., & Airasian, P. (2000). *Educational research: Competencies for analysis and application* (6th ed.). Upper Saddle River, NJ: Prentice Hall.

Gelso, C. J., & Lent, R. W. (2000). Scientific training and scholarly productivity: The person, the training environment, and their interaction. In S. D. Brown & R. W. Lent (Eds.), *Handbook of counseling psychology* (3rd ed.) (pp. 109–139). New York: Wiley.

George, D., & Mallery, P. (2006). *SPSS for windows step by step: A simple guide and reference*. Boston: Pearson Education, Inc.

Gerdes, H., & Mallinckrodt, B. (1994). Emotional, social, and academic adjustment of college students: A longitudinal study of retention. *Journal of Counseling and Development, 72,* 281–288.

Gibson-Davis, C. M., & Duncan, G. J. (2005). Qualitative/Quantitative synergies in a random-assignment program evaluation. In T. S. Weisner (Ed.), *Discovering successful pathways in children's development: Mixed methods in the study of childhood and family life* (pp. 283–303). Chicago: University of Chicago Press.

Glaser, B. G. (1978). *Theoretical sensitivity.* Mill Valley, CA: The Sociology Press.

Glaser, B. G., & Strauss, A. L. (1967). *The discovery of grounded theory: Strategies for qualitative research.* New York: Aldine de Gruyter.

Glense, C. (1999). *Becoming qualitative researchers: An introduction* (2nd Ed.). New York: Longman.

Gluck, S. B., & Patai, D. (Eds.). (1991). *Women's words: The feminist practice of oral history.* New York: Routledge.

Gravetter, F. J., & Wallnau, F. B. (2006). *Statistics for the behavioral sciences* (7th ed.). Belmont, CA: Wadsworth Publishing Company.

Green, E., & Christensen, T. M. (2006). Elementary school children's perceptions of play therapy in school settings. *International Journal of Play Therapy, 15* (1), 65–85.

Gregg, G. S. (1991). *Self-representation: Life narrative studies in identity and ideology.* New York: Greenwood Press.

Grumet, M. (1988). *Bitter milk: Women and teaching.* Amherst: University of Massachusetts Press.

Guba, E. G., & Lincoln, Y. S. (1981). *Effective evaluation.* San Francisco: Jossey-Bass.

Gysbers, N. C. (2004). Comprehensive guidance and counseling programs: The evolution of accountability. *Professional School Counseling, 8,* 1–14.

Gysbers, N. C., & Henderson, P. (2000). *Developing and managing your school counseling program* (3rd ed.). Alexandria, VA: American Counseling Association.

Hadley, R. G., & Mitchell, L. K. (1995). *Counseling research and program evaluation.* Pacific Grove, CA: Brooks/Cole.

Haig, B. D. (1995). Grounded theory as scientific method. *Philosophy of Education 1995.* Retrieved February 20, 2007, from http://www.ed.uiuc.edu/EPS/PES-Yearbook/95_docs/haig.html

Hair, J. F., Anderson, R. E., Tatham, R. L., & Black, W. C. (1998). *Multivariate data analysis* (5th ed.). Upper Saddle River, NJ: Prentice Hall.

Hall, G. C. N. (2001). Psychotherapy research with ethnic minorities: Empirical, ethnical, and conceptual issues. *Journal of Consulting and Clinical Psychology, 69,* 502–510.

Hambleton, R. K. (2001). The next generation of the ITC test translation and adaptation guidelines. *European Journal of Psychological Assessment, 17,* 164–172.

Hambleton, R. K., & Bollwark, J. (1991). Adapting test for use in different cultures: Technical issues and methods. *Bulletin of the International Test Commission, 18,* 3–32.

Hambleton, R. K., & de Jong, J. H. A. L. (2003). Advances in translating and adapting educational and psychological tests. *Language Testing, 20*(2), 127–134.

Hambleton, R. K., & Patsula, L. (1998). Adapting tests for use in multiple languages and cultures. *Social Indicators Research, 45,* 153–171.

Haring-Hidore, M., & Vacc, N. A. (1988). The scientist-practitioner model in training entry-level counselors. *Journal of Counseling and Development, 6,* 286–288.

Hartmann, D. (1977). Considerations in the choice of inter-observer reliability estimates. *Journal of Applied Behavior Analysis, 10,* 103–116.

Haverkamp, B. E., Morrow, S. L., & Ponterotto, S. L. (2005). A time and place for qualitative and mixed methods in counseling psychology research. *Journal of Counseling Psychology, 52,* 123–125.

Hayes, R. L., & Dagley, J. C. (1996). Restructuring school counselor education: Work in progress. *Journal of Counseling and Development, 74*(4), 378–383.

Hayes, S. C., Barlow, D. H., & Nelson-Gray, R. O. (1999). *The scientist-practitioner: Research and accountability in the age of managed care.* Boston: Allyn and Bacon.

Hays, D. G., Chang, C. Y., & Havice, P. A. (2008). White racial identity statuses as predictors of white privilege awareness. *Journal of Humanistic Counseling, Education and Development, 47*(1), 134–145.

Hays, D. G., McLeod, A. L., & Erford, B. T. (in press). The culturally competent counselor. In D. G. Hays & B. T. Erford (Eds.), *Developing multicultural counseling competency: A systems approach.* Columbus, OH: Pearson, Merrill, Prentice Hall.

Henige, D. (2006). Discouraging verification: Citation practices across the disciplines. *Journal of Scholarly Publishing, 37*(2), 99–119.

Heppner, P. P., & Heppner, M. J. (2004). *Writing and publishing your thesis, dissertation & research: A guide for students in the helping professions.* Belmont, CA: Brooks/Cole-Thomson.

Heppner, P. P., Kivlighan, D. M., & Wampold, B. E. (1999). *Research design in counseling* (2nd ed.). Belmont, CA: Wadsworth Publishing Company.

Hertlein, K. M., & Lambert-Shute, J. (2007). Factors influencing student selection of marriage and family therapy graduate training programs. *Journal of Marital and Family Therapy, 33,* 18–34.

Heyman, B., & Cronin, P. (2005). Writing for publication: Adapting academic work into articles. *British Journal of Nursing, 14*(7), 400–403.

Hitchcock, J. H., Sarkar, S., Nastasi, B. K., Burkholder, G., Varjas, K., & Jayasena, A. (2006). Validating culture and gender-specific constructs: A mixed-method approach to advance assessment procedures in cross-cultural settings. *Journal of Applied School Psychology, 22,* 13–33.

Holcomb-McCoy, C. C., & Myers, J. E. (1999). Multicultural competence and counselor training: A national survey. *Journal of Counseling and Development, 77*(3), 294–302.

Holden, J. D. (2001). Hawthorne effects and research into professional practice. *Journal of Evaluation in Clinical Practice, 7*(1), 65–70.

Horrocks, R. (2001). *Freud revisited: Psychoanalytic themes in the postmodern age.* New York: Palgrave.

Hosie, T. (1994). Program evaluation: A potential area of expertise for counselors. *Counselor Education and Supervision, 33*(4), 349–355.

Howard, G. S. (1991). Culture tales: A narrative approach to thinking, cross-cultural psychology, and psychotherapy. *American Psychologist, 46,* 187–197.

Howard, R. D. (2001). Conceptual models for creating useful decision support. *New Directions for Institutional Research, 112,* 45–55.

Howell, D. C. (2007). *Statistical methods for psychology* (5th ed.). Pacific Grove, CA: Duxbury.

Hulley, S. B., & Cummings, S. R. (1988). *Designing clinical research.* Baltimore: Williams & Wilkins.

Hunter, A., & Brewer, J. (2003). Multimethod research in sociology. In A. Tashakkori & C. Teddlie (Eds.), *Handbook of mixed methods in social and behavioral research* (pp. 577–594). Thousand Oaks, CA: Sage Publications.

Husserl, E. (1970). *Logical investigations.* New York: Humanities Press.

Institute of Medicine. (2002). Integrity in scientific research: Creating an environment that promotes responsible conduct. Washington, DC: The National Academies Press.

Isaac, S., & Michael, W. B. (1997). *Handbook in research and evaluation: For education and the behavioral sciences* (3rd ed.). San Diego: EdiTS/ Educational and Industrial Testing Services.

Ivankova, N. V., Creswell, J. W., & Stick, S. L. (2006). Using mixed-methods sequential explanatory design: From theory to practice. *Field Methods, 18,* 3–20.

Jackson, A. P., & Meadows, F. B. (1991). Getting to the bottom to understand the top. *Journal of Counseling and Development, 70,* 72–76.

Jayaratne, S., & Levy, R. L. (1979). *Empirical clinical practice.* New York: Columbia University Press.

Jick, T. D. (1979). Mixing qualitative and quantitative methods: Triangulation in action. *Administrative Science Quarterly, 24,* 602–611.

Johnson, B., & Christensen, L. (2004). *Educational research: Quantitative, qualitative, and mixed approaches* (2nd ed.). Boston: Pearson Education.

Johnson, R. B., & Onwuegbuzie, A. J. (2004). Mixed methods research: A research paradigm whose time has come. *Educational Researcher, 33*(7), 14–26.

Johnston, J. M., & Pennypacker, H. S. (1980). *Strategies and tactics for human behavioral research.* Hillsdale, NJ: Erlbaum.

Johnston, J. M., & Pennypacker, H. S. (1993). *Strategies and tactics for human behavioral research.* (2nd ed.). Hillsdale, NJ: Erlbaum.

Joiner, R., Gavin, J., Duffield, J., Brosnan, M., Crook, C., Durndell, A., Maras, J. M., Scott, A. J., &

Lovatt, P. (2005). Gender, internet identification, and internet anxiety: Correlates of Internet use. *CyberPsychology & Behavior, 8*(4), 371–378.

Josselson, R. (1995). Imagining the real: Empathy, narrative, and the dialogic self. In A. Lieblich & R. Josselson (Eds.), *Narrative study of lives: Vol. 3. Interpreting experience* (pp. 27–44). Thousand Oaks, CA: Sage Publications.

Kahn, J. H., & Gelso, C. J. (1997). Factor structure of the Research Training Environment Scale-Revised: Implications for research training in applied psychology. *The Counseling Psychologist, 25,* 22–37.

Kaplan, D. (2005). How to fix peer review: Separating its two functions—improving manuscripts and judging their scientific merit—would help. *Journal of Child and Family Studies, 14,* 321–323.

Kelly, A. B., Halford, W. K., & Young, R. M. (2000). Maritally distressed women with alcohol problems: The impact of a short-term alcohol-focused intervention on drinking behavior and marital satisfaction. *Addictions, 95,* 1537–1549.

Kelly, F. D. (1976). The counseling jury: A step toward accountability. *Counselor Education and Supervision, 15,* 228–232.

Kemp, A. W. (1997). *The lives of women as teacher educators: A kaleidoscope of reflections.* Unpublished doctoral dissertation, Texas A&M University, College Station, Texas.

Kennedy, C. H. (2005). *Single-case designs for educational research.* Boston: Allyn & Bacon.

Kent, A. J., & Hersen, M. (2000). An overview of managed mental health care: Past, present & future. In A. Kent & M. Hersen (Eds.), *A psychologist's proactive guide to managed mental health care* (pp. 3–19). Mahwah, NJ: Lawrence Erlbaum Associates.

Kerlinger, F. N., & Lee, H. B. (2000). *Foundations of behavioral research* (4th ed.). Toronto, Canada: Thomson Learning, Inc.

Kerr, A. W., Hall, H. K., & Kozub, S. A. (2002). *Doing statistics with SPSS.* London: Sage Publications Ltd.

Kocet, M. M., & Freeman, L. T. (2005). Report of the ACA ethics committee: 2003–2004. *Journal of Counseling and Development, 83,* 249–252.

Koski-Jännes, A., Cunningham, J. A., Tolonen, K., & Bothas, H. (2007). Internet-based self-assessment of drinking—3-month follow-up data. *Addictive Behaviors, 32*(3), 533–542.

Kottler, J. A., & Shepard, D. S. (2004). *Introduction to counseling: Voices from the field.* Belmont, CA: Thompson Higher Education.

Krathwohl, D. R. (1988). *How to prepare a research proposal: Guidelines for funding and dissertations in the social and behavioral sciences.* Syracuse, NY: Syracuse University Press.

Kratochwill, T. R., Sladeczek, I., & Plunge, M. (1995). The evolution of behavioral consultation. *Journal of Educational and Psychological Consultation, 6,* 145–157.

Krueger, R. A. (1994). *Focus groups* (2nd ed.). Thousand Oaks, CA: Sage.

Lackey, D. P. (1986). A single subject in multiple protocols: Is the risk equitable? *IRB: Ethics and Human Research, 8*(1), 8–10.

LaFountain, R. M., & Bartos, R. B. (2002). *Research and statistics made meaningful in counseling and student affairs.* Pacific Grove, CA: Wadsworth Group.

Lambert, M. J. (1991). Introduction to psychotherapy research. In L. E. Beutler & M. Crago (Eds.), *Psychotherapy Research: An international review of programmatic studies* (pp. 1–23). Washington DC: American Psychological Association.

Lampropoulos, G. K., & Spengler, P. M. (2002). Introduction: Reprioritizing the role of science in a realistic version of the scientist-practitioner model. *Journal of Clinical Psychology, 58,* 1195–1197.

Leedy, P. D., & Ormrod, J. E. (2005). *Practical research: Planning and design* (8th ed.). Upper Saddle River, NJ: Pearson Prentice Hall.

Leedy, P. D., & Ormrod, J. E. (2005). Planning your research project. In Authors (Eds.), *Practical research: Planning and designing* (pp. 85–114). Upper Saddle River, NJ: Pearson.

Lester, S. (1999). *An introduction to phenomenological research.* Retrieved July 22, 2006, from http://www.devmts.demon.co.uk/resmethy.htm

Lincoln, Y. S., & Guba, E. G. (1985). *Naturalistic inquiry.* Newbury Park, CA: Sage.

Loesch, L. C. (2001). Counseling program evaluation: Inside and outside the box. In D. C. Locke, J. E.

Myers, & E. L. Herr (Eds.), *The handbook of counseling* (pp. 513–525). Thousand Oaks, CA: Sage.

Luce, K. H., Winzelberg, A. J., Das, S., Osborne, M. I., Bryson, S. W., & Taylor, C. B. (2007). Reliability of self-report: Paper versus online administration. *Computers in Human Behavior, 23*(3), 1384–1389.

Lundervold, D. A., & Belwood, M. F. (2000). The best kept secret in counseling: Single-case (N=1) experimental designs. *Journal of Counseling & Development, 78*(1), 92–102.

Madey, D. L. (1982). Some benefits of integrating qualitative and quantitative methods in program evaluation, with some illustrations. *Educational Evaluation and Policy Analysis, 4,* 223–236.

Marshall, C., & Rossman, G. B. (1995). *Designing qualitative research* (2nd ed.). Thousand Oaks, CA: Sage.

Marshall, C., & Rossman, G. B. (1999). *Designing qualitative research* (3rd ed.). Thousand Oaks, CA: Sage Publications.

Martella, R. C., Nelson, R., & Marchand-Martella, N. E. (1999). *Research methods: Learning to become a critical research consumer.* Needham Heights, MA: Allyn & Bacon.

Martin, W. E., Swartz-Kulstad, J. L., & Madson, M. (1999). Psychological factors that predict the college adjustment of first-year undergraduate students: Implications for college counselors. *Journal of College Counseling, 2,* 121–133.

Mason, E. J, & Bramble, W. J. (1989). *Understanding and conducting research: Applications in education and the behavioral sciences.* New York: McGraw-Hill.

Mathison, S. (1988). Why triangulate? *Educational Researcher, 17,* 13–17.

Maxwell, J. (1996). *Qualitative research design: An interactive approach.* Thousand Oaks, CA: Sage.

McLeod, A. L., Hays, D. G., & Chang, C. Y. (2008). Female intimate partner violence survivors' experiences with accessing resources. Manuscript submitted for publication.

Merchant, N. (1997). Qualitative research for counselors. *Counseling and Human Development, 30,* 1–19.

Merchant, N., & Dupuy, P. (1996). Multicultural counseling and qualitative research: Shared worldview and skills. *Journal of Counseling and Development, 74,* 537–541.

Merriam, S. B. (1988). *Case study research in education: A qualitative approach.* San Francisco: Jossey-Bass.

Merriam, S. B., & Associates. (2002). *Qualitative research in practice: Examples for discussion and analysis.* San Francisco: Jossey-Bass.

Merriam-Webster. (2005). *Merriam-Webster online dictionary.* Retrieved June 17, 2006, from www.m-w.com/dictionary/beneficence

Michael, J. (1974). Statistical inference for individual organism research: Mixed blessing or curse? *Journal of Applied Behavior Analysis, 7,* 647–653.

Miles, M. B., & Huberman, A. M. (1984). *Qualitative data analysis: A sourcebook of new methods.* Beverly Hills, CA: Sage Publications.

Miles, M. B., & Huberman, A. M. (1994). *Qualitative data analysis* (2nd ed.). Thousand Oaks, CA: Sage.

Miller, C. C. (2006). From the editors: Peer review in the organizational and management sciences: Prevalence and effects of reviewer hostility, bias, and dissensus. *Academy of Management Journal, 49,* 425–431.

Miller, D. C., & Salkind, N. J. (2002). *Handbook of research design & social measurement* (6th ed.). Thousand Oaks, CA: Sage.

Miranda, J., Green, B. L., Krupnick, J. L., Chung, J., Siddique, J., Belin, T., & Revicki, D. (2006). One-year outcomes of a randomized clinical trial treating depression in low-income minority women. *Journal of Consulting and Clinical Psychology, 74,* 99–111.

Mishler, E. G. (1990). Validation in inquiry-guided research: The role of exemplars in narrative studies. *Harvard Educational Review, 60,* 415–441.

Morgan, D. L. (1998). Practical strategies for combining qualitative and quantitative methods: Applications to health research. *Qualitative Health Research, 8*(3), 362–376.

Morrow, S. L., Rakhsha, G., & Castañeda, C. L. (2001). Qualitative research methods in multicultural counseling. In J. G. Ponterotto, J. M. Casas, L. A. Suzuki, & C. M. Alexander (Eds.), *Handbook of multicultural counseling* (2nd ed.). Thousand Oaks, CA: Sage.

Morse, J. A., & Field, P. A. (1995). *Qualitative research methods for health professionals.* Thousand Oaks, CA: Sage.

Morse, J. M. (1991). Approaches to qualitative-quantitative methodological triangulation. *Nursing Research, 40,* 120–123.

Moustakas, C. (1994). *Phenomenological research methods.* Thousand Oaks, CA: Sage.

Murphy, M. J., & Harrop, A. (1994). Observer error in the use of momentary time sampling and partial interval recording. *British Journal of Psychology, 85,* 169–179.

National Commission for the Protection of Human Subjects of Biomedical and Behavioral Research. (1979). *The Belmont Report: Ethical principles and guidelines for the protection of human subjects of research.* Retrieved December 29, 2008, from http:// ohsr.od.nih.gov/guidelines/belmont.html#gob3

National Institute of Health. (2001). NIH policy and guidelines on the inclusion of women and minorities as subjects in clinical research – amended, October 2001. Office of Extramural Research. Retrieved December 29, 2008, from http://grants.nih.gov/grants/funding/women_min/guidelines_amended_10_2001.htm

National Institute of Health. (2002). *Human participant protections education for research teams.* U.S. Department of Health and Human Services. Retrieved December 29, 2008, from http://cme.cancer.gov/clinicaltrials/learning/humanparticipant-protections.asp

Newsome, D., Hays, D. G., & Christensen, T. M. (2008). Qualitative approaches to research. In B. T. Erford (Ed.), *Research and evaluation in counseling.* Boston: Houghton Mifflin / Lahaska Press.

Noell, G. H., & Witt, J. C. (1998). When does consultation lead to intervention implementation. *Journal of Special Education, 33,* 29–35.

Office of Research Integrity. (2003). *Research on research integrity.* Retrieved December 29, 2008, from http:// grants1.nih.gov/grants/guide/rfa-files/RFA-NS-03-001.html

Okech, J. E. A. (2003). A grounded theory of group co-leader relationships. *Dissertation Abstracts International, 62*(02A), 0320 (University Microfilms No. AAI3082996).

Okech, J. E. A., & Kline, W. B. (2005). A qualitative exploration of group co-leader relationships. *Journal for Specialists in Group Work, 30*(2), 173–190.

Ollerenshaw, J., & Lyons, D. L. (2002, January). *Voices in a reservation school: A sonata-form narrative from a professor's and pre-service teacher's story about teaching culturally responsive science.* A paper presented at the Association for Education of Teachers of Science, Charlotte, NC.

Onwuegbuzie, A. J., & Johnson, R. B. (2004). Mixed method and mixed model research. In R. B. Johnson & L. B. Christensen (Eds.), *Educational research: Quantitative, qualitative, and mixed approaches* (pp. 408–431). Needham Heights, MA: Allyn & Bacon.

Onwuegbuzie, A., & Leech, N. (2005). Taking the "Q" out of research: Teaching research methodology courses without the divide between quantitative and qualitative paradigms. *Quality & Quantity, 39,* 267–296.

Parker, R. M. (1993). Threats to the validity of research. *Rehabilitation Counseling Bulletin, 36*(3), 130–138.

Parsonson, B. S. (2003). Visual analysis of graphs: Seeing is believing. In K. S. Budd & T. Stokes (Eds.), *A smaller matter of proof: The legacy of Donald M. Baer* (pp. 35–51). Reno, NV: Context Press.

Parsonson, B. S., & Baer, D. M. (1978). The analysis and presentation of graphic data. In T. R. Kratochwill (Ed.), *Single subject research: Strategies for evaluating change* (pp. 101–165). New York: Academic Press.

Patten, M. L. (1997). *Understanding Research Methods: An overview of the essentials.* Los Angeles: Pyrczak Publishing.

Patton, M. Q. (1990). *Qualitative evaluation and research Methods* (2nd ed.). Newbury Park, CA: Sage Publications.

Patton, M. Q. (2002). *Qualitative research & evaluation methods* (3rd ed.). Thousand Oaks, CA: Sage.

Personal Narratives Group. (1989). *Interpreting women's lives: Feminist theory and personal narratives.* Bloomington: Indiana University Press.

Peshkin, A. (1988). In search of subjectivity—one's own. *Educational Researcher, 17,* 17–21.

Phillips, D. C. (1994). Telling it straight: Issues in assessing narrative research. *Educational Psychologist, 29*(1), 13–21.

Pike, G. R. (1999). The constant error of the halo in educational outcomes research. *Research in Higher Education, 40*(1), 61–86.

Polkinghorne, D. E. (1989). Phenomenological research methods. In R. S. Valle & S. Halling (Eds.), *Existential-phenomenological perspectives in psychology: Exploring the breadth of human experience* (pp. 41–60). New York: Plenum Press.

Polkinghorne, D. E. (1995). Narrative configuration. In J. A. Hatch & R. Wisniewski (Eds.), *Life history and narrative* (pp. 5–23). London: Falmer Press.

Ponterotto, J. G. (1988). Racial/ethnic minority research in the *Journal of Counseling Psychology*. A content analysis and methodological critique. *Journal of Counseling Psychology, 35,* 410–418.

Ponterotto, J. G., Costa, C. I., & Werner-Lin, A. (2002). Research perspectives in cross-cultural counseling. In Pedersen et al. (Eds.), *Counseling across cultures* (pp. 395–420). Thousand Oaks, CA: Sage.

Quintana, S. M., Troyano, N., & Taylor, G. (2001). Cultural validity and inherent challenges in quantitative methods for multicultural research. In J. G. Ponterotto, J. M. Casas, L. A. Suzuki, & C. M. Alexander (Eds.). *Handbook of multicultural counseling* (2nd ed.), pp. 604–630.

Reagles, K. W., & O'Neill, J. (1977). Single-subject designs for client groups: Implications for program evaluation. *Rehabilitation Counseling Bulletin, 21*(1), 13–22.

Reisetter, M., Korcuska, J. S., Yexley, M., Bonds, D., Nikels, H., & McHenry, W. (2004). Counselor educators and qualitative research: Affirming a research identity. *Counselor Education and Supervision, 44,* 2–16.

Riessman, C. K. (1993). *Narrative analysis.* Newbury Park, CA: Sage.

Riniolo, T. C., Johnson, K. C., Sherman, T. R., & Misso, J. A. (2006). Hot or not: Do professors perceived as physically attractive receive higher student evaluations? *Journal of General Psychology, 133,* 19–35.

Ritchie, M. H. (1995). Proper use of literature reviews [electronic version]. *Counselor Education and Supervision, 35*(1), 2–4.

Rosenthal, J. A. (2001). *Statistics and data interpretation for the helping professions.* Belmont, CA: Wadsworth Publishing Company.

Rosenwald, G. C., & Ochberg, R. L. (1992). Introduction: Life stories, cultural politics, and self-understanding. In G. C. Rosenwald & R. L. Ochberg (Eds.), *Storied lives: The cultural politics of self-understanding* (pp. 1–18). New Haven: Yale University Press.

Rosnow, R. L., & Rosenthal, R. (2005). *Beginning behavioral research: A conceptual primer* (5th ed.). Upper Saddle River, NJ: Pearson Prentice Hall.

Rowell, L. L. (2006). Action research and school counseling: Closing the gap between research and practice [electronic version]. *Professional School Counseling, 9*(5), 376–384.

Rubel, D. J. (2002). An exploratory study of expert group leadership. *Dissertation Abstracts International, 63*(02A), 0320 (University Microfilms No. AAI3043134).

Sanchez, L. M., & Turner, S. M. (2003). Practicing psychology in the era of managed care: Implications for practice and training. *American Psychologist, 58,* 116–129.

Sanders, J. L., & Freeman, L. T. (2003). Report of the ACA ethics committee: 2001–2002. *Journal of Counseling and Development, 81,* 251–254.

Schaefer, P. (2006). *Experiences of conservative orthodox Christian students attending public secular CACREP-Accredited counseling graduate programs.* Unpublished doctoral dissertation, University of New Orleans.

Scriven, M. (1967). The methodology of evaluation. In R. E. Stake (Ed.), *Curriculum Evaluation* (American Education Research Association Monograph Series on Evaluation, No. 1. pp 39–83). Chicago: Rand McNally.

Scriven, M. (1973). Goal-free evaluation. *Evaluation Comment, 3*(4), 1–4.

Sechrest, L., & Sidana, S. (1995). Quantitative and qualitative methods: Is there an alternative? *Evaluation and Program Planning, 18,* 77–87.

Seidman, I. (1998) *Interviewing as qualitative research: A guide for researchers in education and the social sciences.* New York: Teachers College Press.

Sexton, T. L. (1999). *Evidenced based counseling: Implications for counseling practice, preparation, and professionalism.* ERIC Clearinghouse on Counseling and Student Services, Greensboro, NC (ERIC Document Reproduction Service No. ED435948).

Sexton, T. L., Whiston, S. C., Bleuer, J. C., & Walz, G. R. (1997). *Integrating outcome research into counseling practice and training.* Alexandria, VA: American Counseling Association.

Sexton, T. L. (1996). The relevance of counseling outcome research: Current trends and practical implications [electronic version]. *Journal of Counseling & Development, 74*(6), 590–600.

Shank, G. D. (2002). *Qualitative research: A personal skills approach.* Upper Saddle River, NJ: Pearson Education.

Shavelson, R. J. (1996). *Statistical reasoning for the behavioral sciences* (3rd ed.). Needham Heights, MA: Allyn & Bacon.

Shuman, A. (1986). *Story telling rights.* Cambridge: Cambridge University Press.

Sieber, S. D. (1973). The integration of fieldwork and survey methods. *American Journal of Sociology, 73,* 1335–1359.

Sim, T. N., & Ng, E. L. (2007). Parental attachment and adjustment to higher learning institutions: The role of stress for a Malaysian sample of late adolescents. *Journal of Counseling & Development, 85,* 467–474.

Simpson, L. R. (2005). *Level of spirituality as a predictor of the occurrence of compassion fatigue among counseling professionals in Mississippi.* Unpublished doctoral dissertation, University of Mississippi.

Skinner, H. A., & Pakula, A. (1986). Challenge of computers in psychological assessment. *Professional Psychology: Research and Practice, 17*(1), 44–50.

Skovholt, T. M., & Ronnestad, M. H. (1995). *The evolving professional self.* New York: Wiley & Sons.

Slavin, R. E. (2007). *Education research in an age of accountability.* Boston: Allyn & Bacon.

Som, R. K. (1973). *A manual of sampling techniques.* New York: Crane, Russak.

Spence, D. P. (1986). Narrative smoothing and clinical wisdom. In T. R. Sarbin (Ed.), *Narrative psychology: The storied nature of human conduct* (pp. 211–232). New York: Praeger.

SPSS Base 9.0 Applications Guide. (1999). Chicago: SPSS, Inc.

Stake, R. (1981). Persuasions, not models. *Educational Evaluation and Policy Analysis, 3*(1), 83–84.

Stake, R. (1990). Responsive evaluation. In H. J. Walberg & G. D. Haertel (Eds.), *The international encyclopedia of educational evaluation* (pp. 75–77). Columbus, OH: Merrill.

Stecker, A., McLeroy, K. R., Goomdan, R. M., Bird, S. T., & McCormick, L. (1992). Toward integrating qualitative and quantitative methods: An introduction. *Health Education Quarterly, 19*(1), 1–8.

Steneck, N. H. (2003). The role of professional societies in promoting integrity in research. *American Journal of Health and Behavior, 27,* S239–S247.

Steneck, N. H. (2006). Fostering integrity in research: Definitions, current knowledge, and future directions. *Science and Engineering Ethics, 12,* 53–74.

Sterling, Y. M., & McNally, J. A. (1992). Single-subject research for nursing practice. *Clinical Nurse Specialist, 6*(1), 21–26.

Stevens, S. S. (1946). On the theory of scales of measurement. *Science, 103,* 677–680.

Stolberg, S. G. (1999). The biotech death of Jesse Gelsinger. *New York Times Magazine,* November 28, 136–140, 149–150.

Stoner, G., & Green, S. K. (1992). Reconsidering the scientist-practitioner model for school psychology practice. *School Psychology Review, 21,* 155–167.

Strauss, A., & Corbin, J. (1994). Grounded theory methodology. In N. K. Denzin & Y. S. Lincoln (Eds.), *Handbook of qualitative research* (pp. 273–285). Thousand Oaks, CA: Sage.

Stricker, G. (2002). What is a scientist-practitioner anyway? *Journal of Clinical Psychology, 58,* 1277–1283.

Stuart, R. B. (2004). Twelve practical suggestions for achieving multicultural competence. *Professional Psychology: Research and Practice, 35,* 3–9.

Stufflebeam, D. L. (1971). The relevance of the CIPP evaluation model for educational accountability. *Journal of Research and Development in Education, 5,* 19–25.

Sussman, A. L., Williams, R. L., Leverence, R., Gloyd, P. W., & Crabtree, B. F. (2006). The art and complexity of primary care clinicians' preventative counseling decisions: Obesity as a case study. *Annals of Family Medicine, 4*(4), 327–333.

Tabachnick, B. G., & Fidell, L. S. (2001). *Using multivariate statistics* (4th ed.). Boston: Allyn & Bacon.

Tashakkori, A., & Teddlie, C. (2003). *Handbook of mixed methods in social and behavioral research.* Thousand Oaks, CA: Sage Publications.

Teddlie, C., & Tashakkori, A. (2003). Major issues and controversies in the use of mixed methods in the social and behavioral science. In A. Tashakkori & C. Teddlie (Eds.), *Handbook of mixed methods in social and behavioral research* (pp. 671–701). Thousand Oaks, CA: Sage Publications.

Thompson, B. (2006a). Role of effect sizes in contemporary research in counseling. *Counseling and Values, 50,* 176–186.

Thompson, B. (2006b). Effect sizes for research: A broad practical approach. *Applied Psychological Measurement, 30,* 75–77.

Thorngren, J. M. (1999). Reciprocal influence between clients and counselors. *Dissertation Abstracts International, 60*(03A), 0663 (University Microfilms No. AAG9923576).

Thorpe, S. J., & Brosnan, M. J. (2007). Does computer anxiety reach levels which conform to DSM IV criteria for specific phobia? *Computers in Human Behavior, 23*(3), 1258–1272.

Tinto, V. (1993). *Leaving college: Rethinking the causes and cures of student attrition* (2nd ed.). Chicago: University of Chicago Press.

Tripodi, T. (1983). *Evaluative research for social workers.* Englewood Cliffs, NJ: Prentice Hall.

Tripodi, T. (1994). *A primer on single-subject design for clinical social workers.* Washington, DC: National Association of Social Workers Press.

Troyka, L. Q. (1999). *Simon & Schuster handbook for writers* (5th ed.). Upper Saddle River, NJ: Prentice Hall.

U.S. Census Bureau. (2006). Fact Finder. Retrieved December 29, 2008, from http://factfinder. census.gov

U.S. Census Bureau. (2000). Total population by race, Hispanic origin, and nativity. Retrieved December 29, 2008, from http://www.census.gov/population/ www/projections/natsum-T5.html

U.S. Department of Commerce. (1996). Current population reports: Population projections of the United States by age, sex, race, and Hispanic origin 1995–2050. Retrieved December 29, 2008, from http://www.census.gov/prod/1/pop/p25-1130/ p251130.pdf

Van der Mescht, H. (1999). *Poetry, phenomenology, and "reality".* Paper presented at the Conference on Qualitative Research, Rand Africaans University, Johannesburg, South Africa.

VanderMey, R., Meyers, V., Van Rys, J., Kemper, D., & Sebrank, P. (2004). *The college writer: A guide to thinking, writing, and researching.* Boston: Houghton Mifflin.

Van de Vijver, F. J. R., & Hambleton, R. K. (1996). Translating tests: Some practical guidelines. *European Psychologist, 1,* 89–99.

Viadero, D. (2005). Mixed methods research examined. *Education Week, 24*(20), 1–20.

Viera, A. J., & Garrett, J. M. (2005). Understanding interobserver agreement: The kappa statistic. *Family Medicine, 37*(5), 360–363.

Vinson, T., & Neimeyer, G. J. (2000). The relationship between racial identity development and multicultural counseling competency. *Journal of Multicultural Counseling and Development, 28*(3), 177–193.

Vogt, W. P. (2007). *Quantitative research methods for professionals.* Boston: Allyn & Bacon.

Wakefield, J. C., & Kirk, S. A. (1996). Unscientific thinking about scientific practice: Evaluating the scientist-practitioner model. *Social Work Research, 20,* 83–95.

Walker, C. A. (2003). A scholar is what a scholar writes: Practical tips on scholarly writing. *The Journal of Theory Construction & Testing, 7*(1), 6–9.

Wells, M. G., Burlingame, G. M., & Rose, P. (1999). *Manual for the Youth Outcome Questionnaire Self-Report.* Wharton, NJ: American Professional Credentialing Service.

Wertz, F. J. (1985). Methods and findings in a phenomenological psychological study of a complex life event: Being criminally victimized. In A. Giorgi (Ed.), *Phenomenology and phenomenological research* (pp. 155–216). Pittsburgh, PA: Duquesne University Press.

Wertz, F. J. (2005). Phenomenological research methods for counseling psychology. Journal of Counseling Psychology, 52, 167–177.

Whiston, S. C. (1996). Accountability through action research: Research methods for practitioners [electronic version]. *Journal of Counseling & Development, 74*(6), 616–623.

Whiston, S. C., & Sexton, T. L. (1998). A review of school counseling research: Implications for practice [electronic version]. *Journal of Counseling & Development, 76*(4), 412–426.

Wijndaele, K., Matton, L., Dubigneaud, N., Lefevre, J., Duquet, W., Thomis, M., De Bourdeaudhuij, I., & Philippaerts, R. (2007). Reliability, equivalence and respondent preference of computerized versus paper-and-pencil mental health questionnaires. *Computers in Human Behavior, 23*(4), 1958–1970.

Yeh, C. J., Inman, A. G., Kim, A. B., & Okubo, Y. (2006). Asian American families' collectivistic coping strategies in response to 9/11. *Cultural Diversity and Ethnic Minority Psychology, 12*(1), 134–148.

Young, J. S., Wiggins-Frame, M., & Cashwell, C. S. (2007). Spirituality and counselor competence:

A national survey of American Counseling Association members. *Journal of Counseling and Development*, 85, 47–52.

Young, P. V. (1939). *Scientific social surveys and research* (1st ed.). New York: Prentice-Hall.

Zeller, N. (1995). Narrative strategies for case reports. In J. A. Hatch & R. Wisniewski (Eds.), *Life history and narrative* (pp. 75–88). London: Falmer Press.

INDEX